THE BOOK OF
JUDITH

Dropsie University Edition

JEWISH
APOCRYPHAL LITERATURE
VOLUME VII

Published by
E. J. BRILL, LEIDEN
for
DROPSIE UNIVERSITY, PHILADELPHIA

THE BOOK OF
JUDITH

GREEK TEXT
WITH AN ENGLISH TRANSLATION, COMMENTARY AND
CRITICAL NOTES

BY

MORTON S. ENSLIN

EDITED WITH A GENERAL INTRODUCTION
AND APPENDICES

BY

SOLOMON ZEITLIN

Published by
E. J. BRILL, LEIDEN
for
DROPSIE UNIVERSITY, PHILADELPHIA
1972

ISBN 90 04 03595 8

In Memory of

DOCTOR ABBA HILLEL SILVER

1893 - 1963

איש הרוח ואיש המעשה

A Man of Spirit and Action

ᐒ CONTENT ᐓ

This volume is dedicated to the memory of Abba Hillel Silver, one of the foremost American Jewish leaders in the twentieth century.

There is a saying in the Talmud, "Either the book or the sword." This is to be interpreted that one who produces great scholarly works cannot engage in public affairs, for his place is in an ivory tower; on the other hand, a fighter for ideas and ideals cannot produce great scholarly works. The life of the late Dr. Silver, however, afforded clear proof that this talmudic statement did not apply to a person of superior intellect and gifted with original ideas. Dr. Silver while engaging in scholary research, carried on unceasing struggles for humanity, for justice, for the rights of the Jews; he was the main champion in defending the Jewish rights in Eretz Israel. He was a person with the deep spiritual conviction and endowed with a powerful intellect. He was a dynamic personality and a brilliant orator. His sympathies were as broad as Humanity. To the upbuilding of a Jewish homeland he devoted his immense talent, and an incredible amount of energy and time.

Yet he had enough left over to make extraordinary contributions to Jewish scholarship. The first of his scholarly works was a book entitled *A History of Messianic Speculation in Israel*, in which he traced this aspect of Jewish thought from the first to the seventeenth centuries. This study revealed not only on extraordinary acuteness of mind but also a vast knowledge of sources and literature.

In the volume challenging named *Where Judaism Differed*, Dr. Silver demonstrated his grasp of the historical development of Judaism from the beginning of the era down to the present. He exhibited, moreover, great courage in the expounding of his views.

In expounding the differences between Judaism and Christianity, he says, "The Jewish people did not adopt Judaism as

the Romans, for example adopted Christianity. They created it. Jews and Judaism entered history simultaneously. Its life and that of the Jewish people are inseparably intertwined." He further says, "The predominent hope of the people of Israel was not to convert the whole world to Judaism but to convert the whole world to God. It did not set as its goal the establishment of one universal church to which all true believers must belong." Dr. Silver also has few words to combat the faulty ideas of Professor Toynbee, who maintained that Judaism has survived as a fossil. To this Dr. Silver replied, "What a spry fossil! And what a lively corpse!"

In dealing with Pauline Christianity Dr. Silver said, "Paul wanted to reject the Torah, but he could not reject it outright. The Torah was needed to substantiate and to bear witness to Jesus and to his rôle in history." On another page he drew attention to the relative importance which the doctrine of resurrection has for Christianity in contrast to Judaism. "With Christianity" he writes "it is the *sine qua non*—the chief cornerstone of the entire edifice of its faith. Paul made that point unmistakably clear, 'but if there is no resurrection, then Christ has not been raised; if Christ has not been raised, then our preaching is in vain and your faith is in vain.'" In contrast to Christianity, Dr. Silver writes. A man should serve his God, the teachers of Judaism maintained, regardless of reward, and should endure his share of unavoidable suffering in brave and quiet resignation . . . the Jews produced the first martyrs for religion in history at a time when the belief in personal immortality was not part of their authoritative faith."

Each of the two aspects of Dr. Silver's life would have constituted a distinguished career. As a scholar, his books, monographs, and essays clarified and interpreted Judaism that he so well understood. As a fighter for the Jewish people, as a statesman, he climaxed his career by addressing the United Nations, with dignity and persuasiveness. He forcefully voiced the demand of his people for national recognition and for the right to establish a Jewish state in their ancestral home, Eretz Israel. His persuasive addresses in the United Nations brought a sense

of pride to the Jews the world over. History will record indelibly what Jewish scholarship and the state of Israel owe this man who combined both spirit and action.

The author of the book of Judith depicted Judith as having, by her courage, faith, and self-sacrifice, saved the Jews from destruction. It is fitting, therefore, that a book of this nature be dedicated to the memory of Abba Hillel Silver.

S. Zeitlin
Dropsie University

◄ INTRODUCTION ►

THE BOOKS OF ESTHER AND JUDITH: A PARALLEL

SOLOMON ZEITLIN

JUDITH A CHARMING STORY

The book of Judith, as was well stated by Dr. Enslin in his Introduction, "is an example of Jewish fiction at its best." It is a fine short story of the period of the Second Jewish Commonwealth. It was very well constructed by a vivid imagination, characteristic of the best Jewish stories. The author was a good novelist and composed a popular Jewish novelette. The names mentioned in the book are fictitious and bear no resemblance to actual actions or events. Judith, the heroine of the story, is not an historical character. Similarly, Bethulia, Judith's hometown is fictitious. We seek in vain to identify the names mentioned in the book with kings and generals of the Persian period or with the rulers during the Hellenistic period. The author had no intention to write history; he wrote a charming story.

The book of Judith belongs to the didactic literature. The author wanted to instruct the people and to inflame the Judaeans' patriotism. He propounded the doctrine that the God of Israel was the ruler of heaven and earth and the creator of all things, He was the God of the inheritance of Israel. The author set forth the principle that the God of Israel was omnipotent, *kyrios pantokrator*, and omniscient. He was the God of the humble, the helper of the oppressed, the protector of those in distress, the savior of the helpless. God was merciful and will never forsake His people; He may chastise His people, but will never destroy them. The children of Israel are His people and He is their God. He may test them as He tested Abraham, Isaac and Moses. But the people cannot test God as human beings do not know the

ways of God. The author puts in the mouth of Judith a speech,
to the elders:

> For you will not discover the depth of the human heart, and
> will not lay hold of the thoughts of a man's mind; how then
> will you search out God, who made all these things, and
> understand His mind and comprehend His way of thought?
> Nay, my brethren; stop provoking Adonai, your God, to
> anger . . . Cease seeking to force the counsels of Adonai our
> God, because God is not as a man to be threatened, nor as a
> son of man to be forced to give His decisions.[1]

The threat of annihilation of the Judaeans was only a test, said
Judith to the elders:

> Remember all He did unto Abraham and the ways He
> tested Isaac and what befell Jacob in Mesopotamia of Syria
> while shepherding the sheep of Laban, his mother's brother.
> He hath not put us to the fiery test as He did them to try
> their hearts, and He had not taken vengeance upon us;
> rather for their admonition doth Adonai scourge them who
> draw near to Him.[2]

The author wanted to convey the idea that even during great
danger the Judaeans should not lose heart by assuming that it
was the end of their existence. God will never forsake them. God
will rescue them as he rescued their forefathers. The author
emphasized supplication and repentance.

THE STORIES IN THE BOOKS OF ESTHER AND JUDITH

The stories in the books of Esther and Judith are similar in
plot. In both, the authors narrate that when the Judaeans were
on the verge of destruction, they were saved by a woman. There
is, however, a significant contrast in the narration of the two
books.

The story in Esther may be summarized as follows: King

[1] 8 4-17.
[2] *Ibid.* 26-27.

Ahasuerus on the seventh day of his feasting ordered Queen Vashti to appear before his nobles that they might admire her beauty. The queen refused. The king was greatly incensed; he was advised by his counselors that he should dismiss Vashti from her queenly rank. When the king sobered from his drinking bout, he felt that he missed Vashti and became lonesome for her. His advisors suggested to organize a beauty contest among the virgins of his empire and that the winner should succeed Vashti as queen. The king ordered that this to be done. Among the virgins who were taken to the harem was Hadasah, later called Esther,[3] a cousin and foster daughter of Mordecai [4] who was a descendant of Kish, the father of Saul, first king of Israel. When Esther was taken to the harem she didn't reveal her nationality, for so Mordecai had ordered. What was the underlying reason for Mordecai's order? It is a pertinent question. Was Mordecai apprehensive that if she would reveal her Jewish origin, she would lose the contest? [5] There was also a sexual contest among the maidens. Every maiden would go to the inner chamber of the king in the evening and leave in the morning. She would not return to the king unless he asked for her. Esther likewise went in the evening to the inner chamber of the king but did not return in the morning. The king fell in love with her and crowned her as queen in place of Vashti.

Ahasuerus appointed as grand vizier a certain man by the name Haman the Aggatite. The king ordered everyone to bow and kneel before Haman. Mordecai, who was an official and sat at the palace gate, did not bow or kneel before Haman. The servants of the king reproached Mordecai for disobeying the king's orders. The answer he gave was that he was a Judaean. Was Mordecai's refusal to kneel before Haman due to a personal motive or to a religious one? The author does not say.

When Haman became aware that Mordecai refused to bow and kneel before him because he was Judaean, Haman

---

[3] Esther 2 7
[4] According to Josephus, *Ant.* 11.6.2. (198) Esther was a niece of Mordecai.
[5] *Cf.* Eben Ezra Esther *ad. loc.*

disdained to punish Mordecai alone but decided to take revenge
on the entire Judaean people. Through misrepresentation he
obtained from the king an order to annihilate the Jews, men,
women and children. He told the king there was a certain people
in his empire who had their own laws and disobeyed the king's
laws and that it would be to the royal interest to destroy them.
The date of the extermination of the Judaeans was fixed for the
thirteenth day of the twelfth month, Adar. The day was fixed by
casting *pur*, lots.[6] Hence the name Purim. Orders were dispatched
throughout the entire realm that the people should be ready to
destroy the Judaeans on that day.

When Mordecai became aware of this decree he tore his clothes
and put on sackcloth and ashes on his head and went throughout
the city of Shushan wailing loudly. The Judaeans, when they
learned what they could expect on the thirteenth of Adar, likewise wept bitterly and fasted. The author does not mention that
either Mordecai or the Judaeans offered supplications to God
begging Him to save them. The word God is not mentioned in the
entire book.

When Esther learned that Mordecai was walking through the
streets of Shushan dressed in a sackcloth and crying, she sent
one of her courtiers to find out what was the reason for his
lamentation. Mordecai told to the courtier to tell the queen
about the decree of Haman to exterminate the Judaeans and
charged her to go to the king to plead with him for her people.
In doing so she was bound to reveal her nationality. Esther sent
word to Mordecai that no one could enter the inner court without
being invited and those who did enter without invitation were
put to death. Mordecai then sent a message to Esther saying:
"Think not that by being in the king's palace, you will escape
with your life more than the other Judaeans. For if you keep
silent in this crisis relief and deliverance will come to the Judaeans
from another quarter, and you and your father's house will
perish. And who knows, perhaps you attained royalty at just such
a time as this?" The expression "from another quarter" could be
interpreted to mean from God and also that she reached her

[6] The etomology of the word "pur" is uncertain.

royal position by Providence. Esther then sent a message to Mordecai telling him to assemble all the Judaeans in the city of Shushan and declare a fast in her behalf: "Then I will go to the king and if I perish, I perish."

Esther put on her royal robe and went into the inner court. As soon as the king saw her, he extended to her the golden sceptre, which meant that she was welcome. The king asked her, "What is your petition?" Esther replied, "If it pleases your Majesty that you and Haman should come today for the feast which I prepared." While they feasted, the king asked Esther again, "What is your request and I will grant you?" She answered, "Let the king and Haman come to a banquet tomorrow, and I will then state my petition." Haman was rejoiced that he was invited by the queen to dine with the king. When Haman passed the gates and saw that Mordecai did not kneel before him he became furious. He was advised by his wife and friends to construct gallows and in the morning, when he will be with the king, to ask him to have Mordecai hanged.

On the night before the dinner, the king could not sleep and he asked for the book of memorable deeds to be brought to him. In reading the chronicles the king noticed that Mordecai had reported about two eunuchs who had plotted to kill the king, and when it was found that Mordecai's report was true, the two eunuchs had been hanged. The king asked whether Mordecai had been rewarded for saving his life and he was told that nothing had as yet been bestowed on him. While the king was conversing with his subordinate, Haman came to the court to ask the king to order Mordecai to be hanged. When the king was told that Haman was in the court, he asked that Haman should appear before him. The king asked Haman: "What should be done for a man whom the king desires to honor?" Haman thought that the king was referring to him. He said to the king: "For the man whom the king delights to honor, let the royal robe be brought, which the king had worn, and the horse that the king had ridden when the royal crown was set on his head, and all those shall be put on the man whom the king delights to honor. Let one of the king's princes conduct the man through the open square of the

city heralding before him, 'Thus shall be done for the man the
king desires to honor.'" The king said to Haman: "Do as you
said to Mordecai." So Haman took the royal garb and arrayed
Mordecai and paraded him on the royal horse through the city
proclaiming before him that this was being done for the man
whom the king desired to honor.

The entire episode sounds like a comic opera. The author had
extraordinary imaginative power and knew how to produce
dramatic affect. By chance or providence, the king had a sleepless
night.[7] He occupied himself with the readings of the chronicles
and discovered that Mordecai had once saved his life. Haman
at this moment came to the court to ask the king's permission
to hang Mordecai. The king without knowing the reason for
Haman's coming ordered him to put the royal garb on Mordecai
and like an ordinary servant to run before him proclaiming that
he was the king's favorite. Did the king not know that Haman
was a mortal enemy of Mordecai? The narrator does not tell.

On the following day when the king and Haman were at the
banquet which the queen had prepared for them, Esther revealed
the reasons for her anxiety and said to the king: "My people and
I were sold to be destroyed and annihilated." She did not
mention who were her people. That may be the reason why the
narrator had said that when Esther was first taken to the
harem she did not reveal her nationality. Apparently, the author
wanted to keep the reader in suspense. Similarly, when Haman
came to the king asking him to order to exterminate the Judaeans
he did not mention the name. He referred only to a "certain
people" without specifying the name of the people. When the
king asked Esther who was the man who dared to do this Esther
replied that the man was the villainous Haman. At the same time
the king was informed that Haman prepared a gallow to hang
Mordecai. The king became furious and ordered Haman to the
gallows.

Esther appealed to the king to revoke the letter sent by
Haman to destroy the Judaeans. The king consented and a new
letter was sent out in the name of the king that the Judaeans

[7] According to Josephus (*Ibid.* 248) God deprived the king of sleep.

were allowed to fight for their lives if anyone attacked them. After the fall of Haman, Mordecai presented himself to the king, for Esther had revealed her relationship.

On the thirteenth of Adar, on the day when the enemies of the Judaeans had expected to destroy them, on the very day the Judaeans mustered in their cities and slew those who sought to destroy them. Many people of the land feigned to be Judaeans, "for the fear of the Judaeans had fallen upon them." The Judaeans in the provinces of the empire took revenge on their enemies on the thirteenth of Adar and celebrated the fourteenth of the month. In Shushan, the capital, they continued their slaughtering of their enemies for another day, the fourteenth. Thus the Judaeans of Shushan celebrated on the fifteenth day of the month of Adar.

Mordecai who was appointed grand vizier by the king, together with Queen Esther, sent out another letter to all the Judaeans throughout the country to observe the days of Purim in their proper time, asking that the celebration be observed forever, by every family and in every city. The days of Purim shall be days of festivities and joyfulness, the sending of gifts to one another and alms to the poor.

The book does not record any hymns praising God when the good tidings reached the Judaeans, that Haman, their arch-enemy, was hanged and they were allowed to resist their enemies, even to kill all those who wanted to harm them. There is no mention in the book of divine intervention in the deliverance of the Judaeans from their impending destruction. Now we turn to give a succinct account of the story of Judith.

ANALYSIS OF THE STORY OF JUDITH

Nabouchodonosor, king of Assyria, sent from his capital city, Nineveh, his chief general, Holofernes, with a mighty army to take revenge on all the people who refused to submit to him. He ordered the general to destroy all the gods of the land, so that all nations might worship Nabouchodonosor as god.[8] When the children of Israel who dwelt in Judaea became aware of

[8] 3 8.

what Holofernes had done and how he had destroyed all the shrines, they were in great fear for the safety of Jerusalem and of the temple of God. They had but recently returned from their captivity and the altar of the house of God had recently been purified from defilement.[9]

Joachim, the high priest, and the *gerousia*, council of all the people of Israel in Jerusalem, ordered their brethren in the north to take possession of the passage which led to Judaea. The people followed the order of the high priest. The children of Israel did not rely on strength to prevent Holofernes and his army from taking Jerusalem. They appealed to God not to deliver their babies for booty and their women for spoil and their cities for destruction and their sanctuary for profanation. In Jerusalem the high priest and all the priests offered burnt offerings and cried to God to look with favor upon all the children of Israel.

When Holofernes received word that the Israelites had closed all the passages to Jerusalem and made ready for war, he called a council of war, *synedrion*. One general, Achior, an Ammonite, told the *synedrion* that the Israelites could not be defeated if they were following the precepts of God. Only by disobeying their God could they be brought to defeat by their adversaries. Holofernes was furious and said that the God of Israel could not defend His people since Nabouchodonosor was the sole god; He would exterminate them from the face of the earth and their God could not protect them. The members of the *synedrion* were indignant and were ready to kill Achior. Holofernes ordered to put Achior in fetters and placed at the foot of the hill on which Bethulia stood with a warning that he would be put to death together with all the Israelites.[10]

Upon the advice of the generals, Holofernes decided to lay siege to the city, forcing the inhabitants to capitulate through hunger and thirst. The army of Holofernes encamped in the valley and seized the sources of water. After thirty-four days, the sources of water dried up and the people of Bethulia were in dire

[9] 4 3.
[10] 6 10-13.

distress. The vessels of water utterly failed. People fainted from thirst and were falling prone in the streets. The people accused the leaders of having caused their plight and demanded that they should surrender the city to the Assyrians. The leaders appealed to the people to be patient, saying, "Courage, brethren, let us hold out for five days more, in which Adonai, our God, will turn His mercy towards us, for He will not utterly forsake us. But if these days pass and no succor comes upon us, we will do according to your words." [11]

In this crisis Judith, a very beautiful and devout widow, upon hearing that the leaders promised the people that, if no rain came in five days, they would surrender the city to the enemy, summoned the leaders and rebuked them. She upbraided them for making such a promise by which she thought they were in effect actually trying God. She said to them, "Cease seeking to force the councils of Adonai our God." The elders said to her, "The people were exceedingly thirsty, they forced us to do what we did." The elders appealed to Judith and said that, since she is a very pious widow, she should pray for rain and God may hearken to her prayers. Judith did not reply to their request but said to them: "Hearken unto me, and I will do a thing which will go down through endless generations . . . but you are not to inquire about my act, for I shall not tell it to you until those things which I shall do have been accomplished." [12] Judith apparently made up her mind not to pray for rain but to do something more spectacular, to kill Holofernes, and thus save her people.

Judith, before she undertook her mission, offered an eloquent prayer of intercession, "My God, my God, hearken unto me, a widow, for it was thou who didst do the things which were before those things and those things and the things after them . . . Bring low their might by thy power, for they have planned to pollute thy sanctuary, to defile the tabernacle where thy glorious name doth rest . . . By the guile of my lips smite . . . break in pieces their highest state by the hands of a female . . .

[11] 7 30-31.
[12] 8 33-34.

King of all thy creation, hearken thou to my supplication, and make my word and deceit for the wound and bruise of those who have purposed hard things against thy covenant and thy hallowed house." [13]

After she ceased praying, she adorned herself with costly ornaments and anointed herself daily so as to beguile the eyes of some men as should behold her. The author especially emphasizes among other qualities her extraordinary beauty. In many passages he stresses the fact that she was a most beautiful woman. The elders of the city "wonder at her beauty very exceedingly." The men at the city gate could not turn their eyes from her; they "looked after her until she was going down the mountain." The soldiers at the Assyrian camp marvelled at her beauty. The author portrayed Judith as a perfect seductress, that no man could withstand her. And he made Judith conscious of this power.

With her maid, she went to the city gates where the elders stood, and they invoked a divine blessing on her. She took along with her a bottle of wine, a cruse of oil, a loaf of pure bread, and cheese. [14] When she and her maid passed the gates, the sentries of the Assyrians met her. They arrested her and asked her who she was. She answered that she was a daughter of the Hebrews, fleeing from her people to escape their imminent doom. She said to the guards she would tell the general how to conquer the city without the loss of a man. The guards accompanied her to the tent of Holofernes. They were struck by her beauty and said to each other that no Israelite should be left alive, lest, through beautiful women like Judith they should seduce the whole world. [15] When the guards came to the tent of Holofernes, Holofernes came out to meet her. Judith prostrated herself before him. On his order, they raised her up and all of them marvelled at the beauty of her face. Holofernes said to Judith that she had nothing to fear. Only those who refused to serve Nabouchodonosor, like her people, had reason to fear. Judith said to him that she would tell him the truth and guide him to obtain his objective. She told him that she knew what Achior had

[13] 9 12-13.
[14] So according to the Latin version and the Midrash.

said to the members of the *synedrion*. While his words were
perfectly true, she said to Holofernes that he will prevail over the
children of Israel if they sinned to their God. When the supplies
of food should be exhausted and water became scant they would
resort to eating from the sacrificial victims, from the first fruit
and the tithes sanctified to the temple and they would also
resort to the drinking of the blood of the victims.[15] Being a
religious woman, she decided to flee the city. When the children of
Israel should commit these sins, they would be given over to him
for destruction. She also said to him that she had been commissioned by God to accomplish an outstanding deed.[16] (She
used ambiguous words in saying that God commissioned her to
accomplish an outstanding deed: he took it to mean that she
would help him conquer the Israelites, while she meant that
God commissioned her to kill him.) She requested Holofernes to
permit her to go at night into the valley to pray until God
revealed to her that the Israelites had sinned: then she would
lead Holofernes to the conquest of the city. Holofernes fell
victim to her charm and he believed her. He said to her that if
she fulfilled her words, "Thy God shall be my God and you shall
sit in the house of King Nabouchodonosor."

Judith being a very devout person, could not partake of
Holofernes' food. She brought along her own victuals which
should last for five days. When Holofernes asked her what she
would eat when her provisions were consumed, she laconically
answered him, "Thy handmaid will not use up the things with me
until God by my hand accomplishes what He has purposed." [17]
(Again doubletalk.) For three nights she went with her maid to
the valley to pray to God. On the fourth day, Holofernes, beguiled by her beauty and charm, gave a banquet in her honor and
said to the eunuch, "Go and persuade the Hebrew woman to
come to us and eat and drink with us, for lo, we will be put to
shame if we let such a woman go without having intercourse

---

[15] This is in accordance with the Latin version.
[16] 11 16.
[17] 12 4.
[18] *Ibid.* 12.

with her." [18] Judith appeared willing to yield herself to Holofernes, and joined him at the banquet, eating and drinking wine
only from the provisions which she brought with her. He, in his
exaltation, drank heavily. After the guests had departed, the
eunuch closed the tent and Judith was left alone with Holofernes,
who "was prone on his back, for he was fair swimming in wine."
Judith prayed silently and carried out her designs. She took his
akinaken, a Persian sword, and cut off his head and placed it in a
bag and calmly passed through the camp as on the previous
nights. The sentries, under the instruction of Holofernes, let her
pass. However, this time she did not return to her tent and went
on to Bethulia and asked the guards to open the gate. She said to
them "God is with us" (Emmanuel).

She was joyously welcomed by the people of Bethulia and she
showed them the head of Holofernes. She assured them that she
had enticed Holofernes without being defiled by him. Achior
identified Holofernes' head. Recognizing the power of the God of
Israel, he converted to Judaism and was circumcised. Judith
advised the people to hang the head of Holofernes outside the city
walls.

At dawn, the people of Bethulia marched out as though
preparing to attack. The Assyrians were at first surprised. They
were waiting impatiently for some orders from Holofernes. They
became paralyzed with fear when it was reported that Holofernes
had been slain by the Hebrew woman.[19] The Assyrian soldiers
dispersed in mad terror. The children of Israel fell upon them,
pursuing and slaughtering them. The high priest in Jerusalem,
when he heard of Judith's feat, came to Bethulia to bless Judith.
The people gave the tent of Holofernes and its contents as a gift
of thanks to Judith. Judith and all the women with her went
dancing; and a psalm of thanksgiving was sung by all the women
and all the men. After giving the text of the psalm, the author
briefly describes the last days of the heroine. With this the book
ends.

[19] To be slain by a female was considered a great humiliation. *Cf.*
Judg. 9 54.

The Contrast between the Books of Judith and Esther

After summarizing the narrative as given in the books of Esther and Judith, we readily see that the contrast between the two books is of cardinal significance. It was said above that neither the name of God nor prayers are mentioned in the book of Esther. The author states that a man of Judaea by the name of Mordecai dwelt in Shushan who had been exiled from Jerusalem at the time when King Jechoniah of Judaea had been driven into exile by King Nabouchodonosor. The decree which was sent out by Haman was to exterminate all the Judaeans from all the provinces of the King Ahasuerus. Judaea was a province of the Persian empire. Not a word is said about Jerusalem or the temple. We know that during the Second Commonwealth the temple was the focal point of all the Judaeans regardless where they lived. On the other hand, in the book of Judith, it is said that when the people of Judaea heard that Holofernes was marching with an army toward Judaea, they were in great fear and they were terrified for Jerusalem and the temple of Adonai, their God.

There is a vivid contrast between the two heroines. Judith was depicted as a widow, a devout person. She never ate of Holofernes' food or drank of his wine. She took along her own victuals. Esther according to the author, was beautiful but there was no mention of her religiosity. She ate and drank at the table of the heathen king. When Judith undertook her mission to assassinate Holofernes, she did it at the risk of her life, courageously, without any vacillation. To accomplish her design, she tried to beguile Holofernes, but did not have an affair with him, whereas Esther lived with Ahasuerus. While the book of Esther cannot be stamped as an irreligious work, it is certainly not a religious one. It is written as an epic to delight the readers and it is therefore understandable that the name of God, prayers, the temple are not mentioned in it. Undoubtedly many Judaeans did not like the book, but the story appealed to many others and the book was read on the fourteenth and fifteenth of Adar, the days of Purim.

I venture to postulate that the book of Judith was written to
neutralize the book of Esther. Both books have the same plot:
the children of Israel being saved by a woman. The story of
Judith is clearly intended to give the book a religious character.
The author wanted to have the book serve as a guideline for the
people. It set forth the principles of Judaism of that time. The
God of Israel is omnipotent. God will not allow the annihilation
of the children of Israel. There will be times of trial and suffering but that will only be to chastise the people. The author
also wanted to stress that God demands full obedience to Him, to
observe all of the precepts.

The author depicted Judith as a very courageous person; she
had faith in God and her people and she was ready to sacrifice
herself for them. She reproached the elders who promised the
people that, if God would not give rain in five days, they would
surrender the city to the enemy. She thought that they were
putting God to a test; when she, however, decided to go to the
enemy's camp and to slay Holofernes, she had faith in God that
she would accomplish this in the span of five days, and thus she
took provisions for only five days.

Many writers condemn Judith. While she was devoted to God
and to her people, they say, she was most frivolous, unscrupulous,
and a liar; and used feminine guile and seductiveness to achieve
her noble end by ignoble means. She used ambiguous language in
order to deceive. These accusations against Judith are not
justified. The Judaeans went through a desperate crisis. They
were on the verge of destruction by a powerful army, and rules
of war justified any tactic to combat the enemy. Armies often
engage in espionage and counter-espionage. Each side tries to
lure the other into a position of weakness in order to destroy the
opposing army. This had been going on from time immemorial.
Judith had no army. She had charm and beauty and with this
she was sure she could conquer the enemy by beguiling Holofernes. The Talmud well said that woman had an army with her,
that is sex.[20] This is her main armor. By killing Holofernes, she
knew that the army could not stand up against her people. She

[20] Ab. Zarah 25 b.

killed Holofernes not by the advice of the elders of the people. As a matter of fact, she did not tell them what she expected to do in order to save her people.

In the book of Esther we are told that when Mordecai asked Esther to go to the king and appeal to him for her people, Esther replied that she could not go to the king, for any person, man or woman, who "enters the king's presence in the inner court without having been summoned, there is but one law for him, that he be put to death." Then Mordecai sent a message to Esther: "Do not imagine that you of all the Judaeans will escape with your life by being in the king's palace. On the contrary, if you keep silent in this time, relief and deliverance will come to the Judaeans from another quarter, while you and your father's house will perish." Esther was vacillating. She had not the courage for self-sacrifice like Judith. Finally she told Mordecai that she would go to the king to plead for her people: "If I perish, I perish." Esther, while she was queen, ate in the house of King Ahasuerus and she lived with the pagan king.[20a] The Talmud tried to exonerate her by saying that Esther was merely like a natural ground,[21] i.e., while submitting to the king she did not act her part. The contrast between the two heroines is indeed fundamental.

THE SUPPLEMENTS TO ESTHER

In order to mitigate the ambivalence of some Jews towards the book of Esther for not alluding to divine intervention, passages were inserted into the Septuagint, where prayers were included. There are six supplements which are not found in the Hebrew text. Swete[22] indicates them by the letters A-F. The first supplement (A) is Mordecai's dream; ch. 2 20 adds the following passage. Esther did not disclose her nationality, for so Mordecai commanded her to fear God and perform His commandments as when she was with him; and Esther changed not her manner of

[20a] *Cf.* the Supplement C.
[21] Sanh. 74.
[22] *The Old Testament in Greek according to the Septuagint,* by Henry B. Swete, Cambridge, 1891.

life.[23] (B) is the edict of Artaxerxes against the Jews. (C) is the prayer of Mordecai: "I have done this to refuse obedience to the haughty Haman. For I would gladly have kissed the soles of his feet for the safety of Israel. But I have done this, that I might not set the glory of man above the glory of God, and I will not worship anyone except thee, my Lord." Then comes the prayer of Esther: "Save us by thy power, and help me, who am alone, I have no helper but thee, Lord. Thou knowest all that I hate the glory of transgressors and that I abhor the bed of the uncircumcised or of any heathen . . . I thy servant hath not eaten at the table of Haman, and have not honored the banquet of the king, neither have I drunk wine of libation. Neither has thy handmaid rejoiced in the day of my promotion until now except in thee, Lord God of Abraham." [24]

(D) The story of Esther's admission before the king.

(E) The decree for Artaxerxes on behalf of the Judaeans.

(F) Then comes the interpretation of Mordecai's dream.

At the end comes a colophon. "In the fourth year of the reign of Ptolemy and Cleopatra, Dositheus, who said he was a priest and Levite and his son Ptolemy, brought the above Epistle of Puraia, which they said was authentic and that it had been translated by Lysimachus, son of Ptolemy, who dwelt in Jerusalem." [25]

These supplements to Esther are considered by the Catholics as canonical, while the Protestants consider them Apocrypha. Jerome in his Vulgata places the supplements at the end of the book of Esther and calls this *supplementa deuterocanonica*.

We are faced with pertinent questions. Are the supplements translations from a Semitic (Hebrew Aramaic) original? What are the dates of the supplements? An opinion was expressed that

[23] ἡ δὲ Ἐσθὴρ οὐχ ὑπέδειξεν τὴν πατρίδα αὐτῆς οὕτως γὰρ ἐνετείλατο αὐτῇ Μαρδοχαῖος φοβεῖσθαι τὸν θεὸν, καὶ ποιεῖν τὰ προστάγματα αὐτοῦ, καθὼς ἦν μετ' αὐτοῦ καὶ Ἐσθὴρ οὐ μετήλλαξεν τὴν ἀγωγὴν αὐτῆς.

[24] ... καὶ βδελύσσομαι κοίτην ἀπεριτμήτων, καὶ παντὸς ἀλλοτρίου ...

[25] Ἔτους τετάρτου βασιλεύοντος Πτολεμαίου καὶ Κλεοπάτρας εἰσήνεγκεν Δοσίθεος, ὃς ἔφη εἶναι ἱερεὺς καὶ Λευείτης, καὶ Πτολεμαῖος ὁ υἱὸς αὐτοῦ τὴν προκειμένην ἐπιστολὴν τῶν Φρουραί, ἣν ἔφασαν εἶναι καὶ ἑρμηνευκέναι Λυσίμαχον Πτολεμαίου, τῶν ἐν Ἰερουσαλήμ.

the Greek texts are, in the main, independent translations from different Aramaic originals. The canonical book of Esther is actually an abbreviation of an earlier Aramaic book which was extant in two forms. In the abbreviated book of Esther, all references to God and prayers were removed.[26]

This theory must be disregarded. The Greek translation of Esther and the supplements were not written by one man; they were written by different men and in different periods. Lysimachus did not translate the book of Esther. The Hebrew text, the canonical book of Esther, was composed in the fourth century BCE shortly after the solar calendar was changed to lunar solar. The months were called by name, Nisan, Sivan, no longer by numbers. Whenever the names of the months are given in the book of Esther, the author adds respectively, that this is the first month, the third month, the twelfth: e.g., "On the first month, that is, the month of Nisan." [27] "The king's scribes were summoned at that time, the twenty-third of the third month, that is the month Sivan," [28] "On the thirteenth day of the twelfth month, that is the month of Adar." [29] This indicates that the book was composed shortly after the change of the calendar, when the names Nisan, Sivan, Adar had not as yet came into popular usage, and the author had to indicate each month by number. Similarly, in the first book of Kings, when referring to the months Ziv, Ethanim and Bul, the author always adds that these are the second month, the seventh month and the eighth month respectively, [30] because the Phoenician names of the months Ziv, Ethanim and Bul were no longer familiar to the people at that period, so the author has to indicate the numbers which had recently come into vogue.

In the supplements, however, the names of the months were given without explanatory numbers, "On the twenty-third day

---

[26] See C. C. Torrey, "The Older Book of Esther", *HTR*, Jan. 1944, pp. 1-40, cf. also E. J. Bickerman, "The Colophon of the Greek Book of Esther", *JBL* 1944, pp. 339-362.
[27] Esther 3 7.
[28] 8 9.
[29] 3 13; 8 12.
[30] I Kings 6-7.

of the month of Nisan," [31] "therefore these days shall be unto them in the month Adar, the fourteenth and fifteenth day of the same month." This indicates clearly that the book of Esther was written at a very earlier period, shortly after the calendar was changed and a new one was established, while the supplements were composed at a much later period.

Throughout the book of Esther, the word Judaean occurs, while the word Israel is never mentioned, while in the supplements the word Israel does occur. In the prayer of Mordecai he appealed to God to "save Israel." Again, "and all Israel cried aloud with their might." [32]

In the prayer of Esther, the author says that she prayed to the Lord, God of Israel. She appealed to God saying, "O, Lord, thou took Israel out of all the nations."

Mordecai in interpreting his dream where he saw two dragons: "Are Haman and myself; the nations are those who bothered to wipe out the Judaeans, my nation is Israel, [33] which cried aloud to God and was delivered . . . They shall observe these days, in the month Adar, on the fourteenth and fifteenth days of the month, with an assembly, and joy and gladness before God throughout the generations forever among these people Israel." [34]

From the aforequoted passages from the book of Esther and from the supplements, we must conclude that the book of Esther and the supplements were written neither by one person nor even in the same country. The book of Esther was written in Judaea, where the people were called Judaeans, while the supplements were composed in the diaspora where the term Judaean was not used but Israelite. [35] We may postulate that they were composed in Antioch.

As was noted before, the colophon contains the following, "In the fourth year of Ptolemy and Cleopatra, Dositheus, who said that he was a priest and a Levite, and his son Ptolemy, brought (to Egypt) the above letter of Puraia, as they termed it, saying

---

[31] Τῇ μιᾷ τοῦ Νισάν.
[32] Καὶ πᾶς Ἰσραὴλ ἐκέκραξαν ἐξ ἰσχύος αὐτῶν
[33] Τὸ δὲ ἔθνος τὸ ἀμὸν οὗτος ἐστιν Ἰσραὴλ . . .
[34] . . . ἐν τῷ λαῷ αὐτοῦ Ἰσραήλ.
[35] See below p. 31.

that it had been translated (into Greek) by Lysimachus, son of Ptolemy who dwelt in Jerusalem." Some scholars assign the date of the colophon to the year 114-3 as the fourth year of Ptolemy soter II (Lathyrus) while others give the date 48-7 BCE, the fourth year of Ptolemy XIV. Some suggest the year 78-77.[36]

We are confronted with the problem for whom had Lysimachus translated the book of Esther into Greek in Jerusalem? In those years, there were no Greek readers in Jerusalem. We may consent that there were some intellectuals who knew Greek, but the public at large did not read or know Greek. The knowledge of the Greek language among the Judaeans came at a much later period. It was suggested that Lysimachus made a translation in Egypt and he was a member of the Jerusalem community.[37] The Greek text, however, does not sustain this hypothesis. We may even question the authenticity of the colophon. The phrase "who was a priest and a Levite" is an awkward phrase. It is true that we do have in the Bible the phrase "priest Levites" (some have the reading "the priests and the Levites"). During the Biblical period there were no definite functions assigned to the priests and Levites in the temple, but in the fourth year of Ptolemy, regardless which Ptolemy, there were definite functions for priests and Levites in the temple. The Levites were distinct from the priests. To use the phrase "priest Levites" is not only an anachronistic, but is an awkward phrase.

It seems clear that the colophon is not an authentic document. It was intended to give authority to the statement of Dositheus who claimed that he brought the Greek letter about Prouria (Purim) that it was authentic and had been translated into Greek in Jerusalem by Lysimachus. The fact that this letter about Purim came from Jerusalem was sufficient authority for the Jews of Egypt to establish the fourteenth and fifteenth of Adar as days of joy.

Similarly, we have a letter in the beginning of the Second book

---

[36] Cf. Torrey *Ibid.*; Bickerman *Ibid.*; Robert H. Pfeiffer, *The History of the New Testament Times with an Introduction to the Apocrypha*, New York, 1941, pp. 304-312.

[37] Bickerman *Ibid.*

of Maccabees that purports to be from the Judaeans of Judaea and Jerusalem urging their brethren to celebrate Hanukkah. This letter, as we have demonstrated elsewhere, is a forgery.[38] The intent of this letter was to sanction the festival of Hanukkah as the festival of the purification of the temple, thus making Hanukkah a religious festival and hence it should be celebrated by the Judaeans not only in Judaea but also in diaspora, wherever the Jews lived.

The supplements are undoubtedly translations from Aramaic. The word φρουραί prouria is corrupted from the Aramaic word פוריא *puria*, Purim. The two letters of Artaxerxes are not translations, they were written in Greek, probably by a Jew in Egypt. The first letter is identified as the one King Artaxerxes wrote after Haman had sent out the decree in the name of the king to annihilate the Judaeans. In this letter, the king wrote: "He (Haman) represented to us that in all nations throughout the world there was scattered a certain malicious people, that had laws contrary to all nations, and continually despised the commandment of kings ... Seeing them, we understand that this people alone is continually in opposition to all men, differing in the strange manner of their laws, and evil affected to our empire, working all the mischief they can, that our empire may not be firmly established. Therefore we have commanded ... Shall all, together, with their wives and children be utterly destroyed."

In the second letter which was written after Haman was executed and a letter was sent out in the name of the king that the Judaeans had the right to avenge themselves on the fourteenth and fifteenth days of Adar, the king wrote that he had been beguiled by Haman who was a Macedonian, an alien from the Persian blood. "This man in his unbridled arrogance planned to deprive us of our empire and our lives by using fraud ... For he thought that by this method he would catch us defenseless and transfer to the Macedonians the kingdom of the Persians. But we find that the Judaeans, whom this wicked wretch had consigned to extinction, are no evil-doers, they live by most just

[38] Cf. Introduction to the Second Book of Mac.

laws and they are children of the living God most high, who maintain the kingdom in most wonderful order, for us and for our ancestors." In this letter the Jews of Egypt wanted to show that the hatred of the heathens against them was instigated by unscrupulous people who wanted to destroy not only them but the kingdom. The king had been beguiled by a villain who ordered the destruction of a people whom he did not even know. The destruction of the Judaeans was the first step to betray the kingdom by transferring it to another nation. The Judaeans do have separate laws, but they are just laws and the people were always loyal to the rulers of the land. These two letters were composed for the purpose of combatting the animosity of the heathens towards the Judaeans.

In sum, the book of Esther was written in Judaea in the fourth century BCE. The supplements, however, were written in the diaspora at a much later date. They were intended to soothe the hostility of some Jews towards the book of Esther because neither prayers nor the name of God were mentioned in the book.

THE REASON FOR THE INCLUSION OF THE BOOK OF ESTHER IN THE HOLY SCRIPTURES

The book of Esther is definitely not a religious book. The book of Judith is a religious book. We are faced with a problem. Why is the book of Esther part of the Holy Scriptures, while the book of Judith is outside of the Hebrew canon? To elucidate this problem it is important to trace the high points in the history of the canonization of the Hebrew Bible. The Hebrew Bible consists of three parts. The Torah, the Pentateuch, Prophets, and Holy Scriptures, Hagiographa. The Torah was canonized in the period of Ezra and Nehemiah in the year 444 BCE.[39] The Prophets were canonized in the early Hellenistic period. Ben Sira, in enumerating the prophets, mentioned the twelve Minor Prophets as contained in one book,[40] which indicates that in his time all the Prophets were already canonized. There were other books which

[39] See S. Zeitlin, *The Rise and Fall of the Judaean State*, V. I, pp. 21-22.
[40] Ben Sira 49.10.

were read by the Judaeans and were even recited in the temple, but were not considered holy, they were not canonized. Some of these books were canonized at the conclave of 65 CE. This group of books was called *Ketubim*, Holy Scriptures.[41] The canon at the time of the year 65 CE consisted of twenty-two books,[42] five books of the Torah, eight books of the Prophets, (Joshua, Judges, Samuel, Kings, Isaiah, Jeremiah, Ezekiel and the Twelve Minor Prophets in one book). The *Ketubim* consisted of nine books: Daniel, Ezra-Nehemiah, Chronicles, Psalms, Proverbs, Job, Lamentations, Ruth and Song of Songs. Song of Songs was included in the canon after a long dispute between the schools of Shammai and Hillel. The school of Shammai opposed the inclusion of the book in the canon and the Hillelites favored it and prevailed. The book of Koheleth was brought up before the conclave, but after a long debate it was rejected, it was not made part of the canon.[43]

The Torah, it was held, contained all the laws that God had revealed to Moses. The Prophets, the people believed that they spoke in the name of God and hence their books were second only to the Torah. The third part, the *Ketubim*, was included in the canon because it was maintained that they were "inspired," i.e., their authors had been inspired by the Holy Spirit. Thus they are designated Holy Scriptures, Hagiographa. The canonization of the book of Koheleth was brought up again at the academy of Javneh *ca.* 100 CE. The protagonists of Koheleth succeeded in the inclusion of it in the canon. Thus the Hebrew Bible consisted of twenty-three books. There is no mention whatever about the canonization of the book of Esther. Apparently it was not even considered either in the year 65 or in the year 100.

The book of Esther, as was noted above, was read on the days of Purim. Elsewhere, I quoted Rabban Simeon ben Gemaliel's statement where he said: "The Israelites never had such joyous

[41] S. Zeitlin, *An Historical Study of the Canonization of the Hebrew Scriptures*, 1933.
[42] Josephus, *Against Apion*, 1.8.
[43] Cf. S. Zeitlin, *op. cit.*

days as the fifteenth of Ab and the days of Purim,[44] for on those
days the sons of Jerusalem used to go out dressed in white
garments . . . The daughters of Jerusalem too used to go out on
these days and dance in the vineyard, saying, 'Young man, lift up
thine eyes, and consider what you will select for thyself (as a
wife); do not fix thine eyes upon beauty, but consider the
family.'" The days of Purim were indeed a marriage contest.
Purim were the days of merrymaking, a kind of carnival,
hilarious days. On these days the book of Esther was read, thus it
became a popular book with the people.

After the destruction of the temple, and particularly after the
catastrophe of Bar Kokba, the book of Esther became even more
popular because the Jews felt that the story of the book was a
consolation. Haman strove to annihilate the Jews. He did not
succeed and he himself was destroyed and he was hanged on the
gallows. It happened to those who schemed to destroy the Jews
and it could happen again. The fortunes could again be reversed.
Undoubtedly, there was a popular outcry to include the book of
Esther in the Holy Scriptures. The Talmud relates that Esther
sent a message to the sages saying: "Inscribe my book for
posterity," [45] i.e., canonize the book of Esther. What the Talmud meant was that the people requested the inclusion of the
book of Esther in the canon. The sages were at first reluctant to
include the book of Esther in the Hebrew canon,[46] but finally
yielded. We may say that the canonicity of the book of Esther
was forced on the sages by public pressure.

When the book of Esther was accepted in the Hebrew canon,
the sages endeavored to find in it passages which showed that the
book was "an inspired one," i.e., the author of the book had been
inspired by the Holy Spirit and thus the book of Esther could be
considered a part of the Holy Scriptures, but not all the sages
agreed about the inclusion of the book in the canon.

---

[44] M. Tan. 4.8. The text has כיום הכפורים, however, see my article
"Some Reflections on the text of the Talmud", *JQR,* July 1968 pp. 5-8.

[45] Meg. 7, a שלחה להם אסתר לחכמים קבעוני לדורות.

[46] Ibid. Cf. S. Zeitlin, *"An Historical Study of the Canonization of the
Hebrew Scriptures."*

The technical term for a book which is considered holy was that the book "defiled the hands." Holy books "defile the hands," [47] the secular do not. Samuel an Amora of the third century said that the book of Esther does not defile the hands, i.e., the book of Esther is not a holy book, and thus not a part of the Hebrew Bible. When he was reminded that he, himself had said once, that the book of Esther was "inspired," he retorted that it was "inspired" for reading on the days of Purim but it was not "inspired" for the inclusion in the Hebrew Bible.[48]

The decision to include the book of Esther in the Hebrew Bible was made at the academy of Ousha, *ca.* 140 CE. After its acceptance into the Hebrew Bible, the Mishne Megillah was compiled, dealing with the laws of the writing of the Scroll of Esther and the reading of it on the days of Purim.

WHY THE BOOK OF JUDITH WAS NOT INCLUDED IN THE HEBREW CANON

The book of Judith is not a part of the Hebrew canon. It is an "outside book," the reasons being as follows. The author of the book relates that after the triumph of Judith, an officer in the camp of Holofernes, Achior, an Ammonite, "joined into the house of Israel." According to the Pentateuch, "An Ammonite or a Moabite shall not enter into the assembly of Yahweh, even to the tenth generation shall none of them enter into the assembly of Yahweh forever." [49] If the book of Judith should gain acceptance into the Holy Scriptures, it would contradict the Pentateuchal laws. It is true that Ruth was a Moabite and she converted to Judaism, nevertheless the book of Ruth became a part of the Holy Scriptures. The sages, in order to reconcile the contradictory and opposing view between the book of Ruth and the Pentateuch, declared that the Pentateuchal prohibition regarding the Ammonite and the Moabite referred only to the

---

[47] Ibid. ‎אסתר ברוח הקודש . . .נאמרה לקרות ולא נאמרה לכתוב.
[48] Cf. Ibid.
[49] Deut 23 ₄.

male but not to the female.[50] Thus the book of Ruth could be very well accepted in the Hebrew canon.

It is also true that the sages during the Second Commonwealth encouraged proselytism regardless of race and no obstacles were placed against the Ammonites. However, some sages opposed the conversion of the Ammonites. A Mishne relates: "On that day, came Judah, an Ammonite proselyte, and stood before them in the *Beth Hamidrash*, and said to them, 'May I enter into the community?' Rabban Gamaliel said to him: 'You are not allowed.' Rabbi Joshua said to him: 'You are allowed.'" [51] Thus we have to conclude that in the academy of Javneh there was a division of opinion among the sages regarding the acceptance of Ammonite proselytes. The opinion of Rabbi Joshua became the established law. The opinion of Rabban Gamaliel, however, was enough to keep the book of Judith from inclusion in the Hebrew Bible.

Again, it is stated in the book of Judith that when Achior converted to Judaism, he was circumcised; it does not say that he was baptised. During the Second Jewish Commonwealth, the ritual of immersion was not required for conversion to Judaism. At the Conclave in the year 65 CE, it was decreed that a proselyte must go through the rites of baptism in order to enter the Jewish community.[52] The fact that in the book of Judith it is stated that Achior became a proselyte by circumcision alone without baptism was enough to keep the book out of the Hebrew canon. If this book should be included in the Hebrew Bible, it would mean that the book of Judith was holy and authoritative; thus there would be a contradiction between the statement in Judith and the decree of the sages who maintained that baptism is a *sine qua non*.

The book of Judith was written in a late period, after the time of Antiochus Epiphanes, as we shall subsequently show. According to the rabbinic tradition, books written after the Persian

[50] M. Yeb. 8.3.
[51] Yad. 4 4; Tosefta ibid., 2.17.
[52] Cf. S. Zeitlin, "Proselytes and Proselytism During the Second Commonwealth in the Early Tannaitic Period", 1965 (*Harry Austryn Wolfson Jubilee Volume*).

period were not "inspired," [53] thus they could not be a part of the
Hebrew Bible. Esther's story was placed in the time of Ahasuerus, while the story of Judith was placed after the time of
Antiochus Epiphanes, long after prophecy ceased in Israel.
Again, the book of Esther was written in Judaea, while the book
of Judith was compiled in the diaspora, and that is also a good
reason for its not being included in the Hebrew canon. No books
written in the diaspora were included in the Hebrew Bible.

Although Judith was not a canonical book, it exhorted a
lasting influence on religion and on the medieval literature.
There are Midrashim relating the story of Judith (one Midrash is
given in the Appendix II). Some Midrashim connect Judith with
Hanukkah. Rabbi Samuel b. Meir (Rashbam) ca. 1085-1174 CE
stated that the miracle of Hanukkah came through the inter-
ference of Judith.[54] Nachmanides *ca.* 1194-1270, in his commentary on Deuteronomy, makes a reference to the book of
Judith calling it the Scroll of Shushan.[55] In the liturgy of Sabbath Hanukkah, there is a *piyut* referring to Judith. It refers to
Judith's decapitation of Holofernes, but also the name of
Achior is there mentioned.[56]

DATE OF COMPOSITION

The composition of the book of Judith was placed in the Persian
period, in the fifth or in the fourth century BCE,[57] while some
date the composition in the second century CE after the time of
Emperor Trajan.[58] Most of the scholars believe that the book
was composed during the period of the Hasmoneans. The view
that the book was written in the second century CE, after the
war of Trajan against the Parthians, cannot be taken seriously.
Clement, one of the Apostolic Fathers, in his first epistle to the

[53] Cf. Tos. Yad. 2₁₃. ספרי בן סירא וכל ספרים שנכתבו מכאן ואילך אינן מטמאין את הידים.

[54] Tosefot Meg. 4a בפורים ע״י אסתר, בחנוכה ע״י יהודית.

[55] Deut 21 ₁₄.

[56] ... נבא למלך הנמונו אכיור ... סככתני בלילה היא יהודית.

[57] Cf. R. H. Pfeiffer, *History of the New Testament Times*, the |book of Judith and the literature there quoted.

[58] Ibid.

Corinthiansm, wrote: "The blessed Judith, when her city was besieged, asked the elders to permit her to go out into the camp of the heathens. So she gave herself up to danger, and went forth for love of her country and her people in their siege and the Lord delivered over Holofernes by the hand of a female."[59] Clement, who died in the beginning of the second century CE, already knew about the book of Judith. Thus the theory that Judith was composed in the middle of the second century CE is a pure hallucination. The theories that the book of Judith was composed in the Persian period, in the fifth or in the fourth century BCE, also cannot be seriously considered.

In Chapter IV, 1-3, the author states that when the children of Israel learned that Holofernes and his army were marching towards Judaea, they were terrified for Jerusalem and the Temple. "The sacred vessels and the altar and the House had been sanctified from the profanation." The only time when the holy vessels in the temple were polluted and then purified was in the time of Judah Makkabee when Antiochus Epiphanes profaned and polluted the vessels and the altar in the year 168 BCE. Judah Makkabee, after his victory over the Syrian army, purified and sanctified the temple and the altar in the year 165.[60] This passage in Judith militates against the theory that Judith was composed during the Persian period.

The author said that when the army of Nabouchodonosor invaded Judaea, the people were in terror, "for they had but shortly come up from their captivity, and all the people of Judaea had recently gathered together." The protagonists of dating Judith in the Persian period support themselves by this quotation. But the statement cannot be taken literally; it is incredibily absurd. The author states: "In the twelfth year of the reign of Nabouchodonosor, who reigned over the Assyrians in Nineveh." Nabouchodonosor never reigned in Nineveh, neither was he the king of the Assyrians. He was king of the Babylonians,

---

[59] 'Ιουδὶθ ἡ μακαρία, ἐν συγκλεισμῷ οὔσης τῆς πόλεως, ᾐτήσατο παρὰ τῶν πρεσβυτέρων ἐαθῆναι αὐτὴν ἐξελθεῖν εἰς τὴν παρεμβολὴν τῶν ἀλλοφύλων ... καὶ παρέδωκεν κύριος 'Ολοφέρνην ἐν χειρὶ θηλείας. (55)

[60] Cf. I Mac 4 52-60, Ed. Dropsie.

and he reigned from 605-562. Nineveh was destroyed in 612, seven years before Nabouchodonosor became king over Babylonia. Nabouchodonosor destroyed Jerusalem in 586 and the Judaean return from captivity was in 516. The whole story is full of anachronism and must be considered as fiction.

That Judith was not composed in the early Persian period is indicated from the fact that the author used the expression "night and day," [61] placing the night before the day. In a solar calendar the day preceeds the night, while in a lunar solar calendar, the night preceeds the day. The usage of the phrase "night and day" indicates clearly that Judith was written after the calendar was changed from the solar to a lunar solar.

In the prophetic books, the nomenclature for the temple is "the house of Adonai." [62] In the books of Ezra and Nehemiah, the temple was named "the house of God," no more "the house of Adonai." In the book of Judith, the temple is never referred to as "the house of Adonai," it is named shrine, sanctuary.[63] In only one place is the temple referred to as "the house of God." [64] I doubt if it is the correct text. It is also to note that although the author says that "all the people of Judaea had recently gathered together," he never mentions the word Judaean in the story. He always refers to the children of Israel. The inhabitants of Judaea were called Judaeans, not Israelites. All this militates against the theory that Judith was composed during the early Persian period.

It would be hazardous to set an exact date for the composition of Judith. From a careful analysis of the story, we may readily assume that the book was composed in the late Hasmonean period or in the early Roman period. During these periods, there were many invasions of Judaea. In other words, from the time of the victory of Judah Makkabee over Nicanor in the year 161 BCE to the time of Agrippa I in 40 CE Judaea was invaded many times.

[61] 11 17. νυκτὸς καὶ ἡμέρας.
[62] Cf. I Kings 8 10, 11; II Kings 19 1; 25 9; II Cron. 33 4; 36 14, 18.
[63] 9 8. ... τὰ ἅγιά σου; 4 13.
[64] 9 2. ... τὸν οἶκον τοῦ θεοῦ ... ; καὶ ὁ ναὸς τοῦ θεοῦ ...; 5 18.

From the story given in Judith, it seems that the author reflects the war of Nicanor against the Judaeans. In year 162-161 Demetrius I assumed the rulership over the Selucia empire. Alcimus, who was previously high priest and was removed by Judah Makkabee, went to Demetrius to complain against Judah. The king called a *Synedrion*, a council of war, where Alcimus charged Judah with traitorous acts not only against the king but also against his countrymen. He said: "These Judaeans, who are called Hasideans, whom Judah Makkabee leads, are war mongers and revolutionaries. They will not premit the kingdom to enjoy stability . . . I have now come the second time, primarily with a genuine regard for the interest of the king, secondly, mindful of the welfare of my own countrymen . . . For as long as Judah is alive peace is impossible." [65] The words of Alcimus greatly influenced Demetrius and he appointed Nicanor to invade Judaea, to make war against Judah. Nicanor invaded Judaea, he went to Jerusalem demanding from the priest of the temple to surrender Judah to him. He threatened the priest, saying: "If you do not surrender Judah to me as a prisoner, I will level this sacred enclosure to the ground, tear down the altar, and on this very place erect a magnificant shrine to Dionysus." [66] The priests, who were in great fear for the temple, prayed to God, "Most holy Adonai of all holiness, keep undefiled forever this house so recently purified." [67]

In a battle between the armies of Nicanor and Judah, Judah was victorious. Nicanor was slain, the Judaeans hanged his head "from the citadel as clear and evident proof to all of the help of Adonai." After the victory over Nicanor, the Judaeans praised God with these words: "Praise be He who has preserved His own sacred place from being defiled." The slaying of Nicanor occurred on the thirteenth day of Adar, [68] "a day before the day of Mordecai," which was decreed to be a semi-holiday.

The narration of the war of Nicanor against the Judaeans and

[65] II Mac 9 2.
[66] Ibid.
[67] Ibid.
[68] Ibid.

his defeat, particularly the hanging of Nicanor's head in front
of the temple, undoubtedly left a deep impression on the author
of Judith and he utilized it for his story. There are striking
parallels between the narrations about Nicanor and Holofernes.
It was noted before that Alcimus came to Demetrius charging
Judah Makkabee and his followers of being revolutionaries and
warmongers and causing troubles not only for the empire, but
also for their coreligionists, the Judaeans. The author of Judith
in counterpart to Alcimus relates that a general by the name of
Achior tried to persuade Holofernes not to make war against the
children of Israel. Alcimus, a former high priest, accused his coreligionists. The author of Judith in contrasting him with an
Ammonite general praised the children of Israel, and advised
Holofernes first to find out whether they were loyal to their God
and that if so they were unconquerable. It is significant to note
that King Demetrius called a *Synedrion*, a council of war,
before whom Alcimus appeared. The author of Judith tells that
Holofernes called a *Synedrion*, a council of war, before whom the
Ammonite general, Achior, appeared.

The Second Book of Maccabees was composed sometime
during the early period of Agrippa I (41-44 CE). In the Introduction, Second Book of Maccabees, the present writer wrote
that the book is an epitome of Jason of Cyrene's work who
supplied the basic facts while the epitome elaborated, embellished
and interpreted them.[69] We may safely assume that Jason
wrote the history of Judah Makkabee in the early period of the
Hasmoneans. The author of Judith who read the work of Jason
was deeply affected by the story of Nicanor. His arrogance
towards God and his blasphemous words against the temple
brought his defeat by the intervention of God and his head was
hanged at the cidatel of the temple.

The anonymous author undoubtedly was provoked by the
book of Esther which lacked spirituality and its failure to
mention the intervention of God in saving the Jews. To neutralize
the book of Esther he composed a story based on the same plot
as the book of Esther but replete with religiosity. The saving

[69] Cf. S. Zeitlin, Introduction to the Second Mac.

came through the intervention of God. The heroine of his story was a widow named Judith, in counterpart to the name Esther, who, according to the story, was an orphan. In the Bible the orphan and the widow are equated.

PLACE OF COMPOSITION

To determine the place where the book of Judith was written can be derived from the story of the book. In the book, it is stated: "And the children of Israel who dwelt in Judaea heard of all that Holofernes had done unto the nations." [70] A native of Judaea would not write "the children of Israel who dwelt in Judaea." The inhabitants of Judaea were called Judaeans. In the book of Esther, only the term Judaeans is used. Josephus, in giving the account of the history of the Second Jewish Commonwealth, always refers to the people as Judaeans. He says that the people of Judaea were called Judaeans because the inhabitants were descendants from the tribe of Judah.[71] The name Judaeans is applied to the inhabitants of Judaea in the entire Hellenistic literature as well as in the tannaitic literature of the Second Commonwealth.[71a]

The people who adhere to the same religion as the Judaeans but lived outside of Judaea were called Israelites or Hebrews.[72] This is illustrated by the different nomenclature used by Paul. When he was arrested in Judaea he said "I am a Judaean." [73] In the epistle to the Philippians, however, Paul said he was of the stock of Israel, the tribe of Benjamin, a Hebrew of the Hebrews.[74] In II Corinthians he remarked, "Are they Hebrews? So am I. Are they Israelites? So am I." [75] In the letter to the Romans he said that he was an Israelite.[76] Thus when Paul was in Judaea he called himself a Judaean, while when he was in diaspora he called himself an Israelite or a Hebrew, as the people who

[70] Judith 4 1.   [71] Josephus *Ant.* 11.5. 7 (173).
[71a] Cf. *Megilat Taanit*; M. Ned. 11.12.
[72] See S. Zeitlin, ,,The Names, Hebrew, Jew and Israel, An Historical Study'', *JQR* 1953, pp. 363-370.
[73] Acts 21 30; 22 3. ἐγώ εἰμι ἀνὴρ Ἰουδαῖος.
[74] 35. φυλῆς Βενιαμίν, Ἑβραῖος ἐξ Ἑβραίων.
[75] 1122. Ἑβραῖοί εἰσιν, κἀγώ, Ἰσραηλῖταί εἰσιν, κἀγώ.
[76] 111. ἐγώ Ἰσραηλίτης εἰμί . . . φυλῆς Βενιαμίν.

adhered to the Judaean religion of the diaspora did. The historian Dio Cassius, who lived toward the end of the second century CE, wrote: "The country has been named Judaea, and the people themselves Judaeans." [77] The fact that the word Judaean does not occur at all in the book of Judith but children of Israel stamped the book as written outside of Judaea.

When Judith was encountered by the guards of Holofernes, who asked her who she was, she said she was a daughter of the Hebrews. This is in accordance with the usage of the Bible, when an Israelite spoke to non-Jews he used the term Hebrew. When Moses and Aaron came before Pharoah, king of Egypt, to speak to him about the children of Israel, they said: "The God of the Hebrews has manifested Himself to us." (Ex 5 3). When the sailors asked Jonah: "What people are you?", he replied, "I am a Hebrew." See further my article, "The Names Hebrew, Jew and Israel; An Historical Study," *JQR*, 1953, pp. 365-379.

Again, the author states, "Joachim, the high priest, who was at that time in Jerusalem, wrote. . .." [78] The wording suggests that it was written by a person who lived outside of Judaea. It is unquestionable that the book of Judith was written in the diaspora.

In the late Hellenistic period and the end of the early Roman period, there were three great cities, centers of culture: Rome, Alexandria and Antioch. The first two cities cannot be considered as the place where the book of Judith was composed, for in Rome the Jews spoke either Greek or Latin, mostly Greek. In Alexandria the vernacular language was Greek. They did not write their literary works in Aramaic, certainly not in Hebrew. If we should assume, for the sake of argument that some people knew Aramaic and Hebrew, they would not write in these languages because they would not have sufficient readers. The final analysis is that the book of Judith, which was written in Hebrew, was composed in Antioch, where the epitomist compiled the Second Book of Maccabees. [79]

---

[77] Dio 37 ἥ τε γὰρ χώρα Ἰουδαία οὗτοι Ἰουδαῖοι ὠνομάζεται.

[78] 4 6.

[79] See S. Zeitlin, *Introduction to the Second Mac.*

THE BOOKS OF ESTHER AND JUDITH 33

Religion

The book of Judith is primarily a religious book, emphasizing that righteousness will ultimately triumph and that the children of Israel will be victorious over their enemies as long as they obey the laws of God. The author stressed the obedience to God, to fulfill all His precepts. Judith observed all the dietary laws, Judith did not fast on the Sabbath and holidays. The author stresses the observance of the tithes to the priests and Levites, drinking blood was a cardinal sin, and it was considered a sin to eat of forbidden things. God is omnipotent and omniscient. He will defend Israel only when they observe His laws.

It is to note that the tenet of reward and punishment after death does not occur in the book. The verse: "Woe to the heathens which rise up against my people; Adonai almighty will take vengeance upon them in the day of judgement, to give to their flesh fire and worms." [80] The punishment of "fire and worms" for the heathens cannot be considered a reference to punishment after death. It is literally based on the words of Ben Sira: "For the vengeance of the ungodly is fire and worms"; [81] cf. also Is 66 24. The second book of Maccabees relates that Antiochus Epiphanes was afflicted with worms, "that worms swarmed within the body of this impious, while he was still alive." [82] For the afflictions of worms as a punishment cf. Acts 12 23 where it is stated that Agrippa was punished by worms. The Prophet Zech. preached that "On that day God will punish those who worship idols." [83]

Also to be noted is the lack of reference to physical resurrection and to the immortality of the soul. Neither is there any reference in the book of Judith to Messiah. It seems that the doctrine of resurrection was not yet part of the belief of the Israelites in Antioch. Not only the name of Messiah, but the whole idea of Messiah does not occur not only in the book of Judith but not in the entire apocryphal literature which became a part of the

[80] δοῦναι πῦρ καὶ σκώληκας εἰς σάρκας αὐτῶν.
[81] ὅτι ἐκδίκησις ἀσεβοῦς πῦρ καὶ σκώληξ, 7.17
[82] II Mac 9 14.
[83] Cf. Zech 14 1-12.

Catholic Bible. The idea of a Messiah who will save the Jews
from their oppressors was not known at that time, neither to the
people who lived in Judaea nor to those in diaspora. It was
introduced by the apocalyptist Pharisees.

The Recension of the Book of Judith

Beside the Greek translation of Judith, there are other translations and recensions. There is a Latin rendering of Judith in the
Vulgate. Jerome tells us that he translated Judith from a
Chaldean (Aramaic) text. It is noteworthy that the Vulgate uses
the term Adonai Adonai Domine (16 16). (For a detailed description of the Greek and the Latin texts see below Introduction
pp. 47-50). There is also a Midrash Judith. Both of these recensions
differ considerably from the Greek; they are shorter, they omit
many details, they add, they change the order. There is a great
similarity between the Latin and the Midrash. To cite a few
examples, in ch. 7 13 in the Greek recension we have the generals
of the Assyrian army advise Holofernes, to "hold of the spring of
water which issues from the base of the mountain." In the Latin
version it is stated: "Now Holofernes, in going around about,
found that the fountain which supplied them with water ran
through an aqueduct outside the city on the south side. And he
commanded their aqueduct to be cut off." The same account is
given in the Midrash, that Holofernes himself ordered the
supply of water to be cut off.

Ch. 10 4 The Greek text says that Judith "adorned herself
gaily so as to beguile the eyes of as many as should behold her."
The Latin adds "And the Lord also gave her more beauty;
because all this dressing up did not proceed from sensuality
but from virtue and therefore the Lord increased her beauty so
that she appeared to all men's eyes incomparably lovely." [84]
The Hebrew version is similar to the Latin.[85]

In the victuals which Judith took with her when she went to

---

[84] *Et ideo Dominus hanc in illam pulchritudinem ampliavit ut incomparabili decore omnium oculis appareret.*
[85] וה' נתן לה זיו ויופי הרבה למצוא חן בעיני כל רואיה.

Holofernes cheese is not mentioned; however, in both the Latin and the Hebrew it is stated that she took along cheese.

In the Greek text we have Judith saying to Holofernes that when the water becomes scant they will resort to their cattle.[86] In the Latin version it is stated "And they have a design even to kill their cattle and to drink the blood of them," which is a great offense against God. The offense of the drinking of blood is also recorded in the Midrash.

In the Greek text we read: "When Achior beheld all which the God of Israel had wrought, he believed in God with all his heart and got the flesh of his foreskin circumcised and was added to the house of Israel unto this day." [87] The Latin version reads: "And Achior seeing the power that the God of Israel had wrought, leaving the religion of the heathens, he believed God and circumcised the flesh of his foreskin and was joined to the people of Israel, with all the succession of his kindred until this present day." [88] A similar version is given in the Midrash, that Achior left the religion of the heathens and he and all his descendants joined the people of Israel.[89] In 14 13 the Greek text reads "Waken now, our lord, for the slaves have dared to come down against us for battle." The Latin reads "Go in, and awake him; for the mice, coming out of their holes, have presumed to challenge us to fight." [90] The Midrash also reads: For the mice coming out of their holes.[91] Ozias who was one of the leaders of Bethula in the Latin [92] as well as the Midrash was entitled prince,[93] while the title prince does not occur in the Greek text.

Neither the Latin version nor the Hebrew is a rendition of the

[86] 11.10.

[87] 14.12.

[88] 14.6. *Tunc Achior videns virtutem, quam fecit Deus Israel, relicto gentilitatis ritu credidit Deo, et circumcidit carnem praeputii sui et appositus est ad populum Israel, et omnis successio generis eius usque in hodiernum diem.*

[89] בראות הנס אשר עשה הי אלהי ישראל עזב מעבוד אלילים והאמין בה' והמול בשר ערלתו ובא לחסות תחת כנפי השכינה הואוכל ילידי ביתו עד היום הזה.

[90] 14.12. *quoniam egressi mures de cavernis suis.*

[91] כי יצאו העכברים מחוריהם ופיתו אותנו למלחמה.

[92] 13.23. *Porro Ozias princeps populi Israel.*

[93] ועוזיהו נשיא ישראל.

original Hebrew. The Latin, according to Jerome, was translated
from an Aramaic i.e., Syriac text, which in turn was translated
from a Greek text. It is well established that the original text of
the book of Judith was Hebrew. That the Latin recension was
based on the Greek version can be deduced from the following.
In ch. 16 2 the Greek text has θεὸς συντρίβων πολέμους κύριος "A
Lord who crushes wars." The Hebrew undoubtedly had איש ה′
מלחמה ה′ שמו, which was taken from Ex 15 3 where the Septagint
had Κύριος συντρίβων πολέμους Κύριος ὄνομα αὐτῷ "The Lord
crushes wars, the Lord is His name." The Greek translator in
rendering the verse in the book of Judith just copied the text of
the Septuagint. The Vulgate in rendering this passage of Judith
has, "*Dominus coterens bella, Dominus nomen est illi*, The Lord
putteth an end to wars, the Lord is His name." However, in
translating the Pentateuchal passage, Ex 15 3 the Vulgate has,
Dominus quasi vir pugnator, omnipotens nomen eius, "The Lord
is a man of war, Almighty is His name." In the Pentateuch the
Vulgate has an exact rendition of the Hebrew text. In Judith
however, the Vulgate follows the Greek text. This is a clear indication that the prototype of the Latin version of Judith was
Greek. The Midrash has likewise a rendering from an Aramaic or
Syriac text which again the prototype was a Greek text.

The Greek text is a faithful rendering from the Hebrew. From
the reading of the book of Judith we can readily see that the
author of the book utilized the Biblical style. He copied not only
words, phrases, but entire verses from the Bible. The Greek
translator, in order to translate the Hebrew into Greek, used the
Septuagint which made it easier for him in rendering the Hebrew
text into Greek. It was pointed out previously that the Greek
translator of Judith (16 2) in rendering the Hebrew, איש ה′
מלחמה ה′ שמו, followed the Septuagintal translation of Ex 15 3
Κύριος συντρίβων πολέμους.

V. 7 28 the Greek text has, καὶ Κύριον τῶν πατέρων ἡμῶν, "Our
God and the Lord of our fathers." The term Κύριος, "Lord", is a
rendering of the word *Adonai*. *Adonai* is not a cipher for God,
neither is it a title. Adonai is a proper name. Since the Tetragram-
maton could not be pronounced, the term Adonai was sub-

stituted to take the place of the word Yahweh. *Adonai* is a proper name, it does not suffer declension. It cannot be used as an adjective or as a pronoun. The word *Adonai* cannot have an article. The Hebrew language cannot have the expression *Adonai* of our fathers. It seems to me that this Greek rendering has a Christological implication. The early Christians added the title Κύριος "The Lord," to Jesus. Paul in his Epistles is applying the term "Our Lord," τοῦ Κυρίου, ἐν Κυρίῳ. The Apostolic Fathers do likewise in referring to Jesus . . . τῷ Κυρίῳ, Ἰησοῦ — Χριστοῦ — "Our Lord, Jesus Christ." [94]

The Catholics accepted the book of Judith as a part of the Bible. The Vulgate has after the book of Nehemiah, Tobit, Judith and Esther. The Protestants placed the book of Judith among the apocryphal books. To the Jews, the book of Judith is an "outside book." Although Judith is an extracanonical book it influenced Jewish thought and literature. Jerome in the end of the book has the following, *Dies autem victoriae huius festivitatis, ab Hebraeis in numero sanctorum dierum accipitur, et colitur a Iudaeis ex illo tempore usque im praesentem diem,* "The day of the festivity of this victory is received by the Hebrews in the number of the Holy Days and is religiously observed by the Jews in that time until this day." It is questionable if this passage came from Jerome. However, there is some kernel of history that the story of Judith was connected with the victory of the Hasmoneans over the Syrians. As a matter of fact, the Midrash of Judith gives Holofernes as the king of Greece. It is probable that the book of Judith was read by the Jews in the synagogue during Hanukkah together with the Scroll of Antiochus.[95]

[94] Cf. I Clement. 20.
[95] Cf. above p. 26.

INTRODUCTION
LITERARY CONCERNS

MORTON S. ENSLIN

The story of Judith is an example of Jewish fiction at its best. The purpose of the author of this popular tale is not to recount history as such; rather he is concerned with picturing once again the nature and attempts of world powers hostile to the people of God who are saved by their covenant God from all assaults so long as they keep the law inviolate. But while this emphasis is always to the fore—"And whilst they did not sin before their God good things were theirs because God who hates iniquity was with them" (5 17)—the book is in no sense allegory. Rather the author has given life to this basic religious confidence, not by rewriting any one incident in Israel's history, but rather through the invention of a romantic story, with many colorful details borrowed from earlier stories known to him from the Bible, from history as he had learned it, and from tradition.

Nabouchodonosor, king of the Assyrians, has sent from his capital city Nineveh his chief general Holofernes to the west to exact vengeance on all who had refused to support him in his war against Arphaxad "who reigned over the Medes in Ecbatana." All but the Jews surrendered in terror. Now Holofernes is besieging Bethulia, a hilltop town which controls an important mountain pass to the south, before attempting to proceed against Jerusalem. He had received warning from one of the native leaders, Achior the Ammonite, now conscripted in his own army, that the city could not be taken so long as the people kept inviolate their ancestral law. In contempt, he had sent Achior in chains to the foot of the hill on which Bethulia stood, with the promise that he should die along with the Bethulians when the city fell, as fall it would. Then on the advice of other of his leaders he encamped in the valley before

Bethulia and seized all the sources of water outside the city.

With their source of water now gone the beleagured citizens in dire distress demanded that their leaders surrender the city to the enemy, and the leaders agreed so to do if within the next five days help from the Lord had not come. In this crisis Judith, a beautiful and devout widow of noble descent, rebukes the elders and promises God's intervention by her hand. She proceeds, in enticingly fair attire, to the camp of the enemy, is conducted to Holofernes' tent, and wins his confidence by the promise to inform him the instant their God's protection of the city ceases in consequence of the violation of the law which they are momentarily planning. At the opportune moment, when Holofernes, preluding his expected conquest of the lovely visitor with a banquet, was "fair swimming in wine," she cuts off his head with his own sword, places it in the bag for ritually permitted food which her attendant had brought with them, and hastens back to Bethulia with the news of her triumph.

She is joyously welcomed by her fellow townsmen and the prisoner Achior, who promptly recognizes the might of Israel's God and as a convert gets himself circumcised. The head of Holofernes is affixed to the city wall. The men of the city descend upon the Assyrians, paralyzed by the murder of their leader, rout them, and plunder their tents. The high priest in Jerusalem, to whom the good news is speedily carried, comes to Bethulia and ceremoniously blesses Judith. Following a prayer of thanksgiving led by Judith, they go to Jerusalem where Judith dedicates to the temple the spoils of Holofernes which her grateful fellow townsmen had earlier given her, together with the costly canopy which she herself had taken, along with his head, from the bed of the vanquished foe. The book ends with a brief word concerning the last days of Judith in Bethulia where she had remained in her widowhood, honored throughout the land, and dying at the ripe old age of a hundred and five years.

That the book of Judith, long known only in its Greek dress or in versions (Old Latin, Vulgate, Syriac) made from the Greek,

was originally written in Hebrew is recognized by all scholars.[1] The text as we have it is not Greek with a sprinkling of Hebraisms but is from start to finish not only a translation but a very literal one, regularly following its Hebrew original in both idiom and syntax. But the translation is for the most part very skillfully done, and the Greek version does not materially suffer. Occasionally, in contrast to the regular paratactic sequences of indicatives with the plethora of καί's, not only used as connectives but also added in a way foreign to both English and Greek, examples of more normal Greek syntax occur, with hypotactic participles and even an occasional genitive absolute. But by and large it is the other way, and constantly what must have been the Hebrew original is obvious. In Greek of all periods the noun πρόσωπον ("face") is found, but this does not account for its surfeit in Judith, both with and without accompanying prepositions, ἐπί, εἰς, ἐν, ἐκ, ἀπέναντι, ἀπό, κατά. This one fact alone would be sufficient to raise the question, which finds answer in such phrases as ἡμέρας πολλάς, ἐν ταῖς ἡμέραις, πλῆθος πολὺ σφόδρα; such idioms "mouth of the sword," "inherit" in the sense "take possession," "young man" (נער) in the sense of "servant"; the mild oath, "as thy soul liveth" (akin to our colloquial "as sure as you are alive"); εἰ μήν after a verb of swearing (אם לא); "a month of days" (3 10); and the pleonastic ἐν οἷς ... ἐν αὐτοῖς (7 10) or ὧν ... αὐτῶν (16 4), which inelegance, while not limited to any one language, is definitely more common in good Hebrew than it is in Greek. Not only are these Hebraisms at home on every page but they have definitely choked out elements normally present in Greek idiom. Throughout the book ἄν occurs but four times; ἄρα, τε, and οὖν do not appear at all; μέν occurs but once. Occasionally the Greek as we have it is very obscure, even impossibly awkward. With not too great ingenuity in some of these cases it is possible to visualize the Hebrew which the author had faithfully sought

---

[1] Formerly occasional voices were raised in defense of a Greek original—Fabricius, Jahn, Eichhorn. Eichhorn saw clear evidence of this in the reference to "Titans and giants" (16 7) and also in the perplexing phrase λύειν μίτραν (9 2).

to render, but which in all likelihood he had misread. While it is possible to multiply these genuine cases of mistranslation and to find on every page in every ancient book things obscure to the original translator or scribe which are crystal-clear to the modern scholar who has carefully studied Kautzsch or Hadley and Allen, a few more legitimate cases are to be found— and they add weight to the impressive total evidence pointing to translation.

But while it is certain that had the translator composed the narrative directly in Greek the syntax would have been distinctly different, nonetheless it is unfair to damn it with the easy phrase "translation Greek." Despite his amazingly faithful following of Hebrew idiom and composition, he has produced a very readable book. Occasionally, as in the opening sentence, syntax vanishes in what seems a cluttered congeries of words. That is the fault of the original writer, with what Ball styles "the Hebrew cast" plainly visible. But such cases are comparatively rare. Again, the translator has and has used a very large vocabulary. The way he avoids needless and tiresome repetition with a different word is notable. As an index verborum shows, he uses 1250 different words in all. He uses 183 words beginning with alpha; of these 183 102 are used but once. Compounds and synonyms abound. This is scarcely automatic translation but shows a decided nimbleness on the part of the translator.

In his appreciative appraisal of the book as a whole—and here, of course, it is the Hebrew original, not the Greek translation, that is of moment—Pfeiffer remarked:

The chief literary defect of the book is the lack of simplicity; the gorgeous Oriental *mise en scène*, the turgid style, the patent exaggerations, the stately pomp and ceremony throughout, unrelieved by a sense of humor, give to the book a baroque rather than a classic appearance. A comparison of the story of Judith's deed in prose (12:10-13:10) or in verse (16:6-9) with the similar assassination of a foe by Jael, as sung in Deborah's ode (Judg. 5:24-27) or told in simple prose (Judg.

4:17-22), is a contrast between the extravagantly ornate and the superbly natural, between sophistication and un- adorned reality, between conscious and unconscious art.[2]

This is very true and is characteristic of the period in which each is written. Nonetheless, despite such "literary blemishes" Judith is a superb example of an ancient short story. It may be "unrelieved by a sense of humor," but the patent double-entendre in several of Judith's words to Holofernes, who mistakes their meaning as the wily charmer intended he should, are not lost on the reader who sees entirely aright that they are not promising the loss of her virtue and her people's land and lives, as Holofernes confidently believes, but of his own head and army. Judith herself may be a bit too good to be true, and the reader may be inclined to wonder if her husband Manasseh did not find life with her at times as trying as presumably Xantippe had with Socrates. But these wonderings come as we reflect on the story, not while we are reading it. It may have "stately pomp" and "patent exaggeration," but the author is always master of his material. Never does he have need of an actual or literary *deus ex machina* to resolve what has become a bit too complicated. The entire absence of miracle, even of supernatural portent, is an element often overlooked but nevertheless real and signific- ant. As the story stands, there is nothing impossible or even unlikely in the main plot, save perhaps the size of the bag required to carry Holofernes' head and the bejeweled canopy which had decked his bed, or the utter rout of the panic-stricken Assyrians. And for the early readers of the tale this latter was no problem. It had happened again and again in the days of Asa (II Chron 14 1-15), of Jehoshaphat (II Chron 20 1-30), and Hezekiah (II Kings 19 35-37). In sum, it is a story where patriotism and piety are tightly wedded, where precisely what ought to happen does happen, and moves steadily to its climax and stops when the end has been reached.

Although surely written by a Jew in Hebrew and not im- possibly in Palestine, it failed apparently in winning any lasting

[2] Pfeiffer, *History of New Testament Times*, p. 299.

place in Palestinian Jewry. The fact that it was translated into Greek and is secure, along with Tobit and Esther, in the LXX would suggest that it was prized by Jews to whom the LXX was the Bible until Christian adoption of it rendered it suspect and led to new Greek translations—Aquila, Symmachus, and Theodotion—unspoiled by Christian use and misuse. That neither Philo nor Josephus mentions the book or its heroine has been often remarked. To Volkmar the silence of Josephus was but an added proof of the lateness of the book. Josephus did not mention it for the very good reason that it had not been written until years after his death. That Philo does not mention the book is not surprising and in no way suggests it was not known and in use in Alexandria and elsewhere in Greek-speaking Jewry in his day. Philo's concern is with the Pentateuch. His use, even his mention, of the other books is minimal. Ezekiel he passes by in silence as he does all the Twelve save Hosea and Zechariah. He makes no mention of Daniel or the five Megilloth, and save for Psalms makes little use of the rest of the *Kethubim*—he cites Proverbs twice, Job and Chronicles once each. None of the apocrypha finds mention in his pages. Thus his failure to mention Judith tells nothing of the age of the book or its popularity.

For Josephus the situation is probably much the same. He makes no mention of Job. Caution is well-advised in the matter of confident deductions that the silence of an ancient writer on this point or that is proof of his ignorance of it. On the other hand, the fact that he devotes two pages to Deborah and Jael [3] makes his silence regarding the similar preservation of Israel by the later heroine eloquent. Whatever his opinion about the book, his neglect of the crisis it depicts certainly suggests that he did not regard the incident or its heroine in the domain of historical concern.

Whatever may have been true in the century following the composition of the tale, by the time of Origen there was no use of the book among Palestinian Jews or any known Hebrew text in existence. His word to Africanus is explicit:

[3] *Antt.* 5, 5, 2-4 (§§ 200-09).

Περὶ Τωβίᾳ ὑμᾶς ἐχρῆν ἐγνωκέναι ὅτι τῷ Τωβίᾳ οὐ χρῶνται (οἱ Ἑβραῖοι) οὐδὲ τῇ Ἰουδίθ. οὐδὲ γὰρ ἔχουσιν αὐτὰ καὶ ἐν ἀποκρύφοις Ἑβραϊστί, ὡς ἀπ' αὐτῶν μαθόντες ἐγνώκαμεν. [4]

He knows the book and refers to it several times,[5] as does his predecessor Clement,[6] but it is the Greek text which he knows, and the information he has received from his Jewish sources is that no Hebrew copy was known to exist. A century and a half later than Origen Jerome claims to have interrupted his more pressing work to translate a "Chaldee" text of the book. He did so most unwillingly, but since the book had been recognized by the Council of Nicea as sacred scripture, he yielded to pressure and made a very hasty translation "in one night," in which he "sought to give sense for sense, not word for word." [7]

Great caution is always necessary in evaluating Jerome's claims. It is scarcely an overstatement that whenever an obscure work was mentioned, Jerome made haste to claim that he had translated it. Despite his claim in his preface to Daniel to having studied Aramaic assiduously so that he could read and understand it,[8] it is highly likely that his proficiency in this regard is not understated. It would be quite possible to assume that his "translation" of Judith was essentially a revision of Old Latin texts, with some reference to Greek copies from which the Old Latin had been earlier translated. But Jerome's translation of Judith, which became a part of the Latin Vulgate, is so different in many respects from the common Greek text that

---

[4] *Epist. ad Africanum* 13.
[5] *Hom.* 9 *in Judices*; *Hom.* 19 *in Jerem.*; *Comm. in Joann.* ii, 16.
[6] *Strom.* iv, 19.
[7] *Apud Hebraeos liber Judith inter Hagiographa legitur: cuius auctoritas ad roboranda illa quae in contentionem veniunt, minus idonea iudicatur. Chaldaeo tamen sermone conscriptus, inter historias computatur. Sed quia hunc librum Synodus Nicaena in numero sanctarum legitur computasse, acquievi postulationi vestrae immo exactioni: et sepositis occupationibus quibus vehementer arctabar, huic unam lucubratiunculam dedi, magis sensum e sensu, quam ex verbo verbum transferens. Multorum codicum varietam vitiossimam amputavi: sola est quae intelligentia integra in verbis Chaldaeis invenire potui, Latinis expressi*—Preface to Judith.
[8] *Et ut verum fatear, usque ad praesentem diem magis possum sermonem Chaldaicum legere et intelligere quam sonare.*

many scholars incline to believe that he had become acquainted with an Aramaic translation of the book which he then translated into Latin, with the aid of Jewish scholars who assisted him by translating orally the Aramaic into Hebrew, which latter Jerome then hastily rendered into Latin. But there is no basis for assuming that the supposititious Aramaic text was itself a direct translation from the no longer existent Hebrew original. Rather it, like the Old Latin and Syriac versions, was a translation from the Greek, and made during the years after Origen, in whose days such a version was unknown. Thus the Vulgate would seem to be many stages removed from the supposedly original Hebrew—several more stages removed, in fact, than either our Greek or even the Old Latin.

These further intervening steps (Hebrew→ Greek→ Aramaic→ Hebrew→ Latin), plus Jerome's but hasty clawing over into Latin, with omission of all he either failed to understand or disapproved, are quite sufficient to account for the distinct differences between the resultant Vulgate and our common Greek texts. It is unnecessary to list all these difference here. Those of especial interest are mentioned in the commentary. Suffice it to say that not only is the Vulgate distinctly shorter, omitting many details and incidents, such as the honor guard of 100 men who conducted Judith to the tent of Holofernes or the mention of Judith's freeing of her favorite handmaid and her disposition of her property, but many other details are substantially altered. One notable addition is the high priest Eliakim's—he is so named in the Vulgate—especial commendation of Judith for having remained a widow after her husband's death.[9] Knowing Jerome's misogamy and his fondness for detailing—especially to young ladies—the immeasurable superiority of virgins to those who had enjoyed the marital embrace, one wonders if this little gem was not one of Jerome's own additions.

---

[9] *Tu gloria Ierusalem, tu laetitia Israel, tu honorificentia populi nostri; quia fecisti viriliter et confortatum est cor tuum, eo quod castitatem amaveris, et post virum tuum alterum nescieris* (15 11 Vg).

The earliest mention of the book which we have is by Clement of Rome:

> Many women have received power through the grace of God and have performed many deeds of manly valor. The blessed Judith, when her city was besieged, asked the elders to suffer her to go out into the camp of the strangers. So she gave herself up to danger, and went forth from love of her country and her people in their siege, and the Lord delivered over Holofernes by the hand of a woman.[10]

With Judith Clement lists Esther in his brief encomium. It is of interest to observe that Clement of Alexandria's mention of Judith [11] in his parallel but extended catalogue is obviously a repetition of Clement of Rome's word. His opening word, "In this perfection it is possible for men and women equally to share," and the mention of Judith and Esther as the first two in his Let-us-now-praise-famous-women leave little question as to his literary dependence.

While the date commonly ascribed to I Clement (96 C.E.) is perhaps less certain than is generally assumed, it can scarcely be later than 125 C.E., and is thus clear evidence of the production of Judith well prior to the end of the first Christian century. It is also to be noted that Clement accepts not merely the book, to which he makes no more specific mention, but its story as history.

It is patent and universally recognized that the preservation of what is styled the Old Testament Apocrypha and Pseudepigrapha is due to Christian early acceptance of them rather than due to any Jewish fondness for these writings which failed to gain the approbation of the Jewish pundits in Jamnia. But this commonly voiced pronouncement fails to recognize the fact that the reason that some of these writings had become familiar to Christians was that they were firmly contained in the LXX which they had not unnaturally come to regard

[10] I Clem 55 3-5.
[11] *Strom.* iv, 19.

as their Bible. Only so is its encounter, not to mention its acceptance, to be accounted for by early Christians.

Jerome's claim to have known and translated an Aramaic version of the book would seem to indicate that by his day a belated interest in the story was coming to be felt by some Jews to whom Greek was not the language of their use.[12] Presumably this was well after the days of Origen who attests the absence of anything such, be they copies or translations of the earlier writing. Following Jerome's day there is no further indication of the writing in Hebrew or Aramaic dress for many centuries. We do have several Hebrew versions of the book, all comparatively recent and of little or no value for critical problems in the book. See pp. ..... These are all greatly abridged and modified rewritings of the Greek translation. To regard them, or any of them, as M. Gaster so confidently did, in any sense directly derived from the hypothetical original Hebrew would seem quite unwarranted.

Our Greek text is extant in what may be loosely styled three recensions: (1) that represented by LXX codices B, ℵ, A, N, and many minuscules; (2) that represented by the two minuscules 19 and 108 in the listing by Holmes and Parsons. In the Brooke-McLean-Thackeray *The Old Testament in Greek* these are labeled b' and b respectively. They may conceivably reflect Lucian's recension; (3) that represented by Holmes and Parson 58 (B-M-T, k), which is certainly the type of text followed by both the Old Latin and the Syriac.

All critical editors consider (1) the basic text, although occasionally the variants of the other two, notably 58, are of concern. Rahlffs, whose text is reproduced in this series, tends to follow ℵ (S) more rigorously than does the Cambridge Septuagint, which latter tends to favor B. Holmes and Parsons is still an indispensable tool for both the textual critic and the translator and has not been antiquated by the very useful Cambridge Septuagint. The daughter translations—Old Latin, Syriac, Sahidic, and Ethiopic—are conveniently available in Sabatier,

---

[12] His statement "Apud Hebraeos liber Judith inter Hagiographa legi-tur" (see n. 7) is in striking contrast to the word of Origen (see n. 4).

Bibliorum Sacrorum Latinae Versiones Antiquae, Ceriani and Lagarde for the Syriac, Herbert Thompson, *A Coptic Palimpsest*, for the Sahidic, and Dillmann's *Veteris Testamenti Aethiopici Tomus Quintus, Libri Apocryphi*, for the Ethiopic. In this commentary Rahlffs' text is reprinted, but not his apparatus criticus of variants. Instead, only such variants are listed as appear of consequence for the translation and commentary.

References to Judith are not uncommon in the Fathers. Not only do Clement and Origen refer to her deed of daring heroism but both apparently on occasion quote from the book, as they do other scripture. "And he that is near the Lord is full of stripes" [13] has seemed to most interpreters a likely citation of Judith's word, "The Lord scourges them who draw nigh to him." [14] Even more striking is Origen's word in his Commentary on John.[15] In Jerome's *Against Rufinus* a fragment from Origen's sixth book of *Stromata* is quoted, in which the advice is given that a man under the necessity of lying should do it most discretely and within sober limits, using his falsification as a condiment or medecine, even as Judith did in her contest with Holofernes *et vicit eum prudenti simulatione verborum*.[16] She is frequently referred to, both in connection with Deborah as a valiant champion for Israel and with Anna as a chaste and devout widow. The concluding word of his preface to Judith Jerome begins with the word: *"Accipite Judith viduam castitatis exemplum."* He even sees Judith *de Hebraea historia*, who like Anna spent all her time in the temple with prayer and fasting, *in typo Ecclesiae, diabolum capite truncavit.*[17] Even Tertullian has a kindly word for her, citing along with "Isaac our monogamist father" and "John a noted voluntary celibate of Christ's" "Judith daughter of Merari" with "so many other examples of saints." [18] In the Apostolic Constitutions there are

[13] ὁ ἐγγὺς κυρίου πλήρης μαστίγων—Clem., *Strom.* ii, 7.
[14] μαστιγοῖ κύριος τοὺς ἐγγίζοντας αὐτῷ—Jud 8 27.
[15] ὅτι ταπεινῶν ἐστὶ θεὸς καὶ ἐλαττόνων βοηθός, ἀντιλήπτωρ ἀσθενούντων—*Comm. in Joann.* ii, 22, 16; ταπεινῶν εἶ θεός, ἐλαττόνων εἶ βοηθός, ἀντιλήμπτωρ ἀσθενούντων—Jud 9 11.
[16] *Adv. Rufinum* i, 474 (*P.L.* 23, p. 431).
[17] *Ep.* 79, *ad Salvinam* (*P.L.* p. 732, [508]).
[18] *De Monog.* 17.

several references to her, all laudatory, joining her with Miriam and Deborah and Huldah,[19] with Esther and Mordecai,[20] with Anna,[21] and citing her as a perfect example of true widowhood, because she lived for many years after the loss of her husband "soberly and unblameably and had taken extraordinary care of her family." [22] Methodius (*ob.* 311) in his *Banquet of the Ten Virgins*, a christianized imitation at considerable remove from Plato's *Symposium*, ends with a hymn sung decorously by Thecla, in honor of Christ and his bride the Church. In this paean, after citing such worthies as Abel, Joseph, and Jephthah, Thecla praises "daring Judith, by clever wiles having cut off the head of the leader of the foreign hosts, whom previously she had allured by her beautiful form, without polluting the limbs of her body." [23] Ambrose of Milan saw her as religiously important for her act in saving the chosen people and its holy customs and sacraments from destruction.[24] Thomas Aquinas is also laudatory, but declares Judith praised not because she lied so successfully but because of her great devotion to her people.[25] Martin Luther viewed the book as an allegory, not as history, but listed it as the first of the eight writings in the Apocrypha which are not to be regarded as scripture yet are useful and worthy of being read.

Occasional criticism of this detail or that in the story was raised. Capellus thought the writing "a most silly fable, invented by a most inept, injudicious, impudent, and clownish Hellenist," concocted to praise officious lies and pious frauds.[26] But for the most part whatever doubts were expressed were those regarding the place, not of Judith alone but of all the Apocrypha, in scripture.

[19] *Apostol. Const.* 8, 2.
[20] *Ibid.*, 5, 20.
[21] *Ibid.*, 3,7.
[22] *Ibid.*, 8, 25.
[23] Methodius, *Banquet* xi, 2.
[24] *De Offic. ministr.* iii, 13; cf. *de Viduis* 17, where Judith is highly praised for her bravery and sobriety.
[25] *Summa* ii, 2, quest. 110, art. 3.
[26] L.Cappellus, *Commentaria et notae criticae in Vet. Test.*, p. 575. I am indebted for this citation to Pfeiffer, *op. cit.*, p. 292.

In the Christian church it was different. During the first two centuries all the books of the Greek canon were regarded as Scripture. Frequently, as already noted, Judith is cited and quoted in such a way as to suggest no suspicion as to its value. In the fourth century a change is to be seen. The Eastern church, as represented by Athanasius, Cyril of Jerusalem, and Epiphanius, did not recognize these books as canonical, but frequently cited them. In his famous Festal Letter Athanasius styles them "not canonical but decreed by the fathers to be read." [27] Epiphanius seems to have included Tobit and Judith with Esther and to have introduced an intermediate class of writings "not in the ark" but yet "good and useful." The Western church, as evidenced by Augustine and Innocent I, disregarded Jerome's prejudice against all writings not in the Hebrew scriptures, and considered them canonical, thus seemingly preferring to recognize Christian usage rather than scholarly theories as to origin. The fact that Augustine accepted them as canonical Scripture outweighed Jerome's restriction of them to the rank of books to be read for edification but not "for confirming the authority of church dogma." Thus in the earliest manuscript Bibles—B and ℵ in the fourth century, A in the fifth [28]—they appear and are interspersed, not connected in a limbo at the end.

Somewhat later the Greek church seems to have returned to its earlier view and to have accepted all the books of the Apocrypha. Thus there were two opposing views in the early Christian church: one which regarded them as canonical, the other which viewed them as uncanonical since they were not in Hebrew scripture. This divergent attitude still persists, although in weakened form. For the most part Roman Catholic tradition follows Augustine, disregarding Jerome's scholarly doubts, and views them as canonical, regularly styling them "deuterocanonical," but according them the full authority which Jerome had denied them. Protestant tradition has never regarded them as "sacred Scripture" but has regularly styled them

[27] οὐ κανονιζόμενα μὲν τετυπωμένα δὲ παρὰ τῶν πατέρων ἀναγινώσκεσθαι.
[28] I and II Macc do not stand in B and A.

"apocryphal," a term which Catholic historians tend to use for books in neither the Greek nor Hebrew Bibles, and which Protestants often style "pseudepigraphical."

Despite prevailing opinion some scholars never forgot Jerome's strictures. Nicholas of Lyra (*ob. ca* 1340), a Christian of Jewish parentage, wrote two commentaries, one on the canonical books of the Hebrew Old Testament, the other on the noncanonical scripture. Luther was greatly influenced by Nicholas, and in his famous translation sets them apart from and after the rest of the Old Testament books, with the caption:

Apocrypha. Das sind Bücher: so nicht der heiligen Schrift gleich gehalten: und doch nützlich und gut zu lesen sind.

With the authority of Scripture now a burning one since they had broken from Rome, with texts of the Hebrew Old Testament once more available for scholarly use, with Jerome's words ringing in their ears, and with a dislike for some of the doctrines which Rome had deduced from several of the books of the Apocrypha, this step was natural. A century and a half before Luther Wycliffe had left them out of his translation into English, with the word in the preface that the books which stood outside the Hebrew Old Testament were "without authority of belief."

It was in no small part as a counterblast to the Reformers that the Council of Trent in 1516 made its momentous decision, reaffirming the canon as it stood in the Vulgate, and with the portentous word that whoever did not recognize as sacred and canonical (*sacri et canonici*) all the books contained in the Vulgate would be anathema.

Luther's arrangement of them between the Old Testament and the New was followed by other translations, as the French, Scandinavian, and English. In 1626 copies of the King James began to appear without the Apocrypha, and a growing opposition to them led to their exclusion by the British and Foreign Bible Society and subsequently by the American.

No Protestant denomination has ever officially accepted any of the Apocrypha as canonical Scripture. Opinions regarding their values have differed. The Anglican church recognizes

the books as instructive and edifying, without being inspired; in the words of the Thirty-nine Articles:

> And the other books (as Hierome saith) the Church doth read for example of life and instruction of manners: but yet doth it not apply them to establish any doctrine.

On the other hand, the Calvinistic view, followed by most Protestant bodies and indicated in the Westminster Confession, is that they should be rejected as having no authority in the church and are not to be approved or made use of other than other human writings.

So the stalemate has continued. During recent years, with growing unconcern for their canonical or noncanonical nature, there has been an increasing interest in them, quite apart from their import in shaping doctrine. Once again they are being included in modern editions of the Bible in Christian circles. Not unnaturally there has been no parallel situation in Jewish circles, for the problem of canonicity was settled nearly two millennia ago. On the other hand, a growing recognition of the values in these books long disregarded is to be seen in Jewish circles, notably in the preparation of a new edition of the Apocrypha and Pseudepigrapha, of which this edition of Judith is Volume 7, under the sponsorship of Dropsie University. The Foreword to I Maccabees in this series indicates the growing concern in Jewry for a literature which was produced by Jews only to fall into centurylong disregard.

So far as its position as canonical or noncanonical Scripture and its use in regard to church doctrine or practice is concerned, the situation of Judith is essentially that of the other writings dubbed Apocrypha; but in its influence in popular circles Judith is conspicuous in all centuries. Many are the scenes found on the walls of the catacombs which portray incidents in the story as we know it. In the Anglo-Saxon Chronicle, in what apparently commemorates the prowess of Aethelflaed, Lady of the Mercians, her slaying of "the heathen hound" has seemed to many a clear reflection of the notable deed of

Judith and a lengthy expansion of 13 8a.[29] Certainly Chaucer
made effective use of Judith's prowess several times, notably
in "The Monke's Tale":

> But tak keep of that dethe of Olipherne:
> Amyd his host he dronke lay one night,
> Withinne his tente, large as is a berne;
> And yit, for al his pomp and al his might,
> Judith, a womman, as he lay upright
> Slepying, his heed off smot, and fro his tent
> Ful privily she stole from every wight,
> And with his heed unto hir toun she wente.[30]

To what extent Shakespeare used the story is uncertain. That
he knew it is sure from the name Holofernes which the school-
master in *Love's Labour's Lost* bears. Nor is it to be forgotten
that two of his own daughters bore the names Judith and
Susanna. There can be little question that Judith has exercised
an almost unparalleled influence on writers of all sorts—poets,
dramatists, novelists. Specific references may be found in the
surveys by Herbert Pentin,[31] Edna Purdie,[32] and Rose Glaymen.[33]

[29] Cf. A. S. Cook, *Judith, an Old English Epic Fragment*, p. 11. Cook
discusses in detail an early-tenth-century Old English poem of which the
last three cantos are extant. He raises the possibility that it was from the
pen of Cynewulf, although inclining himself to the guess that it was
composed by St. Swithun (bishop of Winchester) in or about 856 C.E.

[30] Other references are to be found in "the Man of Lawes Tale," in
"The Marchaundes Tale," and in the prose "Tale of Melibeus."

[31] Herbert Pentin, *Judith* (London, 1908), treats the Anglo-Saxon
poem (cf. n. 29) in some detail; then he lists with brief comments allusions to Judith in literature, art, and music. In the last chapter of this
popular treatment he discusses in detail the tragedy *Judith of Bethulia*
by the American poet and littérateur, Thomas Bailey Aldrich.

[32] Edna Purdie, *The Story of Judith in German and English Literature*
(Paris, 1927). Miss Purdie catalogues some 106 works—poems, songs,
cantatas, plays, operas—treating the Judith story, from the ninth-century
fragment "Versus de Judit et Holofernem" to Eugene Goossen's announced opera to be based on Arnold Bennett's play *Judith*. This list
(pp. 1-22) is followed by a detailed study of the various treatments
of the Judith story (pp. 23-137).

[33] R.E. Glaymen, *Recent Judith Drama and its Analogues* (Philadelphia,
1930). This doctoral dissertation treats plays on all biblical themes.

' Among the notable productions of Thomas Augustine Arne was the oratorio *Judith*, first given at Drury Lane in 1761. At a later performance at the Covent Garden Theatre twelve years later Arne introduced for the first time female voices into the oratorio's choruses. In opera too Judith finds herself at home. Marco da Gagliano wrote the music for an Italian opera based on the story *Giuditta* by Andrea Salvadori. Nor did Judith always maintain her rôle as the later poets and musicians found the story rich in possibilities, Von Opitz, who introduced Salvadori's work into Germany, transformed Judith and Holofernes into romantic lovers. Joachim Beccau a century later continued that theme in his *L'Amor insanguinato*. Not only is Holofernes the lover of Judith, but for good measure even Achior is cast as the lover of a Midianite princess.

There is no end of artists who have found in the act of Judith a demand or an excuse for another painting. In his *Mornings in Florence* Ruskin comments on the "million of vile pictures" of Judith "in which the painters thought that they could surely attract the public to the double show of an execution and a pretty woman," and concludes that Botticelli's "The Return of Judith to Bethulia" is the only true picture of the vanquisher of Holofernes: "She is not merely the Jewish Dalilah to the Assyrian Samson; but the mightiest, purest, brightest type of high passion in severe womanhood offered to our human memory." [34]

The bibliography which this dramatic story of the past has occasioned is impressive. Of the many commentaries I have found Fritzsche's the most useful, and have drawn heavily upon that able scholar's findings. C. J. Ball's *Judith* in the volume *Apocrypha*, part of *The Holy Bible*, edited by Henry Wace, is properly to be commended for its full treatment and sometimes almost overconfident pronouncements. A. E.

Ch. 2 considers the more recent Judith plays, of which she lists 17, and discusses in some detail the more important.

[34] Ruskin devotes three pages in the "Third Morning" to the book which he appreciatively styles a "piece of history, or epic poetry"—to him its historicity is a matter of no concern—"which deserves to be read with honourable care."

Cowley's commentary in R. H. Charles' *Apocrypha and Pseudepigrapha*, while brief, contains much of real value. The English translation by Goodspeed was a very great contribution and did much to bring these neglected writings to popular attention. The more recent translation now a part of RSV may also be mentioned with appreciation.

To readers of this volume my translation may at times seem surprising. No attempt has been made to make it seem "better" or "clearer" than the Greek of which it is frankly an attempt to provide a faithful translation. With the popular notion that translation should clear up obscurities by guesswork and should be disdainful of following the text it is purportedly rendering I have no part. The Greek is patently the attempt to render as literally as possible the Hebrew text the translator knew. I applaud his resolve and have sought to follow it in an English version. In addition, the story he is retelling is one which professes to have happened many years in the past. It is not surprising that his diction bears evidence of this recognition. I have deliberately decided to use without apology the "archaic forms"—as some are today pleased to style them— "thou" and "thee," with occasional "ye's" and other reflections of a style which was common when authors sought to make their diction attractive and in keeping with the material with which they were dealing. It need hardly be remarked that no "archaisms" have been introduced for the sake of novelty; but I can see little point to have characters in a story written two thousand years ago use a diction and vocabulary which must seem grossly out of place to anyone at all familiar with the scenes and times under discussion. When such a rendering appears to me to introduce any undue strain on the comprehension of the modern reader, I have either sought regretfully to avoid it or paraphrase it in the commentary. So far as the commentary is concerned, I have tried to throw occasional light on what might seem to the ordinary reader obscure instead of amplifying in detail matters which are perfectly obvious. Since the heavy expense of printing the Greek text in full has been wisely allowed by the editor, it appears to me natural

to assume that it is proper to make use of the Greek as Greek in discussion of style in the commentary, and when in point an occasional Hebrew word or phrase.[35] Those who find these occasional references too great a strain, can usually pass on to the next sentence or skip that particular comment and continue with the fascinating story which the translation has sought to make alive and of interest.

[35] The sole value of transliteration, as it seems to me, is to save the high cost of composition. It is in no sense an aid to the reader. Those who can understand the language involved are properly irked by the nuisance of transliteration. Those who do not know the language are not aided by being provided with a string of English letters which they cannot understand but can only mispronounce.

TEXT, TRANSLATION, COMMENTARY, AND CRITICAL NOTES

1 ¹Ἔτους δωδεκάτου τῆς βασιλείας Ναβουχοδονοσορ, ὃς ἐβασίλευσεν Ἀσσυρίων ἐν Νινευη τῇ πόλει τῇ μεγάλῃ, ἐν ταῖς ἡμέραις
Αρφαξαδ, ὃς ἐβασίλευσεν Μήδων ἐν Ἐκβατάνοις, ²καὶ ᾠκοδόμησεν
ἐπ᾽ Ἐκβατάνων κύκλῳ τείχη ἐκ λίθων λελαξευμένων εἰς πλάτος
πηχῶν τριῶν καὶ εἰς μῆκος πηχῶν ἓξ καὶ ἐποίησεν τὸ ὕψος τοῦ
τείχους πηχῶν ἑβδομήκοντα καὶ τὸ πλάτος αὐτοῦ πηχῶν πεντή-
κοντα ³καὶ τοὺς πύργους αὐτοῦ ἔστησεν ἐπὶ ταῖς πύλαις αὐτῆς
πηχῶν ἑκατὸν καὶ τὸ πλάτος αὐτῆς ἐθεμελίωσεν εἰς πήχεις ἑξή-
κοντα ⁴καὶ ἐποίησεν τὰς πύλας αὐτῆς πύλας διεγειρομένας εἰς ὕψος
πηχῶν ἑβδομήκοντα καὶ τὸ πλάτος αὐτῆς πήχεις τεσσαράκοντα εἰς

---

1   3   αυτου]-της ℵ 74 76 108

---

1. The book begins with a most disconcerting sentence. Following the
words WHO REIGNED OVER THE ASSYRIANS is a lengthy parenthesis
extending through vs. 4. Then in vs. 5 the account of what happened
IN THE TWELFTH YEAR is belatedly resumed. As the Greek is a very
literal translation of the Hebrew, the English attempts to reproduce
this definite cast. The verb of which NABOUCHODONOSOR is the subject
does not appear until vs. 5, and the subject is thus left dangling.   NA-
BOUCHODONOSOR (in Hebr. OT Nebuchadrezzar or -nezzar): king of Babylonia 605-562 B.C.E. In 586 he destroyed Jerusalem and deported many
Judeans. He was never king of the ASSYRIANS and never REIGNED . . . in
NINEVEH, which city had been destroyed in 612 B.C.E. by the combined
forces of the Babylonians and Medes. This mention of Nabouchodonosor
as king of Assyria, with Nineveh his capital city, is but one of the many
historical slips with which the book abounds and which warn the reader
against viewing the tale as a retelling of an historical event in Israel's
history. Rather, these names and places are apparently stage props for
the story. Nebuchadrezzar's act in destroying the temple in Jerusalem
and inaugurating a period of bondage for many, however zealous Jeremiah
might have been in describing it as engineered by Y", had left Nebuchadrezzar in the rôle of archvillain of all time. His is the most apt name for
the foreign tyrant once more to sweep into Palestine and to descend from
the north to menace Jerusalem. Thus without hesitation or concern for
such trivia as dates and exact nationality he is cast in the rôle of the

ঙ্গ JUDITH ৯৯

1 ¹In the twelfth year of the reign of Nabouchodonosor, who reigned over the Assyrians in Nineveh, the great city, in the days of Arphaxad, who reigned over the Medes in Ecbatana ²and who had built round about Ecbatana walls of hewn stone three cubits broad and six cubits long and who had made the height of the walls seventy cubits and the breadth fifty cubits, ³and who had put towers at its gates a hundred cubits high and had made foundations for them sixty cubits broad, ⁴and who had made the gates of the city gates which rise to a height of seventy cubits and with a breadth of forty cubits

---

godless tyrant. And Nineveh: Jonah and Zephaniah incidentally, Nahum with full organ, had blasted the bloody city, epitome of all that Israel loathed and hated. Again its choice by our author is most apt as the capital city of the all-wicked king.   ARPHAXAD: a fictional character quite unknown in history. The name is apparently taken from Genesis where Arpachshad is the third son of Shem (Gen 10 22) and the grand-father of Eber, the eponymous ancestor of the Hebrews. It is possible that the choice of this fictional character as the archenemy of Nabouchodo-nosor is deliberate and intended to heighten his hostility against Hebrews. ECBATANA: modern Hamadan, was in Media, roughly 300 miles n.e. of Babylon and slightly more s.e. of Nineveh. In the sixth century it was captured by Cyrus and made his favorite summer palace. Centuries later it became the summer capital of the Parthians. Herodotus (i, 98) ascribes the building of Ecbatana, surrounded by seven sets of concentric walls, to Deioces. Instead of the text which I have translated, we have the variant Ἐκβάτανα καὶ περιέβαλεν αὐτῇ κύκλῳ τείχη καὶ λίθων (sic) in 19 and 108, which makes Arphaxad the builder as well as the fortifier of the city.

2. For the size of the walls of Babylon, which surpass even these huge walls, see Herodotus i, 178.

3. TOWERS AT ITS GATES: lit. "towers of it" (τοὺς πύργους αὐτοῦ). The pronoun αὐτοῦ presumably refers to τεῖχος (wall), less probably to Arphaxad. The variant αὐτῆς (א, 74, 76, 108), referred to πόλις (city), is probably due to πύλαις αὐτῆς in vs. 4, where αὐτῆς is translated *de facto* OF THE CITY.

ἐξόδους δυνάμεως δυνατῶν αὐτοῦ καὶ διατάξεις τῶν πεζῶν αὐτοῦ.

5 ⁵καὶ ἐποίησεν πόλεμον ἐν ταῖς ἡμέραις ἐκείναις ὁ βασιλεὺς Ναβου
χοδονοσορ πρὸς βασιλέα Αρφαξαδ ἐν τῷ πεδίῳ τῷ μεγάλῳ, τοῦτό
ἐστιν πεδίον ἐν τοῖς ὁρίοις Ραγαυ. ⁶καὶ συνήντησαν πρὸς αὐτὸν
πάντες οἱ κατοικοῦντες τὴν ὀρεινὴν καὶ πάντες οἱ κατοικοῦντες τὸν
Εὐφράτην καὶ τὸν Τίγριν καὶ τὸν ῾Υδάσπην καὶ πεδία Αριωχ βα
σιλέως ᾽Ελυμαίων, καὶ συνῆλθον ἔθνη πολλὰ εἰς παράταξιν υἱῶν
Χελεουδ. ⁷καὶ ἀπέστειλεν Ναβουχοδονοσορ βασιλεὺς ᾽Ασσυρίων ἐπὶ
πάντας τοὺς κατοικοῦντας τὴν Περσίδα καὶ ἐπὶ πάντας τοὺς κατοι
κοῦντας πρὸς δυσμαῖς, τοὺς κατοικοῦντας τὴν Κιλικίαν καὶ Δαμα
σκὸν καὶ τὸν Λίβανον καὶ ᾽Αντιλίβανον, καὶ πάντας τοὺς κατοικοῦν
τας κατὰ πρόσωπον τῆς παραλίας ⁸καὶ τοὺς ἐν τοῖς ἔθνεσι τοῦ
Καρμήλου καὶ Γαλααδ καὶ τὴν ἄνω Γαλιλαίαν καὶ τὸ μέγα πεδίον
Εσδρηλων ⁹καὶ πάντας τοὺς ἐν Σαμαρείᾳ καὶ ταῖς πόλεσιν αὐτῆς
καὶ πέραν τοῦ Ιορδάνου ἕως Ιερουσαλημ καὶ Βατανη καὶ Χελους
καὶ Καδης καὶ τοῦ ποταμοῦ Αἰγύπτου καὶ Ταφνας καὶ Ραμεσση καὶ

---

6 προς αυτον] εις πολεμον ℵ 58

4. OF THE ARMY: this word δύναμις (power, force, strength) is very
common in Judith, and is frequently used where "army" is the only
natural English translation. The gates were built so wide to allow the
infantry to march out in formation.
5. RAGAU: Rages, a city in N.E. Media about five miles s.e. of the Persian
capital Teheran. It is commonly identified with the ruins of Ray or Rai,
is mentioned six times in Tobit (ἐν ῾Ράγοις τῆς Μηδίας —1 14, 4 1, 20,
5 5, 9; τῇ ῾Ράγῃ 6 10), and is mentioned a second time in Judith (1 15) as
the place where Arphaxad was slain. As used in Judith the name would
seem to be of the general region. The PLAIN (tableland of Irak Ajemi)
starts about 100 miles n.e. of Ecbatana and extends to the mountain range
of Elburz, south of the Caspian Sea.
6. WITH HIM i.e., Nabouchodonosor. συναντάω (with dat., 10 11, or with
πρός + acc., as here) may indicate either a friendly or hostile meeting.
Here the former would seem intended, but mss 19 and 108 add εἰς
πόλεμον (for war) and ℵ and 58 substitute εἰς πόλεμον for πρὸς αὐτόν.
HYDASPES: no such river by this name is known in this region. The
Hydaspes (a tributary of the Indus) cannot be meant. The Vg has Iadason,
the Syr Ulai (Eulaeus), which latter is mentioned in Dan 8 22. The most
likely explanation is that the author, whose geographical knowledge
is not profound, meant the Choaspes, which flowed past Susa (Herodotus
i, 188; v, 49) joining the combined Tigris-Euphrates just south of this
point of merger. PLAIN OF ARIOCH (πεδία ᾽Αριώχ): the text is very
uncertain, with πεδίῳ (B) and (τὰ) πεδία (ℵ) as variants. The occasional
spelling παι- is an obvious scribal slip. The change in B to the dative is
surprising, as is the absence of the article. Presumably the plain of Elam

for the going forth of the army of his mighty men and the
drawing up of his foot soldiers.

5   ⁵And in those days King Nabouchodonosor waged war
against King Arphaxad in the great plain: this is a plain in
which Ragau lies. ⁶And there came to meet with him all those
who dwelt in the hill country and all those who dwelt along
the Euphrates and the Tigris and the Hydaspes and in the
plain of Arioch the king of the Elymeans, and many nations
assembled themselves in the battle line of the sons of Cheleoud.
⁷And Nabouchodonosor, king of the Assyrians, sent to
all those who dwelt in Persia and to all who dwelt to the west,
to those dwelling in Cilicia and Damascus and Lebanon and
Antilebanon, and to all who dwelt over against the coast, ⁸and
to those among the nations of Carmel and Gilead, and to those
who dwelt in Galilee and the great plain of Esdraelon, ⁹and
to all those in Samaria and its cities, and beyond Jordan even
to Jerusalem and Batane and Chelous and Kadesh and the

---

is meant.   ARIOCH: apparently a reflection from Gen 14 1 (cf. Dan
2 14). He cannot be identified with any known ancient ruler. As the
text stands, the genitive (βασιλέως) is required; the variant ὁ βασιλεύς
(B, אᶜ, A) is meaningless. It is conceivable that underlying our present
text is a reading joining ARIOCH THE KING with the following ἔθνη (NA-
TIONS) as subject of συνῆλθον.   CHELEOUD: OL reads Chelleoth; Vg
omits; Syr Chaldeans. Probably not "to battle against" but "in the ranks
of." If vs. 6b summarizes 6a, then SONS OF CHELEOUD should be in Nabouchodonosor's army. No such name is otherwise known. RSV (seemingly in agreement with Syr) considers it a corruption of "Chaldeans."
No historical light is to be expected from Judith on such niceties.
8. THOSE AMONG THE NATIONS: this phrase (τοὺς ἐν τοῖς ἔθνεσι) is very
awkward, almost certainly corrupt. Fritzsche conjectures that the Greek
reflects בהרי (ἐν τοῖς ὄρεσιν) or בערי (ἐν ταῖς πόλεσιν) which the translator misread בעמי and rendered ἐν τοῖς ἔθνεσι.
9. BEYOND JORDAN: Palestine west of the Jordan, and from the point of
view of the East looking west. It is surprising for one himself living in
Palestine west of the Jordan to whom the term πέραν τοῦ Ἰορδάνου
normally meant land east of the Jordan (Perea in NT days), so to have
expressed himself.   BATANE or Baitane (B): apparently a town south
of Jerusalem, although Woolf, understanding BEYOND JORDAN to mean
east of the river, saw Bashan indicated. Bethany is scarcely likely; perhaps Beth-anoth (Judg 15 59) is intended.   CHELOUS: often identified
with Halhul in Josh 15 58; by others with Chaluṭsa (so named in late
rabbinic writings), the modern Khalasar.   KADESH: perhaps Kedesh

10 πᾶσαν γῆν Γεσεμ ¹⁰ἕως τοῦ ἐλθεῖν ἐπάνω Τάνεως καὶ Μέμφεως καὶ πάντας τοὺς κατοικοῦντας τὴν Αἴγυπτον ἕως τοῦ ἐλθεῖν ἐπὶ τὰ ὅρια τῆς Αἰθιοπίας. ¹¹καὶ ἐφαύλισαν πάντες οἱ κατοικοῦντες πᾶσαν τὴν γῆν τὸ ῥῆμα Ναβουχοδονοσορ βασιλέως Ἀσσυρίων καὶ οὐ συν-ῆλθον αὐτῷ εἰς τὸν πόλεμον, ὅτι οὐκ ἐφοβήθησαν αὐτόν, ἀλλ᾽ ἦν ἐναντίον αὐτῶν ὡς ἀνὴρ εἷς, καὶ ἀνέστρεψαν τοὺς ἀγγέλους αὐτοῦ κενοὺς ἐν ἀτιμίᾳ προσώπου αὐτῶν. ¹²καὶ ἐθυμώθη Ναβουχοδονοσορ ἐπὶ πᾶσαν τὴν γῆν ταύτην σφόδρα καὶ ὤμοσε κατὰ τοῦ θρόνου καὶ τῆς βασιλείας αὐτοῦ εἰ μὴν ἐκδικήσειν πάντα τὰ ὅρια τῆς Κι-λικίας καὶ Δαμασκηνῆς καὶ Συρίας ἀνελεῖν τῇ ῥομφαίᾳ αὐτοῦ καὶ πάντας τοὺς κατοικοῦντας ἐν γῇ Μωαβ καὶ τοὺς υἱοὺς Αμμων καὶ πᾶσαν τὴν Ιουδαίαν καὶ πάντας τοὺς ἐν Αἰγύπτῳ ἕως τοῦ ἐλθεῖν ἐπὶ τὰ ὅρια τῶν δύο θαλασσῶν. ¹³καὶ παρετάξατο ἐν τῇ δυνάμει

---

11 εις ult.] ισος B   12 δαμασκηνης]-κου ℵ

---

of Josh 15 23, an oasis in the wilderness of Zin.   RIVER OF EGYPT: opinions differ as to whether this means the Nile or the "brook of Egypt" (I Kings 8 65; II Chron 7 8) in the wilderness of Paran, the natural boundary between Palestine and Egypt, the modern Wadi el-Arish. The Assyrian records frequently mention this "brook," once with the descrip-tive addition (to distinguish it from the Nile) "and there is no river" (Pritchard, *ANET*, p. 292).   TAPHNES: Tahpanhes in Jer 43 7ff., a border fortress near Pelusium and mentioned by Herodotus ii, 30 (ἐν Δάφνησι τῆσι Πηλουσίησι).   RAMESSES: a royal residence city in the Egyptian delta. The exact location has long been debated, but there is a strong probability that it is Per-Ramses, capital of Ramses II, and earlier known as Avaris, the capital of the Hyksos; later known as Tanis. It is commonly styled Zoan in the OT.   GESEM: usually regarded as the Greek equivalent of Goshen. The name is not yet attested in Egyptian texts, but the territory is commonly believed to be n.e. of the Delta, the region of the wadi Tumilat.

10. ABOVE (ἐπάνω) = "beyond."   TANIS: see comment on Ramesses (1 9). MEMPHIS: on the west bank of the Nile, 13 miles south of the present Cairo.   To see in these references to Egypt and Nabouchodonosor's demands for allies any exact knowledge of the author of Assyrian con-quests of Egypt or of Nebuchadrezzar's invasion in 568 is surely unwise. As Ball properly remarks: "Such vague and inaccurate knowledge of these matters, as the Book of Judith indicates, hardly requires more than an acquaintance with the O.T. for its adequate explanation" (*op. cit., in loc.,* p. 268). Surely Jer 43 8-13 would have adequately supplied him.

11. IN ALL THE LAND: lit. "all the earth" (πᾶσαν τὴν γῆν). What is ap-parently meant is all the region loosely listed in the preceding verses (7-10). BUT AN ORDINARY MAN (*unus de multis* אחד העם; cf. I Sam 26 15) in contrast to his own exalted opinion of himself. The words ὡς ἀνὴρ εἷς

river of Egypt, and Taphnes and Ramesses and all the land
10 of Gesem, ¹⁰until you come above Tanis and Memphis, and
to all who dwelt in Egypt until you come to the borders of
Ethiopia. ¹¹And all who dwelt in all the land made light of the
word of Nabouchodonosor king of the Assyrians and did not
assemble themselves with him for war, because they did not
fear him, but in their eyes he was but an ordinary man; and
they sent back his messengers emptyhanded and with loss of
face. ¹²And Nabouchodonosor was greatly enraged at all
this land and swore by his throne and his kingdom that he
would surely take vengeance on all the territory of Cilicia
and Damascus and Syria to slay by his sword, and all those
who dwelt in the land of Moab and all the children of Ammon
and all Judea and all those who dwelt in Egypt until you come
to the bounds of the two seas. ¹³And he set his army in battle

---

would seem to be the translation of כאחד האדם. For εἰς B reads ἴσος
(like).

12. BY HIS THRONE AND HIS KINGDOM: the use of κατά with the genitive
instead of the accusative of the thing sworn by is common in Greek of
all periods; one holds out his hand *over* the object and calls *down* the vengeance of the gods *upon* it.   WOULD SURELY TAKE VENGEANCE (εἰμὴν
ἐκδικήσειν): the use of εἰμήν (εἰ μήν) for the classical ἦ μήν in as-
severations is well attested in the papyri as well as in the LXX; cf. also
Heb 6 13. This may be explained as due to iotacism (εἰ *pro* ἤ), but more
particularly to conform with εἰ μή, which also occurs frequently as the
translation of אם לא.   TERRITORY: lit., "coasts," "bounds," but surely
denoting not the lands bordering on Cilicia etc., but those territories
themselves (cf. 4 4).   DAMASCUS: the adjective Δαμασκηνῆς (i.e.,
Δ. χώρας) is to be preferred to the well-attested variant Δαμασκοῦ because
of references to the whole district, not the city alone.   SYRIA: a common designation of the whole territory between the Euphrates and the
Mediterranean and south to Egypt.   TO SLAY BY HIS SWORD: as the text
stands it is uncertain whether this phrase amplifies WOULD TAKE VEN-
GEANCE or whether it is parallel to the preceding infinitive, in the sense of
"(and) to slay" the groups next mentioned (Moab etc.). In the former
case "them" is to be understood; in the latter a καί would seem to be
required before the infinitive.   LAND OF MOAB: the Moabites dwelt
south of the Arnon.   SONS OF AMMON: to the north of the Moabites.
The two comprise loosely the territory abreast of Judea, east of the Jordan.   ALL JUDEA: west of the Jordan.   THE BOUNDS OF THE TWO
SEAS: by some understood to mean the Mediterranean and Red Seas, but
since that would be a strange limit in this campaign, Volkmar took it
to mean the Red Sea and the Persian Gulf, which scarcely lessens the

αὐτοῦ πρὸς Αρφαξαδ βασιλέα ἐν τῷ ἔτει τῷ ἑπτακαιδεκάτῳ καὶ
ἐκραταιώθη ἐν τῷ πολέμῳ αὐτοῦ καὶ ἀνέστρεψεν πᾶσαν τὴν δύναμιν Αρφαξαδ καὶ πᾶσαν τὴν ἵππον αὐτοῦ καὶ πάντα τὰ ἅρματα
αὐτοῦ ¹⁴καὶ ἐκυρίευσε τῶν πόλεων αὐτοῦ καὶ ἀφίκετο ἕως Ἐκβατάνων καὶ ἐκράτησε τῶν πύργων καὶ ἐπρονόμευσε τὰς πλατείας
15 αὐτῆς καὶ τὸν κόσμον αὐτῆς ἔθηκεν εἰς ὄνειδος αὐτῆς ¹⁵καὶ ἔλαβε
τὸν Αρφαξαδ ἐν τοῖς ὄρεσι Ραγαυ καὶ κατηκόντισεν αὐτὸν ἐν ταῖς
σιβύναις αὐτοῦ καὶ ἐξωλέθρευσεν αὐτὸν ἕως τῆς ἡμέρας ἐκείνης.
¹⁶καὶ ἀνέστρεψεν μετ' αὐτῶν αὐτὸς καὶ πᾶς ὁ σύμμικτος αὐτοῦ,
πλῆθος ἀνδρῶν πολεμιστῶν πολὺ σφόδρα, καὶ ἦν ἐκεῖ ῥᾳθυμῶν
καὶ εὐωχούμενος αὐτὸς καὶ ἡ δύναμις αὐτοῦ ἐφ' ἡμέρας ἑκατὸν
εἴκοσι.

2 ¹Καὶ ἐν τῷ ἔτει τῷ ὀκτωκαιδεκάτῳ δευτέρᾳ καὶ εἰκάδι τοῦ πρώ-
του μηνὸς ἐγένετο λόγος ἐν οἴκῳ Ναβουχοδονοσορ βασιλέως Ἀσ-

---

15 εκεινης] ταυτης ℵ   16 αυτων]+εις νινευη A | αυτος 1⁰ ᴧ
                                         2⁰] om. B

---

problem. Not impossibly it signifies the two principal branches of the
Nile—White and Blue.
13. SEVENTEENTH YEAR: not impossibly a reflection of Jer 32 1. Nebuchadrezzar despoiled his other enemies, the Medes, in his seventeenth
year, and was then able to proceed against the Israelites in the eighteenth.
If so, this detail is simply a stage prop for his story.
14. STATELY FASHION INTO SHAME: the general meaning is clear, but the
text is uncertain: many texts, including OL, have substituted: "and he
made it (the city) a reproach"; the Syr has "and all their beauty they made
into a reproach." In all of these renderings the reflection of Ps 44 13 is
clearly to be seen. Cowley sees a play on words in the imagined Hebrew
יפי בדפי.
15. MOUNTAINS OF RAGAU: the Elburz mountains; see 1 5.   DESTROYED
HIM UTTERLY UNTIL THAT DAY: only so can the Greek be translated. The
reading ταύτης (ℵ) is palpably a correction to make it conform to the
common "until this day." Fritzsche valiantly attempts to force a meaning
out of the unaltered text: "From the day of the battle until that day in
which he thrust him through, he was destroying him and his might utterly,"
but this *tour de force* is scarcely convincing. The meaning is clear: the
destruction was final; Arphaxad was killed, and there was no restoration.
While the translation "that day" of the AV has no textual justification, it
may be the original reading which was early changed to the meaningless
UNTIL THAT DAY to express more clearly the note of utter destruction in
the compound ἐξωλέθρευσεν; that is, τὴν ἡμέραν ἐκείνην was altered to
ἕως τῆς ἡμέρας ἐκείνης without realizing that such a change meant substituting ταύτης for ἐκείνης.
16. WITH THEM: presumably in the sense, "with all the spoils and pris-

array against King Arphaxad in the seventeenth year and was victorious in his battle and overthrew the whole army of Arphaxad and all his horse and all his chariots ¹⁴and became master of his cities and came even to Ecbatana and laid hold of the towers and despoiled its broad streets and turned its 15 stately fashion into shame, ¹⁵and he took Arphaxad in the mountains of Ragau and struck him down with hunting spears and destroyed him utterly until that day. ¹⁶And he returned with them, he and all his motley crew, a very great host of men of war, and there he took his ease and banqueted, he and his army, for a hundred and twenty days.

2   ¹And in the eighteenth year, on the twenty-second day of the first month, there was talk in the house of Nabouchodonosor king of the Assyrians to take vengeance on all the land

---

oners." As phrased, it is awkward and was omitted by many texts, including 19, 108, OL, and Syr. Ms A and several others add "to Nineveh" (εἰς Νινευή).   HE AND ALL HIS MOTLEY CREW (πᾶς ὁ σύμμικτος αὐτοῦ); cf. πάντας τοὺς συμμίκτους (Jer 32 20 LXX; cf. 27 37 LXX). The phrase is common in the OT. Herodotus (vii, 55) uses the same term for Xerxes' army: ὁ σύμμικτος στρατὸς παντοίων ἐθνέων. It is apt here in Judith as descriptive of the force which Nabouchodonosor had impounded. The repeated αὐτός ("he and . . . he and") not unnaturally led to the accidental omission of the intervening words (haplography) by B.   RE-TURNED: the repetition of ἀνέστρεψεν (vss. 11, 13, 16) is striking. In the first two cases it is transitive, in the sense "turned back," "repulsed," "routed." In vs. 16 it is intransitive, "returned."   THERE (ἔχει). This abrupt THERE obviously means his home city to which he had RETURNED. This makes the reading εἰς Νινευή (A) a natural smoothing of a suspiciously awkward silence.   FOR A HUNDRED AND TWENTY DAYS: this long period of banqueting is not unnatural in a story of this sort, as a glance at Esther 1 4, with its 180-day feast, will indicate.

---

1. EIGHTEENTH YEAR: cf. comment on "seventeenth" (1 13). Vg reads *anno tertio decimo* since it omits 1 13-16. "Twenty-eighth"—the reading of 58 and Syr—is probably to be explained as due to confusing the two numerals, 18 (ιη) and 22 (κβ), and by transposition 28 (κη). The mention of precise year, month, and day is a familiar biblical touch. That the author is seeking to convince his readers that this is bona fide history is less likely.   IN ALL THE LAND: as in 1 11 (repeated in 1 12), this phrase presumably means in all the territory which had refused to join

συρίων ἐκδικῆσαι πᾶσαν τὴν γῆν καθὼς ἐλάλησεν. ²καὶ συνεκάλεσεν
πάντας τοὺς θεράποντας αὐτοῦ καὶ πάντας τοὺς μεγιστᾶνας αὐτοῦ
καὶ ἔθετο μετ' αὐτῶν τὸ μυστήριον τῆς βουλῆς αὐτοῦ καὶ συνετέλεσεν πᾶσαν τὴν κακίαν τῆς γῆς ἐκ τοῦ στόματος αὐτοῦ, ³καὶ αὐτοὶ ἔκριναν ὀλεθρεῦσαι πᾶσαν σάρκα οἳ οὐκ ἠκολούθησαν τῷ λόγῳ
τοῦ στόματος αὐτοῦ. ⁴καὶ ἐγένετο ὡς συνετέλεσεν τὴν βουλὴν αὐτοῦ, ἐκάλεσεν Ναβουχοδονοσορ βασιλεὺς Ἀσσυρίων τὸν Ολοφέρνην
ἀρχιστράτηγον τῆς δυνάμεως αὐτοῦ δεύτερον ὄντα μετ' αὐτὸν καὶ
5 εἶπεν πρὸς αὐτόν ⁵Τάδε λέγει ὁ βασιλεὺς ὁ μέγας, ὁ κύριος πάσης
τῆς γῆς Ἰδοὺ σὺ ἐξελεύσῃ ἐκ τοῦ προσώπου μου καὶ λήμψῃ μετὰ
σεαυτοῦ ἄνδρας πεποιθότας ἐν ἰσχύι αὐτῶν, πεζῶν εἰς χιλιάδας
ἑκατὸν εἴκοσι καὶ πλῆθος ἵππων σὺν ἀναβάταις χιλιάδας δέκα δύο,
⁶καὶ ἐξελεύσῃ εἰς συνάντησιν πάσῃ τῇ γῇ ἐπὶ δυσμάς, ὅτι ἠπείθη-
σαν τῷ ῥήματι τοῦ στόματός μου, ⁷καὶ ἀπαγγελεῖς αὐτοῖς ἑτοιμά-
ζειν γῆν καὶ ὕδωρ, ὅτι ἐξελεύσομαι ἐν θυμῷ μου ἐπ' αὐτοὺς καὶ
καλύψω πᾶν τὸ πρόσωπον τῆς γῆς ἐν τοῖς ποσὶν τῆς δυνάμεώς
μου καὶ δώσω αὐτοὺς εἰς διαρπαγὴν αὐτοῖς, ⁸καὶ οἱ τραυματίαι
αὐτῶν πληρώσουσιν τὰς φάραγγας αὐτῶν, καὶ πᾶς χειμάρρους καὶ
ποταμὸς ἐπικλύζων τοῖς νεκροῖς αὐτῶν πληρωθήσεται · ⁹καὶ ἄξω

---

in his attack on Arphaxad.　AS HE HAD SAID: his oath of vengeance (1
12).
2. RECOUNTED IN FULL DETAIL: the Greek is very obscure: συνετέλεσεν
πᾶσαν τὴν κακίαν τῆς γῆς ἐκ τοῦ στόματος αὐτοῦ. The translation suggested is at best uncertain, but the literal "completed all the wickedness"
is manifestly absurd. Fritzsche, despairing of finding any meaning in
the common text, imagines a mistranslation. By error the translator read,
or thought he read, ויכלה, which he rendered συνετέλεσεν. This is a
possible hurdle of the difficulty (cf. Esther 3 13), but conjectural emendations are always to be avoided when possible. If this conjecture is
adopted, it requires a similar substitution for the repeated συνετέλεσεν
in vs. 4.
3. AND THEY: Nabouchodonosor's counselors.　DESTROY: ὀλεθρεύω is
nonclassical but frequent in the LXX. Subsequently the medial ε was
changed to ο due to assimilation of the two vowels flanking the liquid (λ),
and has persisted in modern Greek although the noun (ὄλεθρος) remained
unaffected. Though frequent in the LXX, the verb occurs but twice in
Judith (2 3, 8 15).　ALL: lit. "all flesh"—a common Hebraism.
4. HOLOFERNES: No person with this name is known in Mesopotamia. A
Cappadocian Orophernes, aided by Demetrius I of Syria, succeeded
to the throne, ousting his half brother, Ariarathes V, in 158 B.C.E. The
name is properly Ὀροφέρνης. It is so written on coins, in an inscription
from Priene, and regularly in Polybius, Aelian, and Athenaeus. Diodorus

even as he had said. ²And he summoned all his retainers and
all his grandees and laid before them his secret plan and
recounted in full detail, with his own lips, all the wickedness
of the land; ³and they decreed to destroy all who had followed not the word he had uttered. ⁴And it came to pass when
he had given voice to his plan that Nabouchodonosor king of
the Assyrians summoned Holofernes, the chief captain of
5   the army, second only to him, and said to him, ⁵"Thus saith
the great king, the lord of all the earth, Lo, thou shalt go
from before us and shalt take with thee men whose confidence
lies in their strength, of foot soldiers to the number of a
hundred and twenty thousand, and of horse with their riders
twelve thousand, ⁶and thou shalt go forth to fall upon all the
land to the west because they have disobeyed the word of my
mouth, ⁷and thou shalt bid them prepare earth and water, for
I am coming against them in my wrath and shall veil all the
face of the land with the feet of my army, and shall give them
over to rapine, ⁸and their wounded will fill their ravines, and
every mountain torrent and overflowing river will be filled

Siculus fluctuates between 'Ορο- and 'Ολο-. Apparently the author o
Judith, who may well have come to know the name because of the adven
turer's connection with Demetrius, and chose it as the name of his arch
villain, spelled it with a *lamedh*. It is regularly unaspirated. The incorrect
aspiration is due to confusion with compounds of ὁλο-.

5. THE GREAT KING: a term common for the Persian kings (cf. Xenophon)
and for their Assyrian and Babylonian predecessors (cf. II Kings 18 19;
Isa 36 4).   FROM BEFORE ME: ἐκ τοῦ προσώπου μου.   WHOSE CON-
FIDENCE LIES IN THEIR STRENGTH: the Hebrew emphasis is transparent.
A man's confidence is in the Lord—not in his own strength or wealth
(cf. Pss 49 6, 52 7, Prov 11 28). Such is the strength of the Jew, the
weakness of his foes.
6. TO FALL UPON: "to attack." The phrase εἰς συνάντησιν is here manifestly hostile, in contradistinction to συνήντησαν in 1 6.
7. EARTH AND WATER: a Persian demand as a symbol of submission.
Herodotus mentions this demand of Darius sent throughout Greece
(διέπεμπε ὢν κήρυκας ἄλλους ἄλλῃ τάξας ἀνὰ τὴν Ἑλλάδα, κελεύων αἰτέειν
βασιλέϊ γῆν τε καὶ ὕδωρ (vi, 48, 2)). Once again our author ascribes a
Persian practice to their Assyrian predecessors. There is no mention of
such a practice in any cuneiform text.   FOR I AM COMING: i.e., "my
army is."
8. EVERY MOUNTAIN TORRENT AND OVERFLOWING RIVER: that the singular verb indicates the meaning, "every torrent will be a stream filled

10 τὴν αἰχμαλωσίαν αὐτῶν ἐπὶ τὰ ἄκρα πάσης τῆς γῆς. ¹⁰σὺ δὲ ἐξελ-
θὼν προκαταλήμψῃ μοι πᾶν ὅριον αὐτῶν, καὶ ἐκδώσουσίν σοι ἑαυ-
τούς, καὶ διατηρήσεις ἐμοὶ αὐτοὺς εἰς ἡμέραν ἐλεγμοῦ αὐτῶν· ¹¹ἐπὶ
δὲ τοὺς ἀπειθοῦντας οὐ φείσεται ὁ ὀφθαλμός σου τοῦ δοῦναι αὐτοὺς εἰς φόνον καὶ ἁρπαγὴν ἐν πάσῃ τῇ γῇ σου. ¹²ὅτι ζῶν ἐγὼ
καὶ τὸ κράτος τῆς βασιλείας μου, λελάληκα καὶ ποιήσω ταῦτα ἐν
χειρί μου. ¹³καὶ σὺ δὲ οὐ παραβήσῃ ἕν τι τῶν ῥημάτων τοῦ κυρίου
σου, ἀλλὰ ἐπιτελῶν ἐπιτελέσεις καθότι προστέταχά σοι, καὶ οὐ μα-
κρυνεῖς τοῦ ποιῆσαι αὐτά. ¹⁴καὶ ἐξῆλθεν Ολοφέρνης ἀπὸ προσώπου
τοῦ κυρίου αὐτοῦ καὶ ἐκάλεσεν πάντας τοὺς δυνάστας καὶ τοὺς
15 στρατηγοὺς καὶ ἐπιστάτας τῆς δυνάμεως Ασσουρ ¹⁵καὶ ἠρίθμησεν
ἐκλεκτοὺς ἄνδρας εἰς παράταξιν, καθότι ἐκέλευσεν αὐτῷ ὁ κύριος
αὐτοῦ, εἰς μυριάδας δέκα δύο καὶ ἱππεῖς τοξότας μυρίους δισχιλί-
ους, ¹⁶καὶ διέταξεν αὐτοὺς ὃν τρόπον πολέμου πλῆθος συντάσσε-
ται. ¹⁷καὶ ἔλαβεν καμήλους καὶ ὄνους καὶ ἡμιόνους εἰς τὴν ἀπαρτίαν
αὐτῶν, πλῆθος πολὺ σφόδρα, καὶ πρόβατα καὶ βόας καὶ αἶγας εἰς
τὴν παρασκευὴν αὐτῶν, ὧν οὐκ ἦν ἀριθμός, ¹⁸καὶ ἐπισιτισμὸν παντὶ

---

to overflowing," is unlikely, for frequently throughout the book both
verbs and subjects often differ as to number, in what may be styled a
"sense" rather than a severely grammatical agreement. For striking
parallelism of phrase see Isa 66 12—ποταμὸς . . . καὶ . . . χειμάρρους
ἐπικλύζων.
9. THEIR CAPTIVITY: the figure is obvious: "them as captives." The same
figure is to be seen in Isa 20 4: ὅτι οὕτως ἄξει βασιλεὺς 'Ασσυρίων τὴν
αἰχμαλωσίαν; cf. also II Chron 6 36 for the mention of leading captives
afar.
10. BEFOREHAND: that the compound προκαταλήμψῃ means "before I
myself attend to them" is uncertain. The verb is common in Judges,
Kings, and Chronicles, regularly as the translation of לכד (to seize or
get possession of), where no idea of an act preliminary to a subsequent
action is present. It occurs four more times in Judith (4 5; 7 1, 7, 17) in
the sense "before (the enemy) is able to act." But AGAINST THE DAY OF
THEIR CONVICTION or punishment would seem to imply "which I will later
attend to in person." Only those who immediately surrender are to have
this uncertain respite.   ALL THEIR BOUNDS: all their territory (cf.
Exod 10 14, 19; I Sam 11 3, 7).
11. IN ALL THY LAND: only so can ἐν πάσῃ τῇ γῇ σου be translated. The
σου (thy) is awkward and is omitted by many mss (19, 108, 58, 44, 71, 74,
106, 236, Syr, OL), but apparently as an obvious correction, for its
omission is far easier to explain than its addition. It can be explained as
"the land conquered by thee" (so Fritzsche) or "whithersoever thou
goest." It is conceivable that ארצה (with parag. ה) was misread ארצך.
12. BECAUSE AS I LIVE (ὅτι ζῶν ἐγώ): "as surely as I am alive." The

with their corpses. ⁹And I shall lead their captivity to the
10 ends of all the earth. ¹⁰But thou shalt go forth and
take for me beforehand all their bounds, and they shall give
themselves to thee and thou shalt save them for me against
the day of their conviction, ¹¹but for those who disobey,
thine eye shall not spare to give them over to slaughter and
booty in all thy land. ¹²Because as I live, and by the might of
my kingdom, I have spoken, and I will do this with my own
hand. ¹³And thou, thou shalt not transgress aught of the
words of thy lord, but shalt fully accomplish them even as I
have commanded thee, and thou shalt not delay in their
doing."

¹⁴And Holofernes went forth from before his lord and
called all the grandees and generals and officers of the army
15 of Asshur, ¹⁵and he numbered picked men for the battle
line, even as his lord had commanded him, to the number of
one hundred twenty thousand and twelve thousand mounted
archers, ¹⁶and he ordered them as a mighty host is ranged for
war. ¹⁷And he took camels and asses and mules for their
baggage, an exceedingly great multitude, and sheep and
cattle and goats quite beyond number for their provision,

---

participle with the first person pronoun is unusual (cf. Num 14 ₂₁, in
LXX ἀλλὰ ζῶ ἐγὼ καὶ ζῶν τὸ ὄνομά μου) but the variant ζῶ in ℵ and other
mss does not aid Greek syntax.

13. AND THOU, THOU SHALT NOT TRANSGRESS: "as for thee"—the καὶ σὺ
δέ is emphatic—"take care not to deviate in the slightest wise . . ." The
arrogance of Nabouchodonosor is intentionally emphasized.

14. ASSHUR: this form occurs 13 times in Judith for the country; υἱοὶ
Ἀσσούρ and Ἀσσύριοι are used with seeming indifference for the people.
These usages are followed in the present translation.

15. HE NUMBERED PICKED MEN: mustered his forces to the strength
Nabouchodonosor had commanded; ἀριθμέω in this sense is found in Gen
14 ₁₄ (ἠρίθμησεν) where the MT reads וירק, which can scarcely have been
the text the LXX translators read. The presence of many seeming
allusions in Judith to Gen 14 is notable.

16. ORDERED: drew them up in battle formation.

17. BAGGAGE: the meaning "baggage," "light movables," more commonly styled ἔπιπλα, is attested by Pollux (10, 18): τοὔνομα δὲ ἡ ἀπαρτία
ἔστι μὲν Ἰωνικόν, ὠνομασμένων οὕτω παρ' αὐτοῖς τῶν κούφων σκευῶν, ἅ
ἐστι παραρτήσασθαι, ἢ διανοίᾳ καὶ τὰ ἔπιπλα ὠνομάσθαι φαμέν.   QUITE
BEYOND NUMBER: a common Hebrew superlative; cf. Gen 41 ₄₉, Judg
6 ₅, 7 ₁₂.   PROVISION: παρασκευή occurs but six times in the

ἀνδρὶ εἰς πλῆθος καὶ χρυσίον καὶ ἀργύριον ἐξ οἴκου βασιλέως πολὺ
σφόδρα. ¹⁹καὶ ἐξῆλθεν αὐτὸς καὶ πᾶσα ἡ δύναμις αὐτοῦ εἰς πορείαν
τοῦ προελθεῖν βασιλέως Ναβουχοδονοσορ καὶ καλύψαι πᾶν τὸ πρόσωπον τῆς γῆς πρὸς δυσμαῖς ἐν ἅρμασι καὶ ἱππεῦσι καὶ πεζοῖς ἐπι-
20 λέκτοις αὐτῶν · ²⁰καὶ πολὺς ὁ ἐπίμικτος ὡς ἀκρὶς συνεξῆλθον αὐτοῖς
καὶ ὡς ἡ ἄμμος τῆς γῆς, οὐ γὰρ ἦν ἀριθμὸς ἀπὸ πλήθους αὐτῶν.
²¹καὶ ἀπῆλθον ἐκ Νινευη ὁδὸν τριῶν ἡμερῶν ἐπὶ πρόσωπον τοῦ
πεδίου Βεκτιλεθ καὶ ἐπεστρατοπέδευσαν ἀπὸ Βεκτιλεθ πλησίον τοῦ
ὄρους τοῦ ἐπ᾽ ἀριστερᾷ τῆς ἄνω Κιλικίας. ²²καὶ ἔλαβεν πᾶσαν τὴν
δύναμιν αὐτοῦ, τοὺς πεζοὺς καὶ τοὺς ἱππεῖς καὶ τὰ ἅρματα αὐτοῦ,
καὶ ἀπῆλθεν ἐκεῖθεν εἰς τὴν ὀρεινήν. ²³καὶ διέκοψεν τὸ Φουδ καὶ
Λουδ καὶ ἐπρονόμευσεν υἱοὺς πάντας Ρασσις καὶ υἱοὺς Ισμαηλ τοὺς

LXX—twice in Exodus, twice in Judith, and once in I and II Maccabees.
The phrase εἰς τὴν παρασκευήν obviously balances the preceding εἰς
τὴν ἀπαρτίαν, which latter indicates their function was beasts of burden.
This suggests that εἰς τὴν παρασκευήν is different: they were for "ser-
vice," that is, were "part of the military preparation," as a food supply.
Thus the meaning PROVISION, most uncommon for this word, would seem
warranted.
19. THEIR: this pronoun (αὐτῶν) at the end of the phrase refers to those
comprising the ARMY.   PICKED: this adjective may refer specifically
to the last of the three nouns, that is, picked infantry; but it is possible
that it refers to all three: chariots, horsemen, and foot soldiers.
20. A MOTLEY HORDE: cf. 1 16.   LIKE LOCUSTS: ἀκρίς (sg.) regularly
translates ארבה, which latter is usually, as here, used collectively.
LIKE THE SAND OF THE EARTH: the two similes are frequently joined in
Hebrew (cf. Judg 7 12), the one of an advancing army laying bare the
land, the other for a number beyond count. While SAND OF THE EARTH
occurs (cf. Gen 13 16 bis, 28 14), "sand of the sea" or "sand upon the
seashore" is more common.
21. TO THE EDGE: ἐπὶ πρόσωπον τοῦ, the literal translation of על־פני, is
frequently scarcely more than "to" (cf. ἐπὶ πρόσωπον Σοδόμων, Gen 18 16).
PLAIN OF BECTILETH: the name occurs in a great variety of spellings
in different mss. No suggested identification has gained any considerable
support. To identify it with Bakataïlloi, which acc. to Ptolemy (Geogr. v,
14) is near Antioch, involves the same difficulty which the narrative
provides: it is near Cilicia, i.e., 300 miles from Nineveh but reached in the
course of a three-day march; in vs. 24 he is still east of the Euphrates.
Either the author's geography, like his history, was more than hazy or
he was undisturbed by prosy facts in his manufacture of names for
places and individuals. Those who find the fancied derivation of names
rewarding see in the form of the name in Syr—Beth-kṭilath, conjectured
to mean "house of slaughter"—a reflection of the events in vss. 22f.
Thename Ange (OL), Agge (Vg) in the versions and a few Greek mss, has
been conjectured to be an adaptation of ἀγκή = ἀγκάλη. It is more

¹⁸and for every man an ample rationing, and an exceeding great amount of gold and silver from the house of the king. ¹⁹And he went forth on his course, he and all his army, to precede King Nabouchodonosor and to cover all the face of the earth to the west with their chariots and horsemen and
20 picked foot soldiers. ²⁰And there went forth with them a motley horde like locusts and like the sand of the earth, for they were not to be numbered they were so many.

²¹And they went from Nineveh a three-day journey to the edge of the plain of Bectileth, and they encamped hard by Bectileth which is near the mountain on the left of Upper Cilicia. ²²And he took his whole army, his foot soldiers and riders and chariots, and from there moved into the hill country.
²³ And he cut Put and Lud asunder and despoiled all the children of Rassis and the children of Ishmael who were over

likely to be seen as a corruption from the following τῆς ἄνω Κιλικίας. ON THE LEFT: a Hebraism (מִשְּׂמֹאל) for "to the north of."
23. PUT (Φουδ) and LUD (Λουδ) are frequently joined in the OT. In the table of nations Put is a son of Ham (Gen 10 ₆) and Lud is a son of Shem (10 ₂₂). There is much uncertainty as to the location of both, although to many Put is now regarded in connection with Libya and Lud with the far-distant Lydia. Gyges sent aid to his ally Psammetichus against the Assyrians in the late seventh century. This may account for a growing familiarity in Palestine and the Near East with the hitherto unknown Lydians. To the author of Judith PUT and LUD are seemingly but names which he introduces into his narrative. Certainly neither of them can be seen in connection with a region bordering Cilicia and which is reached by a three-day march from Nineveh and apparently east of the Euphrates! CUT ... ASUNDER: by some understood literally as "parted," "broke the ties between" Put and Lud. It is conceivable that to the author, familiar with the combination "Put and Lud" (cf. Ezek 27 ₁₀, 30 ₅), this is meant; but it is far more likely that he meant "cutting asunder," that is, demolishing and destroying. CHILDREN OF RASSIS: no city or district by this name is known. Vg reads *Tharsis* and OL *Thiras et Rassis*. Others identify it with a Rossos mentioned by Strabo (*Geogr.* xiv, 5, 19; xvi, 2, 8) and Ptolemy (*Geogr.* v, 14). Stummer (*op. cit.*, pp. 24-25) accepts this identification and argues that *Ras(s)us* was hellenized to Arsus. Since the battle of Issus was fought hard by Jebel Arsus, it has been conjectured that it was this spectacular military engagement which led our author to hit upon this otherwise obscure name. This may be true, but it seems more likely that he had only the vaguest knowledge of or interest in the exact location of this or many other places he dubs with archaic names. CHILDREN OF ISHMAEL: nomadic desert tribes east of the Jordan in the Syrian desert, north of the Arabian desert.

κατὰ πρόσωπον τῆς ἐρήμου πρὸς νότον τῆς Χελεων. ²⁴καὶ παρῆλθεν τὸν Εὐφράτην καὶ διῆλθεν τὴν Μεσοποταμίαν καὶ κατέσκαψεν
πάσας τὰς πόλεις τὰς ὑψηλὰς τὰς ἐπὶ τοῦ χειμάρρου Αβρωνα ἕως
25 τοῦ ἐλθεῖν ἐπὶ θάλασσαν. ²⁵καὶ κατελάβετο τὰ ὅρια τῆς Κιλικίας
καὶ κατέκοψε πάντας τοὺς ἀντιστάντας αὐτῷ καὶ ἦλθεν ἕως ὁρίων
Ιαφεθ τὰ πρὸς νότον κατὰ πρόσωπον τῆς Ἀραβίας. ²⁶καὶ ἐκύκλω-
σεν πάντας τοὺς υἱοὺς Μαδιαμ καὶ ἐνέπρησεν τὰ σκηνώματα αὐτῶν καὶ ἐπρονόμευσεν τὰς μάνδρας αὐτῶν. ²⁷καὶ κατέβη εἰς πεδίον
Δαμασκοῦ ἐν ἡμέραις θερισμοῦ πυρῶν καὶ ἐνέπρησεν πάντας τοὺς
ἀγροὺς αὐτῶν καὶ τὰ ποίμνια καὶ τὰ βουκόλια ἔδωκεν εἰς ἀφανισμὸν καὶ τὰς πόλεις αὐτῶν ἐσκύλευσεν καὶ τὰ πεδία αὐτῶν ἐξελίκ-
μησεν καὶ ἐπάταξεν πάντας τοὺς νεανίσκους αὐτῶν ἐν στόματι
ῥομφαίας. — ²⁸καὶ ἐπέπεσεν φόβος καὶ τρόμος αὐτοῦ ἐπὶ τοὺς

TO THE SOUTH OF THE LAND OF THE CHELLEANS: who the Chelleans
were is unknown. The mss show the widest variance in spelling the name—
Χαλδιαων, Χελλαιων, Χαλδαιου, Χελλεων, Χελλαιων, Χελλων—and oscillate
between a prefixed τῆς or τῶν, the former understanding an omitted γῆς.
The reference to "children of Ishmael" tends to locate the "Chelleans"
to the north of them. Whether there is any connection between them and
Chellous (1 9, q.v.) is at best uncertain. Some have connected them with
Cholle (modern el-Khalle) between Palmyra and the Euphrates.
24. Certainly as the text stands the confusion is confounded. παρῆλθεν
τὸν Εὐφράτην can scarcely mean "went alongside of" but surely means
"crossed" (PASSED). This would seem to demand that after reaching the
mountains to the north of Upper Cilicia he turned back east and re-
crossed the Euphrates, for to reach Cilicia from Nineveh would have
involved crossing the Euphrates. Then after going through Mesopotamia
and destroying all the HIGH CITIES—i.e., "fortified," not meaning "high
in altitude"; a common OT term—which were on the RIVER (lit. "mountain stream or torrent") ABRON, he came to THE SEA. To have done this
would have involved recrossing the Euphrates, which is not said. All
this is certainly most improbable as a plan of march, especially as in
vs. 25 he makes his inroads into Cilicia. Thus either the text is out of
order and vs. 24 should precede vs. 21, or (rather more likely) the author
has a most confused notion of the relative positions of Cilicia, Mesopotamia, the Euphrates, and the sea, which latter certainly means the
Mediterranean. RIVER ABRON: among the many variants are Χεβρων,
Χευρων, Αρβωναϊ, Mambre (Vg), Jabbok (Syr), Beccon (OL). Some see
it as the Chaboras, which joins the Euphrates fifty miles north of Dura;
but this stream scarcely warrants the descriptive "mountain torrent"
(χειμάρρου). Moreover it seems to be regarded as near Cilicia, not in the
midst of Mesopotamia. Others see it as a mistranslation of בעבר הנהר
("beyond the river"), common in the OT (cf. Josh 24 2, 3, II Sam 10 16,
I Chron 19 16) and regularly translated in the LXX πέραν τοῦ ποταμοῦ.

against the desert to the south of the land of the Chelleans.
²⁴And he passed the Euphrates and went through Mesopotamia and utterly destroyed all the high cities which were on
25 the river Abron until you come to the sea. ²⁵And he laid
hold of the border of Cilicia and slew all who withstood him
and went even to the borders of Japheth which were to
the south over against Arabia. ²⁶And he encompassed all
the children of Midian and burned their tents and despoiled
their sheepfolds. ²⁷And he went down into the plain of
Damascus in the days of the wheat harvest and set fire to all
their fields and gave their flocks and herds to destruction
and sacked their cities and stripped bare their plains and
smote all their youths with the edge of the sword. ²⁸And fear
and trembling before him fell upon those who dwelt on the

On this theory the translator mistook עבר for the name of the river, and
gave it a Greek ending. This is clever, but the popular tendency to find
countless places he failed to comprehend but which modern interpreters
properly reconstruct and then render needs to be kept in check. It is a bit
too like Daniel's ability not only to interpret Nebuchadnezzar's dream,
but to discern what the dream was, when the king had quite forgotten it.
25. BORDER OF CILICIA: territory of. What is meant by BORDERS OF
JAPHETH WHICH WERE TO THE SOUTH OVER AGAINST ARABIA is uncertain.
It is conceivable that this is an unusual way of speaking of the south of
the Phoenician-Palestinian coast, that is, Philistia, which might loosely
be said to be OVER AGAINST (opposite, in the same latitude) ARABIA.
But the mention in vs. 27 of going DOWN INTO THE PLAIN OF DAMASCUS
surely suggests that he was still in Cilicia and had not started south down
the coast. This not done until vs. 28. Thus all one can say is that once
again his geography—or lack of it—eludes us.
26. CHILDREN OF MIDIAN: Cowley, following Scholz, sees in this phrase
an archaism for Arabs in general. Philo says that the old name for Arabs
was Μαδιηναῖοι (de Fort. 34, p. 381 M). Mention of them in the OT would
indicate this location was to the east and south of Palestine, somewhat
north of Arabia and on the east shore of the Gulf of Aqabah, which would
be in accord with Greek and Arabian geographers' location of Madian.
Apparently our author is less concerned with the precise location of the
various peoples than he is with including all who are common in traditions
known to him.
27. IN THE DAYS OF THE WHEAT HARVEST. The wheat harvest was in late
spring—in April in the Jordan valley and extending to August in the
upper Lebanons. Since Holofernes set out in the first month, i.e., Nisan=
March-April (2 1), there would be scanty time—a maximum of four
months—for his exploits before reaching Damascus. There is no indi-

κατοικοῦντας τὴν παραλίαν τοὺς ὄντας ἐν Σιδῶνι καὶ ἐν Τύρῳ καὶ τοὺς κατοικοῦντας Σουρ καὶ Οκινα καὶ πάντας τοὺς κατοικοῦντας Ιεμνααν, καὶ οἱ κατοικοῦντες ἐν ᾿Αζώτῳ καὶ ᾿Ασκαλῶνι ἐφοβήθησαν αὐτὸν σφόδρα.

3   ¹Καὶ ἀπέστειλαν πρὸς αὐτὸν ἀγγέλους λόγοις εἰρηνικοῖς λέγοντες ²᾿Ιδοὺ ἡμεῖς οἱ παῖδες Ναβουχοδονοσορ βασιλέως μεγάλου παρακείμεθα ἐνώπιόν σου, χρῆσαι ἡμῖν καθὼς ἀρεστόν ἐστιν τῷ προσώπῳ σου · ³ἰδοὺ αἱ ἐπαύλεις ἡμῶν καὶ πᾶς τόπος ἡμῶν καὶ πᾶν πεδίον πυρῶν καὶ τὰ ποίμνια καὶ τὰ βουκόλια καὶ πᾶσαι αἱ μάνδραι τῶν σκηνῶν ἡμῶν παράκεινται πρὸ προσώπου σου, χρῆσαι καθὸ ἂν ἀρέσκῃ σοι· ⁴ἰδοὺ καὶ αἱ πόλεις ἡμῶν καὶ οἱ κατοικοῦντες ἐν αὐταῖς δοῦλοί σοί εἰσιν, ἐλθὼν ἀπάντησον αὐταῖς ὡς ἔστιν ἀγαθὸν

5   ἐν ὀφθαλμοῖς σου. ⁵καὶ παρεγένοντο οἱ ἄνδρες πρὸς Ολοφέρνην καὶ ἀπήγγειλαν αὐτῷ κατὰ τὰ ῥήματα ταῦτα. ⁶καὶ κατέβη ἐπὶ τὴν παραλίαν αὐτὸς καὶ ἡ δύναμις αὐτοῦ καὶ ἐφρούρωσε τὰς πόλεις τὰς ὑψηλὰς καὶ ἔλαβεν ἐξ αὐτῶν εἰς συμμαχίαν ἄνδρας ἐπιλέκτους· ⁷καὶ ἐδέξαντο αὐτὸν αὐτοὶ καὶ πᾶσα ἡ περίχωρος αὐτῶν μετὰ στεφάνων καὶ χορῶν καὶ τυμπάνων. ⁸καὶ κατέσκαψεν

---

2   28 ασκαλωνι] + και εν γαζει 58 OL Syr, + και γαζη 𐤀

---

cation that another year has elapsed. Apparently details of this sort did not worry our author.

28. The list of places from north to south on the seacoast is intelligible. It suggests that the author was more familiar with Palestine and its environs, and should be considered in connection with the question of place of composition. Sidon, Tyre, Azotus, Ascalon, are well-known cities on the Phoenician and Palestinian coast and are here listed properly from north to south. ᾿Ιεμνααν is surely JAMNIA (Jabneel, modern Yebna), a base of the Syrian armies during the Maccabean war and burned by Judas. SUR and OCINA are unknown under these names, but the seemingly accurate listing of these coastal towns in their proper order has led some to conjecture that SUR (Σουρ) may represent Dora (Δωρα) and OCINA Akko, later Ptolemais. This learned guesswork is at best uncertain and would disturb the otherwise correct north-south order. Others see Σουρ as dittography for Τυρω. The absence of Gaza is notable. Early scribes shared that feeling and added it to the list: καὶ ἐν Γάζει, 58, OL, Syr; καὶ Γάζῃ, 𐤀.

2. SERVANTS: παῖδες certainly is the translation of עבדים, term common as an actual descriptive of a servant or slave, but also employed from modesty or humility as a self-designation in addressing superiors. Here

seacoast in Sidon and Tyre and upon those who dwelt in Sur and Ocina, and upon all who dwelt in Jamnia; and those who dwelt in Azotus and Ascalon feared him mightily.

3   [1]And they sent to him envoys with words of peace, saying, [2]"Behold, we the servants of Nabouchodonosor the great king lie prostrate before thee; use us as is pleasing in thy sight. [3]Behold, our buildings and all our land and every field of wheat and the flocks and the herds and all our sheepfolds and their tents lie prostrate before thee; use them as is most pleasing to thee. [4]Behold, both our cities and they who dwell in them are thy slaves; come and deal with them as is 5 good in thine eyes." [5]And the men betook themselves to Holofernes and reported to him in accord with these words. [6]And he descended upon the coast, he and his army, and garrisoned all the high cities and took from them chosen men as allies. [7]And they received him, they and all the country round about them with garlands and dancings and timbrels.

---

it may well be rendered "slaves," as is explicitly stated in vs. 4.   LIE PROSTRATE: absolute submission, repeated in the next verse; i.e., all that we are and have is at your disposal.

3. BUILDINGS: our houses, structures—in contrast to lands and fields. Literally the word ἔπαυλις signifies "place to spend the night," hence farm buildings; also used in military parlance for "quarters," "barracks." SHEEPFOLDS AND THEIR TENTS: a phrase as awkward in Greek as in English. The folds were the more permanent and valuable; hence the THEIR in connection with the TENTS pitched by the shepherds hardby their sleeping flocks.

4. SLAVES: in the Greek, as in the translation, this noun is the predicate to the double subject, while the following THEM (αὐταῖς) refers more specifically to CITIES. The phrasing and deliberate repetitions in these verses heighten the picture of groveling terror.

5. IN ACCORD WITH THESE WORDS: the modern English of RSV and Goodspeed ("told them all this [or these things]") fails to suggest their obedient repetition of the precise words (cf. Luke 5 6ff.).

6. GARRISONED: this verb occurs but four times in the LXX—all four in apocryphal writings: I Esd 4 56, Wisd 17 16, I Macc 11 3.   HIGH CITIES: fortified strongholds, as in 2 24.

7. He was welcomed as a conquering hero with dances and music. The GARLANDS (headdresses) were worn by the people as a sign of this ready welcome. The mention of TIMBRELS (τυμπάνων) is probably not intended to limit the instruments to this one form—a sort of drum or tambourine

πάντα τὰ ὅρια αὐτῶν καὶ τὰ ἄλση αὐτῶν ἐξέκοψεν, καὶ ἦν δεδο-
μένον αὐτῷ ἐξολεθρεῦσαι πάντας τοὺς θεοὺς τῆς γῆς, ὅπως αὐτῷ
μόνῳ τῷ Ναβουχοδονοσορ λατρεύσωσι πάντα τὰ ἔθνη, καὶ πᾶσαι
αἱ γλῶσσαι καὶ αἱ φυλαὶ αὐτῶν ἐπικαλέσωνται αὐτὸν εἰς θεόν. ⁹καὶ
ἦλθεν κατὰ πρόσωπον Εσδρηλων πλησίον τῆς Δωταιας, ἥ ἐστιν
10 ἀπέναντι τοῦ πρίονος τοῦ μεγάλου τῆς Ιουδαίας, ¹⁰καὶ κατεστρατοπέδευσαν ἀνὰ μέσον Γαιβαι καὶ Σκυθῶν πόλεως, καὶ ἦν ἐκεῖ μῆνα
ἡμερῶν εἰς τὸ συλλέξαι πᾶσαν τὴν ἀπαρτίαν τῆς δυνάμεως αὐτοῦ.

4   ¹Καὶ ἤκουσαν οἱ υἱοὶ Ισραηλ οἱ κατοικοῦντες ἐν τῇ Ιουδαίᾳ πάν-

---

3   8 και 3⁰] οτι א 58

---

used chiefly by dancing females. The whole picture is that of welcome
with royal honors.
8. To many interpreters HE UTTERLY DESTROYED ALL THEIR BOUNDARIES
seems out of place. Fritzsche and Ball are sure that τὰ ὅρια is a mistranslation of הבמות ("high places"). Certainly in connection with
GROVES and GODS OF THE LAND "high places" would be appropriate,
even though it would make Holofernes follow the practice of an approved
Hebrew king or reformer (II Kings 23 18f.) But why the translator
should have been confused is hard to say. The mistranslation ἔταξα τὰ
ὅρια αὐτοῦ εἰς ἀφανισμόν for ואשׁים את־הריו שׁממה (Mal 1 3) is hardly a
parallel. ἐπάταξεν αὐτούς . . . καὶ τὰ ὅρια I Kingd 5 3 = I Sam 5 6),
καταβαλῶ τὰ ὅρια αὐτῶν (Hag 2 23, A), and τὰ ὅρια αὐτῶν ἠρημώσατε (I
Macc 15 29) indicate that the idiom was not so strange as Fritzsche and
his pedisequi seem to imagine. In addition, the not infrequent reference
to "removing the boundaries" (cf. Deut 19 14; Prov 22 28, 23 10; Isa 10
13; Hos 5 10) may well have influenced the author who saw the godless
Holofernes doing a lawless act instead of following the example of the
more praiseworthy Hebrew kings.   GROVES: ἄλση is the regular Greek
equivalent of (ים) אשׁדות, commonly translated GROVES or "Asherah/
Astarte."   CUTTING DOWN indicates that the objects cut down were
representative of the divinity. The constant repetition of Nabouchodonosor alone being the god to be worshiped is a conspicuous reflection of
the note in Daniel (notably chs. 3 and 6). Both Daniel and Judith may
well have stressed this note because of the blasphemous claims to
divinity of the hated Antiochus Epiphanes.   ALL THEIR TONGUES
AND TRIBES: the awkward "their" refers back to NATIONS. The phrasing
TONGUES AND TRIBES in this context is reminiscent of Daniel (3 4, 4 1,
5 19).   AND IT WAS GIVEN: א, 58 read ὅτι, i.e., *because* it was given to
him (*sc.* by Nabouchodonosor).
9. ESDRAELON: the awkward grecizing of the Hebrew Jezreel; the name
of a plain between Galilee and Samaria and including the valley of Megid-
do. Those who attempt to follow on a map the path of Holofernes will
assume that having reached the southern coastal city Ascalon he had

⁸And he utterly destroyed all their boundaries and cut down their groves, and it was given to him to destroy all the gods of the land that all the nations should worship Nabouchodonosor only, and that all their tongues and tribes should call upon him as god. ⁹And he came towards Esdraelon near Dotaea which is over against the great jagged ridge of
10 Judea, ¹⁰and they pitched their camp twixt Geba and Scythopolis, and he was there a month of days to gather together all the baggage of his army.

4   ¹And the children of Israel who dwelt in Judea heard of all that Holofernes, the chief captain of Nabouchodonosor

---

again turned north to enter Judea (including Samaria) from the north. If, as seems probable, DOTAEA (Δωταια) is to be seen as Dothan (modern Tell Dotha), a very ancient city of central Palestine mentioned in the OT as the place where Joseph's brethren were pasturing their sheep (Gen 37 17) and where Elisha escaped the troops sent to arrest him (II Kings 6 13), it is one of the few places in Judith realistically located. It is just south of the plain of Esdraelon, five mile north of GEBA and fifteen southwest of SCYTHOPOLIS (Beth-shan). The plain of Esdraelon was a logical place of assembly for the coming campaign. Here Sisera had been slain by Jael (a story clearly before the author's eye); here Josiah had been defeated and slain in his rash stand against Pharaoh Necho. If the view expressed in Rev 16 16 that the kings of the earth were to be gathered for the last great encounter was known to our author and Armageddon (Har-magedon) was understood to be הר־מגדו, additional reason, quite apart from actual history, may be seen for the choice of this spot for Holofernes' encampment.   OVER AGAINST THE GREAT JAGGED RIDGE OF JUDEA (ἀπέναντι τοῦ πρίονος τοῦ μεγάλου τῆς Ἰουδαίας): this is palpably awkward, for πρίων ("saw") is otherwise unattested in the tropical sense "great sawlike ridge." In addition, OVER AGAINST (ἀπέναντι) would seem to mean that the object so characterized can be seen from this locale, and RIDGE would probably be Jerusalem, some sixty miles to the south. Fritzsche sees another mistranslation: what the author wrote was מישור ("plain"), but the Greek translator misread it as משור (cf. Isa 10 15).
10. A MONTH OF DAYS: a Hebraism for a full month (Gen 29 14; Deut 21 13; II Kings 15 13).   BAGGAGE: as in 2 17. That this monthlong stay was to get additional supplies for his intended attack on Jerusalem by ravaging the countryside has been occasionally suggested, notably by Volkmar, but nothing in the text warrants the guess. It is more probable that what is meant is the consolidation of his army, increased as it now is by conscription from the territory already overrun.

τα, ὅσα ἐποίησεν Ολοφέρνης τοῖς ἔθνεσιν ὁ ἀρχιστράτηγος
Ναβουχοδονοσορ βασιλέως Ἀσσυρίων, καὶ ὃν τρόπον ἐσκύλευσεν
πάντα τὰ ἱερὰ αὐτῶν καὶ ἔδωκεν αὐτὰ εἰς ἀφανισμόν, ²καὶ ἐφοβήθησαν σφόδρα σφόδρα ἀπὸ προσώπου αὐτοῦ καὶ περὶ Ιερουσαλημ
καὶ τοῦ ναοῦ κυρίου θεοῦ αὐτῶν ἐταράχθησαν. ³ὅτι προσφάτως ἦσαν
ἀναβεβηκότες ἐκ τῆς αἰχμαλωσίας, καὶ νεωστὶ πᾶς ὁ λαὸς συνε-
λέλεκτο τῆς Ιουδαίας, καὶ τὰ σκεύη καὶ τὸ θυσιαστήριον καὶ ὁ οἶκος ἐκ τῆς βεβηλώσεως ἡγιασμένα ἦν. ⁴καὶ ἀπέστειλαν εἰς πᾶν ὅριον
Σαμαρείας καὶ Κωνα καὶ Βαιθωρων καὶ Βελμαιν καὶ Ιεριχω καὶ εἰς
5 Χωβα καὶ Αισωρα καὶ τὸν αὐλῶνα Σαλημ ⁵καὶ προκατελάβοντο πάσας τὰς κορυφὰς τῶν ὀρέων τῶν ὑψηλῶν καὶ ἐτείχισαν τὰς ἐν
αὐτοῖς κώμας καὶ παρέθεντο εἰς ἐπισιτισμὸν εἰς παρασκευὴν πολέμου, ὅτι προσφάτως ἦν τὰ πεδία αὐτῶν τεθερισμένα. ⁶καὶ ἔγρα-
ψεν Ιωακιμ ὁ ἱερεὺς ὁ μέγας, ὃς ἦν ἐν ταῖς ἡμέραις ἐν Ιερουσα-

---

2 σφοδρα 2°] om. אA

---

1. UNTO THE NATIONS: ἔθνος is regularly used in Jewish parlance for
other nations, "gentiles," in contrast to λαός for Jews. In 5 21 ἔθνος is
used by Achior (a gentile) in referring to them. SHRINES: whether τὰ ἱερὰ
is to be understood as "temples" or in the more general sense "holy
things" is uncertain. Some mss (19, 108) read τὰ εἴδωλα and A has τὰ ὅρια.
This is the only occurrence of the word in Judith. Regularly, instead of
τὸ ἱερόν he uses ναός or οἶκος for the Jerusalem temple, as in the immediately following verses (4 2, 3). Perhaps the choice of words here is a
deliberate contrast.
2. IN VERY GREAT FEAR: σφόδρα is a frequent word in Judith (28 times);
here it is doubled, a palpable translation of מְאֹד מְאֹד. Several mss,
including א and A, avoid the repetition, presumably for the sake of style.
3. SHORTLY: once again the author's ignorance of or indifference to
history is manifest in his mention of the return from captivity, and
dedication of the second temple (seemingly without interval) as having
occurred "shortly" before the time of his story (in the twelfth year of
Nabouchodonosor!). Whether the mention of RECENTLY having GATHERED
TOGETHER means for the dedication of the new temple or the reunion of
those in Judea, separated by the exile, is uncertain. It is far from improbable that the author is also mindful of the cleansing of the defiled
sanctuary and rebuilding of the altar by Judas in 165 B.C.E. (I Macc 4 36.51).
This is but one of many reflections of traditional events in Israel's history
which may be seen as stage properties for his story.
4. PART: ὅριον, like גְּבוּל, of which it is the regular translation, has the
force of both "bound," "limit," "border" and the space included within
certain bounds, that is, territory or district or part; so here (cf. 15 4).
SAMARIA: certainly at the date when the author sets this story relations
between Judea and Samaria were such as to make thoughts of support

king of the Assyrians, had done unto the nations, and how he had sacked all their shrines and had given them over to destruction; ²and they were in great fear of him and were terrified for Jerusalem and the temple of Adonai their God. ³For they had but shortly come up from their captivity, and all the people of Judea had recently gathered together, and the sacred vessels and the altar and the house had been sanctified from the profanation. ⁴And they sent to every part of Samaria and to Kona and Beth-horon and Belmain and Jericho and to Choba and Aesora and the vale of Salem, 5 ⁵and they preoccupied all the crests of the high mountains and fortified the villages thereon and laid up provision in preparation for war because their fields had just been reaped. ⁶And Joakim the high priest, who was at the time in Jerusalem,

---

from the latter unlikely. For the most part the places mentioned are quite unknown. If Βαιθωρων and Ιεριχω are to be identified as BETH-HORON (12 miles n.w. of Jerusalem) and JERICHO (in the Jordan valley), they are scarcely to be seen as villages of Samaria, as has seemed plausible to some through regarding the unknown KONA (κωνα) as a scribal misreading of κώμας (villages), six of which are then listed. It is profitless to attempt to guess what places were in the author's mind or his reason for selecting them. The impression given that all of these districts were definitely Jewish and ready to resist one sent to destroy them is in sharp contrast to the attitude of their heathen neighbors (3 28) who had unhesitatingly surrendered and abjectly begged for mercy. This aroused district was to the north of Jerusalem in the path of the would-be conqueror who in good tradition was descending from the north. The reading in Vg: *Et miserunt in omnem Samariam per circuitum usque Jericho*, whether a faithful rendering of the Aramaic text which Jerome claims to have found or his own paraphrase avoiding unknown places, would seem a correct gloss on our text.

6. JOAKIM THE HIGH PRIEST: apparently another creation by the author. In Neh 12 26 mention is made of Joiakim, the son of Jeshua, the son of Jozadak. According to Josephus (*Antt.* 20, 10, 2, §234) Jesus (= Joshua) became high priest at the time of the return from captivity in the stead of his father Josedek, who had formerly held that office. Apparently on the basis of this tradition Joakim is designated by our author as the high priest who shortly after the return had, as Nehemiah seemed to say, come to hold that office. Ms 48 in this chapter and Vg throughout the book names him Eliachim. Does this substitution of El- for Jeho- (so Cowley) reflect a tendency which may account for the marked preference for Elohim over Y″ in Pss 42-83? Joakim is mentioned four times in Judith (4 6, 8, 14, 15 8), always with the title ὁ ἱερεὺς ὁ μέγας.   WHO WAS AT THE TIME IN JERUSALEM: only so can the text be translated. Were it not for IN JERUSALEM, it might well reflect "who was at that

λημ, τοῖς κατοικοῦσι Βαιτυλουα καὶ Βαιτομεσθαιμ, ἥ ἐστιν
ἀπέναντι Εσδρηλων κατὰ πρόσωπον τοῦ πεδίου τοῦ πλησίον Δωθαϊμ,
⁷λέγων διακατασχεῖν τὰς ἀναβάσεις τῆς ὀρεινῆς, ὅτι δι' αὐτῶν ἦν ἡ
εἴσοδος εἰς τὴν Ιουδαίαν, καὶ ἦν εὐχερῶς διακωλῦσαι αὐτοὺς
προσβαίνοντας στενῆς τῆς προσβάσεως οὔσης ἐπ' ἄνδρας τοὺς
πάντας δύο. ⁸καὶ ἐποίησαν οἱ υἱοὶ Ισραηλ καθὰ συνέταξεν αὐτοῖς
Ιωακιμ ὁ ἱερεὺς ὁ μέγας καὶ ἡ γερουσία παντὸς δήμου Ισραηλ, οἳ

---

time high priest." Does this mention of chancing to be in Jerusalem
reflect the tendency of the later Hasmonean high priests to be absent
from the city in crusading campaigns?   BETHULIA: Unlike most
places mentioned casually in this tale this city is repeatedly named,
plays an important rôle in the story, and is definitely located—north of
Jerusalem, near Betomesthaim, over against Esdraelon, near Dothan,
in the hill country, with a spring below the city, and in a position to hold
the narrow mountain pass whereby access to Jerusalem is possible
from the north. To what extent this describes an actual city known to
the author, to what extent these details are supplied as necessary to
the story is uncertain. The name itself tells us nothing. Bethulia is the
form in Vg, which text does not mention the town by name at this
point in the story: *Sacerdos etiam Eliachim scripsit ad universos qui
erant contra Esdraelon, quae est contra faciem campi magni iuxta Dothain,
et universos per quos viae transitus esse poterat* (4 5).The Greek transcription
is Βαιτυλουα, with meaningless variants Βε-, -του, -λαια. No town with
such a name is known. Some have seen it as an echo of Beth-el; others
as an imaginary Beth^{ce}liya (בֵּית עֲלִיָּה, "house of ascent"), serving as a
subterfuge for Shechem which they argued occupied the required geographical position and was so disguised out of unwillingness to herald
the despised Samaritan town in the rôle of savior of Jerusalem. Shechem
may well have been known to the author, but if he utilized it as the site
of his Judean Thermopylae, he has allowed himself full liberty in his
description. Bethulia is high on the mountain; Shechem was not. Whether
Shechem was actually in the pass between Gerizim and Ebal and is to
be seen as Nablous (Josephus, *B.J.* 4, 8, 1, § 449), or a short distance
s.e. at the east end of the pass, is uncertain and would tell us nothing
of the author's thought of the place—if think of it he did—in his description of the habitat of his heroine. Torrey's argument that Shechem is
guaranteed as Bethulia since Judith is "of the tribe of Simeon, which in
the Hebrew tradition took possession of the city when 'the Shechemites'
were exterminated" (*Apocryphal New Testament*, p. 91) is scarcely
definitive. An equally plausible guess would be that the author was
thinking of Beth-el since Deborah dwelt "between Ramah and Beth-el
in the hill country of Ephraim" (Judg 4 5), for surely the figure of Deborah/
Jael is to be seen as a not insignificant source for his romance. Since
Hebrew writing as we know it has no mention of any such campaign
and its collapse as a result of a later Jael's exploit, it would seem pointless
to indulge in plausible attempts to read the storyteller's mind in such

wrote to those who dwelt in Bethulia and Betomesthaim
which is over against Esdraelon toward the plain which is
nearby Dothan, 7telling them to get possession of the passes
into the hill country because through them was the entrance
into Judea, and it was easy to prevent them from approaching, for the approach was narrow, with room for but two men
at the most.

8And the children of Israel did as Joakim the high priest
and the council of all the people of Israel in Jerusalem had

---

details which were necessary for the good story he is telling.   AND
BETOMESTHAIM: another unknown place, set near Bethulia and Dothan.
Torrey, who was certain that Bethulia veiled Shechem, was equally
certain that under Betomesthaim (-masthem) is to be seen a town so
nicknamed by the author: "Beth-masṭēmā" or "Beth Masṭēm" ("place
of enmity" or "house of the devil") in his contempt for Samaria (ibid.,
p. 92).   DOTHAN (Δωθαιμ): mentioned four times (4 6, 7 3, 18, 8 3) and
probably to be equated with Dotaea (Δωταια) in 3 9. The frequency
of mention has led to the guess that it was the author's home.
7. POSSESSION (control) OF THE PASSES: the unfamiliar defiles in rocky
Judea had proved a sore obstacle to the armies of Syria, accustomed to
open fighting, in their attacks upon Judas and his supporters during
the early years of the Maccabean war. Developing this theme was a
most natural piece of realism in our storyteller. Nor does he refrain
from heightening the dramatic by occasional exaggeration, such as the
detail that the pass to be guarded which led to Jerusalem was so NARROW
that not more than TWO MEN might pass through.
8. THE HIGH PRIEST AND THE COUNCIL: the term gerousia (γερουσία), which
occurs three times in Judith (4 8, 11 14, 15 8), indicates the official council
or legislative-judicial-administrative body or senate, presided over by
the high priest. The earliest reference to this or such a council under the
term gerousia is in the letter from Antiochus the Great to Ptolemy, which
Josephus quotes (Antt. 12, 3, 3, § 142). It is the term used by Josephus of
the council in Alexandria (B.J. 7, 10, 1, § 412), while Philo states that this
gerousia was established by Augustus Caesar after the death of the
ethnarch (in Flaccum 10, 74). In II Macc 1 10 quotation is made from a
letter which the gerousia of Judea wrote to their coreligionists in Egypt
about the profanation of the temple. In the same book a letter from
Antiochus IV to the gerousia of Judea is referred to (II Macc 11 28).
A letter by Jonathan the high priest and the council (γερουσία) to the
Spartans is quoted in I Macc 12 6. The only occurrence of the term in the
New Testament is in the perplexing phrase, τὸ συνέδριον καὶ πᾶσαν τὴν
γερουσίαν τῶν υἱῶν Ἰσραήλ (Acts 5 21). What Hebrew term for this council
thetranslator of Judith found in his text is uncertain. In his account of the
young Herod's difficulty with this authoritative Jerusalem council
Josephus had styled it συνέδριον (Antt. 14, 9, 4 f., §§ 168-84). He had also
used the word συνέδρια of the five councils which Gabinius had created

6

ἐκάθηντο ἐν Ιερουσαλημ. — ⁹καὶ ἀνεβόησαν πᾶς ἀνὴρ Ισραηλ πρὸς
τὸν θεὸν ἐν ἐκτενείᾳ μεγάλῃ καὶ ἐταπείνωσαν τὰς ψυχὰς αὐτῶν ἐν
10 ἐκτενείᾳ μεγάλῃ. ¹⁰αὐτοὶ καὶ αἱ γυναῖκες αὐτῶν καὶ τὰ νήπια αὐτῶν
καὶ τὰ κτήνη αὐτῶν καὶ πᾶς πάροικος καὶ μισθωτὸς καὶ ἀργυρώ-
νητος αὐτῶν ἐπέθεντο σάκκους ἐπὶ τὰς ὀσφύας αὐτῶν. ¹¹καὶ πᾶς
ἀνὴρ Ισραηλ καὶ γυνὴ καὶ τὰ παιδία οἱ κατοικοῦντες ἐν Ιερουσαλημ
ἔπεσον κατὰ πρόσωπον τοῦ ναοῦ καὶ ἐσποδώσαντο τὰς κεφαλὰς
αὐτῶν καὶ ἐξέτειναν τοὺς σάκκους αὐτῶν κατὰ πρόσωπον κυρίου·
¹²καὶ τὸ θυσιαστήριον σάκκῳ περιέβαλον καὶ ἐβόησαν πρὸς τὸν θεὸν
Ισραηλ ὁμοθυμαδὸν ἐκτενῶς τοῦ μὴ δοῦναι εἰς διαρπαγὴν τὰ νήπια
αὐτῶν καὶ τὰς γυναῖκας εἰς προνομὴν καὶ τὰς πόλεις τῆς κληρονομίας
αὐτῶν εἰς ἀφανισμὸν καὶ τὰ ἅγια εἰς βεβήλωσιν καὶ ὀνειδισμὸν ἐπί-
χαρμα τοῖς ἔθνεσιν. ¹³καὶ εἰσήκουσεν κύριος τῆς φωνῆς αὐτῶν καὶ

---

when he divided Palestine into five toparchies (*Antt.* 14, 5, 4, § 91), and
which in his earlier *Wars* (*B. J.* 1, 8, 5, § 170) he had styled σύνοδοι. Thus
some, as Cowley in his discussion of Jud 4 8 (*op. cit.*), see סנהדרין· as the
likely term in the Hebrew *Judith*; Solomon Zeitlin, who stresses the
absence of this term in tannaitic literature prior to the destruction of the
temple, and who argues that Josephus' use of the term is anachronistic,
is certain that γερουσία in Judith cannot be the rendering of סנהדרין
but of זקנים, which term in Exod 3 16 and Josh 23 2 is rendered γερουσία
in the LXX. As is true of many other matters, our book of Judith is not
calculated to throw much light on the debated problem of the emergence
of this authoritative council or senate or the exact designation it bore at
the uncertain time in which the author is couching his story. It does
suggest that at the time of the author himself there was such an
authoritative body in close connection with the high priest.
9. IN GREAT EARNESTNESS: twice repeated in the Greek, as in my
translation. Frequently the author indulges in deliberate repetitions
for emphasis. That this is deliberate is indicated by his regular avoidance
of repetition by the use of numberless synonyms.   DID THEY HUMBLE:
humility was in Jewish eyes a cardinal virtue, a view foreign to the Greek
to whom the word, when used at all, indicates groveling.   THEY
HUMBLE THEIR SOULS: Hebrew psychology was simple. A man's body was
an integral part of him. The *ruaḥ* or animating principle was breathed into
the *basar*, and it became a *nephesh* or individual. Thus in our idiom, the
man did not *have* a soul; he *was* one. The reflexive "themselves" is an
exact equivalent of THEIR SOULS in this passage.
10. SACKCLOTH: the putting on of sackcloth, together with other practices
such as putting ashes on the head, was a traditional act of mourning,
penitence, and supplication. The touch AND THEIR CATTLE, omitted in
Syr and Vg, reflects Jonah 3 8. Whether the garment was a small loin
cloth, as the common phrase ON THEIR LOINS, suggests, or was a larger

ordered. ⁹And they raised their cry to God—every man in Israel—in great earnestness, and in great earnestness did 10 they humble their souls. ¹⁰And they put sackcloth on their loins, they and their wives and their babes and their cattle and every sojourner and hireling and purchased slave. ¹¹And every man of Israel and woman and little children, who dwelt in Jerusalem, fell before the temple and cast ashes on their heads and spread out their sackcloth before Adonai. ¹²And they vested the altar with sackcloth, and with one accord they cried fervently to the God of Israel not to give their babes for booty and their women for spoils and the cities of their inheritance for destruction and the sanctuary for profanation and shame to the malicious delight of the heathen. ¹³And Adonai hearkened unto their voice and

---

garment is uncertain. That its use was for the purpose of self-punishment is unlikely, for there is no indication that the coarseness of the cloth was for that purpose. There is no express mention of the practice in the law, but its use throughout Hebrew history seems taken for granted.
11. CAST ASHES: ἐσποδώσαντο τὰς κεφαλὰς αὐτῶν is a most unusual phrase. The verb (σποδόομαι) properly means "to be burnt to ashes." Liddell-Scott-Jones cites this passage in Judith, with the rendering "strewed their heads with ashes," but has no parallel for what is seemingly a hapax. II Sam (II Kingd, LXX) 13 19 has καὶ ἔλαβεν Θημάρ σποδὸν καὶ ἐπέθηκεν ἐπὶ τὴν κεφαλὴν αὐτῆς, which makes the rendering in Judith the more surprising.   SPREAD OUT THEIR SACKCLOTH: apparently to make their mourning clearly visible to God. The other reference to spreading out the sackcloth (II Sam 21 10) is scarcely a parallel. Rizpah spread out the sackcloth she normally would have worn on the rock, presumably to lie upon it.
12. VESTED THE ALTAR: putting sackcloth even on the altar is, like the mention of putting it on the cattle, an exaggeration intended to heighten the picture of their GREAT EARNESTNESS (vs. 9).   OF THEIR INHERITANCE: this view is basic to Jewish thought. The land was given by God, not acquired or merited. Thus it is an "inheritance" and secure possession. By the conquest of Canaan Israel simply entered into actual possession of its inheritance promised to the patriarchs. In this short romance the noun occurs five times (4 12, 8 22, 9 12, 13 5, 16 21), the verb once (5 15), and each reference is in accord with this unshakable confidence.   THE SANCTUARY (τὰ ἅγια): the adjective ἅγιος is used six times (4 12, 13, 8 21, 24, 9 8, 16 20), always in the plural and always in the sense of the temple.
13. HEARKENED: the consequent hearkening of the Lord is in strict accord with the Deuteronomic confidence, and it is the constantly

εἰσεῖδεν τὴν θλῖψιν αὐτῶν· καὶ ἦν ὁ λαὸς νηστεύων ἡμέρας πλείους ἐν πάσῃ τῇ Ἰουδαίᾳ καὶ Ἰερουσαλημ κατὰ πρόσωπον τῶν ἁγίων κυρίου παντοκράτορος. ¹⁴καὶ Ἰωακιμ ὁ ἱερεὺς ὁ μέγας καὶ πάντες οἱ παρεστηκότες ἐνώπιον κυρίου ἱερεῖς καὶ οἱ λειτουργοῦντες κυρίῳ σάκκους περιεζωσμένοι τὰς ὀσφύας αὐτῶν προσέφερον τὴν ὁλοκαύ-τωσιν τοῦ ἐνδελεχισμοῦ καὶ τὰς εὐχὰς καὶ τὰ ἑκούσια δόματα τοῦ
15 λαοῦ, ¹⁵καὶ ἦν σποδὸς ἐπὶ τὰς κιδάρεις αὐτῶν, καὶ ἐβόων πρὸς κύριον ἐκ πάσης δυνάμεως εἰς ἀγαθὸν ἐπισκέψασθαι πᾶν οἶκον Ἰσραηλ.

5   ¹Καὶ ἀνηγγέλη Ολοφέρνῃ ἀρχιστρατήγῳ δυνάμεως Ασσουρ διότι οἱ υἱοὶ Ισραηλ παρεσκευάσαντο εἰς πόλεμον καὶ τὰς διόδους τῆς ὀρεινῆς συνέκλεισαν καὶ ἐτείχισαν πᾶσαν κορυφὴν ὄρους ὑψηλοῦ καὶ ἔθηκαν ἐν τοῖς πεδίοις σκάνδαλα. ²καὶ ὠργίσθη θυμῷ σφόδρα καὶ ἐκάλεσεν πάντας τοὺς ἄρχοντας Μωαβ καὶ τοὺς στρατηγοὺς Αμμων καὶ πάντας σατράπας τῆς παραλίας ³καὶ εἶπεν αὐτοῖς ᾿Αναγ-γείλατε δή μοι, υἱοὶ Χανααν, τίς ὁ λαὸς οὗτος ὁ καθήμενος ἐν τῇ ὀρεινῇ, καὶ τίνες ἃς κατοικοῦσιν πόλεις, καὶ τὸ πλῆθος τῆς δυνάμεως αὐτῶν, καὶ ἐν τίνι τὸ κράτος αὐτῶν καὶ ἡ ἰσχὺς αὐτῶν, καὶ τίς ἀνέστηκεν ἐπ᾽ αὐτῶν βασιλεὺς ἡγούμενος στρατιᾶς αὐτῶν, ⁴καὶ διὰ τί κατενωτίσαντο τοῦ μὴ ἐλθεῖν εἰς ἀπάντησίν μοι παρὰ πάν-

repeated note in the chronicle of the judges.   CONTINUED: the peri-phrastic (ἦν νηστεύων) heightens the familiar theme of a protracted fast.   ADONAI ALMIGHTY (κυρίου παντοκράτορος): a very common title or epithet for Y″ in the LXX, and used to translate both צבאות and שׁדי. Which of the two Hebrew words stands back of this word in Judith (4 13, 8 13, 15 10, 16 5, 17) is uncertain. In all likelihood it had lost its earlier descriptive force and had become an archaic poetic title.
14. WHO MINISTERED: apparently a threefold division of rank—high priest, priest, and (lesser) ministrants. While the third grade (οἱ λει-τουργοῦντες κυρίου) is not otherwise described—the word although common in the LXX occurs only here in Judith—it is far from impossible that by this phrase the author intended Levites.   CONTINUED BURNT OFFERING: τὴν ὁλοκαύτωσιν τοῦ ἐνδελεχισμοῦ = עלת תמיד (Num 28 6, 23); this offering made twice a day was the most important part of Jewish cultus.   VOWS AND FREEWILL GIFTS: (cf. Num 29 39, Lev 7 16, and frequently). This mention is not of special acts, but they were all performed in penitential garb.
15. HEADDRESSES: the linen caps (κιδάρεις λιναῖ worn by priests (cf. Ezek 44 18). κίδαρις is properly a Persian headdress or tiara.

1. THAT: διότι occurs 58 times instead of ὅτι in the LXX with the meaning

looked upon their affliction. And the people continued in
their fast many days in all Judea and Jerusalem before
the temple of Adonai Almighty. ¹⁴And Joakim the high
priest and all the priests who stood before Adonai and those
who ministered to Adonai were offering the continued burnt
offering and the vows and the freewill gifts of the people,
15 with their loins girded with sackcloth. ¹⁵And there were ashes
upon their headdresses, and they were constantly crying
unto Adonai with all their might to look with favor upon
all the house of Israel.

5 ¹And it was reported to Holofernes chief captain of the
army of Asshur that the children of Israel had made ready
for war and had closed all the passes of the hill country
and had fortified the crest of every high mountain and had
set snares in the plains. ²And he was greatly enraged and
summoned all the rulers of Moab and the generals of Ammon
and all the satraps of the seacoast ³and said to them, "Tell
me now, you sons of Canaan, who is this people which lives
in the hill country, and what are the cities in which they
dwell, and what is the size of their army, and wherein is
their power and their strength, and what king has risen over
them, as leader of their army, ⁴and why have they scorned
to come to meet me, they alone of all who dwell in the west?"

"that," usually after a vowel, but in this verse—its other occurrence in
Judith (7 13) is causal—it follows a *rho*.   OBSTACLES: apparently
σκάνδαλα here signifies barricades of some sort, as snares or pitfalls.
2. MOAB, AMMON are listed in II Kings 24 2 as supporters of Nebuchadrezzar against Judah. This may well be the source of the mention of them
here.   RULERS, GENERALS, SATRAPS: the titles chosen are apparently
for variety rather than as precise designations of the leaders of the several
grades. Satrap is a Persian title, not Assyrian or Babylonian.
3. SONS OF CANAAN: hardly apt for Moabites or Ammonites. This indicates
the artificial nature of many of the designations and mentions in the
book.   WHEREIN IS THEIR POWER AND THEIR STRENGTH: this word
put in Nabouchodonosor's mouth instead of the more natural *"What
is their power,"* that is, "How much of an army can they put in the
field against me?" is distinctly Jewish. It is Yʹʹ, not men or weapons,
who is the source of their power and strength.

5 τὰς τοὺς κατοικοῦντας ἐν δυσμαῖς. — ⁵καὶ εἶπεν πρὸς αὐτὸν Αχιωρ
ὁ ἡγούμενος πάντων υἱῶν Αμμων Ἀκουσάτω δὴ λόγον ὁ κύριός
μου ἐκ στόματος τοῦ δούλου σου, καὶ ἀναγγελῶ σοι τὴν ἀλήθειαν
περὶ τοῦ λαοῦ τούτου, ὃς κατοικεῖ τὴν ὀρεινὴν ταύτην, πλησίον
σοῦ οἰκοῦντος, καὶ οὐκ ἐξελεύσεται ψεῦδος ἐκ τοῦ στόματος τοῦ
δούλου σου. ⁶ὁ λαὸς οὗτός εἰσιν ἀπόγονοι Χαλδαίων. ⁷καὶ παρῴκησαν τὸ πρότερον ἐν τῇ Μεσοποταμίᾳ, ὅτι οὐκ ἐβουλήθησαν ἀκο-
λουθῆσαι τοῖς θεοῖς τῶν πατέρων αὐτῶν, οἳ ἐγένοντο ἐν γῇ Χαλ-
δαίων· ⁸καὶ ἐξέβησαν ἐξ ὁδοῦ τῶν γονέων αὐτῶν καὶ προσεκύνησαν
τῷ θεῷ τοῦ οὐρανοῦ, θεῷ ᾧ ἐπέγνωσαν, καὶ ἐξέβαλον αὐτοὺς ἀπὸ
προσώπου τῶν θεῶν αὐτῶν, καὶ ἔφυγον εἰς Μεσοποταμίαν καὶ
παρῴκησαν ἐκεῖ ἡμέρας πολλάς. ⁹καὶ εἶπεν ὁ θεὸς αὐτῶν ἐξελθεῖν
ἐκ τῆς παροικίας αὐτῶν καὶ πορευθῆναι εἰς γῆν Χανααν, καὶ κατῴκησαν ἐκεῖ καὶ ἐπληθύνθησαν χρυσίῳ καὶ ἀργυρίῳ καὶ ἐν κτήνεσιν
10 πολλοῖς σφόδρα. ¹⁰καὶ κατέβησαν εἰς Αἴγυπτον, ἐκάλυψεν γὰρ τὸ

---

5 7 εγενοντο] + ενδοξοι 58 OL Syr

---

5. ACHIOR: the choice of this name for the chief of the Ammonites is
apparently deliberate because of its transparent meaning, "brother
of light." His words are a true and complimentary rescript of Hebrew
history; subsequently he is to become a firm believer and brother Israelite.
Attempts to gain insight into historic characters by playing with the
derivation of their names is profitless, although not infrequently done.
It is quite another matter when the name is the choice of the writer
himself—cf. Judith ("a Jewess"), Esther (Ishtar), Mordecai (Marduk).
Achior is a good Hebrew name, although it does not chance to appear
in the Bible. The name Ahihud occurs in Num 34 27 and is grecized
Ἀχιώρ in the LXX, but it is most unlikely as a spur to our author's
choice.   I PRAY THEE: δή is one of the few Greek particles used by
the translator, and occurs some 14 times. The conspicuous absence
of such common elements of Greek prose, together with the constant
overuse of καί, is among the most impressive arguments that we have
here a piece of translation Greek. Achior's labored profession of the
truthfulness of his words reflects his warranted fear that they will prove
offensive to Holofernes.   HARD BY THEE: the phrase πλησίον σοῦ
οἰκοῦντος is scarcely an awkward and dangling genitive absolute, but
apparently the adjectival participle modifying περὶ τοῦ λαοῦ τούτου,
from which it is awkwardly separated by the intervening relative clause
(ὃς κατοικεῖ . . .).

6. DESCENDANTS OF THE CHALDEANS: this is in accord with the present
text of Genesis (11 28-12 5), where a migration from "Ur of the Chaldees"—
χώρα τῶν Χαλδαίων, LXX—to Haran in Mesopotamia is postulated,
but with no mention (as here) of the reason for the departure.   ARE: an

5   ⁵And Achior, the chief of all the sons of Ammon, said to him, "Let my lord hearken, I prey thee, to a word from the mouth of thy slave, and I will tell thee the truth concerning this people who dwell in this hill country hard by thee, and no lie shall come forth from the mouth of thy slave. ⁶This people are descendants of the Chaldeans. ⁷And formerly did they sojourn in Mesopotamia because they would not follow the gods of their fathers who were born in the land of the Chaldeans. ⁸And they left the way of their parents and worshiped the God of heaven, a god whom they had come to know, and they were driven out from before their gods and fled into Mesopotamia and sojourned there many days. ⁹And their God told them to go forth from the place in which they were sojourning and to go into the land of Canaan, and there they came to dwell and were greatly

10 increased in gold and silver and much cattle. ¹⁰And they went

---

example of the frequent coupling of a collective singular subject with a plural verb in a sense construction.

7. WHO WERE BORN: Syr, OL, and 58 add ἔνδοξοι after οἳ ἐγένοντο, which would make "the gods of their fathers" the antecedent of the relative "who were reverenced," instead of their fathers "who were born."

8. THEY LEFT: apparently Abraham and his family or, as the author is recounting the old story, the Hebrews in general. THEY LEFT THE WAY OF THEIR PARENTS: i.e., abandoned their cultic practices. THE GOD OF HEAVEN: so also in 6 19, 11 17—a title frequently used in the later writings (cf. Tobit 10 11, Dan 2 28, 4 37). WHOM THEY HAD COME TO KNOW: no mention is made of how they had made this discovery. Seemingly the author is familiar with later legend amplifying the Abraham story, as in the *Apocalypse of Abraham*. WERE DRIVEN OUT: lit. "they drove them out." The subject apparently shifts, and the "they" are now the other Chaldeans; less likely their parents.

9. As the story (Gen 12 1ff.) is retold, a far larger number of Hebrews is implied than in the biblical account, in which the number is limited severly to Abraham and Lot and their immediate families. THERE THEY CAME TO DWELL: that is, Canaan became their real home (κατῴκησαν) in contrast to Mesopotamia, in which they simply SOJOURNED (παρῴκησαν; ἐκ τῆς παροικίας). WERE GREATLY INCREASED IN GOLD: inferred from Gen 13 2, although in Genesis this is stated after Abraham's return from Egypt. But in this retelling there is no mention of Abraham's return from Egypt. As the story is here retold, the growth in numbers was not in Canaan but in Egypt. Apparently Abraham's visit to Egypt is omitted—and also the whole story of Joseph—as the words AND THEY

πρόσωπον τῆς γῆς Χανααν λιμός, καὶ παρῴκησαν ἐκεῖ μέχρις οὗ διετράφησαν· καὶ ἐγένοντο ἐκεῖ εἰς πλῆθος πολύ, καὶ οὐκ ἦν ἀριθμὸς τοῦ γένους αὐτῶν. ¹¹καὶ ἐπανέστη αὐτοῖς ὁ βασιλεὺς Αἰγύπτου καὶ κατεσοφίσατο αὐτοὺς ἐν πόνῳ καὶ πλίνθῳ, ἐταπείνωσαν αὐτοὺς καὶ ἔθεντο αὐτοὺς εἰς δούλους. ¹²καὶ ἀνεβόησαν πρὸς τὸν θεὸν αὐτῶν, καὶ ἐπάταξεν πᾶσαν τὴν γῆν Αἰγύπτου πληγαῖς, ἐν αἷς οὐκ ἦν ἴασις· καὶ ἐξέβαλον αὐτοὺς οἱ Αἰγύπτιοι ἀπὸ προσώπου αὐτῶν. ¹³καὶ κατεξήρανεν ὁ θεὸς τὴν ἐρυθρὰν θάλασσαν ἔμπροσθεν αὐτῶν ¹⁴καὶ ἤγαγεν αὐτοὺς εἰς ὁδὸν τοῦ Σινα καὶ Καδης Βαρνη· καὶ ἐξ-
15 έβαλον πάντας τοὺς κατοικοῦντας ἐν τῇ ἐρήμῳ ¹⁵καὶ ᾤκησαν ἐν γῇ Αμορραίων καὶ πάντας τοὺς Εσεβωνίτας ἐξωλέθρευσαν ἐν τῇ ἰσχύι αὐτῶν. καὶ διαβάντες τὸν Ιορδάνην ἐκληρονόμησαν πᾶσαν τὴν ὀρει-

11 κατεσοφισαντο Β | εν] pr. και Α | εταπεινωσεν ℵΑ, pr και ℵ | εθετο Α
15 τους εσεβων ℵΑ

WENT DOWN TO EGYPT reflect Gen 46 5-7, not 12 10-20. It is idle to try to guess the reasons (other than space) for this omission.
10. WHILE THEY WERE SUPPORTED or found food available: the wording is very obscure and led to early and later manipulations. The variant διεστράφησαν ("twisted," "perverted") in 248 and Compl. Ald. indicates that the scribes found the text obscure and altered it to force it to refer to the subsequent enslavement. De Wette sought to translate "until they returned," which would require ἀνέστρεψαν;; Goodspeed, "until they were grown up," which would require ἀνετράφησαν. THERE (bis): in Egypt.
11. This verse reflects Exod 1 8, as the concluding words of vs. 7 do Exod 1 7: the tremendous growth in numbers while in Egypt, which aroused the hostility of the king. While the general purport of the verse is evident, the text is most uncertain, as the variants show. The text as printed reads κατεσοφίσατο, ἐταπείνωσαν, ἔθεντο, with the first parallel with ἐπανέστη and with ὁ βασιλεύς as subject; the other two are plural, with the indefinite "they" (the Egyptians) as subject—essentially equivalent to the passive: "they were humbled and turned into slaves." B has the plural κατεσοφίσαντο, making all three agree. A has all three in the singular. ℵ concurs in reading ἐταπείνωσε, but has the plural ἔθεντο. A inserts καί before ἐν πόνῳ καὶ πλίνθῳ, making this hendiadys modify ἐταπείνωσε. κατασοφίζεσθαι, which occurs here in Judith and also in 10 19, occurs but once more in the LXX, viz., at this precise place in Exod 1 10. Its use here in Judith is obviously a reflection. It means properly to "outwit" or "outsmart"; it is a surprising word, for the action was scarcely one of clever trickery but of superior force. I have translated the unemended text, for the easier variants are palpably secondary. As a somewhat free paraphrase I am tempted to render it: "And the king of Egypt rose up against them and maliciously got the best of them;

down to Egypt, for a famine veiled the face of the land of
Canaan, and they sojourned there while they were supported.
And there they became a great multitude, and it was not
possible to number their people. ¹¹And the king of Egypt
rose up against them and got the best of them with hard
labor in brick; they humbled them and reckoned them as
slaves. ¹²And they raised their cry to their God, and he smote
all the land of Egypt with plagues, in which there was no
healing. And the Egyptians drove them out from before
them. ¹³And God dried up the Red Sea before them ¹⁴and
led them to Sinai and Kadesh Barnea; and they drove
out all those who dwelt in the desert. ¹⁵And they lived in the
land of the Amorites and utterly destroyed by their strength
all the Heshbonites. And having crossed the Jordan, they
took possession of all the hill country, ¹⁶and they drove out

they were humbled by being forced into the making of brick and were
reckoned as slaves."

12. IN WHICH THERE WAS NO HEALING: for this figure cf. Ecclus 21 3
(τῇ πληγῇ αὐτῆς οὐκ ἔστιν ἴασις) and Jer 14 19. FROM BEFORE THEM;
this constant use of πρόσωπον with varied prepositions suggests the
Semitic original.

13. For the phrasing of this verse cf. κατεξήρανεν κύριος ὁ θεὸς τὴν
ἐρυθρὰν θάλασσαν ἀπὸ προσώπου ὑμῶν (Josh 2 10)—this identity of phrasing
is scarcely accidental.

14. TO SINAI: lit. "into the road of S."; probably with the force "on the
road or way to S." εἰς ὁδόν is awkward and led to ὄρος ("mountain")
in 58, 64, 249 and in montem in OL. In Deut 1 2 the sacred mountain
(there Horeb) is also joined with KADESH BARNEA.

15. AND THEY LIVED IN THE LAND OF THE AMORITES: since οἰκέω is very
rare in Judith—only here and 5 5 (q.v.)—and κατοικέω very common, it is
not impossible that ΚΑΙΚΑΤΩΙΚΗΣΑΝ stood here and that the κατ- was
misread καὶ and omitted as a dittograph. THE HESHBONITES: var.,
"the people of Heshbon." The reference to those of Heshbon and the
destruction of their city is joined with the mention of a stay among the
Amorites in Num 21 25.31. BY THEIR STRENGTH: ἰσχύς is a word
constantly used by the author; cf. the similar phrase ἐν τῇ ἰσχύι αὐτῆς
in the account of the climactic act of Judith (13 8). TOOK POSSESSION:
lit. "inherited." The LXX regularly uses κληρονομέω as the equivalent of
both ירש and נחל. This constant emphasis (cf. 4 12) reflects the confidence
that God had promised and delivered the land of Canaan to his people in
consequence of his promise to Abraham (Gen 15 18-21; cf. Josh 1 6, Jer
3 18). While this is the only occurrence of the verb in Judith, the idea
back of it, as expressed by the noun κληρονομία, is frequent (cf. 4 12, 8 22,
9 12, 13 5, 16 21).

16. For the list of dispossessed peoples see Gen 15 19.21, Exod 3 8, 17,

νην ¹⁶καὶ ἐξέβαλον ἐκ προσώπου αὐτῶν τὸν Χαναναῖον καὶ τὸν
Φερεζαῖον καὶ τὸν Ιεβουσαῖον καὶ τὸν Συχεμ καὶ πάντας τοὺς Γερ-
γεσαίους καὶ κατώκησαν ἐν αὐτῇ ἡμέρας πολλάς. ¹⁷καὶ ἕως οὐχ
ἥμαρτον ἐνώπιον τοῦ θεοῦ αὐτῶν, ἦν μετ' αὐτῶν τὰ ἀγαθά, ὅτι
θεὸς μισῶν ἀδικίαν μετ' αὐτῶν ἐστιν. ¹⁸ὅτε δὲ ἀπέστησαν ἀπὸ τῆς
ὁδοῦ, ἧς διέθετο αὐτοῖς, ἐξωλεθρεύθησαν ἐν πολλοῖς πολέμοις ἐπὶ
πολὺ σφόδρα καὶ ἠχμαλωτεύθησαν εἰς γῆν οὐκ ἰδίαν, καὶ ὁ ναὸς
τοῦ θεοῦ αὐτῶν ἐγενήθη εἰς ἔδαφος, καὶ αἱ πόλεις αὐτῶν ἐκρατή-
θησαν ὑπὸ τῶν ὑπεναντίων. ¹⁹καὶ νῦν ἐπιστρέψαντες ἐπὶ τὸν θεὸν
αὐτῶν ἀνέβησαν ἐκ τῆς διασπορᾶς, οὗ διεσπάρησαν ἐκεῖ, καὶ κατ-
έσχον τὴν Ιερουσαλημ, οὗ τὸ ἁγίασμα αὐτῶν, καὶ κατῳκίσθησαν ἐν
20 τῇ ὀρεινῇ, ὅτι ἦν ἔρημος. ²⁰καὶ νῦν, δέσποτα κύριε, εἰ μὲν ἔστιν
ἀγνόημα ἐν τῷ λαῷ τούτῳ καὶ ἁμαρτάνουσιν εἰς τὸν θεὸν αὐτῶν καὶ

Josh 11 3. The addition of SHECHEM in this list is apparently in anticipation
of Judith's denunciation of him for his rape of Dinah (9 2ff.) and the
subsequent taking over of his territory.   GIRGASHITES: the occasional
translation "Gergesites" reflects the Greek modification of גרגשי. This
pre-Israelitic tribe is mentioned only in the table of nations (Gen 10 16 =
1 Chron 1 14) and in the lists in Gen 15 21, Deut 7 1, Josh 3 10, 24 11, and
Neh 9 8. Apparently the change to the plural for this group is due to the
preceding Shechem; perhaps that stylistic change accounts for the ALL.
The group is otherwise unknown. The variant reading "Gergesenes"
in the NT story (Mark 5 1, Matt 8 28, Luke 8 26, 37) is apparently an
arbitrary adaptation of this OT name.   THEREIN: lit. "in it" (ἐν αὐτῇ),
i.e., in that land (χώρᾳ, γῇ).
17. This note, the especial insistence of the Deuteronomists ("Do good
and prosper"), is utilized by our author. For him "doing good," that is,
refraining from sin, which insures prosperity at once, is not limited
to moral probity but includes ceremonial exactness. Unwarranted eating
of first fruits and the tithes of oil and wine (11 13ff.)—even to avoid
the starvation of the people and sanctioned by the high priest and
Jerusalem council—is as certainly to be punished by God as the most
flagrant moral dereliction. This apparently in no wise worries the author
as it surely would an Amos or Hosea.
18. UTTERLY DESTROYED (ἐξωλεθρεύθησαν··· ἐπὶ πολὺ σφόδρα): the
adverbial phrase may simply heighten the force of the ἐξ-, almost in the
sense of "again and again"; at any rate, our author likes to paint with a
full brush. Presumably the CAPTIVITY which resulted was that engineered
by the historic Nebuchadrezzar. Achior recounts this act of past history
to the chief lieutenant of N. now some seventy years later!
19. FROM THE DISPERSION: the word διάσπορα, here used in the sense
of exiles in one place (Babylon), came to be the common term for Jews
settled anywhere outside Palestine. The various conquests by Tiglath-
pileser, Sargon, and Sennacherib and the more systematic deportations

from before them the Canaanites and the Perizzites and the Jebusites and Shechem and all the Girgashites and dwelt therein for many days. ¹⁷And whilst they did not sin before their God, good things were theirs because God who hates iniquity was with them. ¹⁸But when they strayed from the path which he had appointed for them, they were utterly destroyed in many wars and were led into captivity in a land not their own, and the temple of their God was cast to the ground and their cities were taken by the adversaries. ¹⁹And now that they have turned back to their God they have come up from the dispersion where they were dispersed and possessed Jerusalem, wherein is their sanctuary, and have become seated in the hill country because it was desolated. ²⁰And now, most sovereign lord, if there be any fault of ignorance in this people and they sin against their

---

by Nebuchadrezzar, together with subsequent deportations by Artaxerxes Ochus (340 B.C.E.) to the shores of the Caspian and of Pompey (63 B.C.E.) to Rome, very well may have been the reason Jewish writers so regularly regard the dispersion as a great misfortune—which it distinctly was not, at least for those involved—a punishment from God for Israel's sin, which in the golden future would be withdrawn when the time of chastening was past.   SANCTUARY: our author uses various terms for the temple in Jerusalem. Here it is τὸ ἁγίασμα; in the preceding verse it was ναός; in 4 12, 13, 8 21, 24, 9 8, and possibly in 16 20, it is τὰ ἅγια; in 4 3, 8 24, 9 1, 13 it is οἶκος. It is notable that τὸ ἱερόν or τὰ ἱερα—often used of the whole temple area, i.e., not limited to the building itself—is not so used in Judith. The term does occur once (4 1, q.v.), but of heathen shrines.
DESERTED: without people. Apparently the shift of verbs suggests that they simply occupied these places without opposition, in contrast to Jerusalem, which they took back.
20. MOST SOVEREIGN LORD: a term of high compliment = "my lord and master." This term (δέσποτα κύριε) is occasionally used to translate אֲדֹנִי יְהוִה (Gen 15 8, Jer 1 6, 4 10; cf. Dan 9 15). In Judith δέσποτα is used five times in address to Holofernes; once it is a title for God in Judith's word δέσποτα τοῦ οὐρανοῦ καὶ τῆς γῆς (9 12).   IF...BUT IF (vs. 21): the one occasion of μέν in Judith—εἰ μέν... εἰ δέ.   FAULT OF IGNORANCE: in Tobit 3 3 ἀγνοήματα are mentioned together with ἁμαρτίαι as if there were a difference. To what extent the author of Judith is evidencing his insistence on legal and ritual observance, with ignorance no excuse —it was theirs to know—to what extent this word in Achior's mouth is an apologetic note—of course Israel would not sin deliberately—is debatable. The motif for the story is that Holofernes was unable to accomplish his purpose because of the divine aid to Israel who had been

ἐπισκεψόμεθα ὅτι ἔστιν ἐν αὐτοῖς σκάνδαλον τοῦτο, καὶ ἀναβησόμεθα καὶ ἐκπολεμήσομεν αὐτούς· ²¹εἰ δ᾽ οὐκ ἔστιν ἀνομία ἐν
τῷ ἔθνει αὐτῶν, παρελθέτω δὴ ὁ κύριός μου, μήποτε ὑπερασπίσῃ
ὁ κύριος αὐτῶν καὶ ὁ θεὸς αὐτῶν ὑπὲρ αὐτῶν, καὶ ἐσόμεθα εἰς
ὀνειδισμὸν ἐναντίον πάσης τῆς γῆς. — ²²καὶ ἐγένετο ὡς ἐπαύσατο
Αχιωρ λαλῶν τοὺς λόγους τούτους, καὶ ἐγόγγυσεν πᾶς ὁ λαὸς ὁ
κυκλῶν τὴν σκηνὴν καὶ περιεστώς, καὶ εἶπαν οἱ μεγιστᾶνες Ολοφέρνου καὶ πάντες οἱ κατοικοῦντες τὴν παραλίαν καὶ τὴν Μωαβ
συγκόψαι αὐτόν ²³Οὐ γὰρ φοβηθησόμεθα ἀπὸ υἱῶν Ισραηλ, ἰδοὺ
γὰρ λαὸς ἐν ᾧ οὐκ ἔστιν δύναμις οὐδὲ κράτος εἰς παράταξιν ἰσχυ-
ράν· ²⁴διὸ δὴ ἀναβησόμεθα, καὶ ἔσονται εἰς κατάβρωσιν πάσης
τῆς στρατιᾶς σου, δέσποτα Ολοφέρνη.

6 ¹Καὶ ὡς κατέπαυσεν ὁ θόρυβος τῶν ἀνδρῶν τῶν κύκλῳ τῆς συνεδρίας, καὶ εἶπεν Ολοφέρνης ἀρχιστράτηγος δυνάμεως Ασσουρ
πρὸς Αχιωρ ἐναντίον παντὸς τοῦ δήμου ἀλλοφύλων καὶ πρὸς
πάντας υἱοὺς Μωαβ ²Καὶ τίς εἶ σύ, Αχιωρ καὶ οἱ μισθωτοὶ τοῦ
Εφραιμ, ὅτι ἐπροφήτευσας ἐν ἡμῖν καθὼς σήμερον καὶ εἶπας
τὸ γένος Ισραηλ μὴ πολεμῆσαι, ὅτι ὁ θεὸς αὐτῶν ὑπερασπιεῖ

---

able to avoid violation of the divine law.   SUCH A SIN: a somewhat
free paraphrase of σκάνδαλον τοῦτο, which is substantially equivalent
to the preceding ἀγνοήματα.   WE SHALL GO UP: the faithfully repeated
καί preceding the start of the apodosis is but one more example of translation Greek. The future indicatives in this clause are essentially hortatory.
21. LAWLESSNESS: i.e., violation of the law (ἀνομία) and parallel to the
preceding ἀγνόημα and σκάνδαλον, detection of which will make them
vulnerable. The insistence of the prophets, notably Isaiah and Jeremiah,
that disaster at the hands of heathen armies is but the proof of God's
displeasure—the nation may be defeated, but not he whose integrity
is actually thus evidenced—is accepted wholeheartedly by our author.
AND WE SHALL BE SHAMED: this future ἐσόμεθα is scarcely parallel, as
the καί might suggest, to the subjunctive ὑπερασπίσῃ which depends
on μήποτε; rather the καί is logically the equivalent of "for"—for in
that case disaster will be ours.
22. WERE MINDED: lit. "demanded" (εἶπαν + infinitive).   THRASH
HIM WELL: the common translation "put him to death" scarcely renders
συγκόψαι, which is commonly used for "pound well" or "thrash soundly."
23. SAID THEY: this is implied but not expressed in our Greek, for the

God and we discover that such a sin is theirs, we shall go up
and war against them; ²¹but if there be no lawlessness in
their nation, let my lord, I pray thee, pass them by, lest
their Lord and their God cover them with his shield of defense,
and we be shamed in the eyes of all the earth."

²²And it came to pass when Achior ceased speaking these
words, all the people who stood round about the tent began
to murmur, and Holofernes' grandees and all who dwelt
on the coast and in Moab were minded to thrash him well.
²³"For," said they, "we shall not fear the children of Israel,
for lo it is a people in whom there is no power nor might for
a battle line of strength. ²⁴Therefore, we pray thee, let us
go up, and they will be but fodder for thy army, lord Holofernes."

6 ¹And when the uproar of the men who were about the council
ceased, Holofernes, the chief captain of the army of Assyria,
said to Achior and to all the children of Moab, in the presence
of all the foreigners, ²"And who art thou, Achior, and ye
hirelings of Ephraim, that thou shouldest play the prophet
among us, as thou hast this day, and shouldest tell us not
to wage war upon the people of Israel because their God will

---

preceding εἶπαν in vs. 22 is not properly continued as introducing indirect
discourse which changes to direct as Fritzsche contended.

1. WHO WERE ABOUT THE COUNCIL: they were standing around (encircling)
the council, not comprising it (cf. ὁ κυκλῶν τὴν σκηνήν, 5 22). The author
uses ἡ συνεδρία three times (6 1, 17, 11 9). CHILDREN OF MOAB: apparently singled out for emphasis, not for geographical reasons (east of the
Jordan in contrast to those on the coast), but because of their traditional
hostility to Israel.
2. YE HIRELINGS OF EPHRAIM: the precise force of this descriptive—one
of contempt—is uncertain. Presumably they were mercenaries in the
military combine formed by Holofernes against Israel, more specifically
against Jerusalem. Does the mention of Ephraim reflect the traditional
hostility of the south to the north, evidenced in such touches as II Chron
25 7, 9-15, where Amaziah ousted the Ephraimite mercenaries from his
chosen band ? Early uncertainty apparently led to the variant "Ammon"
in 19, 108, 58, OL, Syr. PLAY THE PROPHET: Holofernes' annoyance
at anyone venturing to advise him and even hint at disaster reflects
the earlier rôle of these figures who encouraged—and on rare occasions,
as Micaiah, Isaiah, and Jeremiah, discouraged—the king to engage in

αὐτῶν; καὶ τίς θεὸς εἰ μὴ Ναβουχοδονοσορ; οὗτος ἀποστελεῖ
τὸ κράτος αὐτοῦ καὶ ἐξολεθρεύσει αὐτοὺς ἀπὸ προσώπου τῆς
γῆς, καὶ οὐ ῥύσεται αὐτοὺς ὁ θεὸς αὐτῶν· ³ἀλλ' ἡμεῖς οἱ
δοῦλοι αὐτοῦ πατάξομεν αὐτοὺς ὡς ἄνθρωπον ἕνα, καὶ οὐχ ὑποστήσονται τὸ κράτος τῶν ἵππων ἡμῶν. ⁴κατακαύσομεν γὰρ αὐτοὺς ἐν αὐτοῖς, καὶ τὰ ὄρη αὐτῶν μεθυσθήσεται ἐν τῷ αἵματι
αὐτῶν, καὶ τὰ πεδία αὐτῶν πληρωθήσεται τῶν νεκρῶν αὐτῶν,
καὶ οὐκ ἀντιστήσεται τὸ ἴχνος τῶν ποδῶν αὐτῶν κατὰ πρόσωπον
ἡμῶν, ἀλλὰ ἀπωλείᾳ ἀπολοῦνται, λέγει ὁ βασιλεὺς Ναβουχοδονοσορ ὁ κύριος πάσης τῆς γῆς· εἶπεν γάρ, οὐ ματαιωθήσεται τὰ
5 ῥήματα τῶν λόγων αὐτοῦ. ⁵σὺ δέ, Αχιωρ μισθωτὲ τοῦ Αμμων, ὃς
ἐλάλησας τοὺς λόγους τούτους ἐν ἡμέρᾳ ἀδικίας σου, οὐκ ὄψει
ἔτι τὸ πρόσωπόν μου ἀπὸ τῆς ἡμέρας ταύτης, ἕως οὗ ἐκδικήσω
τὸ γένος τῶν ἐξ Αἰγύπτου· ⁶καὶ τότε διελεύσεται ὁ σίδηρος τῆς
στρατιᾶς μου καὶ ὁ λαὸς τῶν θεραπόντων μου τὰς πλευράς σου,

---

6 ο λαος] ο χαλκος/η λογκη comm. (lancea OL)

---

warfare.   WHO IS GOD SAVE NABOUCHODONOSOR or "What god is
there save N.?": this constant reference to his blasphemous pretensions
may well reflect the undying hatred of Antiochus Epiphanes, reputed
to have made similar claims.
3. AS A SINGLE MAN: so powerless will they be before us. Ball disagrees
and suggests that it implies their annihilation: not one man will be left.
THE MIGHT OF OUR HORSES: references in the Bible to the war horses
of the enemies of Israel, often viewing them as the strength of invading
armies (cf. Hab 1 8), are common.
4. BY THEM WE SHALL CONSUME THEM: obviously this reading is impossible,
for ἐν αὐτοῖς (BY THEM) can only refer to the preceding horses (τῶν
ἵππων); thus κατεκαύσομεν (WE SHALL CONSUME) is more than awkward.
Variants are common—κατακλύσομεν (19, 55, 74, 108, 236), καταπατήσομεν
(52, 64, 243, 248), καταλύσομεν (76), κατακλείσωμεν (106)—but all are
of a sort to be seen as corrections of κατακαύσομεν, which would accordingly
seem a primitive corruption or a stupid mistranslation. If conjectures
are to be made, two seem possible: a primitive miscopying of καταπαύσο-
μεν; deletion of ἐν αὐτοῖς (so א, 58) as a possible dittograph from the
preceding αὐτούς.   TRACK OF THEIR FEET: opinions differ as to the
meaning of this obscure phrase—not only will they be destroyed but
every memory of them; they will run so fast when they see us approaching
that one would believe they never even were there; not by one step
will they withstand us. Perhaps the first of these guesses is the most
likely as expressing the contempt of Holofernes for a group forced to
fight on foot without chariots or horses.   THEY WILL UTTERLY PERISH:
ἀπωλείᾳ ἀπολοῦνται, in imitation of the Hebrew prefixed infinitive

shield them? And who is God save Nabouchodonosor?
He will send forth his might and utterly destroy them from
the face of the earth, and their God will not protect them.
³To the contrary, we, his slaves, will smite them down as a
single man, and they will not stand their ground against
the might of our horses. ⁴For by them we shall consume them,
and their mountains will become drunk with their blood,
and their plains will be filled with their dead bodies, and the
track of their feet will not stand before us, but they will
utterly perish, saith King Nabouchodonosor, the lord of all
the earth. For he hath spoken; the words which he has spoken
5 will not be in vain. ⁵But as for thee, Achior, hireling of Ammon,
who hast spoken these words in the days of thy iniquity,
thou shalt not again see my face from this day until I shall
take my vengeance on the descendants of those who came out
of Egypt. ⁶And then shalt the sword of my army and the
lance of those who serve me pierce thy sides, and thou wilt

---

absolute to strengthen the force.   THE WORDS WHICH HE HAS SPOKEN:
once again the text is very obscure and has led to various alterations.
Some see these words as faulty indirect discourse, with ὅτι omitted;
others alter αὐτοῦ (his) to μοῦ (my) and regard it as direct discourse.
τὰ ῥήματα τῶν λόγων is altered by some to the easier τὰ ῥ. τοῦ στόματος,
an obvious correction. Probably the simplest solution is the one suggested
by the translation. The only alteration of the text required is punctuation:
a colon instead of a comma (εἶπεν γάρ·); with this cf. ἐλάλησα (vs. 9).
τὰ ῥήματα τῶν λόγων αὐτοῦ would seem to mean "the words of his utterance
or declaration" (cf. λόγους in the next sentence), i.e., THE WORDS WHICH
HE HAS SPOKEN. From such as he it is as good as done.
5. HIRELING OF AMMON: the repeated epithet is now applied to Achior,
not serving in the campaign from any sense of loyalty but for the wages
doled out to him in contempt. THESE WORDS: in deliberate contrast
to Nabouchodonosor's words, just quoted.   OFFSPRING: the following
τῶν (τὸ γένος τῶν) suggests "descendants" or "brood" rather than
"race" or "nation."   OUT OF EGYPT: Holofernes seemingly takes this
word from Achior's speech in the sense "a horde of runaway slaves."
6. LANCE: frankly a conjecture. The text reads "and the people of those
who serve me," which is obviously impossible as a parallel to THE SWORD
OF MY ARMY. Surprisingly there are no textual variants save the omission
of this puzzling phrase by 71 (patently a correction) and Vg. OL
(cf. Syr) has *lancea*. Conjectural emendations—ὁ χαλκός or ἡ λόγχη—
are ventured by Fritzsche. Very tentatively I have translated LANCE,
but solely because it seems less grotesque than any other suggestions,
including Cowley's "it may mean 'cut him in two and march between

καὶ πεσῇ ἐν τοῖς τραυματίαις αὐτῶν, ὅταν ἐπιστρέψω. ⁷καὶ ἀπο-
καταστήσουσίν σε οἱ δοῦλοί μου εἰς τὴν ὀρεινὴν καὶ θήσουσίν σε
ἐν μιᾷ τῶν πόλεων τῶν ἀναβάσεων, ⁸καὶ οὐκ ἀπολῇ ἕως οὗ ἐξ-
ολεθρευθῇς μετ' αὐτῶν. ⁹καὶ εἴπερ ἐλπίζεις τῇ καρδίᾳ σου ὅτι οὐ
συλλημφθήσονται, μὴ συμπεσέτω σου τὸ πρόσωπον· ἐλάλησα, καὶ
10 οὐδὲν διαπεσεῖται τῶν ῥημάτων μου. — ¹⁰καὶ προσέταξεν Ολοφέρνης τοῖς δούλοις αὐτοῦ, οἳ ἦσαν παρεστηκότες ἐν τῇ σκηνῇ αὐτοῦ,
συλλαβεῖν τὸν Αχιωρ καὶ ἀποκαταστῆσαι αὐτὸν εἰς Βαιτυλουα καὶ
παραδοῦναι εἰς χεῖρας υἱῶν Ισραηλ. ¹¹καὶ συνέλαβον αὐτὸν οἱ δοῦλοι αὐτοῦ καὶ ἤγαγον αὐτὸν ἔξω τῆς παρεμβολῆς εἰς τὸ πεδίον
καὶ ἀπῆραν ἐκ μέσου τῆς πεδινῆς εἰς τὴν ὀρεινὴν καὶ παρεγένοντο
ἐπὶ τὰς πηγάς, αἳ ἦσαν ὑποκάτω Βαιτυλουα. ¹²καὶ ὡς εἶδαν αὐτοὺς
οἱ ἄνδρες τῆς πόλεως ἐπὶ τὴν κορυφὴν τοῦ ὄρους, ἀνέλαβον τὰ
ὅπλα αὐτῶν καὶ ἀπῆλθον ἔξω τῆς πόλεως ἐπὶ τὴν κορυφὴν τοῦ
ὄρους, καὶ πᾶς ἀνὴρ σφενδονήτης διεκράτησαν τὴν ἀνάβασιν αὐτῶν καὶ ἔβαλλον ἐν λίθοις ἐπ' αὐτούς. ¹³καὶ ὑποδύσαντες ὑποκάτω
τοῦ ὄρους ἔδησαν τὸν Αχιωρ καὶ ἀφῆκαν ἐρριμμένον ὑπὸ τὴν ῥί-
ζαν τοῦ ὄρους καὶ ἀπῴχοντο πρὸς τὸν κύριον αὐτῶν. ¹⁴καταβάν-

---

12 επι την κορυφην του ορους 1°] om 58 OL Syr | 2°] om. cj. MSE

---

the parts.' " WHEN I SHALL RETURN. i.e., from the impending conflict,
as victor.
7. SHALL TAKE THEE BACK: in this contemptuous word BACK (= "out of
my sight") Holofernes is represented as regarding Achior as only one of the
large horde of westerners who have surrendered out of fear and to obtain
pay for fighting against their fellows, of whom Achior is destined, as the
story unfolds, to become one (14 10). Another possibility is a mistranslation. The original Hebrew text had וְהוֹשִׁיבוּךְ "and will place you," the
translator read וְהֵשִׁיבוּךְ "will return you (shall take you back)." CITIES
OF THE ASCENTS: one of these near-by hill cities of the enemy.
8. THOU SHALT NOT PERISH: his delayed fate will let him see the nonsense
of his presumptuous speech.
9. Holofernes final gibe: If you are fool enough to believe your own words,
then stop looking as dismayed as you do! I HAVE SPOKEN: like his
royal master (cf. vs. 4) he has spoken, and his words will not be altered.
10. STANDING BY: i.e., in attendance. LAY HOLD: arrest. BACK:
i.e., "off," "away" (see comment on vs. 7).
11. THE SPRINGS: the springs below the hilltop city are to play a pro-
minent part in the unfolding story.
12. ON THE CREST OF THE MOUNTAIN: this repeated phrase is probably
due to homoioteleuton. Most critics, following 58, OL, and Syr, regard

fall among their wounded when I shall return. ⁷And now
my slaves shall take thee and place thee in the hill country
and put thee in one of the cities of the ascents, ⁸and thou shalt
not perish until thou be utterly destroyed along with them.
⁹And if by any chance thou dost hope in thy heart that they
will not be taken, let not thy face fall! I have spoken, and
not one of my words shall fail to be fulfilled."

10   ¹⁰And Holofernes commanded his slaves who were standing by in his tent to lay hold of Achior and place him in
Bethulia and hand him over to the children of Israel. ¹¹and his
slaves laid hold of him and took him out of the camp into
the plain, and from the midst of the plain they went into the
hill country and came to the springs which were below
Bethulia. ¹²And when the men of the city which was on the
crest of the mountain saw them, they took up their weapons
and went out of the city (which was on the crest of the mountain), and every man that was a slinger withstood their ascent
and kept slinging stones upon them. ¹³And slipping under the
hill, they bound Achior and flinging him down left him lying
at the base of the mountain and returned to their lord.
¹⁴Now when the children of Israel came down from their city,

---

the first instance with suspicion. I am inclined to omit its repetition in
the next line and to regard it as a modifier of THE CITY (τῆς πόλεως),
certainly not of THE MEN (οἱ ἄνδρες). Strictly speaking, a preceding
τῆς might have been expected, but the omission of the article, although
not classical is a far from uncommon tendency even among good writers.
Some who regard the proper location of the repeated phrase in the
following line tend to make it adverbial: they went out of the city
and climbed to the summit. This is on all grounds unlikely. The city
itself was on the summit.   KEPT SLINGING: the change of tense to
the imperfect is vivid. Presumably the way the slingers prevented the
ascent of the enemy was by constant use of their slings.
13. The subject changes from the men of Bethulia to the enemy. SLIPPING
UNDER THE HILL: getting under the overhang to avoid the cascade of
stones.   BOUND: Vg has them bind him to a tree (*ligaverunt Achior
ad arborem manibus et pedibus*).   LEFT HIM LYING: lit. "they left
him flung down."   BASE: lit. "root"; ῥίζα, as the term for base or
foot of a mountain, is vivid but apt (cf. Job 28 ₉ where it is used in this
same sense to translate שֹׁרֶשׁ). Fritzsche's translation "unter die Wurzel,
am Fusse, des Berges," is accurate, but, as is frequently the case, so
compressed as to be ambiguous.

τες δὲ οἱ υἱοὶ Ισραηλ ἐκ τῆς πόλεως αὐτῶν ἐπέστησαν αὐτῷ καὶ
λύσαντες αὐτὸν ἀπήγαγον εἰς τὴν Βαιτυλουα καὶ κατέστησαν αὐ-
15 τὸν ἐπὶ τοὺς ἄρχοντας τῆς πόλεως αὐτῶν, ¹⁵οἳ ἦσαν ἐν ταῖς ἡμέραις ἐκείναις, Οζιας ὁ τοῦ Μιχα ἐκ τῆς φυλῆς Συμεων καὶ Χαβρις
ὁ τοῦ Γοθονιηλ καὶ Χαρμις υἱὸς Μελχιηλ. ¹⁶καὶ συνεκάλεσαν πάντας τοὺς πρεσβυτέρους τῆς πόλεως, καὶ συνέδραμον πᾶς νεανί-
σκος αὐτῶν καὶ αἱ γυναῖκες εἰς τὴν ἐκκλησίαν, καὶ ἔστησαν τὸν
Αχιωρ ἐν μέσῳ παντὸς τοῦ λαοῦ αὐτῶν, καὶ ἐπηρώτησεν αὐτὸν
Οζιας τὸ συμβεβηκός. ¹⁷καὶ ἀποκριθεὶς ἀπήγγειλεν αὐτοῖς τὰ ῥήματα τῆς συνεδρίας Ολοφέρνου καὶ πάντα τὰ ῥήματα, ὅσα ἐλάλησεν ἐν μέσῳ τῶν ἀρχόντων υἱῶν Ασσουρ, καὶ ὅσα ἐμεγαλορρημό-
νησεν Ολοφέρνης εἰς τὸν οἶκον Ισραηλ. ¹⁸καὶ πεσόντες ὁ λαὸς
προσεκύνησαν τῷ θεῷ καὶ ἐβόησαν λέγοντες ¹⁹Κύριε ὁ θεὸς τοῦ

---

16 αυτων ult.] om. ℵ

---

14. CAME UPON HIM. lit. "stood over him."
15. The forms of some of these proper names vary greatly in the several
mss. This is notably the case for CHABRIS, with at least thirteen variants
ranging from "Abris" to "Chambris." Presumably, if our Greek text is a
translation, the names which the author used were Hebrew, some,
but not all of which, are found in the Hebrew OT. Our text, however,
is Greek. It is not easy to determine the wisest form of transliteration
to use in English, especially since in the englishing of Hebrew names a
far from exact transliteration has become conventional, notably of the
sibilants and gutturals. This is palpable in the case of Χαρμις, which
would normally be englished Charmis, but is obviously the Hebrew
Karmi, which is englished in Gen 46 9 and Josh 7 1 "Carmi." Thus
instead of "Uzziah" the Greek equivalent "Ozias" has equal, perhaps
better, claim. "Othniel" surely lies back of "Gothoniel," with *gamma*
replacing the Hebrew *ayin*. In the case of Μελχιηλ (מלכיאל) there seems
to me no preference between "Melchiel" and "Malchiel," since the latter
(the form of the name in the ET of Gen 46 17) may be exact for the
initial vowel but is surely unjustified in *ch* for *kopf*. And to make matters
more confusing, ℵ has Σελλημ, 58 Μοχισηλ, and Syr Mansha'el. The
presumption is that the original author used familiar names, but that
in his choice he meant to refer to specific figures in stories known to
us is in most cases highly improbable. In consequence, the precise spelling
of these names is of minor importance in reading the tale he is telling,
woven as it is from many odds and ends, some historical although amazingly recast and misdated, some from his own gifted imagination. The fact
that OZIAS (Uzziah), the chief elder of Bethulia, and Judith are of the
tribe or lineage of SYMEON (Simeon) is probably deliberate, but to what
extent that aids in the author's choice of Bethulia as the showplace

they came upon him, and having loosed him they brought
him into Bethulia and set him down before the rulers of their
15 city, ¹⁵who in those days were Ozias the son of Micah of
the tribe of Symeon, and Chabris the son of Gothoniel,
and Charmis the son of Melchiel. ¹⁶And they called together
all the elders of the city, and there ran together to the assembly
every one of their young men and the women, and they
stood Achior in the midst of all their people, and Ozias
queried him as to what had happened. ¹⁷And in answer
he told them the words of the council of Holofernes and all
the words which they had spoken in the midst of the leaders
of the children of Asshur, and all that Holofernes had spoken
boastfully against the house of Israel. ¹⁸And the people fell
down and worshiped God and cried aloud saying, ¹⁹"Adonai

---

in his drama is, as has already been remarked, at best uncertain.
16. RAN TOGETHER: assembled or flocked together hastily.   OF THEIR
YOUNG MEN AND THE WOMEN: lit. "every young man of them and the
women." Presumably αὐτῶν refers grammatically to the ELDERS, although
more naturally we might have expected their relationship to be to
the city. The absence of the pronoun with THE WOMEN is surprising,
for the translator regularly so repeats his pronouns. If the THEIR suggests
that the young men were the sons of the elders, are THE WOMEN their
wives? Again, the obscurity is more perplexing than important.
ASSEMBLY: this term (ἐκκλησία) occurs also 6 21, 7 29, 14 6.   OF ALL
THEIR PEOPLE: the omission of the superfluous αὐτῶν after λαοῦ by ℵ
is definitely a betterment of the Greek.
17. IN ANSWER HE TOLD THEM: occasionally, as here, the Greek translates
into its own hypostatic idiom instead of following the Hebrew parataxis
("answered and told") to which we are accustomed in biblical translation.
HE HAD SPOKEN: Achior.   LEADERS: ἄρχων, always a substantive
in Judith, is very hard to translate consistently, for "rulers," "commanders," even "princes," are equally exact. The term refers to those in
authority without specifying the precise rank achieved or even the
exact nature of the assignment (i.e., the "number of stripes" or the
"corps").   AGAINST THE HOUSE: for εἰς, here in the hostile sense of
"with reference to" and so AGAINST, 58 substitutes ἐπί.
18. FELL DOWN (πέσοντες): while standing is a normal posture for
Hebrew prayer and is obligatory for some prayers, kneeling is also
recognized. Additional fervor or intensity was seemingly felt achieved
by falling prostrate (cf. Num 16 45). To what extent the phrase "falling
down" or "falling on their faces" is actual, to what extent increasingly
an equivalent to the Christian "Bow your heads" (or "hearts"!) by those
disinclined to kneel is uncertain.   WORSHIPED...AND CRIED ALOUD:
palpably a liturgical hendiadys.

οὐρανοῦ, κάτιδε ἐπὶ τὰς ὑπερηφανίας αὐτῶν καὶ ἐλέησον τὴν ταπείνωσιν τοῦ γένους ἡμῶν καὶ ἐπίβλεψον ἐπὶ τὸ πρόσωπον τῶν
20 ἡγιασμένων σοι ἐν τῇ ἡμέρᾳ ταύτῃ. ²⁰καὶ παρεκάλεσαν τὸν Αχιωρ
καὶ ἐπῄνεσαν αὐτὸν σφόδρα, ²¹καὶ παρέλαβεν αὐτὸν Οζιας ἐκ τῆς ἐκκλησίας εἰς οἶκον αὐτοῦ καὶ ἐποίησεν πότον τοῖς πρεσβυτέροις, καὶ
ἐπεκαλέσαντο τὸν θεὸν Ισραηλ εἰς βοήθειαν ὅλην τὴν νύκτα ἐκείνην.

7 Τῇ δὲ ἐπαύριον παρήγγειλεν Ολοφέρνης πάσῃ τῇ στρατιᾷ αὐτοῦ καὶ παντὶ τῷ λαῷ αὐτοῦ, οἳ παρεγένοντο ἐπὶ τὴν συμμαχίαν
αὐτοῦ, ἀναζευγνύειν ἐπὶ Βαιτυλουα καὶ τὰς ἀναβάσεις τῆς ὀρεινῆς
προκαταλαμβάνεσθαι καὶ ποιεῖν πόλεμον πρὸς τοὺς υἱοὺς Ισραηλ.
²καὶ ἀνέζευξεν ἐν τῇ ἡμέρᾳ ἐκείνῃ πᾶς ἀνὴρ δυνατὸς αὐτῶν· καὶ
ἡ δύναμις αὐτῶν ἀνδρῶν πολεμιστῶν χιλιάδες πεζῶν ἑκατὸν ἑβδομήκοντα καὶ ἱππέων χιλιάδες δέκα δύο χωρὶς τῆς ἀποσκευῆς καὶ
τῶν ἀνδρῶν, οἳ ἦσαν πεζοὶ ἐν αὐτοῖς, πλῆθος πολὺ σφόδρα. ³καὶ
παρενέβαλον ἐν τῷ αὐλῶνι πλησίον Βαιτυλουα ἐπὶ τῆς πηγῆς καὶ

---

19. The unexplained THEIR (αὐτῶν), obvious to the reader and presumably
so to God, stands in contrast to the subsequent OUR (ἡμῶν).　　ARRO-
GANCE: although this particular word (ὑπερηφανία) occurs but twice in
Judith (here and 9 9), the enemy is regularly stigmatized as having
this quality, surely leading to defeat, in contrast to humility, the ideal
of both Israel and her God. The word ταπεινοφροσύνη does not occur
in the LXX, but the idea was well known, and cognate words ταπεινόφρων
and ταπεινοφρονεῖν each occur once "in honor" in the LXX, while ταπεινός
and ταπεινοῦν occur with great frequency, each occuring twice in Judith.
Very definitely this was a Hebrew, not a Greek, emphasis, and the
quality—in rabbinic eyes the greatest virtue of all—was accordingly
an attitude of God himself (עֲנֹתְךָ תַרְבֵּנִי Ps 18 36). The related word
ταπείνωσις, LOW ESTATE (cf. 7 32, 13 20) is here used, not in the sense
"lack of arrogant pride," but of the strained and depressed position
to which the more powerful foe has reduced them.　　THIS DAY: the
phrase stands at the end of the prayer for emphasis. It should not be
understood in the sense "CONSECRATED this day to thee as not before."
Rather it means "Look with favor this day upon this holy nation, that is,
all Jewry, not those especially devout."
20. COMFORTED: reassured.
21. MADE A FEAST: gave a banquet, lit. "made (gave) a drinking party."
The Greek (ἐποίησεν πότον + dat.) reflects the Hebrew וַיַּעַשׂ לָהֶם מִשְׁתֶּה,
of which it is a very literal translation. The phrase, occurring frequently
in the OT (cf. Gen 19 3, 40 20, Judg 14 10, II Sam [II Kings] 3 20), is

God of heaven, look down upon their arrogance and pity
the low estate of our people and look this day upon the face
20 of those who are consecrated to thee.'' ²⁰ And they comforted
Achior and praised him greatly, ²¹and Ozias took him with
him from the assembly to his own house and made a feast
for the elders, and they besought the God of Israel for succor
all that night.

7   ¹On the morrow Holofernes gave orders to all his army
and to all his people who had joined him as allies to move
against Bethulia and to take aforehand the passes into the
hill country and to wage war against the children of Israel.
²And every mighty man of them moved that day; and their
troops of men of war were one hundred and seventy thousand
foot soldiers and twelve thousand horse, not to mention the
baggage and the men on foot among them, an exceedingly
great host. ³And they encamped in the vale hard by Bethulia

---

repeated in Jud 12 10 of the last feast given by Holofernes. Wine, one of
Israel's principal products throughout her history, was a regular part of
the banquet, as the term for such a meal (מִשְׁתֶּה) indicates. That this was
not limited to Israel (cf. Gk. πότος) but has been the near-universal
practice needs little argument. That this particular moment in Bethulia's
history was the occasion for such a festal meal might at first seem surprising—and would in a work of sober history—for the occasion was the
seeking of God's aid in deadly peril. In this setting our author uses the
customary phrase, untroubled by the concern of a later day at this turn
of phrase.

1. ARMY...PEOPLE: a loose hendiadys, to which as a unit the relative
clause is joined.   TO MOVE AGAINST BETHULIA: ἀναζευγνύειν (lit.
"to yoke or harness up") is the normal word for "break camp" (= Hebr.
נסע), and is so used here and in 7 2; in 7 7 and 16 21 it is used in the
equally common sense of "return."
2. MIGHTY MAN (ἀνὴρ δύνατος): warrior, able to bear arms; another
case of translation Greek. According to 2 15 Holofernes had a force of
120,000, with 12,000 mounted archers. In this muster the former number
has grown to 170,000, presumably including the allies whom he had
collected during the march. The mss and vss have many variants; א*
reads 8,000, which is corrected to 120,000, apparently in agreement with
2 15.

παρέτειναν εἰς εὖρος ἐπὶ Δωθαΐμ ἕως Βελβαιμ καὶ εἰς μῆκος ἀπὸ
Βαιτυλουα ἕως Κυαμωνος, ἥ ἐστιν ἀπέναντι τοῦ Εσδρηλων. ⁴οἱ δὲ
υἱοὶ Ισραηλ, ὡς εἶδον αὐτῶν τὸ πλῆθος, ἐταράχθησαν σφόδρα καὶ
εἶπαν ἕκαστος πρὸς τὸν πλησίον αὐτοῦ Νῦν ἐκλείξουσιν οὗτοι τὸ
πρόσωπον τῆς γῆς πάσης, καὶ οὔτε τὰ ὄρη τὰ ὑψηλὰ οὔτε αἱ φά-
5 ραγγες οὔτε οἱ βουνοὶ ὑποστήσονται τὸ βάρος αὐτῶν. ⁵καὶ ἀναλα-
βόντες ἕκαστος τὰ σκεύη τὰ πολεμικὰ αὐτῶν καὶ ἀνακαύσαντες πυ-
ρὰς ἐπὶ τοὺς πύργους αὐτῶν ἔμενον φυλάσσοντες ὅλην τὴν νύκτα
ἐκείνην. ⁶τῇ δὲ ἡμέρᾳ τῇ δευτέρᾳ ἐξήγαγεν Ολοφέρνης πᾶσαν τὴν
ἵππον αὐτοῦ κατὰ πρόσωπον τῶν υἱῶν Ισραηλ, οἳ ἦσαν ἐν Βαιτυλουα, ⁷καὶ ἐπεσκέψατο τὰς ἀναβάσεις τῆς πόλεως αὐτῶν καὶ τὰς
πηγὰς τῶν ὑδάτων ἐφώδευσεν καὶ προκατελάβετο αὐτὰς καὶ ἐπ-
έστησεν αὐταῖς παρεμβολὰς ἀνδρῶν πολεμιστῶν, καὶ αὐτὸς ἀνέζευξεν εἰς τὸν λαὸν αὐτοῦ. — ⁸καὶ προσελθόντες αὐτῷ πάντες ἄρχοντες υἱῶν Ησαυ καὶ πάντες οἱ ἡγούμενοι τοῦ λαοῦ Μωαβ καὶ
οἱ στρατηγοὶ τῆς παραλίας εἶπαν⁹ Ἀκουσάτω δὴ λόγον ὁ δεσπότης
10 ἡμῶν, ἵνα μὴ γένηται θραῦσμα ἐν τῇ δυνάμει σου. ¹⁰ὁ γὰρ λαὸς
οὗτος τῶν υἱῶν Ισραηλ οὐ πέποιθαν ἐπὶ τοῖς δόρασιν αὐτῶν, ἀλλ'
ἐπὶ τοῖς ὕψεσι τῶν ὀρέων, ἐν οἷς αὐτοὶ ἐνοικοῦσιν ἐν αὐτοῖς· οὐ
γὰρ ἔστιν εὐχερὲς προσβῆναι ταῖς κορυφαῖς τῶν ὀρέων αὐτῶν.

---

5 αυτων ι°] αυτου **א**   7 παρεμβολας om **א**

---

3. DOTHAN (Δωθαΐμ): see 4 6.   BELBAIM: apparently the same as
Belmain (4 4) and Balamon (8 3, q.v.). Once again there is the widest
uncertainty as to the spelling of these names in the mss.   CYAMON:
unknown. Some have fancied the name a corruption of Jokmeam, a city
of Zebulon (I Kings 4 12), in turn identified as Jokneam (modern Tell
Qeimon).
4. WILL LICK UP: the same vivid figure occurs in Num 22 4, expressing
Moab's fear of the inroad of Hebrews.
5. HIS WEAPONS: lit. "their weapons." Frequently this lack of agreement
is found due to the combination of a plural verb or participle with "each
man," apparently for emphasis. The first hand of **א** sought to correct
this infelicity with αὐτοῦ.   TOWERS: Syr and OL agree with 58 in
adding "of the walls."
7. CAMPS OF MEN OF WAR: only so can the Greek be translated. παρεμβολή
is the almost universal translation of מחנה in the LXX. Holofernes
left a detachment for control of the all-necessary springs of water. Thus
they formed an actual camp, apart from the main encampment. As a
patent stylistic betterment **א** omits παρεμβολάς.

at the spring, and they spread out in breadth over Dothan to Belbaim and in length from Bethulia to Cyamon which is over against Esdraelon. ⁴But the children of Israel, when they saw their great host, were greatly disturbed, and each man said to his fellow, "Now these men will lick up the face of all the earth, and neither the high mountains nor the deep ravines nor the hills will bear their weight." ⁵And each man took up his weapons of war, and having kindled watch fires on their towers they remained on watch all that night. ⁶On the second day Holofernes led forth all his horse in full sight of the children of Israel, who were in Bethulia, ⁷and he took note of the ascents to their city, and made visit to the springs of water, and possessed them and set over them to guard them camps of men of war, and then himself returned to his army.

⁸And there came to him all the rulers of the children of Esau and all the leaders of the people of Moab and the commanders of the coast and said, ⁹"Let our lord, we pray thee, give ear to a word, that there be no break in thine army. ¹⁰For this people of the children of Israel do not put their trust in their spears but in the height of the mountains in which they dwell. For it is no light task to mount to the

---

8. CHILDREN OF ESAU: Edomites. The phrase בני־עשו 'υἱοὶ Ησαυ' is common in Hebrew poetry as the title for the Edomites, felt to be close of kin to the Hebrews but for the most part hostile. In consequence of their plundering Judah after the Babylonian conquest (586 B.C.E.) feeling against them ran high. During the Persian period many Edomites moved into Idumea, subsequently to be overrun and foribly converted by John Hyrcanus.

9. OUR LORD: "your highness"; for this title see note on 5 20. Once more Holofernes is advised, but this time, unlike Achior's word, in a way which he approves as good military tactics.   BREAK: several mss substitute θραῦσις for θραῦσμα, but the equivalence in popular usage of these feminine-neuter cognates is too common to demand this orthological alteration.

10. THIS PEOPLE OF THE CHILDREN OF ISRAEL: as awkward and unnecessary a duplication in Greek as it is in English.   IN WHICH: this pleonasm, ἐν οἷς . . . ἐν αὐτοῖς, is often styled a Hebraism, but while it frequently occurs in literal translations of natural Hebrew, it is by no means so limited, as the scarcely Semitic "der du bist" in German or the colloquial "which her name is Mrs. Harris" in Dickens' Martin Chuzzelwit illustrate.

¹¹καὶ νῦν, δέσποτα, μὴ πολέμει πρὸς αὐτοὺς καθὼς γίνεται πόλε-
μος παρατάξεως, καὶ οὐ πεσεῖται ἐκ τοῦ λαοῦ σου ἀνὴρ εἷς. ¹²ἀνά-
μεινον ἐπὶ τῆς παρεμβολῆς σου διαφυλάσσων πάντα ἄνδρα ἐκ τῆς
δυνάμεώς σου, καὶ ἐπικρατησάτωσαν οἱ παῖδές σου τῆς πηγῆς τοῦ
ὕδατος, ἣ ἐκπορεύεται ἐκ τῆς ῥίζης τοῦ ὄρους, ¹³διότι ἐκεῖθεν
ὑδρεύονται πάντες οἱ κατοικοῦντες Βαιτυλουα, καὶ ἀνελεῖ αὐτοὺς ἡ
δίψα, καὶ ἐκδώσουσι τὴν πόλιν αὐτῶν· καὶ ἡμεῖς καὶ ὁ λαὸς ἡμῶν
ἀναβησόμεθα ἐπὶ τὰς πλησίον κορυφὰς τῶν ὀρέων καὶ παρεμβα-
λοῦμεν ἐπ' αὐταῖς εἰς προφυλακὴν τοῦ μὴ ἐξελθεῖν ἐκ τῆς πόλεως
ἄνδρα ἕνα. ¹⁴καὶ τακήσονται ἐν τῷ λιμῷ αὐτοὶ καὶ αἱ γυναῖκες αὐτῶν καὶ τὰ τέκνα αὐτῶν, καὶ πρὶν ἐλθεῖν τὴν ῥομφαίαν ἐπ' αὐτοὺς
15 καταστρωθήσονται ἐν ταῖς πλατείαις τῆς οἰκήσεως αὐτῶν. ¹⁵καὶ
ἀνταποδώσεις αὐτοῖς ἀνταπόδομα πονηρὸν ἀνθ' ὧν ἐστασίασαν καὶ
οὐκ ἀπήντησαν τῷ προσώπῳ σου ἐν εἰρήνῃ. — ¹⁶καὶ ἤρεσαν οἱ
λόγοι αὐτῶν ἐνώπιον Ολοφέρνου καὶ ἐνώπιον πάντων τῶν θεραπόντων αὐτοῦ, καὶ συνέταξε ποιεῖν καθὰ ἐλάλησαν. ¹⁷καὶ ἀπῆρεν
παρεμβολὴ υἱῶν Αμμων καὶ μετ' αὐτῶν χιλιάδες πέντε υἱῶν Ασσουρ καὶ παρενέβαλον ἐν τῷ αὐλῶνι καὶ προκατελάβοντο τὰ ὕδατα
καὶ τὰς πηγὰς τῶν ὑδάτων τῶν υἱῶν Ισραηλ. ¹⁸καὶ ἀνέβησαν οἱ
υἱοὶ Ησαυ καὶ οἱ υἱοὶ Αμμων καὶ παρενέβαλον ἐν τῇ ὀρεινῇ ἀπέναντι Δωθαϊμ. καὶ ἀπέστειλαν ἐξ αὐτῶν πρὸς νότον καὶ ἀπηλιώ-
την ἀπέναντι Εγρεβηλ, ἥ ἐστιν πλησίον Χους, ἥ ἐστιν ἐπὶ τοῦ
χειμάρρου Μοχμουρ. καὶ ἡ λοιπὴ στρατιὰ τῶν Ἀσσυρίων παρεν-

---

17 των υδατων] om. 58 Syr.

---

11. DO NOT WAGE: this imperative, the logical equivalent of a protasis,
"if you do not...," is but one more indication of literal translation
from an idiom more natural to Hebrew than to Greek or English.
12. REMAIN...KEEPING CAREFUL GUARD: i.e., refrain from needlessly
exposing your troops to the certain dangers of dropped stones and other
guerilla tactics.   GAIN HOLD OF THE SPRING: ἐπικρατησάτωσαν is surprising in view of vs. 7 where the springs have already been taken and put
under guard.
14. WILL WASTE AWAY WITH FAMINE: lit. "will melt." In Deut 32 24 the
same figure (τηκόμενοι λιμῷ) is used.
15. REQUITE THEE WITH AN EVIL RECOMPENSE: this repetition with
cognate accusative (ἀνταποδώσεις ἀνταπόδομα) is frequent in the LXX
and not uncommon in Hebrew.   REBELLED: the nature of the "rebellion"
is indicated in the following phrase which is literally "meet thy face in
peace," a palpable bit of translation Greek.

crests of their mountains. ¹¹And now, my lord, do not wage war against them as war is wont to be waged in battle array, and there shall not fall from thy people a single man. ¹²Remain in thy camp, keeping careful guard on every man of thine army, and let thy servants gain hold of the spring of water which issues from the base of the mountain, ¹³because from there all who dwell in Bethulia draw their water, and thirst will slay them, and they will give over their city; and we and our people will go up on the crests of the near-by mountains and will encamp upon them to keep watch that no single man go forth from the city. ¹⁴And they will waste away with famine, they and their wives and their children, and before the sword comes upon them they will be laid low 15 in the streets of their habitation. ¹⁵And thou wilt requite them with an evil recompense because they rebelled and did not meet with thee in peace.''

¹⁶And their words found favor in the sight of Holofernes and in the sight of all his servants, and he gave word to do as they had said. ¹⁷And the force of the children of Ammon departed and with them five thousand children of Asshur and encamped in the valley and seized the sources of water and the springs of water of the children of Israel. ¹⁸And the children of Esau and the children of Ammon went up and pitched camp in the hill country over against Dothaim. And they sent some of their number to the south and to the east toward Egrebel, which is near Chus on the mountain brook Mochmour. And the rest of the army of the Assyrians

---

17. THE FORCE: lit. (the) camp.   THE SOURCES OF WATER AND THE SPRINGS OF WATER: the precise difference intended by this seeming repetition is not clear; τῶν ὑδάτων is omitted by 58 and Syr, apparently to avoid duplication.

18. EGREBEL or Ekrebel: commonly identified as Acraba, near the well of Sychar.   MOCHMOUR: profitless guessing has sought to identify this unknown stream with the Besor, Jordan, and perhaps slightly less unlikely the wadi Makhfurlyeh, south of Nablus. Perhaps our author's geography in this district is less imaginative than in other areas, but it would appear that modern investigators tend to find rather more clues to identity than did the early translators who rival one another in variants for places they obviously had no slightest knowledge of.

ἔβαλον ἐν τῷ πεδίῳ καὶ ἐκάλυψαν πᾶν τὸ πρόσωπον τῆς γῆς, καὶ αἱ σκηναὶ καὶ αἱ ἀπαρτίαι αὐτῶν κατεστρατοπέδευσαν ἐν ὄχλῳ πολλῷ καὶ ἦσαν εἰς πλῆθος πολὺ σφόδρα.

¹⁹Καὶ οἱ υἱοὶ Ισραηλ ἀνεβόησαν πρὸς κύριον θεὸν αὐτῶν, ὅτι ὠλιγοψύχησεν τὸ πνεῦμα αὐτῶν, ὅτι ἐκύκλωσαν πάντες οἱ ἐχθροὶ
20 αὐτῶν καὶ οὐκ ἦν διαφυγεῖν ἐκ μέσου αὐτῶν. ²⁰καὶ ἔμεινεν κύκλῳ αὐτῶν πᾶσα παρεμβολὴ Ασσουρ, οἱ πεζοὶ καὶ ἅρματα καὶ οἱ ἱππεῖς αὐτῶν, ἡμέρας τριάκοντα τέσσαρας. καὶ ἐξέλιπεν πάντας τοὺς κατοικοῦντας Βαιτιλουα πάντα τὰ ἀγγεῖα αὐτῶν τῶν ὑδάτων, ²¹καὶ οἱ λάκκοι ἐξεκενοῦντο, καὶ οὐκ εἶχον πιεῖν εἰς πλησμονὴν ὕδωρ ἡμέραν μίαν, ὅτι ἐν μέτρῳ ἐδίδοσαν αὐτοῖς πιεῖν. ²²καὶ ἠθύμησεν τὰ νήπια αὐτῶν, καὶ αἱ γυναῖκες καὶ οἱ νεανίσκοι ἐξέλιπον ἀπὸ τῆς δίψης καὶ ἔπιπτον ἐν ταῖς πλατείαις τῆς πόλεως καὶ ἐν ταῖς διόδοις τῶν πυλῶν, καὶ οὐκ ἦν κραταίωσις ἔτι ἐν αὐτοῖς. — ²³καὶ ἐπισυνήχθησαν πᾶς ὁ λαὸς ἐπὶ Οζιαν καὶ τοὺς ἄρχοντας τῆς πόλεως, οἱ νεανίσκοι καὶ αἱ γυναῖκες καὶ τὰ παιδία, καὶ ἀνεβόησαν φωνῇ μεγάλῃ καὶ εἶπαν ἐναντίον πάντων τῶν πρεσβυτέρων ²⁴Κρίναι ὁ θεὸς ἀνὰ μέσον ὑμῶν καὶ ἡμῶν, ὅτι ἐποιήσατε ἐν ἡμῖν ἀδι-
25 κίαν μεγάλην οὐ λαλήσαντες εἰρηνικὰ μετὰ υἱῶν Ασσουρ. ²⁵καὶ νῦν οὐκ ἔστιν ὁ βοηθὸς ἡμῶν, ἀλλὰ πέπρακεν ἡμᾶς ὁ θεὸς εἰς τὰς χεῖρας αὐτῶν τοῦ καταστρωθῆναι ἐναντίον αὐτῶν ἐν δίψῃ καὶ ἀπωλείᾳ μεγάλῃ. ²⁶καὶ νῦν ἐπικαλέσασθε αὐτοὺς καὶ ἔκδοσθε τὴν πόλιν πᾶσαν εἰς προνομὴν τῷ λαῷ Ολοφέρνου καὶ πάσῃ τῇ δυνάμει αὐτοῦ. ²⁷κρεῖσσον γὰρ ἡμῖν γενηθῆναι αὐτοῖς εἰς διαρπαγήν· ἐσόμεθα γὰρ εἰς δούλους, καὶ ζήσεται ἡ ψυχὴ ἡμῶν, καὶ οὐκ ὀψόμεθα τὸν θάνατον τῶν νηπίων ἡμῶν ἐν ὀφθαλμοῖς ἡμῶν καὶ τὰς γυναῖκας καὶ τὰ τέκνα ἡμῶν ἐκλειπούσας τὰς ψυχὰς αὐτῶν. ²⁸μαρτυρόμεθα ὑμῖν

---

28 μαρτυρυμεθα] pr. δια � 58 | μη] om. 𝕏 OL Syr Vg

IN GREAT ARRAY: less likely, "with a great throng of people." The concluding clause summarizes the whole verse.
19. THEIR SPIRIT HAD GROWN FAINT: for this same figure cf. Ps 76 4 (LXX), καὶ ὠλιγοψύχησεν τὸ πνεῦμά μου.
20. All the texts agree that the siege was prolonged, but there is little agreement as to the precise length: "fourteen days and a month" (19,108); "four days and two months" (OL, Syr); "twenty days" (Vg). These seemingly purposeless variants in details and the spelling of names are among the most baffling problems the critic faces.

encamped in the plain and covered all the face of the earth, and their tents and their supplies were pitched in great array, and they were an exceeding great multitude.

¹⁹And the children of Israel raised their cry to Adonai their God, because their spirit had grown faint, because all their enemies had compassed them about, and it was impossible 20 to escape from their midst. ²⁰And all the army of Asshur remained encamped around them, their foot soldiers and chariots and horsemen, for thirty-four days. And all their vessels of water utterly failed all those who dwelt in Bethulia, ²¹and their cisterns were going dry, and they did not have enough water to drink their fill for a single day, for by measure were they giving them to drink. ²²And their babies lost heart, and the women and the young men fainted from thirst and were falling prone in the streets of the city and in the ways through the gates, and there was no might left in them.

²³And all the people assembled against Ozias and the rulers of the city, the young men and the women and the little children, and cried out with a loud voice and said, in the presence of all the elders, ²⁴"May God judge between you and us, because you have done us great wrong by not speaking 25 words of peace with the children of Asshur. ²⁵And now we have no helper, but God hath sold us into their hands to be brought low before them in thirst and great destruction. ²⁶And now call them and hand over the whole city for spoils to the people of Holofernes and to all his army. ²⁷For better is it for us to be made their booty. For we shall be their slaves, and our lives will be spared, and we shall not see the death of our babes before our very eyes, and our wives and children gasping out their lives. ²⁸We call to witness

---

21. BY MEASURE: the limited supply was being rationed out.
24f. A complaint not unlike that of the Israelites to Moses in the wilderness of Sin (Exod 16).   GOD HATH SOLD US: for this figure cf. Esther 7 4, Bar 4 6.
26. CALL: not in the sense sometimes read into the word, "appeal," but simply "Summon them and surrender."
27. OUR LIVES WILL BE SPARED: lit. "our souls shall live."

τὸν οὐρανὸν καὶ τὴν γῆν καὶ τὸν θεὸν ἡμῶν καὶ κύριον τῶν πατέρων ἡμῶν, ὃς ἐκδικεῖ ἡμᾶς κατὰ τάς ἁμαρτίας ἡμῶν καὶ κατὰ
τὰ ἁμαρτήματα τῶν πατέρων ἡμῶν, ἵνα μὴ ποιήσῃ κατὰ τὰ ῥήματα ταῦτα ἐν τῇ ἡμέρᾳ τῇ σήμερον. ²⁹καὶ ἐγένετο κλαυθμὸς μέγας
ἐν μέσῳ τῆς ἐκκλησίας πάντων ὁμοθυμαδόν, καὶ ἐβόησαν πρὸς
30 κύριον τὸν θεὸν φωνῇ μεγάλῃ. — ³⁰καὶ εἶπεν πρὸς αὐτοὺς Οζιας
Θαρσεῖτε, ἀδελφοί, διακαρτερήσωμεν ἔτι πέντε ἡμέρας, ἐν αἷς ἐπι-
στρέψει κύριος ὁ θεὸς ἡμῶν τὸ ἔλεος αὐτοῦ ἐφ᾽ ἡμᾶς, οὐ γὰρ
ἐγκαταλείψει ἡμᾶς εἰς τέλος· ³¹ἐὰν δὲ διέλθωσιν αὗται καὶ μὴ ἔλθῃ
ἐφ᾽ ἡμᾶς βοήθεια, ποιήσω κατὰ τὰ ῥήματα ὑμῶν. ³²καὶ ἐσκόρπισεν
τὸν λαὸν εἰς τὴν ἑαυτοῦ παρεμβολήν, καὶ ἐπὶ τὰ τείχη καὶ τοὺς
πύργους τῆς πόλεως αὐτῶν ἀπῆλθον καὶ τὰς γυναῖκας καὶ τὰ τέκνα
εἰς τοὺς οἴκους αὐτῶν ἀπέστειλαν· καὶ ἦσαν ἐν ταπεινώσει πολλῇ
ἐν τῇ πόλει.

8　　¹Καὶ ἤκουσεν ἐν ἐκείναις ταῖς ἡμέραις Ιουδιθ θυγάτηρ Μεραρι

---

32 τον λαον] + εκαστον 58 OL Syr | απεστειλαν] -λε(ν) Bℵ 19, απελυσεν 58

---

28. ADONAI THE GOD OF OUR FATHERS: — The Greek text has "our God and
κύριον (Adonai) of our fathers." There is no such expression in Hebrew.
The word Adonai is a proper name and thus it cannot have an adjective
or pronoun. The Hebrew language cannot suffer the expression Adonai of
our fathers. [s.z.]　　THAT HE MAY NOT ACT . . . SAID: this concluding clause
is far from clear. As the commonly accepted text stands, the ἵνα clause is
presumably not telic but nominal and stands as the content of the
speakers' petition. WE CALL TO WITNESS would then be in the sense
"We beg earnestly," which would make the compound διαμαρτυρόμεθα
(read by ℵ, 58) a bit more natural. The subject HE of this nominal
clause would then be God—the absence of such subject is at best surprising—and the prayer would be that HE not let us die of thirst. This
is possible but definitely awkward. The unusually large number of
variants in the several mss and vss evidence the difficulty felt by early
readers. The most significant variant is the omission of the negative
μή by ℵ, Syr, OL, and Vg. The clause was then understood as the people's
demand that their advice to surrender the city be followed. The verb
ποιήσῃ would then be regarded as middle, 2 sg., and the sense would be:
"that you act in accord with our demand of surrender." This is possible
although nowhere else in this writing is the middle of ποιεῖν used. Greater
difficulty is the singular which would then refer to Ozias, an awkward
shift from the plural ὑμῖν. Apparently this was the way the Syriac and
Latin traditions understood the clause, and they shifted to the active

against you heaven and earth, and Adonai the God of our fathers, who punishes us in accord with our sins and the sinful acts of our fathers, that he may not act in accord with what we have this day said." [29]Then arose with one consent great lamentation in the midst of the assembly, and they cried unto Adonai their God with a loud voice.

30   [30]And Ozias said to them, "Courage, brethren, let us hold out for five days more, in the which Adonai our God will turn his mercy toward us, for he will not utterly forsake us. [31]But if these days pass and no succor come upon us, I will do according to your words." [32]And he dispersed the people, each to his own post, and they departed to the walls and the towers of their city, and they sent the women and children to their homes. And they were greatly humbled in the city.

8   [1]And in those days Judith heard thereof, Judith the daugh-

---

2nd pl.: *ut faciatis* (OL), *ut iam tradatis civitatem in manu Holofernes* (Vg), which certainly implies ποιήσητε. This avoids the awkwardness of IN ACCORD WITH WHAT WE HAVE THIS DAY SAID as a reference to their fear of death through lack of water, and would be in accord with the repeated phrase in Ozias' reply (vs. 31).

30. Presumably Ozias hopes for rain which will fill their empty cisterns (cf. 8 31). UTTERLY FORSAKE US: the striking identity of phrase in 1 Chron 28 9 (καταλείψει σε εἰς τέλος) may well have led to the deletion of ἐγ- in several mss.

32. EACH: ἕκαστον after τὸν λαόν, read by 58 and both the Syr and OL, is an automatic addition of an obvious careless omission. THEY SENT: the well-attested "he sent" is probably to be regarded as a stylistic correction to make the verb parallel to HE DISPERSED. The plural is to be retained as the impersonal equivalent of the passive, rather than the act of the departing husbands and fathers. HUMBLED: that is, "depressed."

1-8. With ch. 8 the second half of the story begins. Chs. 1-7 provide an effective background for the principal incident of the tale, which without this prelude would have been far less effective. It is not accidental that the first two words of this chapter (καὶ ἤκουσεν) are repeated at the start of vs. 9, which resumes the narrative. Thus vss. 1-8 are essentially a parenthesis, although a highly important one, whereby the heroine is introduced, the purity of her descent—it is no accident that her name is Judith, "the Jewess"—is indicated in a genealogy which traces her back to Jacob (ISRAEL), and a quick sketch of her life is given which stresses her exceptional and exemplary piety and purity. All this is essential as a

υἱοῦ Ωξ υἱοῦ Ιωσηφ υἱοῦ Οζιηλ υἱοῦ Ελκια υἱοῦ Ανανιου υἱοῦ Γε-
δεων υἱοῦ Ραφαϊν υἱοῦ Αχιτωβ υἱοῦ Ηλιου υἱοῦ Χελκιου υἱοῦ Ελιαβ
υἱοῦ Ναθαναηλ υἱοῦ Σαλαμιηλ υἱοῦ Σαρασαδαι υἱοῦ Ισραηλ. ²καὶ
ὁ ἀνὴρ αὐτῆς Μανασσης τῆς φυλῆς αὐτῆς καὶ τῆς πατριᾶς αὐτῆς·
καὶ ἀπέθανεν ἐν ἡμέραις θερισμοῦ κριθῶν· ³ἐπέστη γὰρ ἐπὶ τοὺς
δεσμεύοντας τὰ δράγματα ἐν τῷ πεδίῳ, καὶ ὁ καύσων ἦλθεν ἐπὶ
τὴν κεφαλὴν αὐτοῦ, καὶ ἔπεσεν ἐπὶ τὴν κλίνην αὐτοῦ καὶ ἐτελεύ-
τησεν ἐν Βαιτυλουα τῇ πόλει αὐτοῦ, καὶ ἔθαψαν αὐτὸν μετὰ τῶν
πατέρων αὐτοῦ ἐν τῷ ἀγρῷ τῷ ἀνὰ μέσον Δωθαϊμ καὶ Βαλαμων.
⁴καὶ ἦν Ιουδιθ ἐν τῷ οἴκῳ αὐτῆς χηρεύουσα ἔτη τρία καὶ μῆνας
5 τέσσαρας. ⁵καὶ ἐποίησεν ἑαυτῇ σκηνὴν ἐπὶ τοῦ δώματος τοῦ οἴκου
αὐτῆς καὶ ἐπέθηκεν ἐπὶ τὴν ὀσφὺν αὐτῆς σάκκον, καὶ ἦν ἐπ' αὐτῆς τὰ ἱμάτια τῆς χηρεύσεως αὐτῆς. ⁶καὶ ἐνήστευε πάσας τὰς ἡμέρας τῆς χηρεύσεως αὐτῆς χωρὶς προσαββάτων καὶ σαββάτων καὶ

---

prelude to the story in which she is the heroine who, while confronted
with many dangers to her probity, ethical as well as ritual, escapes
completely unsmirched. Since presumably the tale is of an imaginary
incident and the woman herself the product of the storyteller's imagination
rather than of the historian's memory, any serious treatment of the
genealogy is wasted effort. There is the widest divergence in the lists
found in the several mss and vss, with variations not only of spelling
and order but also of additions and omissions. Several of the names
are recognizable in Hebrew history and may well have been chosen
by the author therefrom, but that they provide any actual line of descent
of Judith or of any other actual character is utterly unlikely. The two
names preceding Israel are of interest. SALAMIEL and SARASADAI are
certainly Shelumiel and Zurishaddai, who are respectively the grandson
and son of Simeon (Num 1 6, 2 12, 7 36, 41, 10 19). Why our author here
omits Symeon (Simeon)—if omit him he did, for two mss (23, 108)
include him, and two others append to Israel ἐκ φυλῆς Συμεῶν—is impossible to say, for his dependence upon the repeated references in
Numbers is evident and Judith (9 2) and so her husband (8 2) are of the
lineage of Simeon.
2. BARLEY HARVEST: barley ripened earlier than wheat, and was harvested
during April and May.
3. Manasseh had suffered a sunstroke, had taken to his bed, had died
and been buried in the ancestral tomb. The death by sunstroke was
perhaps suggested by the story of the son of the Shunamite woman
(II Kings 4 18ff.). DOTHAIM AND BALAMON: this is the fourth and last
reference to Dothaim (cf. 4 6). This is the only mention of the seemingly
near-by Balamon, unless Belmain (4 4) is to be regarded as a mere variant.
At any rate, the geography continues to be most uncertain. These places
are to be regarded as near Bethulia since the family grave of Manasseh
was IN THE FIELD, i.e., outside but presumably near by.

ter of Merari, the son of Ox, the son of Joseph, the son of
Oziel, the son of Elkiah, the son of Ananias, the son of Gideon,
the son of Raphaim, the son of Ahitub, the son of Elias,
the son of Chelcias, the son of Eliab, the son of Nathaniel,
the son of Salamiel, the son of Sarasadai, the son of Israel.
²And her husband was Manasseh of her tribe and her family.
And he had died in the days of the barley harvest, ³for he
stood overseeing those who were binding sheaves in the plain,
and the scorching heat came upon his head and he fell upon
his bed and died in Bethulia his city, and they buried him
with his fathers in the field which is betwixt Dothaim and
Balamon. ⁴And Judith had been living as a widow in her
5 house for three years and four months. ⁵And she had made
for herself a tent on the roof of her house and put sackcloth
on her loins, and the garments of her widowhood were upon
her. ⁶And she was wont to fast all the days of her widowhood,
save on the day before the sabbath and the sabbath and the

---

4. HAD BEEN LIVING: since this section (8 1-8) is an earlier interlude,
the use of English pluperfects for the past tenses is certainly allowable,
in some cases, as this, imperative. The specific indications of the length
of Judith's widowhood prior to the siege of Bethulia is presumably
to heighten the picture of her loyalty and devotion, perhaps also to
suggest verisimilitude to the story. The remarriage of widows, while
allowable, was rare in Jewish life; in the whole OT there are but three
mentions (save for the levirate) of such an occasion. Two of these are
widows who became wives of David: Abigail (I Sam 25 39.42) and Bath-
sheba (II Sam 11 27): the third is Ruth of Moab, an ancestress of David.
Judith had apparently escaped the fate of most widows, for she inherited
her husband's property (cf. 8 7) and lived in comfort, with slaves, although
by her own choice she abstained from most of the luxuries which she
enjoyed only on the feast days when mourning was proscribed.
5. ROOF: another evidence of her exemplary piety. The roof of a Palestinian house was frequently used for the purpose of prayer (cf. story of
Peter's experience, Acts 10 9). At times, as for the feast of Tabernacles,
booths were erected on the roof (Neh 8 16). Apparently Judith's actions
—both the constant prayer and the wearing of sackcloth—are to indicate
that what for most was but occasional was for her regular routine.
6. WAS WONT TO FAST: private fasting became increasingly common
in Judaism in the days following the exile, and while not obligatory was
frequently practiced as a voluntary act of devotion by the uncommonly
devout. In her superpiety Judith's fast was continuous, save for the
festal days when fasting was proscribed. The scroll Megillat Taʿanit
gives a list of days on which, because of the events associated with them,

προνουμηνιῶν καὶ νουμηνιῶν καὶ ἑορτῶν καὶ χαρμοσυνῶν οἴκου
Ισραηλ. ⁷καὶ ἦν καλὴ τῷ εἴδει καὶ ὡραία τῇ ὄψει σφόδρα· καὶ
ὑπελίπετο αὐτῇ Μανασσης ὁ ἀνὴρ αὐτῆς χρυσίον καὶ ἀργύριον
καὶ παῖδας καὶ παιδίσκας καὶ κτήνη καὶ ἀγρούς, καὶ ἔμενεν ἐπ' αὐτῶν. ⁸καὶ οὐκ ἦν ὃς ἐπήνεγκεν αὐτῇ ῥῆμα πονηρόν, ὅτι ἐφοβεῖτο
τὸν θεὸν σφόδρα. — ⁹καὶ ἤκουσεν τὰ ῥήματα τοῦ λαοῦ τὰ πονηρὰ
ἐπὶ τὸν ἄρχοντα, ὅτι ὠλιγοψύχησαν ἐν τῇ σπάνει τῶν ὑδάτων, καὶ
ἤκουσεν πάντας τοὺς λόγους Ιουδιθ, οὓς ἐλάλησεν πρὸς αὐτοὺς
Οζιας, ὡς ὤμοσεν αὐτοῖς παραδώσειν τὴν πόλιν μετὰ ἡμέρας πέντε
10 τοῖς Ἀσσυρίοις· ¹⁰καὶ ἀποστείλασα τὴν ἅβραν αὐτῆς τὴν ἐφεστῶ-
σαν πᾶσιν τοῖς ὑπάρχουσιν αὐτῆς ἐκάλεσεν Χαβριν καὶ Χαρμιν τοὺς
πρεσβυτέρους τῆς πόλεως αὐτῆς, ¹¹καὶ ἦλθον πρὸς αὐτήν, καὶ εἶπεν πρὸς αὐτοὺς Ἀκούσατε δή μου, ἄρχοντες τῶν κατοικούντων
ἐν Βαιτυλουα· ὅτι οὐκ εὐθὴς ὁ λόγος ὑμῶν, ὃν ἐλαλήσατε ἐναντίον τοῦ λαοῦ ἐν τῇ ἡμέρᾳ ταύτῃ καὶ ἐστήσατε τὸν ὅρκον τοῦτον,
ὃν ἐλαλήσατε ἀνὰ μέσον τοῦ θεοῦ καὶ ὑμῶν καὶ εἴπατε ἐκδώσειν
τὴν πόλιν τοῖς ἐχθροῖς ἡμῶν, ἐὰν μὴ ἐν αὐταῖς ἐπιστρέψῃ κύριος

---

9 ωμοσεν] pr. ενωτησατο και 58 OL Syr ‖ 11 τουτον] om. B 𝔑

---

fasting was prohibited (cf. S. Zeitlin, *The Rise and Fall of the Judaean
State*, II, pp. 353-55).　　FEASTS: i.e., the other appointed or fixed
festivals.　　DAYS OF JOY: occasional days or times of especial gladness.
7. LOVELY TO BEHOLD: less likely "with lovely face." The identical
Greek phrase (save for emphatic σφόδρα) is used of Rachel (Gen 29 17).
THEREON: in charge of her extensive property. The mention of remaining
in charge seems to disabuse the notion that she had withdrawn from
contacts and responsibilities. She might be in constant mourning and
prayer but, it is implied, she was an able housewife.
8. Her piety—cf. the translator's effective imperfect (ἐφοβεῖτο)—made
her secure against any attack or slander. Early commentators cite
Ausonius: *Quae casta est? de qua mentiri fama veretur.*
9. This verse resumes the narrative, broken by the interlude of vss. 2-8.
The introductory words of vs. 1, καὶ ἤκουσεν ("and she heard"), are
twice repeated in this resuming verse, with the expected subject JUDITH
first appearing between the object of the second HEARD and its qualifying
relative clause. The English translation seeks to duplicate the dangling
Greek.　　HOW HE HAD SWORN: 58 prefixes "how he had hearkened"
(ἐνωτήσατο); this reading is followed by both Syr and OL.
10. FAVORITE SLAVE GIRL: the word ἅβρα occurs seven times in Judith;
in addition it occurs eight times in other books of the LXX, regularly
as the translation of נערה. It is generally referred to ἁβρός ("graceful,"

day before the new moon and the day of the new moon and the feasts and days of joy of the house of Israel. ⁷And she was exceedingly fair of form and lovely to behold; and Manasseh her husband had left her gold and silver and manservants and maidservants and cattle and fields, and she had remained thereon. ⁸And there was none who brought against her an evil report, because she feared God exceedingly.

⁹And she heard the wicked words of the people against the magistrate because they had waxed faint of heart at the lack of water, and Judith heard all the words of reply which Ozias had said to them, how he had sworn to them that he would hand over the city to the Assyrians after 10 five days. ¹⁰And sending her favorite slavegirl, who was over all her possessions, she summoned Chabris and Charmis, the elders of the city, ¹¹and they came to her, and she said unto them, "Hearken to me, I pray you, ye rulers of those who dwell in Bethulia, because your word which you spake before the people on this day is not right, and you have established this oath which you spoke betwixt God and you and have promised to hand over the city to our enemies if Adonai does not turn within those days to aid you. ¹²Pray tell

---

"beautiful"), but many grammarians continue to regard it as a borrowed word, perhaps related to the Aramaic חברה (Dan 7 20). In Judith this favorite was her mistress' major-domo.   CHABRIS AND CHARMIS: cf 6 15. The omission of Ozias, the chief elder, in B, א, A, 19, Syr, OL, Vg indicates its strange absence from the original text, perhaps due to the name having just been mentioned in the preceding verse. Its addition in many mss is easily seen as an obvious correction, for its deletion would be most unlikely, as in vs. 28 it is he who speaks in reply to Judith's lengthy reproof.

11. NOT RIGHT: this so-called Alexandrian spelling εὐθής (for εὐθύς) is frequent in the LXX. This is the only occasion in Judith, save as A's variant for εὐ (10 16), but the more normal feminine εὐθεῖα occurs twice (10 11, 13 20). Their word is not "right" because thereby they are seeking to put God to the test (Deut 6 16).   THIS OATH: B and א omit τοῦτον, perhaps because in the incident (7 27) there is no mention that Ozias' promise was confirmed by an actual oath.   HAVE PROMISED: lit. "said" (εἴπατε + fut. inf.). Since εἶπον does not use the infinitive in indirect discourse, it is clearly the equivalent of a verb of promising. WITHIN THESE DAYS: lit. "in them," i.e., the aforementioned five days.

βοήθειαν ὑμῖν. ¹²καὶ νῦν τίνες ἐστὲ ὑμεῖς, οἳ ἐπειράσατε τὸν θεὸν
ἐν τῇ ἡμέρᾳ τῇ σήμερον καὶ ἵστατε ὑπὲρ τοῦ θεοῦ ἐν μέσῳ υἱῶν
ἀνθρώπων; ¹³καὶ νῦν κύριον παντοκράτορα ἐξετάζετε καὶ οὐθὲν
ἐπιγνώσεσθε ἕως τοῦ αἰῶνος. ¹⁴ὅτι βάθος καρδίας ἀνθρώπου οὐχ
εὑρήσετε καὶ λόγους τῆς διανοίας αὐτοῦ οὐ διαλήμψεσθε· καὶ πῶς
τὸν θεόν, ὃς ἐποίησεν πάντα ταῦτα, ἐρευνήσετε καὶ τὸν νοῦν αὐτοῦ ἐπιγνώσεσθε καὶ τὸν λογισμὸν αὐτοῦ κατανοήσετε; μηδαμῶς,
15 ἀδελφοί, μὴ παροργίζετε κύριον τὸν θεὸν ἡμῶν. ¹⁵ὅτι ἐὰν μὴ βού-
ληται ἐν ταῖς πέντε ἡμέραις βοηθῆσαι ἡμῖν, αὐτὸς ἔχει τὴν ἐξου-
σίαν ἐν αἷς θέλει σκεπάσαι ἡμέραις ἢ καὶ ὀλεθρεῦσαι ἡμᾶς πρὸ
προσώπου τῶν ἐχθρῶν ἡμῶν. ¹⁶ὑμεῖς δὲ μὴ ἐνεχυράζετε τὰς βουλὰς
κυρίου τοῦ θεοῦ ἡμῶν, ὅτι οὐχ ὡς ἄνθρωπος ὁ θεὸς ἀπειληθῆναι
οὐδ' ὡς υἱὸς ἀνθρώπου διαιτηθῆναι. ¹⁷διόπερ ἀναμένοντες τὴν παρ'

---

16 διαιτηθῆναι] διαρτηθῆναι 23 55 74 76, διαρτιθῆναι 19, αναρτιθηναι 106

---

12. IN THE STEAD: the context makes it clear that ὑπέρ has here the force
of "instead of," "in the place of," rather than "in behalf of" or "above."
You have set a time limit for God; if he does not act within this period,
you will no longer depend upon him but will act yourselves. Since it is
God, not men, who makes the decisions, you are attempting to mount
his throne.
13. TRYING: "trying out," "testing." You are trying to estimate and
test the Almighty, usurping his role, and your attempt will be fruitless,
for his thoughts are not your thoughts and his ways are past finding
out.   ANYTHING: οὐθὲν ἐπιγνώσεσθε is scarcely the conclusion expected,
which would be "You will never succeed." It perplexed early readers
as is seen by the complete recasting in 58 (followed by Syr and OL):
καὶ νοῦν κυρίου παντοκράτορος πειράζετε καὶ οὐθεὶς γνώσεται ("you are
testing the mind of the Almighty, and no man will ever know"). It is
possible that οὐθέν is simply a strong negative: you will never succeed
at all. But the following verse rather suggests the severe limits of the
human understanding. It is man's task to obey, not to originate.
14. The construction of this sentence demands that it be regarded as a
new sentence, not a subordinate causal clause to vs. 13. Thus the opening
ὅτι ("for," "because") is elliptical: "You will never succeed in your
quest, for..." If, as is manifestly true, you cannot plumb the human
heart, how can you expect to comprehend the ways and plans of the
Almighty? Logically the first half of this sentence is the protasis of a
condition, actually heightened by being given causal form.   NAY,
NAY: really this word of protest is the answer to the preceding rhetorical
question.   STOP PROVOKING: the present imperative suggests that
(at least to the Greek translator) they were already so doing and should
cease this presumptuous invasion of heaven.

me, who are you who have made trial of God this day and
stand in the stead of God among the sons of men? ¹³And now
ye are trying Adonai Almighty—and ye will never know
anything! ¹⁴For ye will not discover the depths of the human
heart and will not lay hold of the thoughts of a man's mind;
how then will ye search out God, who made all these things,
and understand his mind and comprehend his way of thought?
Nay, nay, brethren; stop provoking Adonai your God to
anger. ¹⁵Because if he be unwilling to succor us within these
five days, he hath the power, within any number of days
which he chooses, to shelter us or even to destroy us in the
face of our enemies. ¹⁶But as for you, cease seeking to force
the counsels of Adonai our God, because God is not as a man
to be threatened nor as a son of man to be forced to give
his decision. ¹⁷Therefore, waiting for the deliverance which

---

15. THESE FIVE DAYS: the definite article in such a phrase is essentially a
demonstrative—the five days under mention. Ms 58, followed by Syr,
omits ἐάν···βοηθῆσαι ἡμῖν, inserts ἡμᾶς after σκεπάσαι, omits ἤ and ἡμᾶς,
thus changing the meaning to: he is able in any length of time to protect
us and destroy our enemies before our eyes.   SHELTER: σκεπάζειν
for God's sheltering protection is common in the LXX, but occurs only
here in Judith. The author (translator?) seems to prefer where possible
synonyms or similar words to bare repetition. In consequence there are
many common words which occur but once or twice in his pages. For a
short book there is a surprisingly long index verborum.   OR EVEN:
only so can the common text (ἤ καί) be properly rendered.
16. BUT AS FOR YOU: the nominative of the personal pronouns, commonly
only for emphasis, is apparently in deliberate contrast to the αὐτὸς
ἔχει of the preceding verse. Many times these nominative forms of the
pronouns (especially αὐτός) are used in a way which the purist finds
"eccentric." Regularly, however, in such cases they carry a deliberate
emphasis and are syntactically quite proper.   CEASE SEEKING TO FORCE:
this verb properly means "take a pledge from one" or "take in pledge."
Apparently it is used here in a compulsive sense: cease trying to force
God to act by threatening to turn to another source of help, viz., surrender
as the lesser of two evils. This is seemingly supported by the two causal
clauses, with the first infinitive TO BE THREATENED in keeping with this
warning. The real problem is the second infinitive. The common reading
διαιτηθῆναι is perplexing and can be understood (a) only by stressing
the derived force of διαιτᾶν ("to umpire or judge") in the somewhat
arbitrary sense TO BE FORCED TO GIVE HIS IMMEDIATE DECISION, or (b)
by regarding is as a manufactured compound of αἰτεῖν and thus "to be
coaxed." This would be a hapax, but since our author (translator) is fond
of compounds, it is conceivable as an intensive of "ask." (c) The synony-

αὐτοῦ σωτηρίαν ἐπικαλεσώμεθα αὐτὸν εἰς βοήθειαν ἡμῶν, καὶ εἰσ-
ακούσεται τῆς φωνῆς ἡμῶν, ἐὰν ᾖ αὐτῷ ἀρεστόν. ¹⁸ὅτι οὐκ ἀνέστη
ἐν ταῖς γενεαῖς ἡμῶν οὐδέ ἐστιν ἐν τῇ ἡμέρᾳ τῇ σήμερον οὔτε
φυλὴ οὔτε πατριὰ οὔτε δῆμος οὔτε πόλις ἐξ ἡμῶν, οἳ προσκυνοῦσι
θεοῖς χειροποιήτοις, καθάπερ ἐγένετο ἐν ταῖς πρότερον ἡμέραις·
¹⁹ὧν χάριν ἐδόθησαν εἰς ῥομφαίαν καὶ εἰς διαρπαγὴν οἱ πατέρες
20 ἡμῶν καὶ ἔπεσον πτῶμα μέγα ἐνώπιον τῶν ἐχθρῶν ἡμῶν. ²⁰ἡμεῖς
δὲ ἕτερον θεὸν οὐκ ἔγνωμεν πλὴν αὐτοῦ· ὅθεν ἐλπίζομεν ὅτι οὐχ
ὑπερόψεται ἡμᾶς οὐδ᾽ ἀπὸ τοῦ γένους ἡμῶν. ²¹ὅτι ἐν τῷ λημφθῆναι ἡμᾶς οὕτως καὶ λημφθήσεται πᾶσα ἡ Ἰουδαία, καὶ προνομευ-
θήσεται τὰ ἅγια ἡμῶν, καὶ ἐκζητήσει τὴν βεβήλωσιν αὐτῶν ἐκ τοῦ
αἵματος ἡμῶν ²²καὶ τὸν φόνον τῶν ἀδελφῶν ἡμῶν καὶ τὴν αἰχμαλωσίαν τῆς γῆς καὶ τὴν ἐρήμωσιν τῆς κληρονομίας ἡμῶν ἐπι-

---

21 καὶ λημφθησεται Ra.] καθησ. ΒΑ, κλιθησ. 19 74 76, MSE, κληθησ, 23
44 64 και θησ. 55,ληφθησ. 58 (om. ουτως και praec.)

---

mous parallelism of the verse calls to mind Balaam's word to Balak in
the form in which it appears in the LXX, which latter is far from an
accurate translation of the masoretic Hebrew:

> οὐχ ὡς ἄνθρωπος ὁ θεὸς διαρτηθῆναι,
> οὐδὲ ὡς υἱὸς ἀνθρώπου ἀπειληθῆναι (Num 23 19).

Aside from the inversion of the two clauses the similarity is too real to
make coincidence likely. The variant readings διαρτηθῆναι (23, 55, 74,
76, 108), διαρτιθῆναι (19, 44), ἀναρτιθῆναι (106) make clear that early
scribes saw the resemblance. The change from διαρ-τηθηναι to διαι- is
trivial. Thus it would appear to me not impossible that the author has
here deliberately made use of the word of Balaam in its Greek mistranslation. Properly the verb should mean "to be kept in suspense,"
and can be interpreted in context as "kept in suspense as to whether
his people will or will not remain obedient to his will." Thus the matters
appears to me at best uncertain, with three possibilities: 1) "to be forced
to immediate action" (διαιτᾶν); 2) "to be coaxed" (διαιτεῖν); 3) "to
waver in indecision" (διαρτᾶν). I am slightly inclined by the context
to the first, but am far from satisfied.
18. IN OUR GENERATION: lit. "among our contemporaries," i.e., "within
our memory," in contrast to the following IN FORMER DAYS.   COUNTRY-
SIDE, δῆμος is here in contrast to πόλις and makes the statement all-
inclusive: none of our folk, whoever they are or wherever they chance
to dwell. This insistence in vss. 18-20, expanded here, is a chief emphasis
in the book, almost its leit motif.
19. OUR ENEMIES: since they were our fathers' enemies they were ours.

comes from him, let us call upon him for succor, and he will hearken to our voice if it be his good pleasure. ¹⁸For there has not risen in our generation nor is there today either a tribe or a family or countryside or city from among us who worship gods made by human hands, as was done in former days; ¹⁹for the which cause our fathers were given over to the sword and for plunder and fell with a great fall before our 20 enemies. ²⁰But as for us, we have known no other God save him; whence we hope that he will not despise us or any of our people. ²¹For if we be taken, so will all Judea lie prostrate, and our sanctuary will be despoiled, and he will require from our blood its profanation, ²²and the murder of our brethren and the captivity of the land and the desolation

---

Our fathers may have sinned; yet they were *our* fathers.
20. DESPISE US: i.e., "overlook us in contempt."   ANY OF OUR PEOPLE: the genitive with ἀπό is simply a partitive, evidencing the ever increasing intrusion of prepositions, which eventuated in the essential conquest of cases, which latter came to be explained as "governed by the preposition."
21. SO WILL...LIE PROSTRATE: the text here is most uncertain, with many variants. Rahlf's conjectured καὶ λημφθήσεται is accepted without comment by Goodspeed and RSV. Cowley had preferred the reading of B, ℵ, A καθήσεται ("shall sit"), but felt some qualifying word such as "desolate" had dropped out. A strong case can be made for κλιθήσεται, which is not, as Fritzsche earlier remarked, a likely correction but rather is itself liable to alteration. The passive may well have the force "to be bent, made to totter, brought down," that is, "lie prostrate" and so be the translation, as it occasionally is in the LXX (cf. Ps 104[103] 5) of כרע. κληθήσεται, καθήσεται, and καὶ θήσεται would be obvious alterations, while the conjectured λημφθήσεται would reflect the preceding λημφθῆναι. Thus Rahlf's conjectured καὶ λημφθήσεται ("so too will Judea be taken") appears to me unlikely because it would be both obvious and unobjectionable. Had this been the reading, it is hard to see why scribes and editors would have attempted alterations. Thus the situation seems definitely κλιθήσεται → καὶ λημφθήσεται, with the reverse quite unlikely. On this basis I prefer the rendering SO WILL JUDEA LIE PROSTRATE.   HE: i.e., God. A few mss add κύριος, OL *deus*.   REQUIRE FROM OUR BLOOD: the common reading ἐκ τοῦ αἵματος ἡμῶν is awkward in the extreme and may well be a mistranslation. The context suggests "from us," that is, God will hold us responsible. Fritzsche, following the conjecture of Holmes and Parsons, reads ἐκ τοῦ στόματος ἡμῶν, and argues that this would indicate that the verb (ἐκζητήσει) does not mean "will take revenge" but "will demand an explanation." Attempts to make the phrase refer

στρέψει εἰς κεφαλὴν ἡμῶν ἐν τοῖς ἔθνεσιν, οὗ ἐὰν δουλεύσωμεν
ἐκεῖ, καὶ ἐσόμεθα εἰς πρόσκομμα καὶ εἰς ὄνειδος ἐναντίον τῶν
κτωμένων ἡμᾶς. ²³ὅτι οὐ κατευθυνθήσεται ἡ δουλεία ἡμῶν εἰς χάριν,
ἀλλ' εἰς ἀτιμίαν θήσει αὐτὴν κύριος ὁ θεὸς ἡμῶν. ²⁴καὶ νῦν, ἀδελφοί, ἐπιδειξώμεθα τοῖς ἀδελφοῖς ἡμῶν, ὅτι ἐξ ἡμῶν κρέμαται ἡ
ψυχὴ αὐτῶν, καὶ τὰ ἅγια καὶ ὁ οἶκος καὶ τὸ θυσιαστήριον ἐπ-
25 εστήρισται ἐφ' ἡμῖν. ²⁵παρὰ ταῦτα πάντα εὐχαριστήσωμεν κυρίῳ
τῷ θεῷ ἡμῶν, ὃς πειράζει ἡμᾶς καθὰ καὶ τοὺς πατέρας ἡμῶν.
²⁶μνήσθητε ὅσα ἐποίησεν μετὰ Αβρααμ καὶ ὅσα ἐπείρασεν τὸν
Ισαακ καὶ ὅσα ἐγένετο τῷ Ιακωβ ἐν Μεσοποταμίᾳ τῆς Συρίας ποι-
μαίνοντι τὰ πρόβατα Λαβαν τοῦ ἀδελφοῦ τῆς μητρὸς αὐτοῦ. ²⁷ὅτι
οὐ καθὼς ἐκείνους ἐπύρωσεν εἰς ἐτασμὸν τῆς καρδίας αὐτῶν, καὶ
ἡμᾶς οὐκ ἐξεδίκησεν, ἀλλ' εἰς νουθέτησιν μαστιγοῖ κύριος τοὺς
ἐγγίζοντας αὐτῷ. — ²⁸καὶ εἶπεν πρὸς αὐτὴν Οζιας Πάντα, ὅσα
εἶπας, ἐν ἀγαθῇ καρδίᾳ ἐλάλησας, καὶ οὐκ ἔστιν ὃς ἀντιστήσεται
τοῖς λόγοις σου· ²⁹ὅτι οὐκ ἐν τῇ σήμερον ἡ σοφία σου πρόδηλός
ἐστιν, ἀλλ' ἀπ' ἀρχῆς ἡμερῶν σου ἔγνω πᾶς ὁ λαὸς τὴν σύνεσίν
30 σου, καθότι ἀγαθόν ἐστιν τὸ πλάσμα τῆς καρδίας σου. ³⁰ἀλλὰ ὁ
λαὸς δεδίψηκεν σφόδρα καὶ ἠνάγκασαν ἡμᾶς ποιῆσαι καθὰ ἐλαλή-

---

30 δεδιψ.] εδιψησεν B

---

back to the rash word of Ozias (7 31) are at best uncertain. WILL HE
BRING UPON OUR HEADS: cf. Judg 9 57 for indentity of figure (ἐπέστρεψεν
ὁ θεὸς εἰς τὴν κεφαλὴν αὐτῶν). WE SHALL BE AN OFFENSE: lit. "for an
offense," i.e., "we shall become."
23. RECKON: our bondage will not be regarded as unjust treatment
and thus eventually to be rewarded, but God will regard it as the proper
consequence of our shameful flouting his will.
24. TO OUR BROTHERS: our fellows, not in Bethulia but throughout
the land, whose safety depends upon how we act. THE SANCTUARY
AND THE HOUSE: i.e., τὸ ἱερόν and all it contains.
26. MESOPOTAMIA OF SYRIA: this designation is common in the LXX,
usually in translation of פדן־ארם (cf. Gen 31 18) for the plain of Syria
and the desert west of the Euphrates. Occasionally it is inverted (ἐκ
Συρίας Μεσοποταμίας, I Chron 19 6); in Judg 3 8 ms A has Συρίας Μεσοποταμίας ποταμῶν.
27. NOT...NOT: attempts have occasionally been made to delete these
two negatives, but this would greatly weaken the argument: we should
give thanks to God, for this test, painful as it is, is far less than the tests
our ancestors underwent, and furthermore, these tests—theirs and ours—
were never in vengeance but for our warning, admonition, and betterment.
SCOURCE: the same figure stands in Prov 3 12. In this climax to her
speech Judith gives expression to what may be styled the saving con-

of our inheritance will he bring upon our heads among the heathen, wherever we shall be in bondage, and we shall be an offense and a reproach in the eyes of those who possess us. ²³For our bondage will not lead to his gracious favor, but rather Adonai our God will reckon it for dishonor. ²⁴And now, my brethren, let us show an example to our brothers because on us does their life hang, and the sanctuary and the 25 house and the altar depend on us. ²⁵On account of all this, let us give thanks to Adonai our God, who is trying us even as he did our fathers also. ²⁶Remember all he did unto Abraham and the ways he tested Isaac and what befell Jacob in Mesopotamia of Syria while shepherding the sheep of Laban his mother's brother. ²⁷For he hath not put us to the fiery test as he did them to try their hearts, and he hath not taken vengeance upon us; rather for their admonition doth Adonai scourge them who draw near to him."

²⁸And Ozias said to her, "All that thou hast said hast thou spoken in good heart, and there is none who will gainsay thy words; ²⁹because today is not the first day that thy wisdom hath been manifest, but from thy earliest day all the people hath known thy understanding, for the fashion 30 of thy heart is good. ³⁰But the people were exceedingly thirsty, and they forced us to do as we spake to them and

---

fidence of Judaism, seemingly evidenced so clearly throughout her history. Through the fires of adversity God was perfecting his chosen people, was subjecting them to constant and bitter punishment, but with the purpose of fitting them for their glorious destiny.

28. IN GOOD HEART: Ozias recognizes the truth and fidelity of her words, not the astuteness of her recommendations.   WHO WILL: who can.

29. HATH BEEN MANIFEST: in Greek, as in German, the present indicative, accompanied by an adverbial phrase indicating duration and referring to past time, is commonly used to describe an action beginning in the past and continuing to the time of speaking, which in English idiom requires the perfect.   FROM THY EARLIEST DAY: as long as they have known thee.   FASHION OF THY HEART: what is formed fully in thy mind, viz., thy thoughts and considered opinions. The Hebrew original of τὸ πλάσμα τῆς καρδίας σου—which Greek phrase occurs only here in the LXX—might well be יֵצֶר לֵב (cf. Gen 8 21).

0. WERE...THIRSTY: the perfect, read by most mss, might better be translated "have (or had) become...thirsty." The aorist in B is a

σαμεν αὐτοῖς καὶ ἐπαγαγεῖν ἐφ' ἡμᾶς ὅρκον, ὃν οὐ παραβησόμεθα.
³¹καὶ νῦν δεήθητι περὶ ἡμῶν, ὅτι γυνὴ εὐσεβὴς εἶ, καὶ ἀποστελεῖ
κύριος τὸν ὑετὸν εἰς πλήρωσιν τῶν λάκκων ἡμῶν, καὶ οὐκ ἐκλεί-
ψομεν ἔτι. ³²καὶ εἶπεν πρὸς αὐτοὺς Ιουδιθ 'Ακούσατέ μου, καὶ ποιήσω πρᾶγμα ὃ ἀφίξεται εἰς γενεὰς γενεῶν υἱοῖς τοῦ γένους ἡμῶν.
³³ὑμεῖς στήσεσθε ἐπὶ τῆς πύλης τὴν νύκτα ταύτην, καὶ ἐξελεύσομαι
ἐγὼ μετὰ τῆς ἅβρας μου, καὶ ἐν ταῖς ἡμέραις, μεθ' ἃς εἴπατε παραδώσειν τὴν πόλιν τοῖς ἐχθροῖς ἡμῶν, ἐπισκέψεται κύριος τὸν Ισραηλ ἐν χειρί μου· ³⁴ὑμεῖς δὲ οὐκ ἐξερευνήσετε τὴν πρᾶξίν μου,
35 οὐ γὰρ ἐρῶ ὑμῖν ἕως τοῦ τελεσθῆναι ἃ ἐγὼ ποιῶ. ³⁵καὶ εἶπεν Οζιας
καὶ οἱ ἄρχοντες πρὸς αὐτήν Πορεύου εἰς εἰρήνην, καὶ κύριος ὁ
θεός ἔμπροσθέν σου εἰς ἐκδίκησιν τῶν ἐχθρῶν ἡμῶν. ³⁶καὶ ἀποστρέ
ψαντες ἐκ τῆς σκηνῆς ἐπορεύθησαν ἐπὶ τὰς διατάξεις αὐτῶν.

9   ¹Ιουδιθ δὲ ἔπεσεν ἐπὶ πρόσωπον καὶ ἐπέθετο σποδὸν ἐπὶ τὴν
κεφαλὴν αὐτῆς καὶ ἐγύμνωσεν ὃν ἐνεδεδύκει σάκκον, καὶ ἦν ἄρτι
προσφερόμενον ἐν Ιερουσαλημ εἰς τὸν οἶκον τοῦ θεοῦ τὸ θυμίαμα

---

31 ευσεβης] θεοσεβης 58 OL Syr

---

stylistic improvement and patently secondary. Ozias' self-excuse is
timeless: cf. Aaron's similar plea (Exod 32 22), not to mention that of
Adam and Eve (Gen 3 12, 13).   WILL NOT VIOLATE: for we cannot, as
an oath, though later repented of, is inviolate; cf. Jephtha's rash vow
(Judg 11 35) and the protest of the princes of the congregation (Josh 9
19.21).
31. PRAY FOR US: the people of Bethulia in their desperate situation;
not for us (the elders) because of a rash word.   DEVOUT: Syr and OL
follow 58 in substituting θεοσεβής (godly). While both are possible,
again the probability is εὐσεβής → θεοσεβής, and not the reverse.   WE
SHALL FAINT NO MORE: here Ozias identifies with his fellow citizens
in their physical distress; not for himself as a spokesman who had slipped
but will not again.
33. MY FAVORITE: see note on 8 10.
34. WHICH I SHALL DO: the present indicative, often the equivalent of a
vivid future, indicates her action has already begun.
35. GO IN PEACE: a common phrase of wishing well to one departing;
that is, "May every good befall thee."   MAY ADONAI GOD GO BEFORE
THEE: the verb is omitted, a literal rendering from the Hebrew אדני
אלהים. For a similar phrase cf. Deborah's word to Barak οὐκ ἰδοὺ κύριος
ἐλεύσεται ἔμπροσθέν σου (Judg 4 14).

to take upon ourselves an oath which we will not violate.
[31]And now, pray for us, because thou art a devout woman,
and Adonai will send rain to fill our cisterns and we shall
faint no more." [32]And Judith said to them, "Hearken unto
me, and I will do a thing which will go down through endless
generations among the children of our people. [33]As for you
men, ye shall stand at the gate this night, and I shall go forth,
I and my favorite, and within the days after which ye said
ye would hand over the city to our foes, Adonai will look
with favor on Israel, by my hand. [34]But ye are not to enquire
about my act, for I shall not tell it to you until those things
35 which I shall do have been accomplished." [35]And Ozias and
the magistrates said to her, "Go in peace, and may Adonai
God go before thee to take vengeance on our foes." [36]And
turning back from the tent they went to their stations.

9   [1]Then Judith fell upon her face and put ashes on her head
and laid bare the sackcloth which she had put on, and at
the moment when that evening's incense offering was being

---

36. AND TURNING BACK FROM THE TENT: occasionally the Greek varies
the literal paratactic succession of verbs joined by "and" by using a
more natural preceding participial phrase; but the initial καί indicate the
ubiquitous *waw*.   THE TENT: on the roof of her house (8 5).   THEIR
STATIONS: or posts of duty from which they had been summoned. Apparently even the magistrates were joined in the common defense.

---

1. THEN: occasionally, as here, the mildly adversative δέ replaces the
almost automatic translational καί. Only once (5 21) does it balance a
preceding μέν, and only once (14 12) does a οἱ δέ occur. The author is at
pains to stress Judith's piety and devotion to religious proprieties, as a
balance and guard against the action she is about to take. The contrast
with the picture of Esther ("corrected,"to be sure, in the Greek rewriting)
is striking. Presumably the two acts of conspicuous lamentation (putting
ashes on her head and bringing into sight the sackcloth worn under her
outer garments) preceded "falling upon her face." The author does not
concern himself with that nicety, but uses aorists for all three acts. Some
later scribes, notably 19 and 108, seek to correct the picture which might
be suggested and rearrange the order of these verbs.   THAT EVENING'S
INCENSE OFFERING: the mention of timing is an obvious heightening
of the holy significance and import of Judith's act—her prayer arose to

τῆς ἑσπέρας ἐκείνης, καὶ ἐβόησεν φωνῇ μεγάλῃ Ιουδιθ πρὸς κύριον
καὶ εἶπεν ²Κύριε ὁ θεὸς τοῦ πατρός μου Συμεων, ᾧ ἔδωκας ἐν
χειρὶ ῥομφαίαν εἰς ἐκδίκησιν ἀλλογενῶν, οἳ ἔλυσαν μήτραν παρθένου εἰς μίασμα καὶ ἐγύμνωσαν μηρὸν εἰς αἰσχύνην καὶ ἐβεβήλωσαν μήτραν εἰς ὄνειδος· εἶπας γὰρ Οὐχ οὕτως ἔσται, καὶ ἐποί-
ησαν· ³ἀνθ' ὧν ἔδωκας ἄρχοντας αὐτῶν εἰς φόνον καὶ τὴν στρω-
μνὴν αὐτῶν, ἣ ᾐδέσατο τὴν ἀπάτην αὐτῶν, ἀπατηθεῖσαν εἰς αἷμα
καὶ ἐπάταξας δούλους ἐπὶ δυνάσταις καὶ δυνάστας ἐπὶ θρόνους
αὐτῶν ⁴καὶ ἔδωκας γυναῖκας αὐτῶν εἰς προνομὴν καὶ θυγατέρας
αὐτῶν εἰς αἰχμαλωσίαν καὶ πάντα τὰ σκῦλα αὐτῶν εἰς διαίρεσιν
υἱῶν ἠγαπημένων ὑπὸ σοῦ, οἳ καὶ ἐζήλωσαν τὸν ζῆλόν σου καὶ
ἐβδελύξαντο μίασμα αἵματος αὐτῶν καὶ ἐπεκαλέσαντό σε εἰς βοη-
5 θόν· ὁ θεὸς ὁ θεὸς ὁ ἐμός, καὶ εἰσάκουσον ἐμοῦ τῆς χήρας. ⁵σὺ
γὰρ ἐποίησας τὰ πρότερα ἐκείνων καὶ ἐκεῖνα καὶ τὰ μετέπειτα καὶ

---

2 μήτραν, 1°] μιτραν cj. | ηδεσατο] ηδεύσατο 23 64 243, ηρδευσατο 248,
εδεξατο 58 | απατην αυτων] om. ℵ* A

God as incense on the holy altar.   WITH A LOUD VOICE: the loud voice,
together with the prostration, seemingly intensifies her fervor.
2. SYMEON: the mention of Symeon (cf. 6 15) is plainly to cite the deed
of revenge on the Shechemites by Simeon and his brother Levi for the
rape of Dinah. This act, which shocked Jacob (Gen 34 30) has come in
tradition to be applauded and regarded as directed by Y" himself.
Presumably our author refers to this story as a justifying parallel to the
forthcoming act of Judith in which both "sword" and "bed," not to
mention an intended defilement, are conspicuous details.
The three phrases ἔλυσαν μήτραν παρθένου, ἐγύμνωσαν μηρόν, and ἐβεβήλωσαν
μήτραν are at best surprising, with the repetition of μήτραν. It is possible,
Fritzsche suggested, that the first phrase represents פתח רחם, but although
this phrase is used of God's act of ending a barren woman's plight, it is
not attested for intercourse. Syr reads "hair" instead of μήτραν which is
conceivably a euphemism for "hair of her feet." Frequently μίτραν
has been conjectured for the first μήτραν. In late Greek μίτρα is used for
"zone," instead of its more normal meaning "headdress." This would
be a very possible translation of אזור (cf. Isa 5 27). This would give a
natural progression: loose the girdle, bare the thigh (euphemistic),
and defile the womb. I have translated μίτραν in place of μήτραν, but with
some misgivings, for it is a conjectural reading and is contrary to the
use of μίτρα elsewhere in this book (10 3, 16 8). It may be that the first
phrase has the sense "rob the maiden of her virginity" and that the
second and third phrases are the two steps.   THOU HAST SAID: the

carried into the house of God in Jerusalem, Judith cried
with a loud voice to Adonai and said, ²"Adonai God of my
father Symeon, into whose hand thou didst give a sword
for vengeance upon the strangers who loosed a maiden's zone
to defile her and stripped bare her thigh to shame her and
polluted her womb to disgrace her; for thou hadst said,
'This shall not be done,' and they did it; ³because of this
thou didst give over their rulers for slaughter and their bed,
which blushed for shame for the one so deceived, to blood,
and thou didst smite all together, slaves and princes, rulers
on thrones, ⁴and thou didst give their wives for booty and
their daughters to captivity and all their spoils for division
among the sons beloved by thee, whose zeal for thee was
great and who abhorred the pollution of their blood and
who called on thee for aid. My God, my God, hearken
5 also unto me, a widow. ⁵For it was thou who didst do the
things which were before those things and those things and

phrase THIS SHALL NOT BE DONE is the LXX's conclusion to Gen 34 ₇;
here it is ascribed to God, for Torah has come to be regarded as God's,
not man's, composition.
3. FOR THE ONE SO DECEIVED: again the text is most uncertain, as is
evidenced by the many variants, notably for ἠδέσατο: ἠδεύσατο (23, 64,
243 [74, 76]); ἠρδεύσατο (248); ἐδέξατο (58). Modern conjectures are no
more satisfactory. I am inclined to omit ἀπάτην αὐτῶν (with ℵ*, A),
thus reading τὴν ἀπατηθεῖσαν (the girl, not the bed). Very possibly,
however, we have a primitive corruption which is not to be solved by
scholarly guesswork.   ALL TOGETHER: this is the apparent meaning
of the phrase. ἐπί is used twice here, once with the dative where it apparently
has the force "with" (= Hebr. על) as in vs. 10; but the second ἐπί (with
the accusative) is not parallel but has its normal force "on." The words
are a paraphrase of the older story, where "all the males" were slain
(Gen 34 ₂₅), but then the principals are mentioned.   THE SONS BELOVED
BY THEE: Israelites ("sons of Jacob," Gen 34 ₂₇).
4. ALSO: this plea concludes Judith's rehearsal of the acts of her ancestor,
and she prays that as God had supported him in his action so he will
aid her to accomplish her intended plan.
5f. This is followed and supported by the repetitious insistence in these
next two verses, where THOSE THINGS are the act of Symeon, but this
is but an example of God's control. What has been done has been done
by God is a fundamental insistence, endlessly repeated in the OT. God
is primarily a God who does things: "What is done, I do it." FOR: it is
no surprise that all has happened as it has, for God has already designed it.
In a religion which took itself seriously as one of revelation there can

τὰ νῦν καὶ τὰ ἐπερχόμενα διενοήθης, καὶ ἐγενήθησαν ἃ ἐνενοήθης, [6]καὶ παρέστησαν ἃ ἐβουλεύσω καὶ εἶπαν Ἰδοὺ πάρεσμεν· πᾶσαι γὰρ αἱ ὁδοί σου ἕτοιμοι, καὶ ἡ κρίσις σου ἐν προγνώσει. [7]ἰδοὺ γὰρ Ἀσσύριοι ἐπληθύνθησαν ἐν δυνάμει αὐτῶν, ὑψώθησαν ἐφ' ἵππῳ καὶ ἀναβάτῃ, ἐγαυρίασαν ἐν βραχίονι πεζῶν, ἤλπισαν ἐν ἀσπίδι καὶ ἐν γαίσῳ καὶ τόξῳ καὶ σφενδόνῃ καὶ οὐκ ἔγνωσαν ὅτι σὺ εἶ κύριος συντρίβων πολέμους. [8]κύριος ὄνομά σοι· σὺ ῥάξον αὐτῶν τὴν ἰσχὺν ἐν δυνάμει σου καὶ κάταξον τὸ κράτος αὐτῶν ἐν τῷ θυμῷ σου· ἐβουλεύσαντο γὰρ βεβηλῶσαι τὰ ἅγιά σου, μιᾶναι τὸ σκήνωμα τῆς καταπαύσεως τοῦ ὀνόματος τῆς δόξης σου, καταβαλεῖν σιδήρῳ κέρας θυσιαστηρίου σου. [9]βλέψον εἰς ὑπερηφανίαν αὐτῶν, ἀπόστειλον τὴν ὀργήν σου εἰς κεφαλὰς αὐτῶν, δὸς ἐν χειρί μου τῆς χήρας ὃ διενοήθην κράτος. [10]πάταξον δοῦλον ἐκ χειλέων ἀπάτης μου ἐπ' ἄρχοντι καὶ ἄρχοντα ἐπὶ θεράποντι αὐτοῦ, θραῦσον αὐτῶν τὸ ἀνάστεμα ἐν χειρὶ θηλείας. [11]οὐ γὰρ ἐν πλήθει τὸ κράτος σου, οὐδὲ ἡ δυναστεία σου ἐν ἰσχύουσιν, ἀλλὰ ταπεινῶν εἶ θεός, ἐλαττόνων εἶ βοηθός, ἀντιλήμπτωρ ἀσθενούντων, ἀπεγνωσμένων σκεπαστής, ἀπηλπισμένων σωτήρ. [12]ναὶ ναὶ ὁ θεὸς τοῦ πατρός μου καὶ θεὸς κληρονομίας Ισραηλ, δέσποτα τῶν οὐρανῶν καὶ τῆς γῆς, κτίστα τῶν ὑδάτων, βασιλεῦ πάσης κτίσεώς σου, σὺ εἰσάκουσον τῆς δεήσεώς μου [13]καὶ δὸς λόγον μου καὶ

---

be no sudden surprises: God has foreseen and devised all that is to occur. Thus the soon-to-come judgment (Assyria's downfall) is no new decision but part of God's plan and thus certain of accomplishment.

7f. ADONAI WHO IS A WARRIOR. ADONAI IS THY NAME: these words are a literal transcript (σου pro αὐτῷ) from Exod 15 3. The Greek text has "A Lord who crushes wars" the translator followed the LXX rendering of Exod 15 3. Cf. ibid. 14 25 אֲדֹנָי נִלְחָם לָהֶם בְּמִצְרָיִם "Adonai is fighting for them against Egypt"; cf. also 14 4. [s.z.].   BY THY POWER: a deliberate contrast to the preceding IN THEIR ARMED MIGHT. Regularly our author uses δύναμις for the enemies' "army" or "armed might." Theirs will be brought low by the POWER or ARMED MIGHT of God.

8. The three descriptives—SANCTUARY, TABERNACLE. ALTAR—stress the sanctity of the temple, the abiding place of Y", whose presence is his people's security; cf. Deut 12 11, I Kings 8 10.11, II Chron 5 13.14, 7 1.3. In Ezekiel's vision (43 5.8) Y" returns to the temple, and his glory fills the house. This imagery, so constant in all parts of the OT, is stressed by Judith to indicate the unspeakable effrontery of the enemy in their godless attempt, not against Israel but against Israel's God.

10. WITH: as in vs. 3 ἐπί with the dative has the force "with." Again

the things after them, and who didst purpose the things which are now and those to come, and what thou didst have in mind have come to pass, ⁶and what thou didst will have presented themselves and said, 'Behold we are here.' For all thy paths are ready, and thy judgment is with fore-knowledge. ⁷For lo the Assyrians have waxed large in their armed might; they are exalted with horse and rider, they pride themselves in the strength of their foot soldiers, they rest their hope in shield and in javelin and bow and sling, and they know not that thou art Adonai who is a warrior. ⁸Adonai is thy name. Bring low their might by thy power and shiver to bits their force by thine anger. For they have planned to pollute thy sanctuary, to defile the tabernacle where thy glorious name doth rest, to lay low with the sword the horn of thy altar. ⁹Look upon their arrogance, send thy wrath upon their heads, give to my—the widow's—hand

10 the strength for what I have purposed. ¹⁰By the guile of my lips smite slave with prince and prince with his servant; break in pieces their high estate by the hand of a female. ¹¹For thy might is not in numbers nor thy rule in men of strength, but thou art a God of the humble, thou art the helper of the oppressed, the champion of the weak, the protector of those in despair, the savior of the hopeless. ¹²Yea, verily, God of my father and God of the inheritance of Israel, ruler of the heaven and the earth, creator of the waters, king of all thy creation, hearken thou to my supplication; ¹³and make my word and deceit for the wound and bruise of those who

---

the figure of speech—PRINCE and SLAVE, i.e., all together—reflects the fate of all the Shechemites, made responsible for the deed of the leader which they (in theory) approved and thus shared in.   FEMALE: the use of θήλεια in place of γυνή is deliberate; it adds to the extraordinary victory of Judith and to the disgrace of the defeated foe.

11. HUMBLE: a Jewish, not a Greek encomium (cf. 6 19).   OPPRESSED: lit. "the lesser," akin to our "underdogs."

13. MY WORD AND DECEIT: hendiadys, "my deceitful word." The Psalmist may pray to be delivered from "lying lips," but Judith prays to be successful (as had Jael earlier) in an act normally castigated but quite proper as a device against an enemy who has purposed the destruc-

ἀπάτην εἰς τραῦμα καὶ μώλωπα αὐτῶν, οἳ κατὰ τῆς διαθήκης σου καὶ οἴκου ἡγιασμένου σου καὶ κορυφῆς Σιων καὶ οἴκου κατασχέσεως υἱῶν σου ἐβουλεύσαντο σκληρά. ¹⁴καὶ ποίησον ἐπὶ παντὸς ἔθνους σου καὶ πάσης φυλῆς ἐπίγνωσιν τοῦ εἰδῆσαι ὅτι σὺ εἶ ὁ θεὸς θεὸς πάσης δυνάμεως καὶ κράτους καὶ οὐκ ἔστιν ἄλλος ὑπερασπίζων τοῦ γένους Ισραηλ εἰ μὴ σύ.

10   ¹Καὶ ἐγένετο ὡς ἐπαύσατο βοῶσα πρὸς τὸν θεὸν Ισραηλ καὶ συνετέλεσεν πάντα τὰ ῥήματα ταῦτα, ²καὶ ἀνέστη ἀπὸ τῆς πτώσεως καὶ ἐκάλεσεν τὴν ἄβραν αὐτῆς καὶ κατέβη εἰς τὸν οἶκον, ἐν ᾧ διέτριβεν ἐν αὐτῷ ἐν ταῖς ἡμέραις τῶν σαββάτων καὶ ἐν ταῖς ἑορταῖς αὐτῆς, ³καὶ περιείλατο τὸν σάκκον, ὃν ἐνεδεδύκει, καὶ ἐξεδύσατο τὰ ἱμάτια τῆς χηρεύσεως αὐτῆς καὶ περιεκλύσατο τὸ σῶμα ὕδατι καὶ ἐχρίσατο μύρῳ παχεῖ καὶ διέξανε τὰς τρίχας τῆς κεφαλῆς αὐτῆς καὶ ἐπέθετο μίτραν ἐπ' αὐτῆς καὶ ἐνεδύσατο τὰ ἱμάτια τῆς εὐφροσύνης αὐτῆς, ἐν οἷς ἐστολίζετο ἐν ταῖς ἡμέραις τῆς ζωῆς

---

14 σου] om. 58 248 249 OL|| 3 διεξανε ℵ] διεταξεν rell.

---

tion of Jerusalem and its holy temple.   AGAINST THY COVENANT: the similarity with Dan 11 28 is striking and may well be a reflection. CREST OF ZION: κορυφή is not uncommon in the LXX and has already occurred six times in Judith. With Zion, regularly "Mt. Zion" (ὄρος), it is unparalleled in the LXX. By it Jerusalem is meant.

14. The common tendency is to understand the opening words of this concluding verse of Judith's prayer as concerned with Israel: "thy whole nation and every tribe." Whether the Greek can be so forced is far from clear, and it involves the use of ἔθνους and γένους as essential synonyms. This interpretation seems suggested by the qualifying σου ("thine") after ἔθνους, which inclines translators to neglect the absence of the definite article, certainly natural if the phrase means "thy whole nation." Several mss (58, 248, 249, OL) omit σου, apparently understanding the phrase to mean "foreign nation," I am inclined to accept the omission as a sort of dittograph ΕΘΝΟΥΣΣΟΥ, and to render the Greek as it naturally stands, in the sense: "Let all men know full well that opposition to us is opposition to the all-powerful God who is our source of strength." This rendering avoids the problem of understanding EVERY NATION in the sense of Israel and of equating ἔθνος (a term hardly to be expected in the mouth of a Jew when referring to Israel) and γένος, and brings Judith's prayer to a proper climax.

1. The similarities between this next section (10 1.11 5) and the Greek

have purposed hard things against thy covenant and thy hallowed house and the crest of Zion and the house of thy sons' possession. [14]And make every nation and every tribe to know full well that thou art God, the God of all power and might, and that there is none other shielding the people of Israel save thee."

10 [1]And it came to pass that when she had ceased crying unto the God of Israel and had finished all these words, [2]she arose from where she lay prostrate and called her maid and went down into the house where she was wont to stay during the sabbaths and her feast days; [3]and she laid aside the sackcloth which she had put on, and divested herself of her widow's garb, and washed her body all over with water, and anointed herself with costly ointment, and vamped up the hair of her head, and put upon it a tire, and clad herself in her gayest attire, with which she had been wont to be garbed in the days

---

Esther 15 1.16 (= 5 1.2b) are too striking to be accidental, but suggest that the two passages are definitely related. Ball viewed the account in Esther as the model employed by the author of Judith. I am inclined to reverse this and to see the addition in the Greek Esther as a reflection of this passage in Judith. That fact that in Esther two maids—the word is ἄβραι—accompany their mistress is not to be disregarded.

2. The apodosis begins with the words SHE AROSE. The presence of the preceding pleonastic καί, similar to copulative and adversative δέ in Greek authors, may well reflect here, as frequently, the Hebrew text; its omission by 44, 71, 74, 106, 58, Syr, OL is plainly secondary. DURING THE SABBATHS AND THE FEAST DAYS: cf. 8 6; regularly she lived in a tent on the roof, going into the house below only on these special occasions.

3. WASHED HER BODY ALL OVER WITH WATER: the verb περιεκλύσατο —its only other appearance in the LXX is in connection with Tobias' bath in the Tigris (Tobit 6 2)—makes the substitution of "face" (πρόσωπον) in Syr unwarranted. COSTLY: lit. "thick," "heavy." Never sparing in any of her acts, Judith was financially able to make this normal preparation (cf. Ruth 3 3) lavish. VAMPED UP: the several variants suggest uncertainty by the masculine scribe as to the precise action involved: combing it out (*pectinavit*, OL), parting it (*discriminavit*, Vg), anointing (Syr). The majority reading διέταξεν ("ordered") is probably to be seen as a variant for διέξανε (ℵ), In the later song of triumph Judith styles this beauty treatment: "and bound her hair with a tire" (16 8). TIRE: or tiara, headdress (cf note on 9 2).

τοῦ ἀνδρὸς αὐτῆς Μανασση, ⁴καὶ ἔλαβεν σανδάλια εἰς τοὺς πόδας
αὐτῆς καὶ περιέθετο τοὺς χλιδῶνας καὶ τὰ ψέλια καὶ τοὺς δακτυ-
λίους καὶ τὰ ἐνώτια καὶ πάντα τὸν κόσμον αὐτῆς καὶ ἐκαλλωπί-
σατο σφόδρα εἰς ἀπάτησιν ὀφθαλμῶν ἀνδρῶν, ὅσοι ἂν ἴδωσιν
5 αὐτήν. ⁵καὶ ἔδωκεν τῇ ἄβρᾳ αὐτῆς ἀσκοπυτίνην οἴνου καὶ καψά-
κην ἐλαίου καὶ πήραν ἐπλήρωσεν ἀλφίτων καὶ παλάθης καὶ ἄρτων
καθαρῶν καὶ περιεδίπλωσε πάντα τὰ ἀγγεῖα αὐτῆς καὶ ἐπέθηκεν
αὐτῇ. ⁶καὶ ἐξήλθοσαν ἐπὶ τὴν πύλην τῆς πόλεως Βαιτυλουα καὶ
εὕροσαν ἐφεστῶτα ἐπ' αὐτῇ Οζιαν καὶ τοὺς πρεσβυτέρους τῆς
πόλεως Χαβριν καὶ Χαρμιν· ⁷ὡς δὲ εἶδον αὐτὴν καὶ ἦν ἠλλοιωμένον τὸ πρόσωπον αὐτῆς καὶ τὴν στολὴν μεταβεβληκυῖαν αὐτῆς,
καὶ ἐθαύμασαν ἐπὶ τῷ κάλλει αὐτῆς ἐπὶ πολὺ σφόδρα καὶ εἶπαν
αὐτῇ ⁸Ὁ θεὸς τῶν πατέρων ἡμῶν δῴη σε εἰς χάριν καὶ τελειῶσαι
τὰ ἐπιτηδεύματά σου εἰς γαυρίαμα υἱῶν Ισραηλ καὶ ὕψωμα Ιερουσαλημ. ⁹καὶ προσεκύνησεν τῷ θεῷ καὶ εἶπεν πρὸς αὐτούς Ἐπιτά-
ξατε ἀνοῖξαί μοι τὴν πύλην τῆς πόλεως, καὶ ἐξελεύσομαι εἰς τελεί-

---

4 απατησιν]απαντησιν BNA, αρπαγην 58|| 9 προσεκυνησαν 23 44 52 55 64
74 76 106 236 248|

4. ANKLETS: many of these ornamental rings worn upon the ankles
have been found in Palestine. Together with bracelets, rings, and headtires
they are mentioned in Isa 3 18 as the lavish adornment of the daughter
of Zion.   ADORNED HERSELF GAYLY: Vg adds that due to her virtuous
object the Lord added to her beauty (*cui etiam Dominus contulit splendorem, quoniam omnis ista compositio, non ex libidine, sed ex virtute
pendebat; et ideo Dominus hanc in illam pulchritudinem ampliavit, ut
incomparabili decore omnium oculis appareret.*   TO BEGUILE: this
unashamed purpose of Judith has resulted in occasional ponderous
and labored comments by modern interpreters, disturbed at the thought
of such barefaced deceit even for the good of God's chosen people. Early
copyists apparently shared this concern, as the variants εἰς ἀρπαγήν (58)
and εἰς ἀπάντησιν (B, ℵ, A) attest. Very obviously the teller of the story
was quite undisturbed by such ethical niceties.
5. Judith is careful to avoid ceremonial defilement through eating other
than ritually permitted food or through its preparation in foreign dishes
and utensils which might well prove "unclean." The same attitude is
seen in Daniel's avoidance of unclean food; Esther, on the contrary,
apparently is quite unconcerned about such niceties, but in the later
Greek additions she is made to express horror at such violations of ritual
purity (Add. to Esther 14 17).   BARLEY-GROATS: parched grain (קלי)
roasted in the ear and then rubbed out (cf. I Sam 25 18, Ruth 2 14).
CAKE OF FIGS: a round cake of figs pressed together in a mass. These
articles of food were the usual provision for a journey; cf Abigail's

while Manasseh her husband was alive, ⁴and she took sandals for her feet, and put on anklets and bracelets and rings and her earrings and all her finery, and adorned herself gayly so as to beguile the eyes of as many as should behold her. 5 ⁵And she gave to her maid a leathern bottle of wine and a cruse of oil, and filled a pouch with barley-groats and a cake of figs and loaves of fine bread, and she carefully wrapped up all her dishes and put them upon her. ⁶And they went forth to the gate of the city of Bethulia and found standing at it Ozias and the elders of the city, Chabris and Charmis. ⁷When they saw her and that her face was altered and her apparel changed, they marveled very greatly at her beauty and said to her, ⁸"May the God of our fathers cause thee to find favor and to accomplish thy purposes that the sons of Israel may be filled with pride and Jerusalem exalted." ⁹And she worshiped God and said to them, "Give order to open for me the gate of the city, and I shall go forth for the accomplishment of

---

provision (I Sam 25 18).   FINE BREAD: lit. "clean bread." Probably this does not mean unfermented (unleavened) but rather in contrast to the bread to be found among the heathen to whom she is going (cf. 12 1.2). Many mss (58, 19, 108, Syr, OL) add "cheese."   CAREFULLY WRAPPED UP: this verb is seemingly a hapax.   DISHES: vessels, utensils, gear for the journey.   UPON HER: the maid (ἄβρα).
7. Very awkward translation Greek: τὸ πρόσωπον is in the nominative, the subject of the periphrastic ἦν ἠλλοιωμένον; then the construction changes with the accusative and participle of indirect discourse depending upon the main verb εἶδον. The apodosis starts with ἐθαύμασεν preceded by the pleonastic καί. That both participles are in the perfect tense heightens the impression of the great change in Judith's appearance.
8. CAUSE THEE TO FIND FAVOR: εἰς χάριν is an overliteral translation of the Hebrew, which the variant δῴη σοι χάριν (58, 71, 108) seeks to correct. That the thought here is "in the eyes of our enemy" that thou mayest be successful in thy endeavor is possible, but not likely. Rather it would seem to means simply. "May God give thee success."   PRIDE: the author is especially fond of the εἰς + acc. construction. The repetition of the uncommon γαυρίαμα in 15 9 indicates that here, as in the subsequent song of thanksgiving (16 1.17), the speeches are the free composition of the author, not the preservation of tradition.
9. AND SHE WORSHIPED GOD: the number of variant readings here evidence early perplexity at the seeming abruptness of the phrase. Mss 19 and 108 add αὐτή, perhaps to avoid the impression that the subject was Ozias, but more likely to correct the plural προσεκύνησαν attested by 23, 44, 52, 55, 64, 74, 76, 106, 236, and 248. Several simply amplify the phrase

ωσιν τῶν λόγων, ὧν ἐλαλήσατε μετ' ἐμοῦ· καὶ συνέταξαν τοῖς
10 νεανίσκοις ἀνοῖξαι αὐτῇ καθότι ἐλάλησεν. ¹⁰καὶ ἐποίησαν οὕτως.
καὶ ἐξῆλθεν Ιουδιθ, αὐτὴ καὶ ἡ παιδίσκη αὐτῆς μετ' αὐτῆς· ἀπ-
εσκόπευον δὲ αὐτὴν οἱ ἄνδρες τῆς πόλεως ἕως οὗ κατέβη τὸ ὄρος,
ἕως διῆλθεν τὸν αὐλῶνα καὶ οὐκέτι ἐθεώρουν αὐτήν. — ¹¹καὶ ἐπο-
ρεύοντο ἐν τῷ αὐλῶνι εἰς εὐθεῖαν, καὶ συνήντησεν αὐτῇ προφυ-
λακὴ τῶν Ἀσσυρίων. ¹²καὶ συνέλαβον αὐτὴν καὶ ἐπηρώτησαν Τίνων
εἶ καὶ πόθεν ἔρχῃ καὶ ποῦ πορεύῃ; καὶ εἶπεν Θυγάτηρ εἰμὶ τῶν
Εβραίων καὶ ἀποδιδράσκω ἀπὸ προσώπου αὐτῶν, ὅτι μέλλουσιν
δίδοσθαι ὑμῖν εἰς κατάβρωμα· ¹³κἀγὼ ἔρχομαι εἰς τὸ πρόσωπον
Ολοφέρνου ἀρχιστρατήγου δυνάμεως ὑμῶν τοῦ ἀπαγγεῖλαι ῥήματα
ἀληθείας καὶ δείξω πρὸ προσώπου αὐτοῦ ὁδὸν καθ' ἣν πορεύσεται
καὶ κυριεύσει πάσης τῆς ὀρεινῆς, καὶ οὐ διαφωνήσει τῶν ἀνδρῶν
αὐτοῦ σὰρξ μία οὐδὲ πνεῦμα ζωῆς. ¹⁴ὡς δὲ ἤκουσαν οἱ ἄνδρες
τὰ ῥήματα αὐτῆς καὶ κατενόησαν τὸ πρόσωπον αὐτῆς — καὶ ἦν
ἐναντίον αὐτῶν θαυμάσιον τῷ κάλλει σφόδρα —, καὶ εἶπαν πρὸς

9 ελαλησεν]-σαν B al.

by inserting πεσοῦσα ἐπὶ πρόσωπον (58,Syr, OL). F.C. Movers conjectured a
slip in translation. The translator misread וַתִּשְׁתַּחוּ אֱלֹהִם ("and she bowed
unto them") as וַתִּשׁ׳ לֵאלֹהִים ("and she bowed unto God"). Thus Judith's
action was a deferential gesture to the elders of the city. It appears to
me that all the variants may be disregarded. In answer to the pious word
of the elders in vs. 8, Judith's act of "worship" is essentially a devout
"Amen." THOSE MATTERS: Fritzsche notes the similarity in this word
of Judith (εἰς τελείωσιν τῶν λόγων, ὧν ἐλαλήσατε μετ' ἐμοῦ) with the word
of Elizabeth ἔσται τελείωσις τοῖς λελαλημένοις αὐτῇ παρὰ κυρίου—Luke
1 45. EVEN AS SHE HAD SPOKEN: the variant ἐλάλησαν, read by many mss
including B, apparently under the influence of the plural ἐλαλήσατε,
would thus be a reflection of their tacit promise in 8 35.
10. THEY: the young men. KEPT THEIR EYES FIXED ON HER: the
imperfect tense heightens the picture. Disregarding all else, they watched
her as long as she was in sight. VALE: Bethulia, high up on a mountain,
was approached by a valley in which the Assyrians were now encamped
(7 1-4).
11. STRAIGHT ON: εἰς εὐθεῖαν sc. ὁδόν; cf. Gen 33 12. They were not
trying to avoid the enemy but rather to meet them; so they took the
regular path through the valley.
12. DAUGHTER OF THE HEBREWS: "Hebrew" is the natural word for
Judith to use of herself in speaking to foreigners. Similarly in 12 11 and
14 18 it is properly used by foreigners in reference to her. It is not a word
normally used by Hebrews in speaking to or of others of their own people.
So in 15 12 the phrase is appropriately πᾶσα γυνὴ Ἰσραήλ. The author is

those matters whereof ye spake with me"; and they gave order
10 to the young men to open for her even as she had spoken. ¹⁰And
they did so. And Judith went forth, she and her handmaid
with her. And the men of the city kept their eyes fixed on
her until she had gone down the mountain, until she had
passed through the vale and they could no longer see her.
¹¹And they went straight on in the vale, and an outpost of
the Assyrians met her. ¹²And they arrested her and demanded,
"Of what folk art thou, and whence hast thou come and
whither dost thou go?" And she said, "A daughter of the
Hebrews am I, and am fleeing from them because they are
about to be given to you for fodder. ¹³And I am on my way
to the presence of Holofernes, the chief captain of your army,
to tell to him words of truth, and I will show him a way
whereby he shall go and master all the hill country, and
there shall not be lost of his men one person or one life."
¹⁴When the men heard her words and remarked her face—her
beauty was in their eyes exceeding great—they said to her,

---

quite unconcerned with such details as the language employed by Judith
and her captors or whether an interpreter was necessary. He is telling a
story, not writing a textbook.　　FROM THEM: lit. "from face of them"
(מפניהם). The host of periphrases with πρόσωπον—the word occurs 68
times in Judith—which far exceeds the idiomatic limits of Greek and
which renders with overliteralness common Hebrew locutions, is one of
the most obvious signs of translation Greek.　　FOR FODDER: a reflection
of Achior's word to Holofernes (5 24), where B, 58, L read εἰς κατάβρωμα;
for the common εἰς κατάβρωσιν, not impossibly in harmony with Judith's
word.
13. TO THE PRESENCE: once again the ubiquitous εἰς τὸ πρόσωπον; cf. the
immediately following and still more ungreek πρὸ προσώπου αὐτοῦ, which
latter may indicate that she will not communicate the secret to any save
Holofernes himself, but is more likely an overliteral translation of words
instead of idioms.　　LOST: διαφωνήσει, a late use of διαφωνεῖν, which
properly means "to be dissonant," "to disagree," but in the LXX is
occasionally used in the sense "to be lost." Apparently the Hebrew
phrases underlying ONE PERSON OR ONE LIFE (σὰρξ μία οὐδὲ πνεῦμα ζωῆς)
are simply repetitive parallelisms with the heightened force οὐδὲ εἰς
("not a single one"). Seemingly, however, the Greek translator understood
them in the sense "no one will be taken prisoner or slain."
14. HER BEAUTY: lit. "and it [sc. her face] was in their opinion exceedingly
wondrous with respect to beauty." Their words are really a parenthesis,
and the apodosis begins with THEY SAID (καὶ εἶπαν).

15 αὐτήν ¹⁵Σέσωκας τὴν ψυχήν σου σπεύσασα καταβῆναι εἰς πρόσωπον τοῦ κυρίου ἡμῶν· καὶ νῦν πρόσελθε ἐπὶ τὴν σκηνὴν αὐτοῦ,
καὶ ἀφ' ἡμῶν προπέμψουσίν σε, ἕως παραδώσουσίν σε εἰς χεῖρας
αὐτοῦ· ¹⁶ἐὰν δὲ στῆς ἐναντίον αὐτοῦ, μὴ φοβηθῇς τῇ καρδίᾳ σου,
ἀλλὰ ἀνάγγειλον κατὰ τὰ ῥήματά σου, καὶ εὖ σε ποιήσει. ¹⁷καὶ
ἐπέλεξαν ἐξ αὐτῶν ἄνδρας ἑκατὸν καὶ παρέζευξαν αὐτῇ καὶ τῇ
ἅβρᾳ αὐτῆς, καὶ ἤγαγον αὐτὰς ἐπὶ τὴν σκηνὴν Ολοφέρνου. ¹⁸καὶ
ἐγένετο συνδρομὴ ἐν πάσῃ τῇ παρεμβολῇ, διεβοήθη γὰρ εἰς τὰ
σκηνώματα ἡ παρουσία αὐτῆς· καὶ ἐλθόντες ἐκύκλουν αὐτήν, ὡς
εἱστήκει ἔξω τῆς σκηνῆς Ολοφέρνου, ἕως προσήγγειλαν αὐτῷ περὶ
αὐτῆς. ¹⁹καὶ ἐθαύμαζον ἐπὶ τῷ κάλλει αὐτῆς καὶ ἐθαύμαζον τοὺς
υἱοὺς Ισραηλ ἀπ' αὐτῆς, καὶ εἶπεν ἕκαστος πρὸς τὸν πλησίον αὐτοῦ Τίς καταφρονήσει τοῦ λαοῦ τούτου, ὃς ἔχει ἐν ἑαυτῷ γυναῖκας τοιαύτας; ὅτι οὐ καλόν ἐστιν ὑπολείπεσθαι ἐξ αὐτῶν ἄνδρα
ἕνα, οἳ ἀφεθέντες δυνήσονται κατασοφίσασθαι πᾶσαν τὴν γῆν.
20 ²⁰καὶ ἐξῆλθον οἱ παρακαθεύδοντες Ολοφέρνῃ καὶ πάντες οἱ θεράποντες αὐτοῦ καὶ εἰσήγαγον αὐτὴν εἰς τὴν σκηνήν. ²¹καὶ ἦν Ολοφέρνης ἀναπαυόμενος ἐπὶ τῆς κλίνης αὐτοῦ ἐν τῷ κωνωπίῳ, ὃ
ἦν ἐκ πορφύρας καὶ χρυσίου καὶ σμαράγδου καὶ λίθων πολυτελῶν

---

15. SOME OF US: ἀφ' ἡμῶν. Periphrasis with the preposition ἀπό or ἐκ is
common in late Greek for the partitive genitive. Frequently, as here,
the indefinite τινὲς is omitted.
16. IF: although this "if" is essentially equal to "when," it may well
heighten the event as seen by the soldiers, almost in the sense "even
if"—not that it is improbable, but rather awesome.
17. A HUNDRED: the soldiers, less aware than the storyteller of the significance of Judith's mission, properly provide an escort rather greater than
necessary; another conspicuous example of this imposed propriety
is the number of soldiers sent to arrest Jesus (John 18 3).   SET THEM
AS ESCORTS: lit. "yoked them beside her and her maid" (adiunxerunt—
OL).   AND THEY: the 100 escorts.
18. GREAT CONCOURSE: συνδρομή ("tumultuous concourse of people")
occurs only here and in III Macc 3 8 in the LXX. It is but another example
of the author's wide and colorful vocabulary.   ANNOUNCED: frequently
the active with the unexpressed "they" is simply the equivalent of the
passive.
19. MARVELED: the verb is repeated for emphasis. They were amazed
at her beauty and in consequence at a people who could produce such a
woman.   ISRAELITES: lit. "sons of Israel."   SURELY: the answer

15 ¹⁵"Thou hast saved thy life by hastening to come down to the presence of our lord. And now draw nigh to his tent, and some of us will accompany thee until they deliver thee into his hands. ¹⁶But now, if thou standest before him, have no fear in thy heart, but announce to him as thou hast said, and he will treat thee well." ¹⁷And they chose a hundred of their number and set them as escorts for her and her maid, and they led her to the tent of Holofernes. ¹⁸And there arose a great concourse in the whole camp, for her presence was noised about from tent to tent. And when they came up, they stood around her as she stood outside the tent of Holofernes, until she had been announced to him. ¹⁹And they marveled at her beauty and because of her marveled at the Israelites, and each said to his neighbor, "Who shall despise this people who have women such as she among them? Surely it is not best that a single man of them be left alive, for if they be let go they will be able to get the best of the whole earth." ²⁰And Holofernes' trusted attendants and all those who served him came out and led her into the tent. ²¹And Holofernes was resting on his bed, under the canopy

---

to the preceding rhetorical question is obviously "no one." There is thus an ellipse in construction, with the introductory ὅτι suggesting some equivalent to "it is evident that."   BE LET GO: the present campaign to blot them out is imperative.   GET THE BEST OF: cf. 5 11. In both passages the basic meaning of κατασοφίσασθαι, viz., "outwit," or "outsmart," is suggested as the way they will "get the best of," "triumph over." That the speakers have any inkling of Judith's deceitful purpose is not to be read in, but this may well have led the author to use the phrase.

20. TRUSTED ATTENDANTS: lit. "those who slept beside"; 58 and Syr "those who sat beside" or were in constant attendance (παραδρεύοντες).

21. UNDER THE CANOPY: prop. "in." The κωνωπεῖον was a mosquito net, common in the Orient, especially in Egypt, as a protection against gnats and other insects. Horace refers to them contemptuously in reference to Antony's weakness (*sol adspicit conopium*—*Ep.* 9 16), as symbolic of the abomination of oriental luxury. The same attitude may be seen here by the author. Often of fine gauze, this one was of purple and gold —cf. the ephod (Exod 28 6)—and adorned with precious stones, and is subsequently referred to (13 9, 15, 16 19) as a valuable prize and the symbol

καθυφασμένων. ²²καὶ ἀνήγγειλαν αὐτῷ περὶ αὐτῆς, καὶ ἐξῆλθεν εἰς
τὸ προσκήνιον, καὶ λαμπάδες ἀργυραῖ προάγουσαι αὐτοῦ. ²³ὡς δὲ
ἦλθεν κατὰ πρόσωπον αὐτοῦ Ιουδιθ καὶ τῶν θεραπόντων αὐτοῦ,
ἐθαύμασαν πάντες ἐπὶ τῷ κάλλει τοῦ προσώπου αὐτῆς· καὶ πεσοῦσα ἐπὶ πρόσωπον προσεκύνησεν αὐτῷ, καὶ ἤγειραν αὐτὴν οἱ
δοῦλοι αὐτοῦ.

11   ¹Καὶ εἶπεν πρὸς αὐτὴν Ολοφέρνης Θάρσησον, γύναι, μὴ φοβηθῇς τῇ καρδίᾳ σου, ὅτι ἐγὼ οὐκ ἐκάκωσα ἄνθρωπον ὅστις
ᾑρέτικεν δουλεύειν βασιλεῖ Ναβουχοδονοσορ πάσης τῆς γῆς. ²καὶ
νῦν ὁ λαός σου ὁ κατοικῶν τὴν ὀρεινὴν εἰ μὴ ἐφαύλισάν με, οὐκ ἂν
ἦρα τὸ δόρυ μου ἐπ' αὐτούς· ἀλλὰ αὐτοὶ ἑαυτοῖς ἐποίησαν ταῦτα.
³καὶ νῦν λέγε μοι τίνος ἕνεκεν ἀπέδρας ἀπ' αὐτῶν καὶ ἦλθες πρὸς
ἡμᾶς· ἥκεις γὰρ εἰς σωτηρίαν· θάρσει, ἐν τῇ νυκτὶ ταύτῃ ζήσῃ
καὶ εἰς τὸ λοιπόν· ⁴οὐ γὰρ ἔστιν ὃς ἀδικήσει σε, ἀλλ' εὖ σε ποιήσει, καθὰ γίνεται τοῖς δούλοις τοῦ κυρίου μου βασιλέως Ναβου-
5 χοδονοσορ. ⁵καὶ εἶπεν πρὸς αὐτὸν Ιουδιθ Δέξαι τὰ ῥήματα τῆς

---

21 καθυφασμενον ℵ 58 OL Syr   23 ηλθεν] εστη 58 OL Syr

---

of the spoiler spoiled. The participle WOVEN (καθυφασμένων) which should
probably modify κωνωπεῖον has been attracted to the case of the preceding
λίθων. ℵ, 58, Syr, OL correct this seemingly obvious and not unnatural
error. It is possible that the genitive plural is correct in the sense "inter-
woven stones."
22. THEY GAVE WORD: once again the impersonal equivalent of the
passive.   SILVER LAMPS GOING BEFORE HIM: an added touch of the
opulence which was to be despoiled, even though, since it was night
(8 ₃₃), a light was necessary.
23. CAME: since Judith was already in the forechamber of the tent and
awaiting Holofernes' pleasure, the reading ἔστη (58, OL, Syr) is super-
ficially more appropriate and to be seen as a scribal alteration. Judith's
act of obeisance before Holofernes—into whose presence she had "come"—
is described in identical terms with that of Abigail before David (I Sam
25 ₂₃) and of Ruth before Boaz (Ruth 2 ₁₀).

2. AS FOR THY PEOPLE: for emphasis, the subject precedes the conjunctive
"if," and is balanced by the following THEY (αὐτοί), which is essentially
an intensive, not simply a loose "they."   MADE LIGHT: disparaged,
slighted (cf. 1 ₁₁).   LIFTED MY SPEAR: for this figurative idiom (II Sam
23 ₁₈) cf. Jer 50 ₁₀ (LXX), which passage may well account for the word
of Holofernes in our Greek translation, although in the Hebrew (43 ₁₀)

which was woven of purple and gold and emerald and precious
stones. ²²And they gave word to him about her, and he went
out to the fore part of the tent, with silver lamps going before
him. ²³When Judith came before him and his attendants,
they all marveled at the fairness of her face. And falling upon
her face she did obeisance to him, and his slaves raised her up.

11 ¹And Holofernes said to her, "Be of good cheer, woman;
have no fear in thy heart, because I am not one to harm any
one who has seen fit to serve Nabouchodonosor, the king
of all the earth. ²And now, as for thy people who dwell
in the hill country, if they had not made light of me, I would
not have lifted my spear against them. But it is they who have
brought all this upon themselves. ³And now, tell me for what
reason thou hast fled from them and come to us. For thou
art come into safety. Be of good cheer, this night thou shalt
live and henceforth, ⁴for there is none who will harm thee;
rather, all will treat thee well as is the case with the slaves
5 of my lord, King Nabouchodonosor." ⁵And Judith said to

"he shall spread his royal canopy"? replaces the Greek "he will lift
his weapons against thee."

3. AND NOW: the opening word of vs. 2 (καὶ νῦν—is here repeated; it
occurs 20 times in this short book.   FOR: scarcely in the sense Goodspeed reads in, "for you have come to save yourself"; for in that case
the question would be pointless. Rather it seems a somewhat loose
assertion: "Tell me what leddest thee to take this step which hath freed
thee from the certain doom of thy fellows."   BE OF GOOD CHEER:
attempts to find a difference between the earlier (vs. 1) aorist and the
more common present imperative are pointless. In vs. 1 the aorist may
have been used deliberately in connection with the following μὴ φοβηθῆς
("Don't be scared").   AND HENCEFORTH: a not too deft attempt
to avoid an overliteral understanding of THIS NIGHT. Since the phrase
εἰς τὸ λοιπόν occurs in the LXX only here and in II Macc 11 19 (cf.
εἰς τὰ λοιπά in II Macc 12 31), there is no direct evidence of what Hebrew
phrase it seeks to translate. It is possible that it renders עד־עולם thus,
instead of by the more usual εἰς τὸν αἰῶνα or ἕως αἰῶνος which might
well be misunderstood.

4. AS IS THE CASE WITH: i.e., "as men do to."   SLAVES OF KING
NABOUCHODONOSOR: Assyrians in general; i.e., thou wilt be safe from
outside molestation, as a member of a nation whom all the world respects
and fears.

5. That Judith very deliberately seeks to deceive Holofernes and to lure

δούλης σου, καὶ λαλησάτω ἡ παιδίσκη σου κατὰ πρόσωπόν σου, καὶ οὐκ ἀναγγελῶ ψεῦδος τῷ κυρίῳ μου ἐν τῇ νυκτὶ ταύτῃ. ⁶καὶ ἐὰν κατακολουθήσῃς τοῖς λόγοις τῆς παιδίσκης σου, τελείως πρᾶγμα ποιήσει μετὰ σοῦ ὁ θεός, καὶ οὐκ ἀποπεσεῖται ὁ κύριός μου τῶν ἐπιτηδευμάτων αὐτοῦ. ⁷ζῇ γὰρ βασιλεὺς Ναβουχοδονοσορ πάσης τῆς γῆς καὶ ζῇ τὸ κράτος αὐτοῦ, ὃς ἀπέστειλέν σε εἰς κατόρθωσιν πάσης ψυχῆς, ὅτι οὐ μόνον ἄνθρωποι διὰ σὲ δουλεύουσιν αὐτῷ, ἀλλὰ καὶ τὰ θηρία τοῦ ἀγροῦ καὶ τὰ κτήνη καὶ τὰ πετεινὰ τοῦ οὐρανοῦ διὰ τῆς ἰσχύος σου ζήσονται ἐπὶ Ναβουχοδονοσορ καὶ πάντα τὸν οἶκον αὐτοῦ. ⁸ἠκούσαμεν γὰρ τὴν σοφίαν σου καὶ τὰ πανουργεύματα τῆς ψυχῆς σου, καὶ ἀνηγγέλη πάσῃ τῇ γῇ ὅτι σὺ μόνος ἀγαθὸς ἐν πάσῃ βασιλείᾳ καὶ δυνατὸς ἐν ἐπιστήμῃ καὶ θαυ-

---

7 δια 2° pr. και 108 | om επι B𝕏 | πας ο οικος 19 (108) OL

---

him to destruction by encouraging him to expect to seduce her is in no way an adverse criticism of her probity in the eyes of the author. It is a perfectly proper attitude and entirely approved by God, as was the case with Jael, not to mention other worthies such as Joshua, Jephthah, Samson, and David, whose lauded exploits disturb many modern readers. To deceive one's fellow Israelite was outrageous, but to deceive and lure to destruction the nation's enemies was completely different. The writer we dub "J" assumes this as a matter of course, with no apology or subterfuge. Through the succeeding centuries the same basic position has been held by most nations, but with an increasingly heavyhanded attempt to disguise and explain away what their earlier brethren had felt needed no justification or apology.

6. As frequently, Judith's words are in *double entente*. God will assuredly accomplish his purpose with Holofernes. It is even possible that in the words AND MY LORD WILL NOT FALL SHORT OF HIS DESIGN Judith is made to think of the epithet MY LORD in a sense far different from what she intended Holofernes to understand it.

7. I SWEAR TO THEE: lit. "as the king liveth"; ζῇ γὰρ βασιλεύς reflects the common formula of an oath, "as surely as Y" liveth," i.e., "I swear by the living God." Here Judith makes the oath binding (in Holofernes' eyes) by swearing by his lord and master; cf. also 2 12, 12 4, 13 16.

KING OF ALL THE EARTH: as in 11 1 the genitive OF ALL THE EARTH depends upon KING (βασιλεύς), which is separated from it by the name N. While this separation of the genitive from the *nomen regens* occurs, it is exceptional and not to be found elsewhere in the LXX.   FOR THE SETTING STRAIGHT: another example of the translator's inordinate fondness for the telic use of εἰς + an accusative. Needless to say, the "setting straight" is definitely from the point of view of Assyria. EVERY LIVING SOUL; i.e., both men and animals; cf. Dan 2 38.   SERVE: lit. "are his slaves," the condition of all Nabouchodonosor's subjects (cf. 11 4). The future,

him, "Receive the words of thy slave, and let thy handmaid speak before thee, and I will tell my lord nothing false
this night. ⁶And if thou wilt follow out the words of thy
handmaid, God will accomplish with thee a deed to the full,
and my lord wilt not fall short of his design. ⁷For I swear
to thee by the life of Nabouchodonosor, king of all the earth,
and by the might of him who sent thee for the setting straight
of every living soul, that because of thee not only do men
serve him, but also the beasts of the field and the cattle and
the birds of the heaven, and due to thy strength shall Nabouchodonosor and all his house be secure. ⁸For we have
heard of thy wisdom and the wonderful feats of clever cunning
of thy brain, and report has come to all the earth that thou
alone art good in all the kingdom and able in knowledge

parallel to the following ζήσονται would have been more natural; a few
mss (106, 249) read the future (δουλεύσουσιν).   BUT ALSO...BE
SECURE: the text is most uncertain here and probably corrupt. ἐπί with
the accusative is untranslatable. The conjecture (followed by ER) of the
genitive, "in the days of," is no better. There is no warrant to render
it "under the sway of." Even worse, why those who "shall live" (whatever
ἐπί means) is limited to beasts, cattle, and birds is far from clear. B,
ℵ omit ἐπί, but retain the accusative καὶ πάντα τὸν οἶκον αὐτοῦ; 19 [108]
read ζήσεται ... καὶ πᾶς ὁ οἶκος; OL reads sciet N. et omnis domus sui.
In this medley of confusion any attempt at reconstruction is hazardous,
but obviously something is necessary. To me the least unwarranted
conjecture is 1) move the comma after δουλεύουσιν αὐτῷ to follow οὐρανοῦ,
making the three following nouns parallel to ἄνθρωποι and thus part of
the subject of δουλεύουσιν;; 2) omit ἐπί and read πᾶς ὁ οἶκος; 3) insert
καί before διὰ τῆς ἰσχύος σου. ζήσονται would then be understood in the
sense "will be secure." To the charge that this is pretty heavy flattery
for Holofernes and might seem even treasonable, it may be replied
that it scarcely exceeds the encomia of the following vs. 8. The translation
I am venturing embodies this modest reconstruction. All unsupported
textual emendation is hazardous; in rare cases, if a translation of any
intelligible sort is to be attempted, it seems necessary.
8. WONDERFUL FEATS OF CLEVER CUNNING: πανουργεύματα (var. -ήματα)
is properly in the sense "knavish tricks" or "villainy," although less
frequently in the sense of "cunning," "craft." In the LXX it occurs
only here and in Sir 1 ₆ and 42 ₁₈. Here Judith in her flattery seems
to use it in a superficial good sense. Is this another case of deliberate
double meaning? To outwit a deceiver, as Jacob did Laban, was, of course,
an admirable quality, as Judith is herself demonstrating. BRAIN: lit.
"soul."   GOOD: scarcely in the ethical sense, but rather "able,"
especially as a soldier. This ultralavish flattery is deliberate, evidencing

μαστὸς ἐν στρατεύμασιν πολέμου. ⁹καὶ νῦν ὁ λόγος, ὃν ἐλάλησεν
Αχιωρ ἐν τῇ συνεδρίᾳ σου, ἠκούσαμεν τὰ ῥήματα αὐτοῦ, ὅτι περι-
εποιήσαντο αὐτὸν οἱ ἄνδρες Βαιτυλουα, καὶ ἀνήγγειλεν αὐτοῖς πάντα,
10 ὅσα ἐξελάλησεν παρὰ σοί. ¹⁰διό, δέσποτα κύριε, μὴ παρέλθῃς τὸν
λόγον αὐτοῦ, ἀλλὰ κατάθου αὐτὸν ἐν τῇ καρδίᾳ σου, ὅτι ἐστὶν
ἀληθής· οὐ γὰρ ἐκδικᾶται τὸ γένος ἡμῶν, οὐ κατισχύει ῥομφαία
ἐπ᾽ αὐτούς, ἐὰν μὴ ἁμάρτωσιν εἰς τὸν θεὸν αὐτῶν. ¹¹καὶ νῦν ἵνα
μὴ γένηται ὁ κύριός μου ἔκβολος καὶ ἄπρακτος καὶ ἐπιπεσεῖται
θάνατος ἐπὶ πρόσωπον αὐτῶν, καὶ κατελάβετο αὐτοὺς ἁμάρτημα,
ἐν ᾧ παροργιοῦσιν τὸν θεὸν αὐτῶν, ὁπηνίκα ἂν ποιήσωσιν ἀτοπίαν. ¹²ἐπεὶ παρεξέλιπεν αὐτοὺς τὰ βρώματα καὶ ἐσπανίσθη πᾶν
ὕδωρ, ἐβουλεύσαντο ἐπιβαλεῖν τοῖς κτήνεσιν αὐτῶν καὶ πάντα, ὅσα
διεστείλατο αὐτοῖς ὁ θεὸς τοῖς νόμοις αὐτοῦ μὴ φαγεῖν, διέγνωσαν
δαπανῆσαι. ¹³καὶ τὰς ἀπαρχὰς τοῦ σίτου καὶ τὰς δεκάτας τοῦ οἴνου
καὶ τοῦ ἐλαίου, ἃ διεφύλαξαν ἁγιάσαντες τοῖς ἱερεῦσιν τοῖς παρ-

---

11 και 3° om Bℵ 23 (19 108 pr. γνωθι οτι)

---

how completely Judith is playing with her intended victim, whose
"amazing cleverness" is thus held up to ridicule before the eyes of the
partisan reader.
9. AS TO: the so-called *nominativus pendens*, common in animated
discourse in every language, is not infrequently, as here, free from the
charge of being a solecism; rather it is an effective rhetorical touch.
SPARED HIM: i.e., kept him alive, rescued him.   MADE KNOWN: reported,
told.
10. MY SOVEREIGN LORD: for this term cf. 5 20, where Achior uses it of
Holofernes.   IS NOT TO BE CHASTENED: whether ἐκδικᾶται is to be
seen as simply an inconsequential variant in --αω for the more natural
-εω, or (as in Lev 19 18, Deut 32 43) as a contracted future from ἐκδικάζω is
debatable. In view of the author's frequent use of ἐκδικέω and the parallelism here with κατισχύει, it is probable that the α is a simple inter-
change for ε, increasingly common in koine Greek. Both verbs, while
presents, have the force of futures: is not to be = will not be = cannot
be.   SWORD: a natural and most effective personification of the enemy
wielding the sword. In the concluding phrase the central emphasis of
the book is struck: so long as they do not sin—and this involves ritual
as well as morality—God's people are sure of his protection.
11. THWARTED: disappointed in his endeavor. The obscurity of the verse
is evidenced by the wide variations in mss and vss. The principal problem
is to determine where the apodosis begins. Some, including Rahlfs, see
it beginning with καὶ κατελάβετο. This would allow the third καί to be a
simple connective but would demand that a ἵνα (suggested by the preceding ἵνα μή) be understood as introducing the future indicative ἐπιπεσεῖται.

and wondrous in the arts of war. ⁹And now, as to the matter of which Achior spake in thy council, we have heard his words because the men of Bethulia spared him, and he made known to them all that he had spoken in thy presence. ¹⁰Wherefore, my sovereign lord, do not disregard his word, but store it in thy heart because it is true; for our people is not to be chastened, sword will not prevail against them, if they do not sin against their God. ¹¹And now that my lord be not thwarted and fail to achieve his goal, death will fall upon them, for a sin has laid hold of them, whereby they will enrage their God whenever they do amiss. ¹²When their supply of food had completely failed them and all their water had become scant, they determined to resort to their cattle and decided to spend all that God had commanded them in his laws not to eat. ¹³And the first fruits of wheat and the tithes of wine and oil, which they had consecrated and set aside for the priests

---

Others prefer to see the apodosis beginning with ἐπιπεσεῖται. This was the understanding of B, ℵ, and 23, who omit the superfluous καί. 19 and 108 omit the καί and read γνῶθι ὅτι. I am inclined to accept that understanding but see no reason to omit the καί, which omission was clearly a case of stylistic improvement. To see καί as an editorial addition is quite unlikely. It is another case (see 5 20) of the Hebrew *waw* which was far from limited to the joining of actual co-ordinate phrases or sentences, but could introduce not only an apodosis after a conditional protasis but a causal clause or serve to express emphasis (= "and especially"). The fourth καί (preceding κατελάβετο) is to be understood as causal ("for"). That is, by the decision so to act (as had been evidenced by their demand to their leaders) they had brought the penalty near to hand; when they actually do act as they have determined, their doom will be sure. A final minor obscurity lies in the concluding phrase. 58 reads αὐτό for ἀτοπίαν, which is natural after the future protasis ὁπηνίκα ἄν. Actually it is far from certain that there is not a mingling of two protases here: 1) whenever they actually do what they wickedly planned to do, and 2) as has been true in the past whenever they did wrong.
12. RESORT TO THEIR CATTLE: i.e., "fall upon," "make use of." The impropriety lies in this planned disregard of those portions belonging to God and his priests, as is laboriously explained in the next verse. OL seeks to indicate the wicked nature of this intended act—to non-Jews the act of eating the cattle would have seemed common sense—by adding the phrase *et bibere sanguinem eorum.*   SPEND: i.e., expend, utterly consume. The choice of this verb is deliberate to indicate vividly the entire consumption without regard for the portions not theirs to eat.   BY HIS LAWS: the addition of the preposition ἐν in many mss is easier to explain than its omission; it is accordingly to be deleted.

εστηκόσιν ἐν Ἰερουσαλημ ἀπέναντι τοῦ προσώπου τοῦ θεοῦ ἡμῶν, κεκρίκασιν ἐξαναλῶσαι, ὧν οὐδὲ ταῖς χερσὶν καθῆκεν ἅψασθαι οὐδένα τῶν ἐκ τοῦ λαοῦ. ¹⁴καὶ ἀπεστάλκασιν εἰς Ἰερουσαλημ, ὅτι καὶ οἱ ἐκεῖ κατοικοῦντες ἐποίησαν ταῦτα, τοὺς μετακομίσοντας αὐτοῖς
15 τὴν ἄφεσιν παρὰ τῆς γερουσίας. ¹⁵καὶ ἔσται ὡς ἂν ἀναγγείλη αὐτοῖς καὶ ποιήσωσιν, δοθήσονταί σοι εἰς ὄλεθρον ἐν τῇ ἡμέρᾳ ἐκείνη.
¹⁶ὅθεν ἐγὼ ἡ δούλη σου ἐπιγνοῦσα ταῦτα πάντα ἀπέδρων ἀπὸ προσώπου αὐτῶν, καὶ ἀπέστειλέν με ὁ θεὸς ποιῆσαι μετὰ σοῦ πράγματα, ἐφ᾽ οἷς ἐκστήσεται πᾶσα ἡ γῆ, ὅσοι ἐὰν ἀκούσωσιν αὐτά.
¹⁷ὅτι ἡ δούλη σου θεοσεβής ἐστιν καὶ θεραπεύουσα νυκτὸς καὶ ἡμέρας τὸν θεὸν τοῦ οὐρανοῦ· καὶ νῦν μενῶ παρὰ σοί, κύριέ μου, καὶ ἐξελεύσεται ἡ δούλη σου κατὰ νύκτα εἰς τὴν φάραγγα καὶ προσεύξομαι πρὸς τὸν θεόν, καὶ ἐρεῖ μοι πότε ἐποίησαν τὰ ἁμαρτήματα αὐτῶν. ¹⁸καὶ ἐλθοῦσα προσανοίσω σοι, καὶ ἐξελεύσῃ σὺν πάσῃ τῇ δυνάμει σου, καὶ οὐκ ἔστιν ὃς ἀντιστήσεταί σοι ἐξ αὐτῶν. ¹⁹καὶ ἄξω σε διὰ μέσου τῆς Ἰουδαίας ἕως τοῦ ἐλθεῖν ἀπέναντι Ἰερουσα-

---

13. THEY HAVE DECIDED: the perfect is vivid. Their act of folly was no unpremeditated suggestion, speedily repented, but a deliberate and abiding decision, speedily to be realized; hence the certainty of their doom. CONSUME: another vivid word parallel to "spend" in the preceding verse, with its repeated note of completeness. The translator has a wide vocabulary and a marked ability for a word fitly chosen.
NOT PROPER: "not lawful," i.e., "no such thing ought be done in Israel." The imperfect is frequent in verbs expressing propriety or obligation, where English usage prefers a present—but cf. our "ought" (= "owed"). The obligation existed and should have been met, but has not been; cf. Acts 22 22.
14. COUNCIL: cf. note on 4 8.
15. AND IT SHALL BE: the order of the sentence, with this abrupt opening phrase (καὶ ἔσται) and the delayed subject (δοθήσονται ...ἐκείνη) ending with the ominous ON THAT VERY DAY, suggests that this is not a simple future—"the result will be"—but is a part of the divine plan from which there can be no escape; thus it is essentially the equivalent of the prophetic "Thus saith Adonai."
16. Once again Judith's words have occasioned moralizing by interpreters hard put to justify her deliberate violation of truth which they regard as inviolate. To escape this dilemma many laborious efforts have been attempted. All this is quite unnecessary, for certainly the author would not have understood them. To outwit one who is seeking to destroy you is, as has been already remarked, entirely warranted in his eyes, and matters of ethical nicety do not obtrude. He is telling a story, not writing a treatise on ethics. It may well be that once again

who stand in Jerusalem before the face of our God, which things it is not proper for any of the people even to touch with their hands, them they have decided to consume. [14]And to Jerusalem, because even they who dwell there have done these deeds, have they sent messengers to bring back 15 to them permission from the council. [15]And it shall be that when the word reaches them and they so do, on that very day will they be given over to thee for destruction. [16]Wherefore, I thy slave, having learned all this, fled from before them, and God has sent me to do things with thee at which the whole earth will be astounded, as many as shall hear of them, [17]because your slave is God-fearing and worships the God of heaven night and day; and now I will remain with thee, my lord, and thy slave shall go forth each night into the valley, and I shall pray to God, and he will tell me when they have committed these deeds of sin. [18]And I will come and bring thee word, and thou shalt go forth with all thine army, and there is no one of them who will withstand thee. [19]And I will guide thee through the midst of Judea until thou comest

---

he is intentionally phrasing himself so that a deeper meaning is evident: Judith means the success of her venture; Holofernes infers that the God of the Hebrews is angry with them and is giving them into his hand for destruction. Very possibly the author expects his readers to see this and chuckle over it. A more real problem lies in Holofernes' ready acceptance of Judith's insistence that the real and controlling power is her God. If Holofernes fails to hearken, his plan will fail; if he is successful, it will be because the God of the Hebrews has so willed it. All this is in sharp contrast to his earlier expressed views about the all-supremacy of Nabouchodonosor. But these inconsistencies are of no moment to the author as he tells his story, although they may well reflect his own theological views.

17. BECAUSE: this sentence is somewhat loosely attached to the preceding. The awkward "because," with which it opens, apparently indicates an ellipse. The reason God has chosen her for this deed is her exemplary piety.   GOD OF HEAVEN: cf. 5 8.   INTO THE VALLEY: the regular nightly excursion of Judith is here alluded to, but with no mention of her nightly bath. Its purpose is to render her available for the divine communication, which will be made while she is in prayer. That this may involve a bit of delay in receiving the report, for Israel's defection is not likely to coincide with Judith's nocturnal trip outside the camp does not disturb Holofernes—or the author.

18. WILL (shall?) WITHSTAND THEE: i.e., "will be able to withstand."

λημ καὶ θήσω τὸν δίφρον σου ἐν μέσῳ αὐτῆς, καὶ ἄξεις αὐτοὺς
ὡς πρόβατα, οἷς οὐκ ἔστιν ποιμήν, καὶ οὐ γρύξει κύων τῇ γλώσσῃ
αὐτοῦ ἀπέναντί σου· ὅτι ταῦτα ἐλαλήθη μοι κατὰ πρόγνωσίν μου
20 καὶ ἀπηγγέλη μοι, καὶ ἀπεστάλην ἀναγγεῖλαί σοι. — ²⁰καὶ ἤρεσαν
οἱ λόγοι αὐτῆς ἐναντίον Ολοφέρνου καὶ ἐναντίον πάντων τῶν θεραπόντων αὐτοῦ, καὶ ἐθαύμασαν ἐπὶ τῇ σοφίᾳ αὐτῆς καὶ εἶπαν ²¹Οὐκ
ἔστιν τοιαύτη γυνὴ ἀπ' ἄκρου ἕως ἄκρου τῆς γῆς ἐν καλῷ προσώπῳ καὶ συνέσει λόγων. ²²καὶ εἶπεν πρὸς αὐτὴν Ολοφέρνης Εὖ
ἐποίησεν ὁ θεὸς ἀποστείλας σε ἔμπροσθεν τοῦ λαοῦ τοῦ γενηθῆναι
ἐν χερσὶν ἡμῶν κράτος, ἐν δὲ τοῖς φαυλίσασι τὸν κύριόν μου ἀπώλειαν. ²³καὶ νῦν ἀστεία εἶ σὺ ἐν τῷ εἴδει σου καὶ ἀγαθὴ ἐν τοῖς
λόγοις σου· ὅτι ἐὰν ποιήσῃς καθὰ ἐλάλησας, ὁ θεός σου ἔσται
μου θεός, καὶ σὺ ἐν οἴκῳ βασιλέως Ναβουχοδονοσορ καθήσῃ καὶ
ἔσῃ ὀνομαστὴ παρὰ πᾶσαν τὴν γῆν.

12 ¹Καὶ ἐκέλευσεν εἰσαγαγεῖν αὐτὴν οὗ ἐτίθετο τὰ ἀργυρώματα αὐ-

---

Again Judith's word is not simply futurity, but a certainty ordained
and directed by God.
19. SEAT: lit. "chariot board," but common in the sense of "seat" or
"stool." The variant "throne" is obvious as an interpreter's substitution.
  SHEEP: again there is the probability of double meaning here in the
mention of sheep scattered without a shepherd, which was to be the fate
of Holofernes' forces panic-struck by his murder.   GROWL WITH
HIS TONGUE: a typical piece of awkward translation Greek attempting
to render literally the Hebrew idiom "a dog shall not move (point) his
tongue."
19. BECAUSE: Judith ends her speech with this somewhat turgid assurance
that what she is saying is not guesswork but has been revealed to her by
God. Apparently Holofernes is to conclude that she has come not merely
to escape the doom of her city but to bring him the word that he will
be successful if he follows her (God's!) plan.
21. UNDERSTANDING: wisdom—"for beauty and brains."
22. BEFORE THE PEOPLE: this phrase is most obscure. Apparently by
"people" those in Bethulia are meant, although it is possible to understand
it in the florid sense "to us." The simplest meaning would be "from
before thy people": thy coming has the purpose of giving strength to us,
defeat to them. The infinitive τοῦ γενηθῆναι is telic with κράτος and
ἀπώλειαν as subjects. The ungrammatical nominative ἀπώλεια (and so
presumably κράτος) in B, A suggests that some early interpreter saw the
subject of the infinitive σέ (i.e., Judith) and the two nouns predicates.

before Jerusalem, and I will set thy seat in her midst, and
thou shalt drive them like sheep who have no shepherd,
and before thee shall no dog dare to growl with his tongue;
because these things were told me according to my fore-
knowledge and were reported to me, and I have been sent
to announce them to thee."

20   ²⁰And her words were pleasing in the eyes of Holofernes
and of all who attended him, and they marveled at her wisdom
and said, ²¹"There is not such a woman from one end of
the earth to the other, for fairness of face and understanding
of words." ²²And Holofernes said to her, "God hath done
well in sending thee before the people that might should be in
our hands but destruction for those who made light of my
lord. ²³And now, thou art pretty of face and able of speech.
If thou doest as thou hast spoken, thy God shall be my God,
and thou shalt sit in the house of King Nabouchodonosor
and shalt be of note throughout the whole earth."

12   ¹And he gave command to conduct her where his silver
plate was kept and gave order to spread before her some of

Several OL mss add a concluding word: *quia abominati sunt me et dominum
meum Nabuchodonosor.*

23. IF: the force of ὅτι which precedes "if" is uncertain. It may pick up
Holofernes' last word in the sense "Thou hast really shown intelligence
in coming to me, *for* if thou doest what thou hast said, thou wilt be richly
rewarded." Conceivably, however, it may be elliptical in the sense
"I swear *that*...." In all probability it is Judith's beauty, not her brains,
that qualify her for her promised seat in the house of Nabouchodonosor!
        THY GOD SHALT BE MY GOD: there has been much debate whether
this word is simply flattery to render Judith's seduction the easier,
or whether it is in earnest, as in the case of Naaman. There may be point
in debating how our author intended the word to be taken; certainly
as far as Holofernes is concerned such a word is most unlikely in view of
his constant attestation that N. is the only god. Actually the taking of
Bethulia and conquest of Judea is from Holofernes' point of view hardly
as dependent upon a miracle as had been the cure of Naaman's leprosy.
All of these words of Holofernes but indicate once again that speeches
very regularly express the view of the author, not of the speaker who is
made to enunciate them.   OF NOTE: Once again the double entendre.
This fame did come to Judith (16 21), but scarcely as Holofernes meant.

1. WAS KEPT: or, giving force to the imperfect, "where his silver plate

τοῦ καὶ συνέταξεν καταστρῶσαι αὐτῇ ἀπὸ τῶν ὀψοποιημάτων αὐτοῦ
καὶ τοῦ οἴνου αὐτοῦ πίνειν. ²καὶ εἶπεν Ιουδιθ Οὐ φάγομαι ἐξ αὐτῶν, ἵνα μὴ γένηται σκάνδαλον, ἀλλ' ἐκ τῶν ἠκολουθηκότων μοι
χορηγηθήσεται. ³καὶ εἶπεν πρὸς αὐτὴν Ολοφέρνης Ἐὰν δὲ ἐκλίπῃ
τὰ ὄντα μετὰ σοῦ, πόθεν ἐξοίσομέν σοι δοῦναι ὅμοια αὐτοῖς; οὐ
γάρ ἐστιν μεθ' ἡμῶν ἐκ τοῦ γένους σου. ⁴καὶ εἶπεν Ιουδιθ πρὸς
αὐτόν Ζῇ ἡ ψυχή σου, κύριέ μου, ὅτι οὐ δαπανήσει ἡ δούλη σου
τὰ ὄντα μετ' ἐμοῦ, ἕως ἂν ποιήσῃ κύριος ἐν χειρί μου ἃ ἐβουλεύ-
5 σατο. ⁵καὶ ἠγάγοσαν αὐτὴν οἱ θεράποντες Ολοφέρνου εἰς τὴν σκηνήν, καὶ ὕπνωσεν μέχρι μεσούσης τῆς νυκτός· καὶ ἀνέστη πρὸς
τὴν ἑωθινὴν φυλακήν. ⁶καὶ ἀπέστειλεν πρὸς Ολοφέρνην λέγουσα
Ἐπιταξάτω δὴ ὁ κύριός μου ἐᾶσαι τὴν δούλην σου ἐπὶ προσευχὴν

---

3 εξοισομεν] εξομεν A al. || 4 κυριος] om. B 155, θεος 19 106, κυριος ο
θεος 23

---

was wont to be set"; i.e., his dining room.   DAINTIES: ὀψοποίημα,
a very rare word (although the verb and other derivatives are not uncommon), found only here in the LXX.   TO DRINK: epexegetic infinitive, common in Greek and Hebrew as well as in English.
2. OFFENSE: not in the eyes of men, who would regard it as entirely
proper, but in the eyes of God, where it would be sin. Once again Judith is
portrayed as the pink of propriety so far as religious niceties are concerned.
To what extent commentators are justified in emphasizing this point
and using it as an example of the way ritual details of this sort had
ecclipsed the moral virtues in a Judaism which had degenerated into
an "arid legalism" is more than questionable. To be sure, it is stressed
also in such a book as Daniel and in the later rewriting of Esther, but in
all these cases the writer is telling a good story and painting with a full
brush. To harp on this detail in Judith, in contrast with her apparent
perfect willingness to sleep with Holofernes should that prove necessary,
and then to find determinative evidence for the comparative scales of
ethics and religious values is as utterly unwarranted as to decide from
Tobit that the only duty of a really pious Hebrew was to spend his
days hunting for dead bodies to bury. A bit of common sense when
reading fiction is essential. These authors are storytellers, trying to tell
a story effectively, not careful historians or professors of ethics arranging
lists of ethical demands in the exact order of importance.   WHICH
HAVE COME WITH ME: lit. "which have followed me," i.e., "which I
have brought for the purpose."
3. GET: the perfectly grammatical ἐξοίσομεν offended some scribes who
substituted ἕξομεν, in the sense "be able." As is so frequently the case,
there is no possible doubt as to which is the original reading, for while
ἐξοίσομεν could easily lead to ἕξομεν, the reverse is utterly unlikely.
FOR...: i.e., from whom we could get such stuff.

his own dainties and of his own wine to drink. ²And Judith said, "I shall not eat them lest it be an offense, but provision will be made from the things which have come with me." ³Holofernes said to her, "But if the things with you fail, where will we get things like them to give thee, for there is none of thy race with us?" ⁴And Judith said to him, "As thy soul liveth, my lord, thy handmaid will not use up the things with me until Adonai by my hand accomplishes what he hath 5 purposed." ⁵And the servants of Holofernes led her to the tent, and she slept until midnight; and toward the morning watch she arose. ⁶And she sent word to Holofernes, "Please let my lord give order to permit thy handmaid to go forth for prayer."

4. AS THY SOUL LIVETH: a mild sort of oath akin to our colloquialism "as sure as you are alive." WITH ME: Syr, OL, and a few others change this to "with her," although at other places they allow the author a bit more latitude in the case of *constructiones ad sensum.* ADONAI the omission of κύριος by B and 155 is unexplainable; other more understandable variants as θεός (19, 106) or κύριος ὁ θεός (23) are found. 5. THE TENT: presumably the one assigned to her use. It is surprising that none of the copyists found it necessary to amplify this bare remark, with indications that scrupulous privacy was given her. TOWARD THE MORNING WATCH: the Hebrew division of the night into three watches, the last of which was the morning watch (Exod 14 24, I Sam 11 11), yielded by the first century C.E. to the Roman fourfold division. TOWARD THE MORNING WATCH, in connection with the mention of midnight, would suggest "during the last hours of the middle watch," i.e., between midnight and 2 a.m. That Holofernes would not appreciate being awakened at that hour, when his permission could easily have been asked a few hours earlier, does not disturb the author. 6. PLEASE: the particle δή—one of the few which the translator employs— makes the request seemingly less demanding. The reason for her nocturnal visits to the spring for prayer and washing has occasioned much argument as there would seem no especial reason for this ablution. In a late Hebrew version of this legend (cf. pp. 182-190), much briefer and with no mention of Bethulia or Holofernes, a reason for the bath is assigned. When Seleucus (who replaces Holofernes as the luckless villain) asks Judith to lie with him, she replies; "My lord king, for this very thing I came hither with all my heart, but now it is impossible, as I am in my impurity; tonight is the time of my purification; I therefore desire the king to herald throughout the camp that no one should stay the woman and her handmaid, when she goes out in the night to the fountain of water. When I return I will give myself over to the king, that he may do what is pleasing in his sight." Here, to be sure, a satisfactory explanation might seem to be provided (cf. 12 9), but the probability is real that this is an explanation provided to explain the enigma. In addition to heightening the aura

ἐξελθεῖν· ⁷καὶ προσέταξεν Ολοφέρνης τοῖς σωματοφύλαξιν μὴ δια-
κωλύειν αὐτήν. καὶ παρέμεινεν ἐν τῇ παρεμβολῇ ἡμέρας τρεῖς· καὶ
ἐξεπορεύετο κατὰ νύκτα εἰς τὴν φάραγγα Βαιτυλουα καὶ ἐβαπτίζετο
ἐν τῇ παρεμβολῇ ἐπὶ τῆς πηγῆς τοῦ ὕδατος· ⁸καὶ ὡς ἀνέβη, ἐδέετο
τοῦ κυρίου θεοῦ Ισραηλ κατευθῦναι τὴν ὁδὸν αὐτῆς εἰς ἀνάστημα
τῶν υἱῶν τοῦ λαοῦ αὐτοῦ· ⁹καὶ εἰσπορευομένη καθαρὰ παρέμενεν ἐν
τῇ σκηνῇ, μέχρι οὗ προσηνέγκατο τὴν τροφὴν αὐτῆς πρὸς ἑσπέραν.
10 ¹⁰Καὶ ἐγένετο ἐν τῇ ἡμέρᾳ τῇ τετάρτῃ ἐποίησεν Ολοφέρνης πότον
τοῖς δούλοις αὐτοῦ μόνοις καὶ οὐκ ἐκάλεσεν εἰς τὴν κλῆσιν οὐδένα
τῶν πρὸς ταῖς χρείαις. ¹¹καὶ εἶπεν Βαγώᾳ τῷ εὐνούχῳ, ὃς ἦν ἐφ-
εστηκὼς ἐπὶ πάντων τῶν αὐτοῦ Πεῖσον δὴ πορευθεὶς τὴν γυναῖκα
τὴν Εβραίαν, ἥ ἐστιν παρὰ σοί, τοῦ ἐλθεῖν πρὸς ἡμᾶς καὶ φαγεῖν

10 κλησιν] χρησιν B

of holiness in which the author clothed Judith, her action is intended
further to convince Holofernes of her sincerity and her expectation
of receiving the divine word that the moment has come. Even more,
it enables Judith and her maid to move about the camp without restraint
during the night, which freedom is essential to her escape when she has
carried out her plan.
The exact location of the spring—within or outside the camp—has also
been debated. According to 7 3 it was within the Assyrian control.
Apparently the "going out" each night was from her tent to a more
remote part of the camp. The words IN THE CAMP (vs. 7) are nonetheless
awkward. Some mss simply omit the phrase.
7. THREE DAYS: those who are content to regard the story as an edifying
tale, not a historical chronicle, will probably be inclined to view "three"
as a natural and common designation of a small number. It is needless
to list its frequent use in such contexts. BATHED: one of the very
few occurrences of the verb βαπτίζειν for a purificatory bath. It suggests,
as do the following words in the next verse, AND WHEN SHE HAD COME
OUT OF THE WATER, that Judith immersed herself in the water at the
spring, not that she took a sponge bath.
8. The use of tenses in the verbs in this verse is apparently careful:
ὡς + aorist is clearly WHEN SHE HAD COME OUT, not "as she was coming
out"; the imperfect ἐδέετο suggests the continued practice each night
(SHE WAS WONT...). ELEVATION: her prayer was that Adonai might
direct her to aid in accomplishing the triumph of Israel, *raising* them
from the gloom of despair into which they had fallen. HIS PEOPLE:
i.e., Y" 's. The variant "her" is a natural alteration of a certainly original
"his."
9. PARTOOK: Judith is the subject of the verb; the middle of προσφέρω
is regularly used in the sense "to take to oneself," "to enjoy," particularly
of food and drink. To regard it as transitive, with her maid as the un-

⁷And Holofernes bade his bodyguard not to hinder her. And she abode in the camp three days. And each night she went forth to the vale of Bethulia and bathed in the camp at the spring of water. ⁸And when she had come out of the water, she was wont to beseech Adonai the God of Israel to make straight her way for the elevation of the children of his people. ⁹And coming in clean, she was wont to stay in the tent until she partook of her food toward evening.

10 ¹⁰And it came to pass on the fourth day that Holofernes made a feast for his slaves only, and he did not include in the invitation any of those on duty. ¹¹And he said to Bagoas, the eunuch who was in charge of all his possessions, "Come, now, go and persuade the Hebrew woman, who is with thee, to come to us and eat and drink with us, ¹²for lo, we will

---

expressed subject ("until she brought her...") is quite foreign to Greek diction.

10. FEAST: lit. "drinking bout" (cf. 6 21).   DID NOT INCLUDE IN THE INVITATION: the text is very obscure. οὐκ ἐκάλεσεν εἰς τὴν κλῆσιν οὐδένα is well attested and can only mean "called to the calling," "invited to the invitation," or, as I have rendered it. It is awkward and led to the correction χρῆσιν, apparently in the sense of "use," "participation" (i.e., of the wine), perhaps influenced by the concluding τῶν πρὸς ταῖς χρείαις. This latter must mean "none of those on duty," i.e., his officers. Instead, the party was solely for his personal intimates. Whether the colorless term SLAVES is here to be understood in the sense of "intimates," "friends," or those especially honored by the invitation, or whether it indicates those regularly in attendance because of especial duties is uncertain, although the last appears to me the most likely. Since the purpose of the party was the conquest of Judith, there was little need of a large attendance. In the late Hebrew midrashic rewriting of the story this detail is overlooked: rather it is a great feast for all his princes and servants.

11. BAGOAS: a Persian word thought to mean "eunuch," and a frequent proper name; cf. Pliny, *N.H.* 13, 4, 9, *Babylone natae uno in horto Bagou; ita enim vocant spadones qui apud eos etiam regnavere.* The best known of these was the confidential minister of Artaxerxes III, who became the real master of the kingdom, eventually making Darius III king; but when later he sought to poison him, he was himself forced to drink the poison. Another eunuch by the same name was a favorite of Alexander the Great. The choice of this name for the major-domo of Holofernes, in charge of all his affairs, was most appropriate. In Vg the name is spelled Vagao.   WITH THEE: Judith was not unnaturally under his oversight.

καὶ πιεῖν μεθ' ἡμῶν· ¹²ἰδοὺ γὰρ αἰσχρὸν τῷ προσώπῳ ἡμῶν εἰ
γυναῖκα τοιαύτην παρήσομεν οὐχ ὁμιλήσαντες αὐτῇ· ὅτι ἐὰν ταύτην μὴ ἐπισπασώμεθα, καταγελάσεται ἡμῶν. ¹³καὶ ἐξῆλθεν Βαγώας
ἀπὸ προσώπου Ολοφέρνου καὶ εἰσῆλθεν πρὸς αὐτὴν καὶ εἶπεν Μὴ
ὀκνησάτω δὴ ἡ παιδίσκη ἡ καλὴ αὕτη ἐλθοῦσα πρὸς τὸν κύριόν
μου δοξασθῆναι κατὰ πρόσωπον αὐτοῦ καὶ πίεσαι μεθ' ἡμῶν εἰς
εὐφροσύνην οἶνον καὶ γενηθῆναι ἐν τῇ ἡμέρᾳ ταύτῃ ὡς θυγάτηρ
μία τῶν υἱῶν Ασσουρ, αἳ παρεστήκασιν ἐν οἴκῳ Ναβουχοδονοσορ.
¹⁴καὶ εἶπεν πρὸς αὐτὸν Ιουδιθ Καὶ τίς εἰμι ἐγὼ ἀντεροῦσα τῷ κυρίῳ μου; ὅτι πᾶν, ὃ ἔσται ἐν τοῖς ὀφθαλμοῖς αὐτοῦ ἀρεστόν,
σπεύσασα ποιήσω, καὶ ἔσται τοῦτό μοι ἀγαλλίαμα ἕως ἡμέρας θα-
15 νάτου μου. ¹⁵καὶ διαναστᾶσα ἐκοσμήθη τῷ ἱματισμῷ καὶ παντὶ τῷ
κόσμῳ τῷ γυναικείῳ, καὶ προσῆλθεν ἡ δούλη αὐτῆς καὶ ἔστρωσεν
αὐτῇ κατέναντι Ολοφέρνου χαμαὶ τὰ κώδια, ἃ ἔλαβεν παρὰ Βαγώου
εἰς τὴν καθημερινὴν δίαιταν αὐτῆς εἰς τὸ ἐσθίειν κατακλινομένην
ἐπ' αὐτῶν. ¹⁶καὶ εἰσελθοῦσα ἀνέπεσεν Ιουδιθ, καὶ ἐξέστη ἡ καρδία
Ολοφέρνου ἐπ' αὐτήν, καὶ ἐσαλεύθη ἡ ψυχὴ αὐτοῦ, καὶ ἦν κατεπί-

---

13 πιεσαι] πιειν A 64 243 248 249 | γενηθηναι]γενησει 19, γενηση 108,
γενηθησει cj. MSE || 15 προσηλθεν] προηλθ. B 55

---

12. WILL BE PUT TO SHAME: lit. "it is/will be a shame to our face."
LET SUCH A WOMAN GO: almost the equivalent of the colloquial "let her
off." To read in the thought of "enticing" or "coaxing" is as false to
the Greek as it would have been to Holofernes.   FORCE HER is surely
more accurate than "allure" or "persuade," as is indicated by the concluding WILL LAUGH US TO SCORN.
13. Bagoas' word is studiedly courteous, with the use of the third person
and the softening of the blunt imperative "Come," by the auxiliary
ὀκνησάτω and the particle δή—a common device in all languages.
DRINK: the syntax abruptly changes, with the future indicative middle,
THOU SHALT DRINK (πίεσαι). Several mss (including A) substitute the
more natural infinitive (πιεῖν), but this is a palpable correction of the
awkward indicative, for the received text continues with another parallel
infinitive, γενηθῆναι, depending upon the auxiliary. Two mss substitute
future indicatives (γενήσει, 19; γενήση, 108) for the infinitive. While there
is no ms evidence, I would hazard the suggestion that the original text
read γενηθήσει, which was altered to γενηθῆναι to harmonize with the
earlier δοξασθῆναι. Nor is it impossible that the alteration was prompted
by considering πιεσαι a first aorist active infinitive. Somewhat hesitantly

be put to shame if we let such a woman go without having intercourse with her, because if we do not force her, she will laugh us to scorn." [13]And Bagoas went out from before Holofernes and came to her and said, "Let not this fair maid, I pray, hesitate to come to my lord to be honored in his presence, and thou shalt drink wine and make merry with us and become this day as a daughter of the children of Asshur who attend in the house of Nabouchodonosor." [14]And Judith said to him, "And who am I to say nay to my lord? Because all which will be pleasing in his eyes will I hasten to do, and this will be a source of joy to me till the day of 15 my death." [15]And arising, she arrayed herself in her apparel and all her woman's finery, and her slavegirl came forward and strewed on the ground for her before Holofernes the lambskins which she had received from Bagoas for her daily use, that she might recline on them as she ate. [16]And Judith came in and reclined, and the heart of Holofernes was delighted to ecstasy at her, and his soul reeled, and he was

---

I have translated the text to preserve πίεσαι, which appears to me the original reading.

14. TO MY LORD: Holofernes, not Bagoas.   SOURCE OF JOY: Syr "It will be to me a boast."

15. CAME FORWARD: presumably after Judith had entered Holofernes' presence. As the account is given, with Judith entering the tent in the next verse, it was not unnatural to avoid this by reading προῆλθεν, that is, the maid preceded her, with the laying of the skins somewhat akin to strewing the path for the following dignitary. Although this reading is attested by B and 55, it is a quite needless alteration, for vs. 16 does not properly imply that Judith entered after her maid, but that having entered she reclined. The surprising element is that Judith felt it necessary to have her maid tote along the skins which had been given her for use in her own tent. Perhaps it is to be explained as another indication that Judith, unlike Esther, in this dangerous moment guarded herself zealously against all ceremonial defilement. Not only did she take her own food, but even the equipment on which she was to recline. In this overtouch the fact is, of course, disregarded that these had come from the foreigner. Perhaps, however, it is but one more of the colorful details in this lush picture. No further mention of the skins is made as the story proceeds. After this final banquet Judith will eat no more in the camp of the enemy.   AS SHE ATE: Bagoas had given them to her for use in her own tent. The words do not mean that she might recline on them as she ate this last supper with Holofernes.

θυμος σφόδρα τοῦ συγγενέσθαι μετ' αὐτῆς· καὶ ἐτήρει καιρὸν τοῦ ἀπατῆσαι αὐτὴν ἀφ' ἧς ἡμέρας εἶδεν αὐτήν. ¹⁷καὶ εἶπεν πρὸς αὐτὴν Ολοφέρνης Πίε δὴ καὶ γενήθητι μεθ' ἡμῶν εἰς εὐφροσύνην. ¹⁸καὶ εἶπεν Ιουδιθ Πίομαι δή, κύριε, ὅτι ἐμεγαλύνθη τὸ ζῆν μου ἐν ἐμοὶ σήμερον παρὰ πάσας τὰς ἡμέρας τῆς γενέσεώς μου. ¹⁹καὶ λαβοῦσα ἔφαγεν καὶ ἔπιεν κατέναντι αὐτοῦ ἃ ἡτοίμασεν ἡ δούλη αὐτῆς.
20 ²⁰καὶ ηὐφράνθη Ολοφέρνης ἀπ' αὐτῆς καὶ ἔπιεν οἶνον πολὺν σφόδρα, ὅσον οὐκ ἔπιεν πώποτε ἐν ἡμέρᾳ μιᾷ ἀφ' οὗ ἐγεννήθη.

13   ¹Ὡς δὲ ὀψία ἐγένετο, ἐσπούδασαν οἱ δοῦλοι αὐτοῦ ἀναλύειν. καὶ Βαγώας συνέκλεισεν τὴν σκηνὴν ἔξωθεν καὶ ἀπέκλεισεν τοὺς παρεστῶτας ἐκ προσώπου τοῦ κυρίου αὐτοῦ, καὶ ἀπῴχοντο εἰς τὰς κοίτας αὐτῶν· ἦσαν γὰρ πάντες κεκοπωμένοι διὰ τὸ ἐπὶ πλεῖον γεγονέναι τὸν πότον. ²ὑπελείφθη δὲ Ιουδιθ μόνη ἐν τῇ σκηνῇ, καὶ Ολοφέρνης προπεπτωκὼς ἐπὶ τὴν κλίνην αὐτοῦ· ἦν γὰρ περικεχυμένος αὐτῷ ὁ οἶνος. ³καὶ εἶπεν Ιουδιθ τῇ δούλῃ αὐτῆς στῆναι ἔξω τοῦ κοιτῶνος αὐτῆς καὶ ἐπιτηρεῖν τὴν ἔξοδον αὐτῆς καθάπερ καθ' ἡμέραν, ἐξελεύσεσθαι γὰρ ἔφη ἐπὶ τὴν προσευχὴν αὐτῆς· καὶ τῷ Βαγώᾳ ἐλάλησεν κατὰ τὰ ῥήματα ταῦτα. ⁴καὶ ἀπῆλθοσαν πάντες ἐκ προσώπου, καὶ οὐδεὶς κατελείφθη ἐν τῷ κοιτῶνι ἀπὸ μικροῦ

---

4 προσωπου]αυτου 4 76 106, +αυτης A 23 52 64 71 243 248 | ολοφερνου 58

---

16. EXCEEDINGLY EAGER: the adjective κατεπίθυμος—a heightened equivalent of ἐπίθυμος (cited by Fritzsche as a hapax)—while not found elsewhere in either the LXX or NT, occurs in Hermas, *Vis.* 3, 8, 2, together with the similar κατεπιθυμεῖς (*Vis.* 3, 2, 2). The picture of the lusting Holofernes, frantic in his desire to seduce Judith, tends to quiet the reader's scruples as to Judith's coldly planned act. Actually "deceit" is more descriptive of Judith's purpose than of Holofernes.'
18. MY LIFE HAS BEEN EXALTED: in this highfaluting word again Judith's double entendre is conspicuously to the fore. The beguiled Holofernes thinks, as Judith intends that he shall, that she is thrilled at the honor of being in his presence; the reader knows that she is thinking of the realization of her mission now so soon to be accomplished.
19. WHAT HER SLAVE HAD PREPARED: once again the mention of her ritually permitted victuals. If worst comes to worst, she may be defiled, but not through eating unclean food.
20. The highly chromoed picture continues. Holofernes' passion for her,

exceedingly eager to lie with her; and he had been biding his time to deceive her, from the day when he had first seen her. [17]And Holofernes said to her, "Drink, I pray thee, and make merry with us." [18]And Judith said, "Indeed yes, my lord, I will drink, because my life hath been exalted today to a height beyond that of all the days since my birth." [19]And taking, she ate and drank before him what her slave had 20 prepared. [20]And Holofernes was enraptured with her and drank exceeding much wine, more than he had ever drunk in one day since he was born.

13 [1]But when the hour had become late, his slaves made haste to withdraw. And Bagoas closed the tent from without and excluded the attendants from the presence of his lord, and they went off to bed, for all were weary since the party had lasted so long. [2]And Judith was left alone in the tent, and Holofernes was prone on his bed, for he was fair swimming in wine. [3]And Judith had bidden her slavegirl to stand outside her chamber and to await her departure even as she did every day, for she had said that she would go out for her prayers. And she had spoken to Bagoas in the same wise. [4]And all had gone away, and no one was left in the chamber,

---

artfully anticipated by Judith, leads to his gross overuse of wine, which proves definitely to our heroine's advantage.

1. HOUR: the context suggests that the conventional rendering "when it became evening," is scarcely apt. The PARTY—"banquet"—had been protracted, and it was high time for bed. The melodramatic stage setting continues: the tactful haste of the guests to leave; the barring of the door of the tent from the outside; the careful exclusion of all attendants who might normally have assisted their master in bedtime preparation. WEARY: worn-out; the perfect of κοπόω is commonly used as a passive of κοπιάω.
2. PRONE: Holofernes had fallen headlong (προπεπτωκώς) on his bed in a drunken stupor.   FAIR SWIMMING IN WINE: *madidus vino.*
3. HAD BIDDEN: while on the way to Holofernes. She would thus be in a position to unbar when Judith was ready to leave. Seemingly Judith has not apprised the maid of her plans.   HER CHAMBER: strictly Holofernes'.   HAD SPOKEN TO BAGOAS: i.e., before he had left. Both aorists are equivalents of English pluperfects.
4. HAD GONE AWAY: the common reading ἐκ προσώπου disturbed later

ἕως μεγάλου· καὶ στᾶσα Ιουδιθ παρὰ τὴν κλίνην αὐτοῦ εἶπεν ἐν
τῇ καρδίᾳ αὐτῆς Κύριε ὁ θεὸς πάσης δυνάμεως, ἐπίβλεψον ἐν τῇ
ὥρᾳ ταύτῃ ἐπὶ τὰ ἔργα τῶν χειρῶν μου εἰς ὕψωμα Ιερουσαλημ·
5 ⁵ὅτι νῦν καιρὸς ἀντιλαβέσθαι τῆς κληρονομίας σου καὶ ποιῆσαι τὸ
ἐπιτήδευμά μου εἰς θραῦσμα ἐχθρῶν, οἳ ἐπανέστησαν ἡμῖν. ⁶καὶ
προσελθοῦσα τῷ κανόνι τῆς κλίνης, ὃς ἦν πρὸς κεφαλῆς Ολοφέρνου, καθεῖλεν τὸν ἀκινάκην αὐτοῦ ἀπ᾽ αὐτοῦ ⁷καὶ ἐγγίσασα τῆς
κλίνης ἐδράξατο τῆς κόμης τῆς κεφαλῆς αὐτοῦ καὶ εἶπεν Κραταί-
ωσόν με, κύριε ὁ θεὸς Ισραηλ, ἐν τῇ ἡμέρᾳ ταύτῃ. ⁸καὶ ἐπάταξεν
εἰς τὸν τράχηλον αὐτοῦ δὶς ἐν τῇ ἰσχύι αὐτῆς καὶ ἀφεῖλεν τὴν
κεφαλὴν αὐτοῦ ἀπ᾽ αὐτοῦ. ⁹καὶ ἀπεκύλισε τὸ σῶμα αὐτοῦ ἀπὸ τῆς
στρωμνῆς καὶ ἀφεῖλε τὸ κωνώπιον ἀπὸ τῶν στύλων· καὶ μετ᾽ ὀλί-
γον ἐξῆλθεν καὶ παρέδωκεν τῇ ἅβρᾳ αὐτῆς τὴν κεφαλὴν Ολοφέρ-
10 νου, ¹⁰καὶ ἐνέβαλεν αὐτὴν εἰς τὴν πήραν τῶν βρωμάτων αὐτῆς.
καὶ ἐξῆλθον αἱ δύο ἅμα κατὰ τὸν ἐθισμὸν αὐτῶν ἐπὶ τὴν προσευ-
χήν· καὶ διελθοῦσαι τὴν παρεμβολὴν ἐκύκλωσαν τὴν φάραγγα ἐκεί-

---

10 επι την προσευχην] om. B, pr. ως 58 OL Syr

---

scribes who added αὐτοῦ (44, 76, 106), αὐτῆς (A, 23, 52, 64, 71, 243, 248),
Ολοφέρνου (58). Presumably the Hebrew was מלפני, reflecting vs. 1.
It is tempting to wonder if the original translator did not write ἐκ προσώπου
(without pronoun), considering it essentially the equivalent of ἐκποδών
("out of the way"), but accomodating this apt Greek idiom to the Hebrew
fondness for "face."   BY HIS BED: 58, Syr, OL read "by his head."
IN HER HEART: Vg, presumably to parallel Hannah's prayer (I Sam 1 13),
has *orans cum lacrymis et labiorum motu in silentio*.
5. NOW IS THE TIME: "the moment has come." That in this word Judith
is comparing unfavorably the earlier attempt of her fellow townsmen to
set a time limit for God's intervention is unlikely.   TO COME TO THE AID:
presumably God is the unexpressed subject ("for thee to come to the aid"),
although this act will be by Judith's hand.   FOR THE SHATTERING:
εἰς θραῦσμα is inexact for εἰς θραῦσιν, but nouns in -μα and -σις had come
to be used with little or no difference in meaning (cf. κρίμα/κρίσις; δόμα/
δόσις).
6. BEDPOST the precise nature of this "rod" or "bar" (τῷ κανόνι τῆς
κλίνης) is uncertain, but apparently it was a vertical pole at the head of
the bed. There is no textual variant, and Vg, probably correctly, renders
it *ad columnam quae erat ad caput lectuli eius*. C. Badwell's conjecture
κίονι ("pillar") for κανόνι is clever but unconvincing in the face of the
unanimous (and most unusual) ms attestation.   SWORD: a short
straight Persian sword. The word ἀκινάκης is frequently used by Herodotus—cf. Περσικὸν ξίφος, τὸν ἀκινάκην καλέουσι (vii, 52).
8. TOOK HIS HEAD FROM HIM: a vivid figure; she had hold of his hair

small or great. And taking her stand by his bed, Judith
said in her heart, "Adonai God of all power, look down with
favor in this hour upon the works of my hand for the exalta-
5 tion of Jerusalem; ⁵because now is the time to come to the
aid of thine inheritance and to carry out my designs for the
shattering of the enemies who have risen up against us."
⁶And going to the bedpost which was at Holofernes' head,
she took down from it his sword, ⁷and nearing the bed, she
seized hold of the hair of his head and said, "Give me strength
this day, Adonai God of Israel." ⁸And with all her might
she smote him twice in the neck and took his head from him.
⁹And she rolled his body from the couch and took the canopy
from the poles; and a moment later she went out and gave
10 Holofernes' head to her maidservant, ¹⁰and she put it in her
pouch of victuals. And the two went forth together according
to their wont for prayer. And having traversed the camp
they compassed that valley and went up the mountain of

---

and thus "pulled his head from him" as the sword did its work. Actually,
to behead a man, lying on a soft bed, with a sword held by one hand
was in itself no mean feat. Our author has no time for such trivia. The
scene is further heightened by the fact that the sword was the victim's
own (cf. David and Goliath, I Sam 17 51).
9. Neither act—the rolling Holofernes' headless body onto the ground
and the pulling down the canopy—is explained, although occasional
commentators have sought somewhat ponderously the reason: the former,
to stop the sound of the splashing blood; the latter, as a means of wrapping
the head. Rather more probably the acts are to be explained as 1) adding
insult to injury and 2) to secure a valuable trophy of the happy event;
see note on canopy at 10 21.   FROM THE POLES: presumably the frame
over which the net was draped. According to the Midrash Judith, after
cutting off the head Judith beat the body with a weapon also hanging
on the pole so that his whole body was a mass of wounds and gore.
But in none of these later versions is there any mention of the canopy.
10. AND SHE PUT IT: the maid placed the head and presumably the canopy
(cf. 13 15) in the pouch (10 5). This latter must have been of considerable
size, for in addition to these two new trophies it presumably held the
dishes and other gear—not to mention food stuff—for the expedition.
But details of this sort were not likely to worry a storyteller or his audience.
    FOR PRAYER: that is what they seemed to be doing; thus 58, Syr,
OL prefix ὡς ("as if"). B omits the phrase. Despite the heavy support,
the absence of the word in B is probably original. The addition was
early made to explain ACCORDING TO THEIR WONT. The addition of "as if"
is a patent and prosy explanation.   COMPASSED THAT VALLEY: i.e.,

νην καὶ προσανέβησαν τὸ ὄρος Βαιτυλουα καὶ ἤλθοσαν πρὸς τὰς πύλας αὐτῆς.

¹¹Καὶ εἶπεν Ιουδιθ μακρόθεν τοῖς φυλάσσουσιν ἐπὶ τῶν πυλῶν Ἀνοίξατε ἀνοίξατε δὴ τὴν πύλην· μεθ' ἡμῶν ὁ θεὸς ὁ θεὸς ἡμῶν ποιῆσαι ἔτι ἰσχὺν ἐν Ισραηλ καὶ κράτος κατὰ τῶν ἐχθρῶν, καθὰ καὶ σήμερον ἐποίησεν. ¹²καὶ ἐγένετο ὡς ἤκουσαν οἱ ἄνδρες τῆς πόλεως αὐτῆς τὴν φωνὴν αὐτῆς, ἐσπούδασαν τοῦ καταβῆναι ἐπὶ τὴν πύλην τῆς πόλεως αὐτῶν καὶ συνεκάλεσαν τοὺς πρεσβυτέρους τῆς πόλεως. ¹³καὶ συνέδραμον πάντες ἀπὸ μικροῦ ἕως μεγάλου αὐτῶν, ὅτι παράδοξον ἦν αὐτοῖς τὸ ἐλθεῖν αὐτήν, καὶ ἤνοιξαν τὴν πύλην καὶ ὑπεδέξαντο αὐτὰς καὶ ἅψαντες πῦρ εἰς φαῦσιν περιεκύκλωσαν αὐτάς. ¹⁴ἡ δὲ εἶπεν πρὸς αὐτοὺς φωνῇ μεγάλῃ Αἰνεῖτε τὸν θεόν, αἰνεῖτε· αἰνεῖτε τὸν θεόν, ὃς οὐκ ἀπέστησεν τὸ ἔλεος αὐτοῦ ἀπὸ τοῦ οἴκου Ισραηλ, ἀλλ' ἔθραυσε τοὺς ἐχθροὺς ἡμῶν
15 διὰ χειρός μου ἐν τῇ νυκτὶ ταύτῃ. ¹⁵καὶ προελοῦσα τὴν κεφαλὴν ἐκ τῆς πήρας ἔδειξεν καὶ εἶπεν αὐτοῖς Ἰδοὺ ἡ κεφαλὴ Ολοφέρνου ἀρχιστρατήγου δυνάμεως Ασσουρ, καὶ ἰδοὺ τὸ κωνώπιον, ἐν ᾧ κατέκειτο ἐν ταῖς μέθαις αὐτοῦ· καὶ ἐπάταξεν αὐτὸν ὁ κύριος ἐν χειρὶ θηλείας· ¹⁶καὶ ζῇ κύριος, ὃς διεφύλαξέν με ἐν τῇ ὁδῷ μου, ᾗ ἐπορεύθην, ὅτι ἠπάτησεν αὐτὸν τὸ πρόσωπόν μου εἰς ἀπώλειαν αὐτοῦ, καὶ οὐκ ἐποίησεν ἁμάρτημα μετ' ἐμοῦ εἰς μίασμα καὶ αἰσχύνην. ¹⁷καὶ ἐξέστη πᾶς ὁ λαὸς σφόδρα καὶ κύψαντες προσεκύνησαν τῷ θεῷ καὶ εἶπαν ὁμοθυμαδόν Εὐλογητὸς εἶ, ὁ θεὸς ἡμῶν ὁ ἐξουδενώσας ἐν τῇ ἡμέρᾳ τῇ σήμερον τοὺς ἐχθοὺς τοῦ λαοῦ σου. ¹⁸καὶ εἶπεν αὐτῇ Οζιας Εὐλογητὴ σύ, θύγατερ, τῷ θεῷ τῷ ὑψίστῳ παρὰ πάσας τὰς γυναῖκας τὰς ἐπὶ τῆς γῆς, καὶ εὐλογημένος κύριος ὁ θεός, ὃς ἔκτισεν τοὺς οὐρανοὺς καὶ τὴν γῆν, ὃς κατεύθυνέν σε

---

10 το ορος]προς ℵ, εις 58

---

with a circuitous route around the valley, presumably to escape being seen. MOUNTAIN OF BETHULIA: i.e., they ascended the mountain on which Bethulia was located. ℵ substitutes πρός for τὸ ὄρος; 58 has εἰς.
11. CALLED OUT: lit. "said." I BEG YOU: for δή, one of the few Greek particles used by this translator, see 5 5. TO SHOW: not "he will do" but "he has done" and so has shown you the folly of doubting him or trying to force his hand, as some of you sought to do.
13. CIRCLED THEM AROUND: gathered around them.
14. BY MY HAND: lit. "through my hand"; it was God who did it.

Bethulia and came to its gates. ¹¹And Judith called out from afar to those on guard at the gates, "Open, open the gate, I beg you! God, our God, is with us, to show yet again his strength in Israel and his might against the enemies, even as he hath done this day." ¹²And it came to pass that when the men of her city heard her voice they hastened to go down to the gate of their city, and summoned the elders of the city. ¹³And all, both great and small, ran together because it seemed incredible that she had come, and they opened the gate and welcomed them, and having lit a fire for light, they circled them around. ¹⁴Then she said to them with a loud voice, "Praise God, give praise; praise God who hath not withdrawn his mercy from the house of Israel but hath

15 shattered our enemies this night by my hand." ¹⁵And drawing out from the pouch the head, she showed it and said, "Behold, the head of Holofernes, the chief captain of the army of Asshur, and behold, the canopy under which he lay in his drunken stupor. And Adonai smote him down by the hand of a female. ¹⁶And as Adonai liveth, who watched over me on the way I went, (I swear to you) my face deceived him to his undoing, and he wrought no deed of sin with me to defile or cause me shame." ¹⁷And all the people were exceeding amazed and bowed down and worshiped God and said with one accord, "Blessed art thou, our God, who hath brought to naught this day the enemies of thy people." ¹⁸And Ozias said to her, "Blessed art thou, my daughter, to the most high God, beyond all the women of the earth, and blessed is Adonai God who created the heavens and the earth,

---

15. BY THE HAND: here ἐν,, the natural equivalent of ב.   FEMALE: cf. 9 10.

16. DECEIVED: beguiled or tricked him. Judith swears by God himself that she has escaped untouched.

18. BLESSED ART THOU...OF: this non-Greek construction (εὐλογητή + dat.) reflects the Hebrew ל ברוכה (cf. Gen 14 19; Ruth 3 10. This blessing reflects the blessing of Abraham by Melchizedek (Gen 14 19f.), with the combination of εὐλογητός and εὐλογημένος and the mention of God's creative acts; cf. also Deborah's blessing of Jael (Judg 5 24) for her similar

εἰς τραῦμα κεφαλῆς ἄρχοντος ἐχθρῶν ἡμῶν· ¹⁹ὅτι οὐκ ἀποστήσε-
ται ἡ ἐλπίς σου ἀπὸ καρδίας ἀνθρώπων μνημονευόντων ἰσχὺν θεοῦ
20 ἕως αἰῶνος· ²⁰καὶ ποιήσαι σοι αὐτὰ ὁ θεὸς εἰς ὕψος αἰώνιον τοῦ
ἐπισκέψασθαί σε ἐν ἀγαθοῖς, ἀνθ' ὧν οὐκ ἐφείσω τῆς ψυχῆς σου
διὰ τὴν ταπείνωσιν τοῦ γένους ἡμῶν, ἀλλ' ἐπεξῆλθες τῷ πτώματι
ἡμῶν ἐπ' εὐθεῖαν πορευθεῖσα ἐνώπιον τοῦ θεοῦ ἡμῶν. καὶ εἶπαν
πᾶς ὁ λαός Γένοιτο γένοιτο.

14 ¹Καὶ εἶπεν πρὸς αὐτοὺς Ιουδιθ 'Ακούσατε δή μου, ἀδελφοί, καὶ
λαβόντες τὴν κεφαλήν ταύτην κρεμάσατε αὐτὴν ἐπὶ τῆς ἐπάλξεως
τοῦ τείχους ὑμῶν. ²καὶ ἔσται ἡνίκα ἐὰν διαφαύσῃ ὁ ὄρθρος καὶ
ἐξέλθῃ ὁ ἥλιος ἐπὶ τὴν γῆν, ἀναλήμψεσθε ἕκαστος τὰ σκεύη τὰ
πολεμικὰ ὑμῶν καὶ ἐξελεύσεσθε πᾶς ἀνὴρ ἰσχύων ἔξω τῆς πόλεως
καὶ δώσετε ἀρχηγὸν εἰς αὐτοὺς ὡς καταβαίνοντες ἐπὶ τὸ πεδίον
εἰς τὴν προφυλακὴν υἱῶν Ασσουρ, καὶ οὐ καταβήσεσθε. ³καὶ ἀναλα-
βόντες οὗτοι τὰς πανοπλίας αὐτῶν πορεύσονται εἰς τὴν παρεμβολὴν αὐτῶν καὶ ἐγεροῦσι τοὺς στρατηγοὺς τῆς δυνάμεως Ασσουρ·
καὶ συνδραμοῦνται ἐπὶ τὴν σκηνὴν Ολοφερνου καὶ οὐχ εὑρήσου-
σιν αὐτόν, καὶ ἐπιπεσεῖται ἐπ' αὐτοὺς φόβος, καὶ φεύξονται ἀπὸ
προσώπου ὑμῶν. ⁴καὶ ἐπακολουθήσαντες ὑμεῖς καὶ πάντες οἱ κατ-

---

deed.   WOUNDING lit. "wound" (εἰς τραῦμα)—a vivid but somewhat
awkward and inexact expression.
19. BECAUSE THY HOPE: ambiguous—1) men will remember thy realized
hope; 2) (more probably) the hope which was yours that God would
never forsake his people. Thus greatly blessed art thou BECAUSE.
FROM THE HEARTS OF MEN: in Hebrew thinking the heart is the center of
the intellectual life (cf. Gen 6 5, Prov 16 9) and the storehouse of his
memory (Prov 3 3).
20. THESE DEEDS: lit. "them" (αὐτά).   TO VISIT THEE: or "look with
favor upon (cf. 4 15).   FOR REASON OF THE HUMILITY: not that Judith
was not deterred because of her shame for the low estate of her nation;
rather, this humbled state of the nation was the spur to her action.
DIDST GO FORTH TO AVENGE: lit. "didst go out against + dat.   WALKING:
the aorist participle emphasizes that it was this specific act—not her
normal probity of life—which was right in the eyes of God.   AND ALL
THE PEOPLE SAID, "AMEN": cf. Deut 27 15-26 for this traditional phrase of
concurrent approval.

1. This display of the head of Holofernes on the wall is not unlikely
a reflection of the act of Judas in cutting off the head and right hand of

who did guide thee aright for the wounding of the head of the
prince of our enemies. ¹⁹Because thy hope will never depart
from the hearts of men as they remember the strength of God.
20 ²⁰May God make these deeds a perpetual exaltation for thee,
to visit thee with good, because thou didst not spare thine
own life for reason of the humility of thy people but didst
go forth to avenge our fall, walking in the straight path
before our God." And all the people said, "Amen, amen."

14 ¹And Judith said to them, "Hearken to me, I pray thee,
brethren, and take this head and hang it on the battlement
of your wall. ²And it shall be, as soon as morning dawns
and the sun comes forth upon the earth, that ye shall take
up your weapons of war, each of you, and ye shall go forth,
every able man of you, from the city and shall give them a
leader as though you were about to descend upon the plain
against the outpost of the children of Asshur, and ye shall
not descend. ³And these fellows will take up their arms and
go to their camp and will arouse the generals of the army
of Asshur; and they will rush to the tent of Holofernes and
will not find him; and fear will fall upon them, and they will
flee from before you. ⁴And do ye and all who dwell within

Nicanor and displaying them "just outside Jerusalem" (I Macc 7 47;
cf. II Macc 15 30ff.).
2. AND IT SHALL BE: the construction of this verse is very loose. These
introductory words (καὶ ἔσται) are scarcely predictive ("this will happen")
but hortative ("this shall be," i.e., "this is what is to be done") and make
the four future indicatives essentially imperatives. My translation
attempts to indicate the combination of 2nd pers. pl. verbs and pronouns
with inserted 3rd sing. subjects ("each of you"). Judith's speech may be
vivid, but it certainly is couched in the loosest sort of translation Greek.
  GIVE THEM A LEADER: another infelicity, which most modern translations have sought to english with such paraphrases as "set a
captain over them," but the awkward "them" remains.   AND YE
SHALL NOT DESCEND: of course, the "and" (καί) is a transparent overliteral rendering of the Hebrew ו, here with the adversative force "but."
3. THOSE FELLOWS: the demonstrative (οὗτοι) not only looks back to
the group just mentioned but may well have a pejorative overtone of
contempt.   THEY WILL FLEE: as did the troops of Nicanor—"When
his army saw that Nicanor had fallen, they threw down their arms and
fled" (I Macc 7 44). These resemblances are scarcely accidental.

οἰκοῦντες πᾶν ὅριον Ισραηλ καταστρώσατε αὐτοὺς ἐν ταῖς ὁδοῖς
5 αὐτων. ⁵πρὸ δὲ τοῦ ποιῆσαι ταῦτα καλέσατέ μοι Αχιωρ τὸν Αμ-
μανίτην, ἵνα ἰδὼν ἐπιγνοῖ τὸν ἐκφαυλίσαντα τὸν οἶκον τοῦ Ισραηλ
καὶ αὐτὸν ὡς εἰς θάνατον ἀποστείλαντα εἰς ἡμᾶς. ⁶καὶ ἐκάλεσαν
τὸν Αχιωρ ἐκ τοῦ οἴκου Οζια· ὡς δὲ ἦλθεν καὶ εἶδεν τὴν κεφαλὴν
Ολοφέρνου ἐν χειρὶ ἀνδρὸς ἑνὸς ἐν τῇ ἐκκλησίᾳ τοῦ λαοῦ, ἔπεσεν
ἐπὶ πρόσωπον, καὶ ἐξελύθη τὸ πνεῦμα αὐτοῦ. ⁷ὡς δὲ ἀνέλαβον
αὐτόν, προσέπεσεν τοῖς ποσὶν Ιουδιθ καὶ προσεκύνησεν τῷ προσώπῳ αὐτῆς καὶ εἶπεν Εὐλογημένη σὺ ἐν παντὶ σκηνώματι Ιουδα
καὶ ἐν παντὶ ἔθνει, οἵτινες ἀκούσαντες τὸ ὄνομά σου ταραχθήσον-
ται· ⁸καὶ νῦν ἀνάγγειλόν μοι ὅσα ἐποίησας ἐν ταῖς ἡμέραις ταύ-
ταις. καὶ ἀπήγγειλεν αὐτῷ Ιουδιθ ἐν μέσῳ τοῦ λαοῦ πάντα, ὅσα
ἦν πεποιηκυῖα ἀφ' ἧς ἡμέρας ἐξῆλθεν ἕως οὗ ἐλάλει αὐτοῖς. ⁹ὡς
δὲ ἐπαύσατο λαλοῦσα, ἠλάλαξεν ὁ λαὸς φωνῇ μεγάλῃ καὶ ἔδωκεν
10 φωνὴν εὐφρόσυνον ἐν τῇ πόλει αὐτῶν. ¹⁰ἰδὼν δὲ Αχιωρ πάντα,

---

7 ανελαβεν Aℵ 19 108 OL Sah | αυτης]αυτου 108 248

4. AS THEY FLEE: lit. "in their ways" (cf. 15 2).
5. BUT BEFORE YOU DO THIS: by these words the concluding chapter
of the story of Achior is not too felicitously introduced. Some see this
section misplaced. Vg makes it the conclusion of ch. 13, reserving the
account of Achior's conversion to Judaism to follow 14 1.4. That this
arrangement is secondary and an attempt to avoid the abruptness in
the common text is sure. Other difficulties remain. Aside from the fact
that Achior had to be specially summoned—seemingly all the others
in Bethulia had flocked to the gate—Judith's report of how she had
accomplished her mission follows her detailed directions for the military
move and is given primarily to Achior, not to Ozias and his fellow elders.
This arrangement may make the scene "more significant and colorful,"
as Fritzsche remarks, but it leaves some unanswered questions for the
reader. The whole episode is a necessary detail in the story: it gives
those in Bethulia necessary information about Holofernes' plans and
aids Judith in entangling Holofernes. The conversion of Achior is a
colorful addition and adds a vivid detail to the picture of Holofernes'
complete failure. But in addition the question is raised as to the reason
for making Achior an Ammonite. That this is incidental appears to me
improbable. Our author has not elaborated here. To his readers (unlike us)
the choice may have been obvious.
6. ONE OF THE MEN: lit. "in (the) hand of one man." The numeral "one"
is increasingly common in late Greek in the sense of the indefinite article.
ASSEMBLY: "gathering," rather than "council." BECAME AS ONE DEAD:

the borders of Israel follow and lay them low as they flee.
5 ⁵But before you do this, summon to me Achior the Ammonite,
that he may see and recognize the one who made of small
account the house of Israel and sent him to us, as he thought
for death." ⁶And they summoned Achior from the house of
Ozias, and when he came and saw the head of Holofernes
in the hand of one of the men in the assembly, he fell upon his
face and became as one dead. ⁷When they picked him up,
he fell at Judith's feet and did obeisance unto her and said,
"Blessed shalt thou be in every tent of Judah, and in every
nation those who hear thy name will be terror-struck. ⁸And
now tell me what thou hast done in these days." And Judith
told him in the midst of the people all that she had done from
the day she went forth until the moment she spake to them.
⁹When she had ceased speaking, the people shouted aloud
10 and gave cries of joy in their city. ¹⁰When Achior beheld

---

i.e., he fainted away, and not unnaturally, for the sight of Holofernes'
head meant his own release from the promised threat.
7. PICKED HIM UP: several mss read the singular ἀνέλαβεν, naturally
employing αὐτόν for αὐτόν, i.e., "when he came to" or "recovered."
This sense is excellent, but it is a palpable editorial improvement, easily
deduced from the common and better attested reading. Had it been the
original, it would scarcely have been altered.   DID OBEISANCE UNTO
HER: the common text προσεκύνησεν τῷ προσώπῳ αὐτῆς is almost certainly
due to the translator's misunderstanding of the Hebrew (cf. Gen 19 1)
or (cf. Num 22 31), in both of which cases the LXX translates προσεκύνησεν τῷ προσώπῳ (αὐτοῦ). In translating the Hebrew here the author
repeated the non-Greek idiom, but assumed the dative referred to the
one reverenced, thus adding αὐτῆς. It is of interest to note that both 108
and 248 read αὐτοῦ instead of αὐτῆς. Certainly no pronoun is needed
as the preceding phrase, HE FELL AT JUDITH'S FEET, guards against
misunderstanding. The Hebrew phrase, often completed by אַרְצָה, is
frequently used of reverent homage to another person.   IN EVERY
TENT OF JUDAH: Achior' word may well be reminiscent of the not unlike
adulation of Jael: "Blessed shall she be above women in the tent"
(Judg 5 24).
8. AND NOW TELL ME: that Judith makes her report—cf. ἀνάγγειλον
and ἀπήγγειλεν—to Achior in answer to his bidding and only incidentally
to her fellow townsmen is surprising, and the combination TOLD HIM
and SPAKE TO THEM is awkward. That this was early recognized is seen
in the not too felicitous variant λαλεῖ μετ' αὐτῆς (19, 108).

ὅσα ἐποίησεν ὁ θεὸς τοῦ Ισραηλ, ἐπίστευσεν τῷ θεῷ σφόδρα καὶ περιετέμετο τὴν σάρκα τῆς ἀκροβυστίας αὐτοῦ καὶ προσετέθη εἰς τὸν οἶκον Ισραηλ ἕως τῆς ἡμέρας ταύτης.

¹¹ʽΗνίκα δὲ ὁ ὄρθρος ἀνέβη, καὶ ἐκρέμασαν τὴν κεφαλὴν Ολοφέρνου ἐκ τοῦ τείχους, καὶ ἀνέλαβεν πᾶς ἀνὴρ τὰ ὅπλα αὐτοῦ καὶ ἐξῆλθοσαν κατὰ σπείρας ἐπὶ τὰς ἀναβάσεις τοῦ ὄρους. ¹²οἱ δὲ υἱοὶ Ασσουρ ὡς εἶδον αὐτούς, διέπεμψαν ἐπὶ τοὺς ἡγουμένους αὐτῶν· οἱ δὲ ἦλθον ἐπὶ τοὺς στρατηγοὺς καὶ χιλιάρχους καὶ ἐπὶ πάντα ἄρχοντα αὐτῶν. ¹³καὶ παρεγένοντο ἐπὶ τὴν σκηνὴν Ολοφέρνου καὶ εἶπαν τῷ ὄντι ἐπὶ πάντων τῶν αὐτοῦ ῎Εγειρον δὴ τὸν κύριον ἡμῶν, ὅτι ἐτόλμησαν οἱ δοῦλοι καταβαίνειν ἐφ᾽ ἡμᾶς εἰς πόλεμον, ἵνα ἐξολεθρευθῶσιν εἰς τέλος. ¹⁴καὶ εἰσῆλθεν Βαγώας καὶ ἔκρουσε τὴν αὐλαίαν τῆς σκηνῆς· ὑπενόει γὰρ καθεύδειν αὐτὸν
15 μετὰ Ιουδιθ. ¹⁵ὡς δ᾽ οὐθεὶς ἐπήκουσεν, διαστείλας εἰσῆλθεν εἰς τὸν κοιτῶνα καὶ εὗρεν αὐτὸν ἐπὶ τῆς χελωνίδος ἐρριμμένον νεκρόν, καὶ ἡ κεφαλὴ αὐτοῦ ἀφήρητο ἀπ᾽ αὐτοῦ. ¹⁶καὶ ἐβόησεν φωνῇ μεγάλῃ μετὰ κλαυθμοῦ καὶ στεναγμοῦ καὶ βοῆς ἰσχυρᾶς καὶ διέρρηξεν τὰ ἱμάτια αὐτοῦ. ¹⁷καὶ εἰσῆλθεν εἰς τὴν σκηνήν, οὗ ἦν Ιουδιθ κατα-

---

15 η κεφαλη αυτου αφηρητο] την κεφαλην αυτου αφηρημενην 13 108

---

10. WITH ALL HIS HEART: the translator's favorite word of intensity (σφόδρα = "exceedingly") is, as Cowley observed, "not very suitable here." UNTO THIS DAY: Vg understands this word to refer to his descendants: *et appositus est ad populum Israel, et omnis successio generis eius usque in hodiernum diem.* In his treatment of Achior the author is seemingly unconcerned with the prohibition of Ammonites from entry into the assembly of Y" "even to the tenth generation" (Deut 23 3).
11. CAME: ἀνέβη suggests the rise of the sun. IN GROUPS: that this word σπεῖρα (occurring only here and in II Macc 8 23 and 12 20 in the Greek OT and Apocrypha) is intended in the technical sense of "cohort" (Lat. *cohors* or *manipulus*) is doubtful; rather it would seem to mean simply "in large groups."
12. WORD WAS SPREAD: lit. "they sent hither and thither." SUPERIORS: the account is vivid. Word was raced by the soldiers to their squad leaders, who in turn repeated it to their superiors until all knew of the enemy's action.
13. TO THE ONE: Bagoas (cf. 12 11 where he is so described), as the next verse makes clear. The reading τῷ Βάγωᾳ occuring in several mss and reflected in Syr and OL is a secondary but correct gloss. THE SLAVES: some have conjectured a mistranslation here of העברים ("Hebrews")

all which the God of Israel had wrought, he believed in God with all his heart and got the flesh of his foreskin circumcised and was added to the house of Israel unto this day.

[11]When morning came, they hung the head of Holofernes from the wall, and each man took up his weapons, and they went forth in groups to the mountain passes. [12]When the children of Asshur saw them, word was spread to their superiors; and they in turn to the generals and chiliarchs and every other officer. [13]And they betook themselves to the tent of Holofernes and said to the one in charge of all his possessions, "Waken, now, our lord, for the slaves have dared to come down against us for battle, that they may be utterly destroyed." [14]And Bagoas entered and knocked on the curtain of the tent, for he supposed that he was sleeping with Judith.
15 [15]When no one paid heed, he parted the curtains and entered the chamber and found him thrown down upon the bedstool, dead, and his head had been taken from him. [16]And he cried out with a loud voice, with weeping and groaning and a loud cry, and rent his garments. [17]And he went into the tent where Judith had been lodging, and he did not find her. And he

---

read mistakenly as העבדים ("slaves"), and support their guess by the variants *filii Israel* or *Iudaei* in OL. But vs. 18, as Fritzsche properly insisted, with presumably the same epithet ("slaves"/"Hebrews") repeated and then immediately followed by "one Hebrew woman," makes this otherwise plausible suggestion unlikely. "Slaves" was a not unnatural characterization of their opponents by the Assyrians certain that their delayed defeat was now at hand. Cf. above p. 35.

14. CURTAIN: i.e., what closed the entry in place of a door and which was "parted," not "opened" (vs. 15).

15. PAID HEED: the reading ὑπήκουσεν ("answered") in several mss is a transparent editorial improvement.   BEDSTOOL: the word χελωνίς ("tortoise") is here used apparently of some article in the tent. Hesychius writes: χελωνίς: οὐδὸς τῆς θύρας τῆς σκηνῆς, apparently on the basis of this passage which he seemingly misunderstood. Since the bed was scarcely near the door, it is hard to see why the corpse should be found on the threshold, as Hesychius seems to understand. Possibly it is the stepstool, used in climbing up into bed, upon which the body sprawled when Judith tumbled it out.   AND HIS HEAD: the parataxis adds a vivid touch, reflecting Judith's act (13 8). Several mss (13, 108) attempt to smooth the style: τὴν κεφαλὴν ἀφηρημένην·

λύουσα, καὶ οὐχ εὗρεν αὐτήν· καὶ ἐξεπήδησεν εἰς τὸν λαὸν καὶ
ἐβόησεν ¹⁸'Ηθέτησαν οἱ δοῦλοι, ἐποίησεν αἰσχύνην μία γυνὴ τῶν
Ἑβραίων εἰς τὸν οἶκον τοῦ βασιλέως Ναβουχοδονοσορ· ὅτι ἰδοὺ
Ολοφέρνης χαμαί, καὶ ἡ κεφαλὴ οὐκ ἔστιν ἐπ' αὐτῷ. ¹⁹ὡς δὲ ἤκουσαν ταῦτα τὰ ῥήματα οἱ ἄρχοντες τῆς δυνάμεως Ασσουρ, τοὺς χι-
τῶνας αὐτῶν διέρρηξαν, καὶ ἐταράχθη αὐτῶν ἡ ψυχὴ σφόδρα, καὶ
ἐγένετο αὐτῶν κραυγὴ καὶ βοὴ μεγάλη σφόδρα ἐν μέσῳ τῆς παρεμβολῆς.

15 ¹Καὶ ὡς ἤκουσαν οἱ ἐν τοῖς σκηνώμασιν ὄντες, ἐξέστησαν ἐπὶ
τὸ γεγονός, ²καὶ ἐπέπεσεν ἐπ' αὐτοὺς τρόμος καὶ φόβος, καὶ
οὐκ ἦν ἄνθρωπος μένων κατὰ πρόσωπον τοῦ πλησίον ἔτι, ἀλλ'
ἐκχυθέντες ὁμοθυμαδὸν ἔφευγον ἐπὶ πᾶσαν ὁδὸν τοῦ πεδίου καὶ
τῆς ὀρεινῆς· ³καὶ οἱ παρεμβεβληκότες ἐν τῇ ὀρεινῇ κύκλῳ Βαιτυλουα καὶ ἐτράπησαν εἰς φυγήν. καὶ τότε οἱ υἱοὶ Ισραηλ, πᾶς ἀνὴρ

---

17 και εβοησεν] κραζων Β, λεγων ℵ

---

17. BURST FORTH...PEOPLE: lit. "leaped out to the people and cried."
In place of the paratactic καὶ ἐβόησεν, repeated from vs. 16, B reads
κράζων, an obvious stylistic improvement. Many editors, including
Holmes-Parsons and Fritzsche, somewhat surprisingly accept this
reading despite the fact that it is attested alone by B and introduces a
word not otherwise employed in Judith. The fact that it is manifestly
a stylistic improvement cannot fail to make its originality unlikely.
18. THE SLAVES: as in vs. 13 (q.v.) "Hebrews" would seem more likely,
but the immediately following ONE HEBREW WOMAN must render it
unlikely.   TRICKED US: the verb properly means "have disregarded
or set aside an oath or agreement." Apparently Bagoas uses it—the
absence of a direct object is surprising—in connection with Judith's
promise to Holofernes, which she has treacherously broken, thus applying
or attributing her act to the whole Hebrew people who have outwitted
or tricked them.   SHAME: disgrace. Unwittingly Bagoas is anticipating
the rout the Assyrians are to suffer.   ONE HEBREW WOMAN: once again
the pill is made more bitter—Our mighty nation has been worsted by
one individual, and that one a woman!   BEHOLD: the interjection,
as frequently, followed by a nominative (cf. ἰδού, ὁ ἄνθρωπος= ecce
homo). Once again in the climactic word, AND HIS HEAD IS NOT ON HIM!
our author shows himself to be a master at melodrama.
19. TUNICS: properly an undergarment, but often used of leather coats of
mail (for soldiers). Here the phrase would seem the translation of the
Hebrew קָרְעוּ בִגְדֵיהֶם. (I Kingd 20[21] 27).   THEIR CRIES: as the text stands,
there is no apparent change of subject; i.e., the cries were raised by the

burst forth and cried aloud to the people, ¹⁸"The slaves have
perfidiously tricked us! One Hebrew woman has brought
shame on the house of King Nabouchodonosor. Behold,
Holofernes on the ground, and his head is not on him!"
¹⁹When they heard these words, the commanders of the army
of Asshur rent their tunics, and were thrown into great
dismay, and their cries and shouts exceedingly great arose
in the midst of the camp.

15 ¹And when those who were in the tents heard, they were
aghast at what had come to pass, ²and fear and trembling
fell upon them, and there was not a man who longer stayed
to face his neighbor, but streaming forth with one accord
they sought to make their escape by every path in the plain
and the hill country. ³And those encamped in the hill country
about Bethulia also took to flight. And then the children
of Israel, every man of them who was a warrior, streamed

---

commanders. This would seem to be assumed in the next verse (15 1).
But the reference in 14 17 to the people (εἰς τὸν λαόν) would not seem
limited to the commanders. Nice points such as this were apparently of
no concern to the author, as he paints the scene of mounting confusion.

2. FEAR AND TREMBLING: a stereotyped phrase (cf. Exod 15 16).
STAYED TO FACE: a vivid picture of the pandemonium that resulted,
with all vestiges of military ordered vanished. The picture is clear but
the phraseology very definitely translation Greek.   STREAMING:
lit. "pouring forth" as a freshet. The same verb is repeated in the next
verse, and a compound in vs. 4. This is characteristic of the author:
to employ a word otherwise not used several times in the immediate
context or to echo an earlier statement.   WITH ONE ACCORD: perhaps
better, "with one common impulse," "simultaneously," for there was
no concerted plan. Attempts to understand the meaning of the word
by the fancied derivation of ὁμοθυμαδόν are pointless; the translator
simply seeks to render יחדיו. He may well have avoided using ἅμα or
ἐπὶ τὸ αὐτό, also common in the LXX for יחד, because the only thing
"in common" or "together" was their frantic attempt to escape, not
their common path, for one ran this way, another that. The vividness is
heightened by the conative force of the imperfect, SOUGHT TO MAKE
THEIR ESCAPE, which was tastelessly altered by some copyists to the
aorist.
3. THOSE ENCAMPED IN THE HILL COUNTRY: the Edomites ("children
of Esau"; cf. note on 7 8) and Ammonites (acc. to 7 18) had occupied

πολεμιστὴς ἐξ αὐτῶν, ἐξεχύθησαν ἐπ' αὐτούς. ⁴καὶ ἀπέστειλεν Ο-
ζιας εἰς Βαιτομασθαιμ καὶ Βηβαι καὶ Χωβαι καὶ Κωλα καὶ εἰς πᾶν
ὅριον Ισραηλ τοὺς ἀπαγγέλλοντας ὑπὲρ τῶν συντετελεσμένων καὶ
ἵνα πάντες ἐπεκχυθῶσιν τοῖς πολεμίοις εἰς τὴν ἀναίρεσιν αὐτῶν.
5 ⁵ὡς δὲ ἤκουσαν οἱ υἱοὶ Ισραηλ, πάντες ὁμοθυμαδὸν ἐπέπεσον ἐπ'
αὐτοὺς καὶ ἔκοπτον αὐτοὺς ἕως Χωβα. ὡσαύτως δὲ καὶ οἱ ἐξ Ιερουσαλημ παρεγενήθησαν καὶ ἐκ πάσης τῆς ὀρεινῆς, ἀνήγγειλαν
γὰρ αὐτοῖς τὰ γεγονότα τῇ παρεμβολῇ τῶν ἐχθρῶν αὐτῶν· καὶ οἱ
ἐν Γαλααδ καὶ οἱ ἐν τῇ Γαλιλαίᾳ ὑπερεκέρασαν αὐτοὺς πληγῇ μεγάλῃ, ἕως οὗ παρῆλθον Δαμασκὸν καὶ τὰ ὅρια αὐτῆς. ⁶οἱ δὲ λοιποὶ
οἱ κατοικοῦντες Βαιτυλουα ἐπέπεσαν τῇ παρεμβολῇ Ασσουρ καὶ
ἐπρονόμευσαν αὐτοὺς καὶ ἐπλούτησαν σφόδρα. ⁷οἱ δὲ υἱοὶ Ισραηλ
ἀναστρέψαντες ἀπὸ τῆς κοπῆς ἐκυρίευσαν τῶν λοιπῶν, καὶ αἱ κῶ-
μαι καὶ ἐπαύλεις ἐν τῇ ὀρεινῇ καὶ πεδινῇ ἐκράτησαν πολλῶν λαφύρων, ἦν γὰρ πλῆθος πολὺ σφόδρα.

⁸Καὶ Ιωακιμ ὁ ἱερεὺς ὁ μέγας καὶ ἡ γερουσία τῶν υἱῶν Ισραηλ
οἱ κατοικοῦντες ἐν Ιερουσαλημ ἦλθον τοῦ θεάσασθαι τὰ ἀγαθά,
ἃ ἐποίησεν κύριος τῷ Ισραηλ, καὶ τοῦ ἰδεῖν τὴν Ιουδιθ καὶ λα-
λῆσαι μετ' αὐτῆς εἰρήνην. ⁹ὡς δὲ εἰσῆλθον πρὸς αὐτήν, εὐλόγησαν

this position.   UPON THEM: commonly understood as "against" or
"after them." Apparently the figure is of a raging torrent engulfing them.
4. Three of these unknown towns were earlier mentioned (cf. 4 4, 6);
Kola, if it is different from Kona (4 4), only here. Further guesswork
about these localities is profitless. They are represented as near enough
to Bethulia to join in the butchery. PART: the literal meaning of
ὅριον—"bound," "border," "coast" (Cowley)—is apt to be misleading
(cf. 4 4); certainly so here. ὅριον, very common in the LXX, is the regular
translation of גְּבוּל, which though properly "bound," "limit," "border,"
is very often used of the territory within these bounds (Gen 10 19). So here
the meaning is "every place within the limits of Israel." AND TO BID:
the καί before the ἵνα clause makes the latter essentially correlative
with the preceding τοὺς ἀπαγγέλλοντας, which is scarcely a model for
Greek syntax, although clear and vigorous.
5. AS FAR AS CHOBA: Chobai in vs. 4 and Choba here are surprising.
Are they the same? Apparently the scribe of א thought so and omitted
the repetition. In 4 4 a Choba is mentioned with Jericho, Aesora, and
the vale of Salem. The reference to Damascus (vs. 5), together with the
descriptive ἐπέπεσον ἐπ' αὐτούς, raises the question if the author is not
borrowing from the account in Gen 14 15, where Abraham fell upon his
routed foes and pursued them ἕως Χωβα ἥ ἐστιν ἐν ἀριστερᾷ Δαμασκοῦ.
CAME: or perhaps "came to their aid" (παρεγενήθησαν). MEN: the
unexpressed subject may be understood as messengers from Bethulia;

forth upon them. ⁴And Ozias sent to Betomasthaim and Bebai and Chobai and Kola and to every part of Israel men to tell what had been accomplished and to bid them 5 all stream forth upon the enemy to destroy them. ⁵When the children of Israel heard, all with one accord fell upon them and set to cutting them to pieces as far as Choba. In like manner, both those from Jerusalem and from all the hill country came, for men had told them what had taken place in the camp of their enemies. And those in Gilead and those in Galilee outflanked them with great losses until they passed Damascus and its borders. ⁶And the rest of those who dwelt in Bethulia fell upon the camp of Asshur and despoiled them and became exceeding wealthy. ⁷When the children of Israel returned from the slaughter, they took possession of what was left, and the towns and villages in the hill country and in the plain got hold of much spoils, for the amount was exceedingly great.

⁸And Joakim the high priest and the council of the children of Israel who dwelt in Jerusalem came to behold the good deeds which Adonai had wrought for Israel and to see Judith and to hail her. ⁹And when they came to her, all with one

---

more probably it is simply the impersonal active in the sense of the passive.   IN THE CAMP: to the camp (?).   GREAT LOSSES: suffered by the routed Assyrians (THEY) as far north as Damascus.   ITS BORDERS: see comment on vs. 4.

6. THE REST: those who had not engaged in the sally recounted in 14 11. DESPOILED THEM: a few mss somewhat pedantically alter "them" to "it" since no Assyrians had remained.   AND BECAME EXCEEDINGLY WEALTHY: rifling the deserted camp, first by noncombattants and subsequently by the returning victorious heroes, is obviously very proper in the eyes of the author and no anticlimax to the godly patriotism which had so gloriously routed the foe. To the winner belongs the spoils, or, as the Deuteronomist styled it, "Do right and you will prosper." Thus very properly, once again, as when leaving Egypt (Exod 12 36), the spoiler is spoiled. Philosophy, not history, would seem to lie behind vss. 6-7 as the author tells his tale.

8. JOAKIM: see 4 6.   COUNCIL: see 4 8.   WHO DWELT: in apposition with Joakim and the council.   HAIL: or greet; lit. "speak peace," reflecting the Hebrew idiom (cf. Pss 28 3, 85 9, 122 8, Jer 9 7), natural from the use of "Peace" as a friendly salutation or greeting.

9. THEY CAME (in) TO HER: corrected by 58, 19, 108, Syr, OL to "she

αὐτὴν πάντες ὁμοθυμαδὸν καὶ εἶπαν πρὸς αὐτήν Σὺ ὕψωμα Ιερουσαλημ, σὺ γαυρίαμα μέγα τοῦ Ισραηλ, σὺ καύχημα μέγα τοῦ γένους
10 ἡμῶν· ¹⁰ἐποίησας ταῦτα πάντα ἐν χειρί σου, ἐποίησας τὰ ἀγαθὰ
μετὰ Ισραηλ, καὶ εὐδόκησεν ἐπ' αὐτοῖς ὁ θεός· εὐλογημένη γίνου
παρὰ τῷ παντοκράτορι κυρίῳ εἰς τὸν αἰῶνα χρόνον. καὶ εἶπεν πᾶς
ὁ λαός Γένοιτο. ¹¹καὶ ἐλαφύρευσεν πᾶς ὁ λαὸς τὴν παρεμβολὴν
ἐφ' ἡμέρας τριάκοντα· καὶ ἔδωκαν τῇ Ιουδιθ τὴν σκηνὴν Ολοφέρνου καὶ πάντα τὰ ἀργυρώματα καὶ τὰς κλίνας καὶ τὰ ὁλκεῖα καὶ
πάντα τὰ κατασκευάσματα αὐτοῦ, καὶ λαβοῦσα αὐτὴ ἐπέθηκεν ἐπὶ
τὴν ἡμίονον αὐτῆς καὶ ἔζευξεν τὰς ἁμάξας αὐτῆς καὶ ἐσώρευσεν
αὐτὰ ἐπ' αὐτῶν. ¹²καὶ συνέδραμεν πᾶσα γυνὴ Ισραηλ τοῦ ἰδεῖν
αὐτὴν καὶ εὐλόγησαν αὐτὴν καὶ ἐποίησαν αὐτῇ χορὸν ἐξ αὐτῶν,
καὶ ἔλαβεν θύρσους ἐν ταῖς χερσὶν αὐτῆς καὶ ἔδωκεν ταῖς γυναιξὶν
ταῖς μετ' αὐτῆς· ¹³καὶ ἐστεφανώσαντο τὴν ἐλαίαν, αὐτὴ καὶ αἱ
μετ' αὐτῆς, καὶ προῆλθεν παντὸς τοῦ λαοῦ ἐν χορείᾳ ἡγουμένη
πασῶν τῶν γυναικῶν, καὶ ἠκολούθει πᾶς ἀνὴρ Ισραηλ ἐνωπλισμέ-
νοι μετὰ στεφάνων καὶ ὕμνουν ἐν τῷ στόματι αὐτῶν. ¹⁴καὶ ἐξῆρχεν

---

came out to them," in reference to the dignity of the high priest.
EXALTATION: i.e., the cause or reason for the exaltation.   PRIDE:
lit. "boast." These words echo the elders' word of felicitation in 10 8.
10. IS WELL PLEASED: B substitutes for the indicative the optative
εὐδοκήσαι ("may God be pleased therewith"). This liturgical nicety,
suggested by the next phrase, is surely editorial. The author is quite
certain that the profitable triumph they have enjoyed is definitely
in consequence of God's entire approval and direct assistance.   EVER:
the addition of χρόνον gives the τὸν αἰῶνα an adjectival force akin
to εἰς τὸ νῦν (χρόνον). This phrase occurs several times in the LXX
(Isa 9 7, 13 20, 14 20, 18 7, Baruch 3 32) as the translation of varying
Hebrew terms. Not infrequently some mss omit χρόνον, as do 44 and 106
in this passage.
11. DESPOILED: = "sacked": another example of the author's repetition
of a word (ἐλαφύρευσεν) just previously used (λαφύρων, vs. 7) not otherwise
occurring in the book.   THIRTY DAYS: scarcely intended as a record
of the precise time but to suggest the thoroughgoing and complete job;
cf. our colloquial "for a month," and also this period in Dan 6 7, 12, Esth
4 11. The spoils given to Judith, as here listed, were a sizable collection.
With somewhat ponderous literalness several mss decide that one mule
was not sufficient to tote it away and so substitute the plural. Since
wagons were employed, probably more than one animal was needed.
Presumably what is meant is: she hitched up her mule(s) and wagons and
loaded on all the loot.   THEM UPON THEM: the spoils upon the wagons.

accord blessed her and said to her, "Thou art the exaltation
of Jerusalem, thou art the great glory of Israel, thou art
10 the great pride of our people. ¹⁰By thy hand hast thou done
all this, thou hast done a great deed for Israel, and God is
well pleased therewith. Mayest thou be ever blest in the
eyes of the Almighty." And all the people said, "Amen."
¹¹And all the people despoiled the camp for thirty days;
and they gave to Judith the tent of Holofernes and all his
silver vessels and the beds and the basins and all his gear;
and she took it and loaded it upon her mule, and yoked up
her wagons and piled them on them. ¹²And all the women
of Israel flocked to see her, and they blessed her, and some of
them made for her a dance; and she took branches in her hands
and gave them to the women with her. ¹³And they gar-
landed themselves with olive, she and the women with her,
and she went before all the people in the dance, leading all
the women, and all the men of Israel followed, wearing their
arms, crowned with garlands, with songs of praise on their
lips. ¹⁴And Judith began this hymn of thanksgiving in the

---

12. SOME OF THEM: ἐξ αὐτῶν (with τινὲς understood), equivalent to a
partitive genitive, increasingly common in koine Greek.　　FOR HER:
in her honor.　　BRANCHES: a surprising word, for strictly the thyrsos
(θύρσος) was a Bacchic wand, wreathed in ivy and carried by his devotees.
Hesychius remarks (very possibly with this passage in mind) that the
word could be used for a ῥαβδός or κλάδος. In addition to this passage
the word occurs in the LXX only once (II Macc 10 7).
13. WITH OLIVE: the olive branch was the especial symbol of peace,
joy, and thanksgiving (cf. Neh 8 15); but crowning themselves with olive
seems more a Greek than Hebrew usage. It is scarcely a primitive touch.
　　DANCE: in the OT the dance appears frequently in both sacred and
secular celebrations. It was a natural part of the celebration of a military
victory and the return of a hero (cf. Judg 11 34, I Sam 18 6). Apparently
most commonly it was performed by groups of women, but occasionally,
as in this instance, by both women and men. It was naturally regularly
accompanied by music, frequently by castanets in the hands of the
women. Not unnaturally, in a celebration where the exemplary Judith
was featured the music was a hymn of thanksgiving and praise.
14. BEGAN: prob. "led" (cf. 16 1).　　HYMN OF THANKSGIVING: strictly
"confession" of either sins or benefits. Here it is definitely the latter.
Frequently in the LXX ἐξομολόγησις renders תּוֹדָה, which may well be

Ιουδιθ τὴν ἐξομολόγησιν ταύτην ἐν παντὶ Ισραηλ, καὶ ὑπερεφώνει
πᾶς ὁ λαὸς τὴν αἴνεσιν ταύτην·

16 ¹Καὶ εἶπεν Ιουδιθ
   Ἐξάρχετε τῷ θεῷ μου ἐν τυμπάνοις,
   ᾄσατε τῷ κυρίῳ ἐν κυμβάλοις,
   ἐναρμόσασθε αὐτῷ ψαλμὸν καὶ αἶνον,
   ὑψοῦτε καὶ ἐπικαλεῖσθε τὸ ὄνομα αὐτοῦ,
   ²ὅτι θεὸς συντρίβων πολέμους κύριος,
   ὅτι εἰς παρεμβολὰς αὐτοῦ ἐν μέσῳ λαοῦ
   ἐξείλατό με ἐκ χειρὸς καταδιωκόντων με.
   ³ἦλθεν Ασσουρ ἐξ ὀρέων ἀπὸ βορρᾶ,
   ἦλθεν ἐν μυριάσι δυνάμεως αὐτοῦ,
   ὧν τὸ πλῆθος αὐτῶν ἐνέφραξεν χειμάρρους,

---

15 14 υπερφωνει B𝔸A] υπεφωνει ℵ 107 106 311 130 || **16** 2 οτι θεος]συ
ει ο θεος 58 OL Syr| κυριε 58 OL Syr

---

the case here.   IN THE MIDST OF ALL ISRAEL: not only is Judith for
the moment the center of all Israel's attention, but in her song she is,
as her name ("the Jewess") makes doubly appropriate, their mouthpiece.
   ECHOED: the text is uncertain, with both ὑπερεφώνει and ὑπεφώνει
attested. Both words are hapaxlegomena in the LXX. Certainly the
compound with ὑπερ- is surprising in this context, for the word properly
means "outbawl" or cry exceedingly loud. It is possible, but awkward
in the sense "sang with all their might." With ὑπο— it would mean
"echo" or "sing in answer" and would be most apt, especially if Judith
is represented as leading, if not actually lining-out, the hymn. Just
because it is the far easier reading and less likely to have led to the rival,
it must be regarded with caution, especially since the ms evidence for
ὑπερ- is far more impressive.

1. BEGIN: "strike up," "sing"; ἐξάρχετε is common in the LXX, as
the opening word of a song (Ps 147[146] 7; cf. Num 21 17), but this is
scarcely translation Greek as it is frequent in Homer, Hesiod, Pindar,
and Xenophon.   TIMBRELS: used by dancing females in both secular
and religious frolics. It was of the nature of a tambourine and was shaken
or beaten by hand.   CYMBALS: small percussion instruments held
either vertically or horizontally and struck together to produce a clashing
or clanging sound.   TALE OF PRAISE: i.e., a song with that content.
The common reading αἶνον is probably to be understood in the sense
of ἔπαινον. Mss A, N, and 107 read καινόν ("new"), which would be
most appropriate: God's deliverance has been so great that the old
songs are inadequate to express thanks or at least demand new verve

midst of all Israel, and all the people echoed this song of praise.

16 ¹And Judith said,
> "Begin unto my God on the timbrels,
> Sing unto Adonai with cymbals,
> Tune for him a psalm and tale of praise.
> Exalt his name and call upon it,
> ²For Adonai is a warrior;
> For into his camps in the midst of his people
> He delivered me from the hand of those who pursued me.
> ³Asshur came out of the mountains from the north;
> He came with the ten thousands of his host,
> Whose multitude stopped up the mountain torrents,

---

and enthusiasm. This is a frequent note in the OT—cf. Pss 33 3, 40 3, 96 1, 144 9, Isa 42 10. In vs. 13 ὕμνον καινόν is the common reading, with but slight attestation for καὶ αἶνον. Thus the suspicion is real that A's reading in vs. 1 is a scribal alteration to harmonize with καινόν in vs. 13, which latter may well have been a conscious reflection of the idiom in the psalms.   EXALT...IT: "exalt him and call upon his name."
2. ADONAI IS A WARRIOR: the Greek text has "A Lord who crushes wars"; cf. above 9 7. The Vulgate has *Dominus conterens bella, Dominus nomen illi*.58, Syr, and OL insert "thou art" and change κύριος to κύριε: "Thou art the God who crushes wars, O Lord." Some OL add *nomen est illi* ("the Lord is his name"). 44 and 106 delete the whole line.   FOR INTO HIS CAMPS...PURSUED ME: almost certainly the text is corrupt, but whether the corruption is due to faulty transmission or to an original misunderstanding of the Hebrew by the first translator appears to me uncertain. The various mss and vss show an unusual number of variants, obviously due to unsuccessful attempts to remedy the confusion. The translation offered appears to me the only rendering of the present text. That a translation should attempt to give a fictitious clarity to what is patently obscure is to me more than doubtful. It is possible to assume the meaning that God encamps with his people and that in his camp, to which he brings Judith back, there is safety as there was not in the camp of her enemies. This pious thought would reflect Ps 23, but it is at best eisegesis. It is equally possible that the original thought was a continuance of the preceding ascription of praise: "Our God crushes wars, destroying his enemies, and has done so by delivering me from the camp of Holofernes who had sought to violate me." But while this would make sense of words otherwise awkward, the sense has to be read in before it can be read out.
3. HOST: lit. "power," and regularly used in Judith in the sense of "army."   WHOSE MULTITUDE: lit. "of whom the multitude of them."

καὶ ἡ ἵππος αὐτῶν ἐκάλυψεν βουνούς·
⁴εἶπεν ἐμπρήσειν τὰ ὅριά μου
καὶ τοὺς νεανίσκους μου ἀνελεῖν ἐν ῥομφαίᾳ
καὶ τὰ θηλάζοντά μου θήσειν εἰς ἔδαφος
καὶ τὰ νήπιά μου δώσειν εἰς προνομὴν
καὶ τὰς παρθένους μου σκυλεῦσαι.
5   ⁵κύριος παντοκράτωρ ἠθέτησεν αὐτοὺς
ἐν χειρὶ θηλείας.
⁶οὐ γὰρ ὑπέπεσεν ὁ δυνατὸς αὐτῶν ὑπὸ νεανίσκων,
οὐδὲ υἱοὶ τιτάνων ἐπάταξαν αὐτόν,
οὐδὲ ὑψηλοὶ γίγαντες ἐπέθεντο αὐτῷ,
ἀλλὰ Ιουδιθ θυγάτηρ Μεραρι
ἐν κάλλει προσώπου αὐτῆς παρέλυσεν αὐτόν,
⁷ἐξεδύσατο γὰρ στολὴν χηρεύσεως αὐτῆς
εἰς ὕψος τῶν πονούντων ἐν Ισραηλ,
ἠλείψατο τὸ πρόσωπον αὐτῆς ἐν μυρισμῷ
⁸καὶ ἐδήσατο τὰς τρίχας αὐτῆς ἐν μίτρᾳ
καὶ ἔλαβεν στολὴν λινῆν εἰς ἀπάτην αὐτοῦ·
⁹τὸ σανδάλιον αὐτῆς ἥρπασεν ὀφθαλμὸν αὐτοῦ,

---

6 υπεπεσεν ΒΑ] επεσεν rell.

For this frequent redundancy, often unwarrantably styled a Hebraism, see comments on 7 10.

4. BORDERS: i.e., territory.

5. FOILED: brought to naught. This same word is used by Bagoaz (14 18) where the context suggests trickery, breaking their agreement. Here this element is not to the fore, but rather their downfall.

6. THEIR CHAMPION: the same ὁ δυνατὸς αὐτῶν is used to translate גבורם, "their champion," viz., the Philistine Goliath, by David (I Sam 17 51). The choice of phrase here is scarcely accidental.   FALL: the compound ὑπέπεσεν followed by ὑπό is very awkward, and most mss read ἔπεσεν. The strongest argument for ὑπέπεσεν is not that it is attested by B, A but that it is inconceivable as a scribal substitution for the apt ἔπεσεν.   YOUNG MEN: they were strong and able warriors; to have fallen at their hands would have been far less a disgrace than what befel him. This note—not only the defeat but the shameful loss of face—is almost the leit motif of the tale as the author pens it.   TITANS AND GIANTS: γίγαντες is the word regularly employed in the LXX to translate the several terms *Anakim, Nephaim,* and *Rephaim.* Presumably the out-of-place TITANS, scarcely likely on the lips of Judith, is because

And their horsemen covered the hills.

⁴He said that he would burn up my borders,

And slay my young men by the sword,

And would cast to the ground my nurslings.

And give my babes for spoils

And would despoil my maidens.

⁵Adonai Almighty hath foiled them by the hand of a
female.

⁶For their champion did not fall by the hand of young men,

Nor did the sons of the Titans smite him,

Nor did towering giants lay their hands upon him;

But Judith, the daughter of Merari,

Undid him by the beauty of her face;

⁷For she put off the garb of her widowhood

To raise on high those in distress in Israel.

She anointed her face with an ungent

And bound her hair with a tire

And took linen garb for his deceit.

⁹Her sandal ravished his eye,

---

two of these groups were mentioned in the Hebrew and thus two terms
were necessary. In II Sam 5 18 and as a variant: in 23 13 τῶν τιτάνων
is used to translate רפאים; also in two mss of Josephus at *Antt.* 7, 4, 1
(§ 71) τιτάνων is read instead of γιγάντων.   TOWERING: lit. "high,"
"tall," somewhat redundant when applied to giants. It may well reflect
the description of the "sons of the Anakim," viz., "great and tall" (Deut
9 2). The Hebrew גדול ורם is regularly μέγα καὶ πολύ, but ὑψηλοί would be
an accurate translation of רם. The probability would seem to be that in
the Hebrew original the reference was to sons of the Rephaim and Anakim.
Normally both words would have been rendered γίγαντες ("giants") in
Greek, but since both occur in the same context, τίτανες ("Titans") was
employed for one, for which rendering there was, as mentioned above,
earlier precedent.   UNDID: a vivid word, lit. "deprived him of his
strength," "disrupted him," "paralyzed him."

7. FOR: in explanation of Holofernes' undoing.   UNGENT: μυρισμῷ
(otherwise found only in Athenaeus, p. 547 F) means "an anointing":
several mss alter it to μύρῳ.

8. TIRE: or tiara (see 10 3).   TOOK: selected; this heightens the picture
of her deliberate and careful preparation, as the prosy "she put on a
linen dress" does not.

9. SANDAL: in this quick résumé of Judith's astute choices of garb

καὶ τὸ κάλλος αὐτῆς ἠχμαλώτισεν ψυχὴν αὐτοῦ,
διῆλθεν ὁ ἀκινάκης τὸν τράχηλον αὐτοῦ.

10 ⁱⁿ⁰ἔφριξαν Πέρσαι τὴν τόλμαν αὐτῆς,
καὶ Μῆδοι τὸ θράσος αὐτῆς ἐταράχθησαν·
¹¹τότε ἠλάλαξαν οἱ ταπεινοί μου,
καὶ ἐφοβήθησαν οἱ ἀσθενοῦντές μου καὶ ἐπτοήθησαν,
ὕψωσαν τὴν φωνὴν αὐτῶν καὶ ἀνετράπησαν·
¹²υἱοὶ κορασίων κατεκέντησαν αὐτοὺς
καὶ ὡς παῖδας αὐτομολούντων ἐτίτρωσκον αὐτούς,
ἀπώλοντο ἐκ παρατάξεως κυρίου μου.
¹³ὑμνήσω τῷ θεῷ μου ὕμνον καινόν
Κύριε, μέγας εἶ καὶ ἔνδοξος,
θαυμαστὸς ἐν ἰσχύι, ἀνυπέρβλητος·
¹⁴σοὶ δουλευσάτω πᾶσα ἡ κτίσις σου·
ὅτι εἶπας, καὶ ἐγενήθησαν·
ἀπέστειλας τὸ πνεῦμά σου, καὶ ᾠκοδόμησεν·
καὶ οὐκ ἔστιν ὃς ἀντιστήσεται τῇ φωνῇ σου.

---

10 εταραχθησαν] ερραχθησαν B ℵ
11 εφοβηθησαν BℵA 542 249] εβοησαν rell. OL Syr
14 ωκοδομηθησαν ℵ

---

sandal is entirely appropriate (cf. Song 7 1, Ezek 16 10).   SWORD:
see 13 6; while our translator has a very large vocabulary and does not
hesitate to use it to the full, he deliberately repeats key words when
referring back to what has previously been said or done.
10. TERROR-STRUCK: in place of ἐταράχθησαν B, ℵ * read ἐρράχθησαν
("shattered," "overthrown"). Fritzsche feels the common reading an
anticlimax after SHIVERED. To me TERROR-STRUCK is more apt and a
neater parallel. The real problem is that ἐρράχθησαν is less obvious an
alteration; that is, it is easier to see this less common word being altered to
one so apt than is the reverse; and our translator has already used
ῥάσσω (9 8). The passive of neither verb is properly followed by an accusative. This apparently led to the occasional omission of the verb, making
τὸ θράσος depend, like τὴν τόλμαν, on ἔφριξαν.   PERSIANS AND MEDES:
a strange slip by the author, for according to him the opponents were
Assyrians. Nabouchodonosor had sent to Persia demanding support
against Arphaxad (1 7), but his army could scarcely be so constituted
or described. Nabouchodonosor had defeated the Medes (1 12.15). The
mention of Persians naturally led to the counterbalancing "and Medes."
11. This verse is easily misconstrued because of the change of subject.
The opening words refer to the Hebrews who raised a shout of triumph
and a cry of joy at the rout of the enemy; with the words WERE FILLED

> Her beauty made captive his soul,
> The sword passed through his neck.
> 10   ¹⁰Persians shivered at her daring,
> And Medes were terror-struck at her boldness.
> ¹¹Then my humble ones raised their shout of triumph,
> And my weak ones uttered their cry;
> And (the enemy) were filled with dismay.
> They raised their voices and were turned in panic.
> ¹²The sons of maidens pierced them through
> And wounded them as fugitives' children;
> They perished from the battle line of Adonai.
> ¹³I will sing to my God a new song:
> Adonai, great and glorious art thou,
> Marvelous of strength, invincible.
> ¹⁴Let all thy creation serve thee,
> Because thou didst speak, and they were made.
> Thou didst send forth thy spirit, and it builded them;
> And there is none who wilt withstand thy voice.

WITH DISMAY (καὶ ἐπτοήθησαν) the subject is shifted to the terror = struck enemy, who in their panic raised their cry of terror. Thus ἐβόησαν, read by many minuscules and reflected in Syr and OL, is to be preferred to ἐφοβήθησαν which latter apparently reflects ἐπτοήθησαν.

12. SONS OF MAIDENS: sons of still young mothers and so mere children themselves—in sharp contrast to "sons of Titans and tall giants" of vs. 6.   FUGITIVES' CHILDREN: or with a slight shift (-ας for -ων) "runaway slaves."   THEY PERISHED FROM: this literal translation English tries to reproduce the equally obvious translation Greek which in turn reflects the very common Hebrew phrase, "they shall perish from the land" (cf. Deut 4 26, 11 17, Josh 23 13, 16). It is apt here. This destruction came from the very thing of which they were so contemptuous (5 23).   BATTLE LINE: the army of the Lord of Hosts was Israel. The Assyrians' expectation of worsting it and making the land theirs had dramatically failed; instead destruction and death had come forth.

13. A NEW SONG: see 16 1.   INVINCIBLE: the adjective, while common in classical Greek, occurs only here in the LXX. It is another example of the translator's wide vocabulary. What the Hebrew word it sought to translate is uncertain.

14. THY SPIRIT: God's word (Gen 1) is here personified as the creative agent, and is apparently the subject of the following BUILDED, which latter (without an object) is awkward. ℵ alters to the passive "and they were built"; cf Pss 33 6-9, 104 30.   VOICE: in Hebrew thinking a word once spoken takes on a life of its own and accomplishes its purpose

15   ¹⁵ὄρη γὰρ ἐκ θεμελίων σὺν ὕδασιν σαλευθήσεται,
        πέτραι δ᾽ ἀπὸ προσώπου σου ὡς κηρὸς τακήσονται·
        ἔτι δὲ τοῖς φοβουμένοις σε,
        σὺ εὐιλατεύσεις αὐτοῖς.
        ¹⁶ὅτι μικρὸν πᾶσα θυσία εἰς ὀσμὴν εὐωδίας,
        καὶ ἐλάχιστον πᾶν στέαρ εἰς ὁλοκαύτωμά σοι·
        ὁ δὲ φοβούμενος τὸν κύριον μέγας διὰ παντός.
        ¹⁷οὐαὶ ἔθνεσιν ἐπανιστανομένοις τῷ γένει μου·
        κύριος παντοκράτωρ ἐκδικήσει αὐτοὺς ἐν ἡμέρᾳ κρίσεως
        δοῦναι πῦρ καὶ σκώληκας εἰς σάρκας αὐτῶν,
        καὶ κλαύσονται ἐν αἰσθήσει ἕως αἰῶνος.

        ¹⁸ʽΩς δὲ ἤλθοσαν εἰς Ιερουσαλημ, προσεκύνησαν τῷ θεῷ, καὶ
        ἡνίκα ἐκαθαρίσθη ὁ λαός, ἀνήνεγκαν τὰ ὁλοκαυτώματα αὐτῶν καὶ
        τὰ ἑκούσια αὐτῶν καὶ τὰ δόματα. ¹⁹καὶ ἀνέθηκεν Ιουδιθ πάντα τὰ
        σκεύη Ολοφέρνου, ὅσα ἔδωκεν ὁ λαὸς αὐτῇ, καὶ τὸ κωνώπιον, ὃ

---

15 ετι BℵA]επι pl. | ευιλατευσεις]ιλατευσ. ℵ, ευιλατευεις B

---

by its own innate power. This potentiality of the word may well have
aided in its more serious personification.
15. WITH THE WATERS: the obscurity of this phrase has led to the
conjecture "like waters" (Goodspeed), but the ὡς ("like") in the next
line makes this at best uncertain. Not improbably the author is reflecting
here Ps 18, where both figures appear: "The foundations also of the
mountains quaked" (vs. 7); "Then the channels of waters appeared,
and the foundations of the world were laid bare" (vs. 15). Our author
combines them: the mountains were shaken by ("with") the waters
that laid the foundations bare.   MELT LIKE WAX: a clear reminiscence
of Ps 97 5.   PROPITIOUS: these two concluding lines of vs. 15 have
many minor obscurities. The opening word ἔτι ("still"), read by B, ℵ, A, is
awkward and is not improbably a correction of ἐπί, to avoid the incon-
sistent ἐπὶ τοῖς φοβουμένοις and αὐτοῖς. The verb εὐιλατεύσεις is apparently
a hapax—at least Liddell-Scott do not list it, and the only mention of
it in Lampe's *Patristic Greek Lexicon* is a solitary occurrence in the 7th
cent. John of Thessaly. ℵ deletes the εὐ-, while B reads it as a present.
16. All offerings and sacrifices, regardless of size and cost, are in themselves small and inconsequential in the eyes of the God; it is the attitude
of the man who offers them that makes them of moment. Attempts to
read into these lines a minimizing of acts demanded by the law are
quite unwarranted in the light of Judith's almost excessive care for their
fulfillment; cf. also 16 18.
17. The song ends with the prediction of certain doom and torment
for the foreign nations who have risen against the people of God. At the

15   ¹⁵For the mountains will be shaken from their foundations
with the waters,
And before thy face rocks will melt like wax;
But to them who fear thee wilt thou be propitious.
¹⁶Because every sacrifice for a sweet savor is a little thing,
And all fat for a whole burnt offering is to thee exceed-
ingly small;
But he who fears Adonai is forever great.
¹⁷Woe to the gentiles which rise up against my people;
Adonai Almighty will take vengeance upon them in the
day of judgment,
To give to their flesh fire and worms,
And they will wail forever alive to the pain."
¹⁸Now when they came to Jerusalem, they worshiped God, and when the people were purified, they offered their whole burnt offerings and their freewill offerings and gifts. ¹⁹And Judith dedicated all the vessels of Holofernes which the people had given her; and the canopy, which she had taken for her-

---

day of final judgment they will be given over to unceasing torment. The imagery—unquenchable fire and consuming worms—reflects Isa 66 24: "their worm shall not cease, neither shall their fire be quenched," and Ecclus 7 17: "for fire and worms are the punishment of the ungodly," notably in the case of Antiochus Epiphanes (II Macc 9 9). These pictures are endlessly expanded in the apocalyptic writings, notably Enoch, IV Ezra, and the NT Apocalypse. That the specific mention of the eternity of this punishment (ἕως αἰῶνος) indicates that the author has broken with earlier orthodoxy and is reflecting the Pharisees' point of view is at best uncertain. Rather it would seem a rhetorical flourish or heightening of phrases long familiar.

18. NOW WHEN THEY CAME: the mention of the arrival in Jerusalem seems to the modern reader abrupt, for there has been no reference to a departure from Bethulia, but only the loading of the wagons (15 11). Apparently the author intends the dances and songs of triumph, not as an act in Bethulia, but descriptive of the festal pilgrimage to Jerusalem.
     PURIFIED: from their contact with the dead bodies of the routed enemy.

19. VESSELS: stuff or gear, viz., the various objects mentioned in 15 11.
CANOPY: the repeated mention of this object—she had displayed it along with the head of Holofernes (13 5)—suggests that aside from its considerable intrinsic value it was particularly appropriate to be hung up in the temple as had been the head on Bethulia's walls.   FOR

ἔλαβεν ἑαυτῇ ἐκ τοῦ κοιτῶνος αὐτοῦ, εἰς ἀνάθημα τῷ θεῷ ἔδωκεν.
20 ²⁰καὶ ἦν ὁ λαὸς εὐφραινόμενος ἐν Ιερουσαλημ κατὰ πρόσωπον τῶν ἁγίων ἐπὶ μῆνας τρεῖς, καὶ Ιουδιθ μετ' αὐτῶν κατέμεινεν.

²¹Μετὰ δὲ τὰς ἡμέρας ταύτας ἀνέζευξεν ἕκαστος εἰς τὴν κληρονομίαν αὐτοῦ, καὶ Ιουδιθ ἀπῆλθεν εἰς Βαιτυλουα καὶ κατέμεινεν ἐπὶ τῆς ὑπάρξεως αὐτῆς· καὶ ἐγένετο κατὰ τὸν καιρὸν αὐτῆς ἔνδοξος ἐν πάσῃ τῇ γῇ. ²²καὶ πολλοὶ ἐπεθύμησαν αὐτήν, καὶ οὐκ ἔγνω ἀνὴρ αὐτὴν πάσας τὰς ἡμέρας τῆς ζωῆς αὐτῆς, ἀφ' ἧς ἡμέρας ἀπέθανεν Μανασσης ὁ ἀνὴρ αὐτῆς καὶ προσετέθη πρὸς τὸν λαὸν αὐτοῦ. ²³καὶ ἦν προβαίνουσα μεγάλη σφόδρα καὶ ἐγήρασεν ἐν τῷ οἴκῳ τοῦ ἀνδρὸς αὐτῆς ἔτη ἑκατὸν πέντε· καὶ ἀφῆκεν τὴν ἅβραν αὐτῆς ἐλευθέραν. καὶ ἀπέθανεν εἰς Βαιτυλουα, καὶ ἔθαψαν αὐτὴν ἐν τῷ σπηλαίῳ τοῦ ἀνδρὸς αὐτῆς Μανασση, ²⁴καὶ ἐπένθησεν αὐτὴν οἶκος Ισραηλ ἡμέρας ἑπτά. καὶ διεῖλεν τὰ ὑπάρχοντα αὐτῆς πρὸ τοῦ ἀποθανεῖν αὐτὴν πᾶσι τοῖς ἔγγιστα Μανασση τοῦ

---

21 εις βαιτ.] pr. εις τον οικον αυτης אּ

HERSELF: possibly simply as indirect object; more probably it is in contrast to the other things which her grateful fellow townsmen had given her: this she had taken with her own hand, and so it was doubly hers to offer as a VOTIVE OFFERING, which meaning ἀνάθημα apparently has here. This word occurs frequently in the LXX—the variant spelling -ημα and -εμα is apparently without significance. It is the normal translation of חרם; cf. Lev 27 28.

20. BEFORE THE SANCTUARY: grammatically the adjective might be regarded as masculine ("holy men"), but it is far more probable as a term for the temple—its building and surrounding courts (cf. 4 12).

FOR THREE MONTHS: a surprisingly long time; Syr substitutes "for a month of days."

21. EACH MAN...TO HIS INHERITANCE: apparently reflecting Josh 1 15.

TO BETHULIA: אּ laboriously prefixes "to her house."   IN HER TIME: during the rest of her life. It is possible that ἐγένετο has here its proper force "became" and that the author means "her fame spread as time went on throughout the land."

22. KNEW HER: had intercourse with her (cf. Matt 1 25). RSV avoids the common idiom by the delicate paraphrase "she remained a widow."

GATHERED TO HIS PEOPLE: for this idiom cf. Gen 25 8. This term came to be the stereotyped phrase for the departure of a revered man.

23. The Greek is here very obscure. Most interpreters understand the adjective "great" in the sense "great in fame," and render the phrase "and her fame grew even greater." This appears to me improbable.

self from his bed, she gave to Adonai for a votive offering. ²⁰And the people continued their celebration of joy in Jerusalem before the sanctuary for three months, and Judith remained with them.

After these days each man returned to his inheritance, and Judith went back to Bethulia and remained on her own estate; and she was famous in her time throughout the land. ²²And many desired her, but no man knew her all the days of her life, from the day when Manasseh her husband died and was gathered to his people. ²³And she advanced very greatly in years and reached the age of a hundred and five years in the house of her husband. And she set her favorite handmaid free. And she died in Bethulia, and they buried her in the cave of her husband Manasseh, ²⁴and the house of Israel mourned for her seven days. And she had divided her possessions before she died among all those closest to Manasseh her

---

The verb προβαίνω is common in Greek of every period in the sense of advancing in age. The absence of any indication to the contrary suggests that "great" is to be understood of her age, not her fame; the second half of the sentence would then be a deliberate synthetic parallelism. With this may be compared the prophetess Anna (Luke 2 36) who "was of great age."   A HUNDRED AND FIVE YEARS: if, as has been frequently remarked, Judith is the author's own creation, this unusual age is not to be seen as reflecting historical tradition but as due to the author. For a possible explanation see Appendix I.   CAVE: a common place of interment throughout the history of Palestine; cf. Abraham (Gen 25 9) and Lazarus (John 11 38).

24. HOUSE OF ISRAEL: all Israel.   SEVEN DAYS: the customary period acc. to Hebrew practice; cf. Ecclus 22 12: "mourning for the dead lasts seven days." This was the period Joseph mourned for his father Jacob, once they had reached Palestine (Gen 50 10), although, acc. to Egyptian custom, there had been a period of seventy days (Gen 50 3). Seven days was the period of mourning for Saul and his sons (I Sam 31 13, I Chron 10 12). In the case of Moses and Aaron the mourning lasted thirty days (Deut 34 8, Num 20 29).   SHE HAD DIVIDED HER POSSESSIONS: this portion of the narrative is told with the utmost economy of words. How long before her death this division was made is not indicated; nor is there any indication in the codes known to us regarding the division of the property of a widow who died without children. What part of her husband's property had come to her is not indicated (8 7). Apparently the intent is to indicate that in this final deed, as throughout her life, she had acted in strict compliance with the law (cf. Num 27 6.11).

25 ἀνδρὸς αὐτῆς καὶ τοῖς ἔγγιστα τοῦ γένους αὐτῆς. ²⁵καὶ οὐκ ἦν
ἔτι ὁ ἐκφοβῶν τοὺς υἱοὺς Ισραηλ ἐν ταῖς ἡμέραις Ιουδιθ καὶ μετὰ
τὸ ἀποθανεῖν αὐτὴν ἡμέρας πολλάς.

---

25 fin.]+ αμην B 19 108|| Subscr. ιουδειθ BℵA

---

25. B adds "Amen" as it does to Tobit. Vg adds a final verse to the
effect that a festival commemorating Judith's act was inaugurated:

25 husband and those who were closest of her own kin. ²⁵And there was no longer any who spread fear among the children of Israel throughout the days of Judith and for many days after she had died.

Dies autem victoriae huius festivitatis ab Hebraeis in numero sanctorum dierum accipitur, et colitur a Judaeis ex illo tempore usque in praesentem diem. Nothing is known of any such festival; this coda seems a palpable reflection of Esth 9 ₂₇ff. Some are inclined to see in this word of Jerome a reference to the feast of Hanukkah. Cf. above p. 37.

JUDITH THE WIDOW

That Judith was an historical figure to whom traditions bore word of some notable deed, even if by now replete with legendary accretion, appears to me unlikely. Her name Judith—"a Jewess"—is transparent. While the book is no allegory, nonetheless again and again in this romantic tale where the leading figure is a woman—and a widow—the author, while never losing sight of the good story he is creating and its key figure, lets her reflect unobtrusively true Jewish piety. This is notably so in the concluding psalm of ch. 16 where Judith conspicuously personifies all Israel as she leads—almost lines-out—the chant which the obedient chorus repeats. But Judith is the author's own creation. That Jael who slew Sisera in her tent in the course of the notable conflict where Deborah had played so leading a part is the prototype of Judith appears to me certain. Several of the details in the two stories are worth mentioning: the assembly of the tribes at the insistence of Deborah, the assembly of Nabouchodonosor's army; the triumphal song of Deborah and Judith, not to mention Miriam.

There are numerous places where familiarity with the story of Esther may well be reflected in this touch or that in the tale of Judith. Conspicuous here are the prolonged beauty treatment which Esther undergoes at the hands of Hegai the chamberlain prior to her reception by the king and the care of Judith by Bagoas when she was in the camp of Holofernes. But, in addition, is it not likely that the almost overemphasis on Judith's devout godliness and concern for even more than the letter of the law in her personal habits, with the lengthy insistence upon her carrying her own proper diet and utensils, is in quiet correction of the almost scandalous disregard for such matters in the Hebrew Esther? Judith corrects a patriotism like Esther's with her never-failing regard for a ceremoniously correct life. Nor at this spot should one forget Daniel's scruples against eating the king's meats and dainties. These touches do not appear accidental but indicative of familiarity and use of the earlier tales.

It is often overlooked that Judith is a widow. It appears to me well worth considering whether this is not a deliberate and purposed touch by the author. There is really no especial need that Judith be a widow. No such detail is found in the stories of Jael, Deborah, the woman of Thebez (Judg 9 53), or the wise woman of II Sam 20 14.22, all of whom may well have combined to suggest to the author the propriety of having a woman once more as the one who delivered Israel. Judith is another Deborah who will rise a mother in Israel, another Jael who will slay the enemy of God in the tent, another Miriam who will break forth into singing at the discomforture of the enemy. But why a widow? Perhaps the presence of a husband would have been an awkward hurdle

for our storyteller, but an unmarried prototype of Joan of Arc would certainly have been equally convenient. Why this emphasis that she is a widow and a descendant of Symeon, whose bloody deed is heartily approved and applauded in somewhat sharp contrast to the original account in Genesis? Since numerous other emphases in the book suggest a date well beyond the Maccabean days, it is to my mind far from improbable that this choice is deliberate as a reflection of Alexandra, idealized in the eyes of later Pharisees under the name Salome, who ruled for nine years (78-69) as queen, weathering the storm which her husband, Alexander Jannaeus, had made ominously likely. Her brother,[1] Simon ben Shetach, a leading Pharisee, may well have been her confidant and adviser. That the Pharisees were in actual control during her reign, as they later popularly believed, is far from probable; that she had given them far more voice than they had had during the reign of her husband is likely. While no act of Alexandra is to be seen as prompting the story, it does seem to me not unlikely that the author casts his heroine, unlike the other famous heroines of Israel's history, out of compliment to this doughty queen. That this would suggest that he wrote during the nine-year reign and did so to gain favor is possible but perhaps improbable. One detail has escaped most interpreters of the book. Judith died at the age of 105 (16 23). If, as certainly seems probable, this precise figure is not to be seen as "external tradition" known to the author but as "internal inference," that is, as is commonly the case, a guess, the question rises, Why this not particularly natural choice of years? It was in 168 that the mad act of Antiochus Epiphanes started the Maccabean revolution; it was in 63 that Pompey's advent in Jerusalem ended the reign of the Hasmonean successors of the Maccabees. This period (168-63) was precisely 105 years in length. The ground is a bit more solid under our feet and free from the perils of sacred arithmetic when we note that the way Judith addresses the elders of Bethulia and issues unqualified directions and commands is rather more natural for a queen than from a laywoman, wealthy and pious though she might be. The years following the advent of Rome may not seem a likely time for the composition of the book, which might seem to some, as does Esther, to have been written in a time of prosperity when foreign foes were for the moment neither in control nor feared. On the other hand, it is conceivable that in the author's mind is the prayerful hope, later to be expressed as the concluding word of some of the midrashic versions of Judith and of the Megillath Antiochus: "May God in his mercy work signs and wonders in this time and at this hour as he has done in the days of our fathers." While in no sense a call to arms, the book may well be intended as a call to renewed and confident hope. God is not dead nor one to desert his people so long as their loyal obedience is manifest.

---

[1] So styled in Berakot 48a.

מעשה יהודית:

ויהי בימי אליפורני מלך יון מלך גדול וחזק והוא כבש מדינות רבות ומלכים חזקים והחריב טירוות והיכליהם שרף· באש· בשנת עשר שנים למלכותו שם פניו לעלות ולכבוש ירושלים עיר הקדש וקיבץ ק"ך אלפי שולפי חרב וצ"ב אלף בעלי חצים ויאמר המלך אליהם הנה עם בני ישראל אשר בירושלים משנים בדתיהם ואת דתי המלך אינם עושים בקרבם ולא ימיש מרחובם תוך ומרמה עתה קומו ונקומה עליהם למלחמה ולא יזכר שם ישראל עוד· ויען מלך א' אשר היה כבוש תחת ידו במלחמה ויאמר לו חדל לך המלך מאלהי עולם אלהי ישראל אלהי האלהים ה' גבור מלחמה מושל בגבורתו עולם עיניו תצפינה הסוררים להלחם עם עמו ונחלתו לא ימלט· ולא עוד אלא שכל א"ה נקראים נכרים וישראל הם עם קרובו ומי יגש ויערב אל לבו להלחם עמם· לך התבונן במלכים הראשונים שעברו על שפשטו ידיהם בישראל מה עלתה בהם כמו פרעה וסנחריב ויתר המלכים נבול נבול אתה וכל העם אשר ברגליך ולא תוכל להלחם בישראל אשר מנשרים קלו מאריות גברו הלא המה הגברים אשר מעולם אנשי שם· ויהי כשמוע אליפורני המלך את דברי המלך ההוא ויקצף המלך מאד וחמתו בערה בו לאמר מי זה ואיזה הוא אשר מלאו לבו לאמר כי עם בני ישראל רב וعצו ממני ואשר כח בהם לעמוד בפני חיילי רבים כחול הים ומי בכל אלהי הארצות אשר הצילו את ארצם מידי כי יציל ה' את ירושלים מידי ויחר אפו מאד ויצו לייסר את המלך ההוא בשפטים גדולים כי דיבר סרה על עוצם חייליותיו לאמר כי לא יעצרו כח בפני עם בני ישראל ויצו המלך לאנשי הצבא לאוסרו בנחשתי ולהוליכו אל מחנה העברים לירושלים באף ובחמה ובקצף גדול לאמר ככה יעשה לאיש אשר דיבר טוב על ישראל קום לך אתם ואם באבדי את ישראל תפול גם עתה כמוהם כנפול בני עולה ויקחו אותו עבדיו ויביאו אותו מחנה ישראל פתח שערי ירושלים וישבו אל אדוניהם· והמלך בא ברחובות ירושלים אסור בכבלי ברזל וימצא שם שרי צבאות ישראל עוזיהו בן מיכה וכרמי ותמנו איש אל אחיו וישאלו את פיו ויספר להם את כל אשר קרהו על כי דיבר טוב על ה' ועל ישראל עמו ואשר צוה המלך למסור אותו ביד ישראל להמיתו בחרב בהריק חרבו בישראל ואשר אמר ארדוף אשיג אריק חרבי תורישמו ידי וחירף מערכות אלהים חיים לאמר מי בכל אלהי הארצות אשר הציל את ארצו מידי כי יציל ה'

את ירושלים. ויהי כשומעם שרי ישראל את דברי המלך רעדה אחזתם שם חיל
כיולדה ויבאו אל מקדש ה' וישתחוו לה' בבכי ובצעקה גדולה ומרה לאמר ה'
אלהי ישראל יושב הכרובים אתה הוא האלהים לבדך לכל ממלכות הארץ אתה
עשית את השמים ואת הארץ הטה ה' אזנך ושמע פקח עיניך וראה ושמע דברי
אליפורני אשר חירף מערכות אלהים היים ומלך עולם אמנם ה' החריבו מלכי
אשור את העכו"ם ואת ארצם ונתנו את אלהים באש כי לא אלהים המה כי מעשה
ידי אדם עץ ואבן ויאבדם ועתה ה' אלהינו הושיענו נא מידו שפוך חמתך על הגוים
אשר לא ידעוך ועל הממלכות אשר בשמך לא קראו כי לא תעזוב הבוטחים בשמך
וכי תשפיל הגבר אשר הובטח באדם ובגבור' הסוס יבטח. ויהי כבלות את תפלתם
לפני ה' נחמו את המלך ההוא וידברו על לבו לאמר ה' אלהינו ואלהי אבותינו
אשר הודעת את שמו ואת גבורת ו יהיה מגן עזרך והוא יראך את מפלת האויב הרע
הזה בנקום ה' אלהינו נקם נקמת בני ישראל ויהי ה' עמך ואתנו תשב כטוב בעיניך
ובא עוזיהו וקבלו בביתו ויעש לו משתה גדול ואח"כ נתקבצו כל העם ויתפללו
כל הלילה שואלי' עזר מאת ה':

ויהי ממחרת היום הזה צוה אליפורני לעלות למלחמה עליהם והעם הרגליים
אנשי חיל היו ק"ך אלפים איש והפרשים י"ב אלפים נתקבצו יחדיו בכח גדול
וביד חזקה נגד בני ישראל. וכאשר ראו בני ישראל את ריבויים ישבו על הארץ
ויעלו עפר על ראשם ויצעקו בני ישראל אל ה' להושיעם מיד אויביהם ויקחו את
כלי זיניהם וישבו בדרכים הצרים אשר בהם נתיב ההר וישמרו אותם יומם ולילה.
ואליפורני בלכתו סביב ההר מצא סילוני המים אשר חוץ לעיר ויצו לנתוש ולנתוץ
ולהאביד ולהרוס אותם. ויבואו חיילי הצבא אל המלך לאמר לו כי בני ישראל
אינם בוטחים לא בחנית ולא בחיצים ולא בקשת אפס ההרים הרמים וכל הגבעות
מחזיקים אותם ואתה למען תוכל להם בלי מערכת מלחמה שום תשים שומרים על
מקורי המים לבלתי יוכלו לעלות מים מהמה ואתם בצמא ותמית אותם בצמא מבלי חרב אז
ימסרו לך את העיר מפני הצמא. וייטב הדבר בעיני המלך ולפני כל שלישיו וישם
מסביב שרי מאות על מקורי המים ויהי לעשרים יום אחרי שומו משמרת
זאת נתמעטו המים מהבורו' ומהפלגו' לכל יושבי ירושלי' ויצמא העם למים ויאספו
בני ישראל אל עוזיהו כל האנשים והנשים בחורים ונערים יחד כולם פה א' לאמר
ישפוט אלהים ביניכו וביניך כי הרעותה לנו ומאנת לענות מפני המלך ועל כן ימסור
אלהים אותנו בידיהם ואין עוזר ונפלנו לעיניהם ברוב הצמאון ועתה נמסור עצמנו
בלב שלם למלך. הלא טוב לנו לעבוד לה' והיינו עבדים לאליפורני ממותנו בצמא
ומהיותנו דראון לכל בשר בראותנו בנינו ובנותינו מתים לפנינו מעידים אנחנו היום
את השמים ואת הארץ ואת אלהי אבותינו הפוקד עלינו כפי עונותינו כי תמסרו
תכף ומיד את העיר ביד חיל האויב ונמות מהרה לפי חרב. ויהי כשומעם את צעקת

בני ישראל כל שרי צבאות ישראל צעקו צעקה גדולה ומרה ויבכו בכי גדול תוך
ההיכל ויצעקו אל ה' קול א' לאמר חטאנו עם אבותנו העוינו הרשענו אלהים אל
דמי לך אל תחרש ואל תשקוט אל כי הנה אויביך יהמיון ומשנאיך נשאו ראש על
עמך יערימו סוד ויתיעצו על צפוניך לכו ונכחידם מגוי ולא יזכר שם ישראל
עוד אשר אמרו נרשה לנו את נאות אלהים כי נועצו לב יחדיו עליך ברית יכרותו·
אלא האל אב הרחמן חמול על עמך ועל נחלתך ואל תמסור בני בריתך
ביד העמים אשר לא ידעוך למה יאמרו הגוים איה אלהיהם וברוב גאונך תהרוס
קמיך עשה להם כמדין כסיסרא כיבין בנחל קישון נשמדו בעין דאר היו
דומן לאדמה שיתמו נדיבמו כעורב וכזאב וכזבח וכצלמונע כל נסיכמו· וכאשר
כלו הצעקות והבכי קם עוזיהו ועיניו זולגות דמעה ויאמר אליהם חזקו ויאמץ
לבבכם אחי ונקוה חסד מה' עוד ה' ימים אולי ישוב חרון אף ה' ויתן כבוד לשמו
ואם אחרי ה' ימים לא יושיע ה' לנו נעשה כאשר דברתם:

ויהי כשמוע את הדברים האלה יהודית האלמנה בת בארי והיא היתה יראת
ה' מאד ותעש לה יהודית בעליות ביתה חדר מיוחד להתפלל בה ותשב שם
עם נערותיה והיא היתה מענה בצום נפשה כל ימי חייה והיא היתה יפת תואר
מאד ותהי יהודית נושאת חן בעיני כל רואיה כי היתה יראת את ה' והיא כאשר
שמעה כי דבר עוזיהו למסור את העיר אחר ה' ימים שלחה לקרוא את הכהנים
חברי וכרמי ויבאו אליה ותאמר אליהם יהודית מה זה הדבר אשר חשב עוזיהו
לעשות למסור את העיר ביד האויב אם לא יבא ישועתנו תוך ה' ימים ומי אתם
נסיתם את ה' לא זו הדרך לקבל חסד המקום ב"ה רק להעיר חרון אף ה' האפס
לנצח חסדו כי שמתם גבול לחסדיו ולרחמיו לשום לכם יום כפי בחירתכם חלילה
לסור מאחרי ה' חסדי ה' כי לא תמנו כי לא כלו רחמיו טוב ויחיל ודומ' לתשועת
ה' כי לא יזנח לעולם ה' כי אם הוגה ורחם כרוב חסדיו רגע ידבר על
גוי ועל ממלכה ונחם על הרעה ועתה לכו ונשבוה אל ה' כי ארך אפים הוא ונשאלה
ממנו סליחה וכפרה על זה העון ובצום ובבכי ונשבה אל אלהינו כי ירבה לסלוח ועת
צרה הוא ליעקב וממנו יושע וכאשר נבהלה נפשינו מפני זדונם כן נגילה ונשמחה
בישועתו כי לא הרשענו כאבותנו אשר עזבוהו ויקטרו לאלהים אחרים· ועל כן נמסרו
לחרב ולשבי ולחרפה ולכלימה ביד שונאיהם ואנחנו לא נדע אל אחר זולתו
אלהינו אין עוד מלבדו והוא ידרוש דמינו מיד קמינו למען כבד שמו ועתה אחי
אתם הכהנים לה' ונפש כל עמו ישראל תלויות בכם ואתם חזקו ויאמץ לבבכם ולב
כל ישראל לאמר אליהם כי אבותינו הובאו בנסיון לנסות אותם אם באמת אהבו
את ה' אלהיהם ואתם תאמרו אליהם כי אברהם אבינו עמד בנסיונו של מקום וה'
אהבו וכן יצחק ויעקב ומשה ושאר האבות נמצאו נאמנים לפני ה' ביסורין· וכל
מי שלא עמד בנסיון ביראת ה' והתלוננו לפני ה' נגפו לפני המשחית וימותו במכת

הנחשי' ועתה התכוננו וראו כי כאשר ייסר איש את בנו ה' אלהינו מיסרנו ולמות
לא נתננו בעבור שמו הגדול והנורא:

וּיאמרו אליה עוזיהו והכהנים צדק כל אמרי פיך אין בהם נפתל ועקש נואלנו
ואשר חטאנו לשום גבול לישועת ה' ולכן העתר בעדינו כי ישרה ויראת את ה' את·
ותאמר להם יהודית אנכי אתפלל לה' בעדיכם· וגם אתם העתירו אל ה' בעדי
להקים את עצתי אשר חשבתי לעשות לנקום נקמת בני ישראל מאת היונים ולכן
לעת ערב תעמדו בשערי העיר ואצא אני ושפחתי עמי בלילה ואתם אל תחקרו
ממני אנה אני בא אפס כי תמיד תהיה תחינתכם בפיכם לה' אלהי ישראל לפקוד
את עמו בעבור כבוד שמו· ויאמר אליה עוזיהו לכי לשלום ואלהי ישראל יתן את
שאלתך אשר שאלת מעמו ויהי ה' עמך לנקום אותנו מאויבינו אמן· ויהודית נכנסה
בחדרה ותלבש שק ואפר ותעל עפר על ראשה ותשתחוה לה' ותשפוך את נפשה
בצום ובבכי ותתפלל לפני ה' וכה אמר בתפלתה ה' אלהי שמעון אבי אשר שמת
בידו חרב להתנקם מהנכרים אשר טמאו וגילו את ערות דינה אחותם ונתת את
נשיהם בשבי ואת בנותיהם וכל שללם לבוז ביד עבדיך אשר קנאו את קנאתך פקדני
נא ה' אלהי כרוב חסדך כי כל דרכיך צדק ומשפטיך תהום רבה והבט נא את
מחנה האויב הרע הזה אשר חירף מערכות אלהים כאשר ראיתה את מחנה מצרים
ברודפם חמושים אחרי ישראל עמך ונחלתך אשר בטחו במרכבותיהם ובסוסיהם
וברוב חילם והשקפת על מתניהם והבהלת אותם במחשכים תהומות יכסיומו ירדו
במצולות כמו אבן במים אדירים כמזהב יהיו גם אלה ה' אלהי הבוטחים על חילם
וברכב ובפרשים ובחיצים ובקשת המתהללים בחניתותיהם ולא ידעו ולא יבינו
כי אתה ה' אלהינו ה' איש מלחמות יעיר קנאה יריע אף יצריח על אויביו יתגבר
חשוף זרוע גבורתך כבראשונה ושפוך כאש גבורתך אל הגוים אשר לא ידעוך ועל
ממלכות אשר בשמך לא קראו אשר אמרו נרשה לנו את נאות אלהים לבא במקדש
ולטמא היכל קדשיך ולנתק קרן מזבחך אנא ה' עשה למענך אם לא למעניגו חרבם
תבא בלבם וקשתותם תשברנה ולצר הצורר הרע הזה אליפורני המלך קדמה פניו
הכריעיהו וילכד בפת עיניו לאהוב אותי ותחלהו בחולי החשק בי ותן בנפשי חזק
למאסו ובידי כח ואל להשמידו יפלו במכמוריו רשעי· יחד אנכי עד אעבר· ויהי·
זה זכר לשמך הגדול כי תמכור אותו ה' אלהי ביד אשה ואתה ה' לא בגבורת הסוס
תחפץ ומלכות זדן לעולם שנאת שועת עניים אתה תשמע צעקת הדל תקשיב
ותושיע חנני שמע תפלתי ושומעי האזינה אל דמעתי אל תחרש ותן דבר בפי ועצה
בלבי לקיום בית מקדשך למען ידעו כל הגוים כי אתה אלהים חיים ואין זולתך
אלהים:

ויהי ככלות יהודית להתפלל לה' את כל התפלה והתחנה הזאת ותקם
מן המקום אשר השתחותה שמה לה' מכרוע על ברכיה וכפיה פרושות השמים

ותקרא את שפחתה ותבא אל היכל ביתה ותסר בגדי אלמנותה והשק מעליה
ותרחץ את גופה ומשחה עצמה בשמן המור ותקלע את קלעות שערותיה ותשם כתר
על ראשה ותלבש בגדים יקרים מוזהבים ותכשיטי' חריטים ושהרוני' ועגילי'
וטבעות ותיפה את עצמה בכל תמרוקי הנשים וכ"ד קישוטיה וה' נתן לה זיו ויופי
הרבה למצוא חן בעיני כל רואיה ותתן ביד אמתה שפחתה נאד חלב וחמת
יין וצלוחית שמן וקמח ולחם וגבינה ותלך לה וכאשר באה אל שערי העיר, ומצאה
את עוזיהו ואת הכהנים המקוין אותה שמה ותעבור לפניהם ויאמרו לכי לשלום
ואלהינו יתן חן וחסד בעיני כל רואיך ויתן לך כלבבך וכל עצתך ימלא לטובה
ותתהלל עליך ירושלים עיר הקדש ותהי שמך בכלל החסידי' ובמספר הצדיקי'
ויענו כל העם אשר שם אמן ותצא יהודית מן העיר ההיא ואמתה:

ויהי כאשר ירדו מן ההר בעת עלות השחר פגעו בה משומרי המלך אליפורני
ויתפשוה לאמר מאין באתה ואנה תלכי ותאמר אליהם יהודית מבנות העברים אנכי
ואברח בהחבא מאתם כי ידעתי כי ימסרו בידכם ולכן חשבתי אצלי לאמר אלכה
נא לי לפני שער אליפורני לגלות לו סודות עם היהודים ולהורות לאנשי הצבא
את הדרך ילכו בה ואת המעשה אשר יעשון ללכוד את העיר ולתופשה ולא יפול
ממחנהו עד א'. וכאשר שמעו את דבריה האנשים אשר תפשוה הביטו את תוארה
ויפיה והמה ראו כן תמהו מנוגם אמרותיה במועצות ודעת ויאמרו אליה
ברוך טעמך כי חלצת נפשך ממות וחכמת בעצתך לבא אל אדונינו ותדע באמת כי
בעמדך לפניו ייטב לך ותמצא חן וחסד בעיניו ויביאו אותה למלך ומיד כאשר
באת לפניו וישא המלך את עיניו וירא את יפיה וזיו הדרה בערה בו אש
החשק והתאוה ויחלה המלך מחולי החשק וכל שריו ועבדיו הפרתמים היושבי'
לפני המלך אמרו מי אשר ימאס עם העברי', אשר יש להם נשים יפות כאלה ומי
לא ילחם עמהם בעבורם וכאשר ראתה יהודית את המלך יושב על כסא מלכותו
השתחוה לו אפים ארצה ויקימוה עבדי המלך כי כן מצות אדוניה'. אז אמר לה
המלך תגילי ותשמחי בלבבך ואל תיראי כי לא אחפוץ במות כל אשר יחפוץ
לעבדני ולא הייתי מרים חרבי ותניחותי על עמך אם לא מאסוני ועתה תאמרי נא
לי על מה נסת וברחת מעמהם ותברחי לבא אלינו. ותאמר לו יהודית אנחנו חטאנו
לפני ה' אלהינו ולכן דבר ביד הנביאים אל העם לייסר אותם על עוונת ועל כן
בני ישראל פחדו ממך כי חטאו לפני ה' אלהיהם וכבד הרעב בהם והנה נחשבו
כמתים מפני הצמאון עד אשר הסכימו לשחוט את צאניהם ולשתות את דמם וחשבו
להתיר את הקדשים אשר צוה ה' אלהיהם בשמירתם ושלא יהנו מהמה בחטים ביין
ובשמן. ואם המה יעשו זה המה יאבדו ואתה תעמוד. וכאשר ידעתי זה אני אמתך נסתי
מאתם ושלחני אלהים להגיד לך ואולם אנכי יהודית אמתך עובדת את ה' אלהי
גם עתה בהיותי אצלך. אשר על כן אנכי אצא ג' פעמים ביום ואתפלל לפני ה'

אלהי ואתנפל לפני אלהי והוא יגיד לי מתי ישלם להם כפעולם וכרוע מעללותם
ואבא ואגיד לך ואעבורך בכל חוצות ירושלים ויהיו כל עדת בני ישראל כצאן
אשר אין להם רועה ולא יחרץ כלב לשונו נגדך כי כל זה נאמר לי במראות
האלהים ולמען חרון אף ה׳ שולחתי להגיד לך כל זה. וייטב הדבר בעיני המלך
ובעיני כל עבדיו ויראו האנשים ויתמהו בראות חכמתה כי רבה ויאמרו איש אל
רעהו אין אשה משכלת כזאת בכל הארץ ביופי בחן ובשכל. ויאמר לה המלך
הטיב אלהים עמך אשר שלחך לפני למען תמסור את עמך בידינו ובעבור דבריך
הטובים אם כה יעשה לי אלהיך. אלהיך אלהי והוא תהיה ראשונה במלכות ויהי
שומעך בכל הארץ. ויצו המלך להביא אותה בבית נכותו ויצו להאכילה מעל
שלחנו ותאמר לו יהודית לא תוכל אמתך לאכול מאשר צוית לתת לי פן יקראני
אסון אבל אוכל מאשר הבאתי עמי ויאמר אליה המלך ואם יחסר לך את אשר
הבאת לך עמך מה נעשה לך. ותאמר יהודית חי נפשך אדוני שלא יחסר לי זה עד
אשר יקים ה׳ את דברי אשר חשבתי לעשות. ותשאל עוד בעת בואה אל
האהל רשות לצאת בלילה ובעת עלות עמוד השחר חוץ מן המחנה להתפלל לה׳
אלהיה ג׳ ימים ויצו המלך את אנשיו להניחה ולעשות כל חפצה ולצאת ולבא להתפלל
לפני ה׳ אלהיה ותצא בכל לילה ולילה מחוץ למחנה לטבול את גופה תוך ברכת
המים ובעלותה מלטבול שפכה את נפשה בבכי ואנקה לפני ה׳ ישראל
לישר את דרכה בישועת עמה ובאה אל האהל בטהרתה ותאכל בסעודת הערב:

ויהי ביום הג׳ ויעש המלך משתה גדול לכל שריו ועבדיו ויאמר אל סריסו שומר
הפלגשים לאמר לך נא ראה אם תוכל לפתות ולרצות את יהודית הזאת שתבא
אליה ואז בא הסריס אל יהודית ויאמר אליה אל תבושי ואל תכלמי לבא אל אדוני
ואולי ייטב לך לאכול ולשתות עמו ותאמר לו יהודית מי אנכי אשר אמנע מאדוני
כל אשר ייטב לו וכל הישר בעיניו אעשה כי כל אשר יחפוץ אדוני המלך הוא טוב
לי כל ימי חיי. ותקח ותלבש בגדי תפארתה ותבא ותעמוד לפניו ויהי כראות המלך
את יפיה תכף הוכה ונחלה מאהבתו אותה ויאמר לה המלך אכלי לחמך בשמחה
ושתי בלב טוב טוב יינך כי מצאת חן בעיני. ותאמר לו יהודית אשתה אדוני כי שמח לבי
ויגל כבודי היום שמחה רבה מכל ימי חיי ותשב ותאכל ותפתח את נאד החלב
ותשת וגם את המלך השקתה וישמח ויגל המלך עמה מאד וישתה יין הרבה מאד
ממה ששתה כל ימי חייו:

ויהי אח״כ הלכו כל עבדי המלך איש איש על מקומו ויסגור סריס המלך את
דלתי האוהל אשר שם יהודית עם המלך וילך לו. ויהודית לבדה באהל עם המלך
במטתו ישן כמת ותאמ׳ יהודית אל אמתה לעמוד בחוץ לשמור לפני האהל
ותעמוד יהודית לפני המטה ותתפלל בדמעות רק שפתיה נעות וקולה לא ישמע
וכה אמרה בתפלתה חזקני ה׳ אלהי ישראל ואנקמה את נקמת עבדיך ישראל לחזק

בריחי שערי ירושלים עיר מקדשך סמכני באמרתך ואל תבישני משברי בחוזק
עוזך· וככלותה להתפלל קרבה אל העמוד אשר בראש מטתו ושלפה חרבו של
אליפורני עצמו אשר היה תלוי בעמוד ובשולפה את החרב תפשה אותו משערי
ראשו ותאמר חזקני נא ה' האלהים והכתה פעמים צוארו ותתכה את ראשו ותשלח
את אמתה ותקח את כלי מלחמתו אשר היו תלויים בעמודים והכתה את כל גופו
מכף רגל ועד ראש אין בו מתום פצע וחבורה ומכה טריה ותבא ותתן ראש אליפורני
ביד שפחתה לשום אותה באמתחתה· ותצאנה שתיהן יחדיו כמנהגן להתפלל
ותעבורנה את כל המחנות ואין פוצה פה ומצפצף עליהן כי כן צוה עליהן המלך
ובסובבן את העמק באו בשערי העיר ותאמר אל שומרי החומות מרחוק
בקול ששון ובקול שמחה פתחו שערים כי עמנו אל אשר עשה הישועה הגדולה
הזאת בישראל:

ויהי כאשר שמעו את קולה אנשי העיר ויקראו את כהני ה' ויאספו כולם מגדול
ועד קטן יצאו לקראתם בשמחה ובשירים ובהלל ובהודות לה' ובהדליקו נרות בכל
חוצות ירושלים ובחצריהם ובטירותם עטרו כולן בבגדים חמודים וכלי יקר ואבנים
טובות ומרגליות לכבוד ולתפארת ויביאו את יהודית אל תוך העיר בשמחה גדולה
כי חשבו לבלתי ראות פניה עוד ויסובבוה כל ישראל סביב· ותעל יהודית במקום
גבוה ותהס את כל העם· ויהס העם עמדו לא ענו עוד· ואז ענתה יהודית בקולה
קול עוז לאמר הללו ירושלים את ה' הללי אלהיך ציון כי חזק בריחי שעריך
בירך בניך בקרבך הללו הללו את ה' אלהינו הללוהו בגבורותיו הללוהו כרוב גודלו
אשר לא עזב חסדו ואמתו למיחלים לחסדו ועשה חסד ביד שפחתו וימכור ה' ביד
אשה שפחתו לשונא ועוכר ישראל בלילה הזה· ותוציא מאמתחת· את ראש האויב
צורר היהודים אליפורני הרשע· ועתה אחי חי ה' כי שמרני מלאך ה' בצאתי מכאן
וביושבי שמה ובשובי הנה ולא נטמאתי והביאני ה' אלהיכם אליכם בשמחה
ובישועה והמליט נפשי בישועכם הודו לה' כי טוב כי לעולם חסדו: וכל ישראל
השתחוו לה' אפים ארצה ויאמרו אליה ברוך ה' אשר בידך השפיל אויבינו
המחרף והמגדף מערכות אלהים כל גוים סבבונו בשם ה' כי אמילם דחה דחיתנו
לנפול וה' עזרנו כי לא בזה ולא שיקץ ענות עני ולא הסתיר פניו ממנו ובשועו אליו
שמע· ועוזיהו נשיא ישראל אמר אליה ברוכה את לה' עליון מכל הנשים מנשים
באהל תבורך ברוך ה' אשר ברא את השמים ואת הארץ ואשר הצליח את דרכיך
להביא ראש מלך אויבנו צורר היהודים והגדיל היום את שמך ולא ימוש
זכר תהלתך מפי כל האנשים אשר יזכרו את חסדי ה' לעולם כי לא חמלת על
נפשך בעת צרה ויגון עמך· ויענו כל העם אמן ואמן· ויקראו אל המלך אשר היה
עומד בבית עוזיהו אשר דיבר טוב על ישראל ותאמר לו יהודית ה' אלהי ישראל
אשר הודעת את שמו ואת גבורתו ואמרת כי הוא יקום נקמתנו מאויבנו הנה הוא

יתברך שבר ראש כל הרשעים בלילה הזה בידי ולמען תדע כי כן הוא הנה ראש
אליפורני אשר בזדון ובעזות לבו מאס את אלהי ישראל וישטום אותך להרגך
לאמר כאשר נכה עם ישראל מוכה תפול ביניהם וחרבי יעבור בך· וכאשר ראה
המלך החסיד ההוא את ראש אליפורני ויפול על פניו ארצה ויאמר כן יאבדו כל
אויבך ה׳ ויפול על רגל יהודית וישתחוה לה ויאמר אליה ברוכה את מאלהיך בכל
אהלי יעקב כי כל גוי ועם ועם אשר ישמע את שמעך יהללו עליך את שם ה׳ אלהי
ישראל:

ותאמר יהודית אל כל העם שמעו נא לי אתי ועמי ותלו את הראש הזה
על ראש חומותינו והיה כאשר יזרח השמש ולקחתם כל אחד מכם את כלי זייניכם
ותצאו בתרועת מלחמה ואל תרדו למטה אפס כי תקעתם ותריעו ובכן שומרי
החומה וילכו אל שר חילם לעוררו למלחמה וכאשר יבאו השרים באהל אליפורני
וימצאו אותו מגולל בדמו עליהם אימתה ופחד ובראותכם אותם בורחים
רדפו מהם אחריהם בחזוק כי ה׳ יתן אותם תחת רגליכם· וכן עשו בני ישראל כאשר
האיר היום תלו על ראש החומות את ראש האויב הצורר ויקח כל איש ואיש את
כלי מלחמתו בידו ויצאו ויתקעו והריעו תרועה גדולה וכאשר ראו כן שומרי
החומות באו באהל מלכם אליפו׳ והשמיעו קול גדול בפתח האהל להעירו וכאשר
באו השרים והשלישים אמרו לסריסים לא עת התמהמה לכו ועוררו את המלך כי
יצאו העכברים מחוריהם ופיתו אותנו למלחמה ואז דחק ונכנם סריס המלך שומר
הפלגשים באהל אליפורני ויעמוד לפני קלעי מטתו ויספוק את כפיו אולי ישן הוא
ויקץ כי חשב כי עודינו ישן עם יהודית וכאשר לא הרגיש דבר קרב אל המטה ויסר
את הקלעים וירא גוף אליפורני מושלך ארצה ומגולל בדמו וראשו איננו ויצעק
צעקה גדולה בבכי ויקרע את בגדיו ויבא באהל יהודית ולא מצאה ויצא החוצה
אל העם ויאמר אליהם אשה א׳ עברית עשתה רעה גדולה הזאת והנה אדונינו
המלך מת ומושלך על הארץ ומגולל בדמו וראשו איננו וכאשר שמעו כן שרי החיל
קרעו כולם את בגדיהם ויפול עליהם אימה ושכיכה גדולה ותהי צעקה גדולה
ומרה במחנותם:

וכאשר שמעו כל החיל כי נהרג ומת גבורם יצאה מהם כל עצה ויברחו כולם
מפני הפחד והיראה ובברחם מלפני העברים הרודפים אחריהם חמושים עזבו כל
רכושם וינוסו במשעול הכרמים ובנתיבות ההרים וכאשר ראו כן בני ישראל ירדומן
ההרים וירדפו אחריהם וירדפו בתרועת חצוצרות ובקול שופר חזק מאד והיו
מכים את כל הנמצאים מכה גדולה מכת חרב וירדפום עד החורמה ויתר העם
ירדו אל מחנה האויב וישללו את כל שלל שללם מאד הרבה מאד אין מספר
בצאן ובבקר ברכב ובסוס ובכל מטלטלי אליהם וכולם נתעשרו מגדול ועד קטן
משלליהם ובזמן ל׳ יום לא נשלם שללם אשר שללו בני ישראל רק כל

עושר אליפורני וכל רכושו ניתן ליהודית זהב וכסף ומרגליות ואבני יקר אשר לו
הכל ניתן לה מאת העם:

ואל המלך אשר בבית עוזיהו אשר דיבר טוב על ישראל בראות הנם אשר עשה
ה' אלהי ישראל עזב מעבוד האלילים והאמין בה' וימול את בשר ערלתו ובא
לחסות תחת כנפי השכינה הוא וכל ילידי ביתו עד היום הזה· וכל עדת
ישראל ששים ושמחים עם יהודית ותצאן כל הנשים אחריה בתופי· ובמחולות והיו
אומרות הודו לה' כי טוב כל"ח את יהודית אם בישראל את תהלת ירושלים את
שמחת ישראל את כבוד עמינו כי עשית בכח וחזק ואמץ לבך ויד ה' היתה עמך
לחזק אותך ומבורכת תהיה לעולם ויען כל העם אמן ואמן וזקנים עם נערים ישמחו
יעלצו במצלתים ובנבלים:

ותשר יהודית את השירה הזאת לה' ותאמר הללו את ה' בתוף שירו לה' במחול
שירו לו שיר חדש הודו וקראו בשמו· ה' איש מלחמה ה' שמו ה' אלהים גדול אתה
ונורא בכח ואין דומה לך כל הבריות יעבדוך ויודוך ה' כל מעשיך כי אמרת ותהי
ושלחת את רוחך ונבראו· ההרים והיסודות ירעשו וכדונג נמסו מלפני גבורתך ימינך
ה' נאדרי בכח ימינך ה' תרעץ אויב מי כמוך באלים ה' מי כמוך נאדר בקדש נורא
תהלות עושה פלא:

ואז אחר התשועה הגדולה הזאת כאשר נטהרו כל ישראל העלו כולם עולות
וזבחי' ונדרים ויהודית הקדיש את כל שללה לבית האלהים ויעשו עם יהודית
שמחת זאת הישועה ג' חדשים ובכל ימי חיי יהודית לא קם מזיק על ישראל ותשקוט
הארץ אחרי מותה שנים רבות ולכל בני ישראל היה אור במושבותם:

תם מעשה יהודית:

Arphaxad aedificavit civitatem Ecbatanis

1 ¹ Arphaxad itaque rex Medorum subiugaverat multas gentes imperio suo; et ipse aedificavit civitatem potentissimam, quam appellavit Ecbatanis, ²ex lapidibus quadratis et sectis. Fecit muros eius in latitudinem cubitorum septuaginta, et in altitudinem cubitorum triginta; turres vero eius posuit in altitudinem cubitorum centum. ³Per quadrum vero earum latus utrumque vicenorum pedum spatio tendebatur; posuitque portas eius in altitudinem turrium. ⁴Et gloriabatur quasi potens in potentia exercitus sui, et in gloria quadrigarum suarum.

Hic a Nabuchodonosor vincitur.

⁵Anno igitur duodecimo regni sui, Nabuchodonosor, rex Assyriorum qui regnabat in Ninive civitate magna, pugnavit contra Arphaxad et obtinuit eum ⁶in campo magno qui appellatur Ragau, circa Euphraten et Tigrin et Iadason, in campo Erioch regis Elicorum.

⁷Tunc exaltatum est regnum Nabuchodonosor, et cor eius elevatum est; et misit ad omnes qui habitabant in Cilicia et Damasco et Libano, ⁸et ad gentes quae sunt in Carmelo et Cedar et inhabitantes Galilaeam in campo magno Esdrelon, ⁹et ad omnes qui erant in Samaria et trans flumen Iordanem usque ad Ierusalem et omnem terram Iesse, quousque perveniatur ad terminos Aethiopiae. ¹⁰Ad hos omnes misit nuntios Nabuchodonosor rex Assyriorum. ¹¹Qui omnes uno animo contradixerunt, et remiserunt eos vacuos, et sine honore abiecerunt.

¹²Tunc indignatus Nabuchodonosor rex adversus omnem terram illam, iuravit per thronum et regnum suum, quod defenderet se de omnibus regionibus his.

Mittitur Holofernes ut omnes subiugaret.

2 [1]Anno tertiodecimo Nabuchodonosor regis, vigesima et secunda die mensis primi, factum est verbum in domo Nabuchodonosor regis Assyriorum ut defenderet se. [2]Vocavitque omnes maiores natu, omnesque duces et bellatores suos, et habuit cum eis mysterium consilii sui; [3]dixitque cogitationem suam in eo esse, ut omnem terram suo subiugaret imperio. [4]Quod dictum cum placuisset omnibus, vocavit Nabuchodonosor rex Holofernem principem militiae suae, [5]et dixit ei: Egredere adversus omne regnum occidentis, et contra eos praecipue qui contempserunt imperium meum. [6]Non parcet oculus tuus ulli regno; omnemque urbem munitam subiugabis mihi.

Holofernes provincias devastat.

[7]Tunc Holofernes vocavit duces et magistratus virtutis Assyriorum; et dinumeravit viros in expeditionem, sicut praecepit ei rex, centum viginti millia peditum pugnatorum, et equitum sagittariorum duodecim millia. [8]Omnemque expeditionem suam fecit praeire in multitudine innumerabilium camelorum, cum his quae exercitibus sufficerent copiose, boum quoque armenta, gregesque ovium quorum non erat numerus. [9]Frumentum ex omni Syria in transitu suo parari constituit; [10]aurum vero et argentum de domo regis assumpsit multum nimis. [11]Et profectus est ipse et omnis exercitus cum quadrigis et equitibus et sagittariis, qui cooperuerunt faciem terrae sicut locustae.

[12]Cumque pertransisset fines Assyriorum, venit ad magnos montes Ange, qui sunt a sinistro Ciliciae; ascenditque omnia castella eorum, et obtinuit omnem munitionem. [13]Effregit autem civitatem opinatissimam Melothi, praedavitque omnes filios Tharsis et filios Ismael, qui erant contra faciem deserti et ad austrum terrae Cellon. [14]Et transivit Euphraten, et venit in Mesopotamiam; et fregit omnes civitates excelsas quae erant ibi, a torrente Mambre usquequo perveniatur ad mare. [15]Et occupavit terminos eius a Cilicia usque ad fines Iapheth

qui sunt ad austrum; ¹⁶abduxitque omnes filios Madian, et
praedavit omnem locupletationem eorum: omnesque re-
sistentes sibi occidit in ore gladii.

¹⁷Et post haec descendit in campos Damasci in diebus
messis; et succendit omnia sata omnesque arbores, et vineas
fecit incidi. ¹⁸Et cecidit timor illius super omnes inhabitantes
terram.

Principes Syriae mittunt legatos pacis ad Holofernem.

3   ¹Tunc miserunt legatos suos universarum urbium ac pro-
vinciarum reges ac principes, Syriae scilicet Mesopotamiae et
Syriae Sobal et Libyae atque Ciliciae; qui venientes ad
Holofernem, dixerunt: ²Desinat indignatio tua circa nos;
melius est enim ut viventes serviamus Nabuchodonosor regi
magno et subditi simus tibi, quam morientes cum interitu
nostro ipsi servitutis nostrae damna patiamur. ³Omnis civitas
nostra omnisque possessio, omnes montes et colles et campi
et armenta boum, gregesque ovium et caprarum, equorumque
et camelorum, et universae facultates nostrae atque familiae in
conspectu tuo sunt; ⁴sint omnia nostra sub lege tua: ⁵nos et
filii nostri servi tui sumus. ⁶Veni nobis pacificus dominus, et
utere servitio nostro sicut placuerit tibi.

Assumpsit de urbibus viros ad bellandum.

⁷Tunc descendit de montibus cum equitibus in virtute
magna, et obtinuit omnem civitatem et omnem inhabitantem
terram. ⁸De universis autem urbibus assumpsit sibi auxiliarios
viros fortes et electos ad bellum. ⁹Tantusque metus provinciis
illis incubuit, ut universarum urbium habitatores, principes et
honorati simul cum populis, exirent obviam venienti, ¹⁰exci-
pientes eum cum coronis et lampadibus, ducentes choros in
tympanis et tibiis. ¹¹Nec ista tamen facientes ferocitatem eius
pectoris mitigare potuerunt; ¹²nam et civitates eorum
destruxit, et lucos eorum excidit. ¹³Praeceperat enim illi
Nabuchodonosor rex ut omnes deos terrae exterminaret,
videlicet ut ipse solus diceretur deus ab his nationibus quae
potuissent Holofernis potentia subiugari.

¹⁴Pertransiens autem Syriam Sobal et omnem Apameam, omnemque Mesopotamiam, venit ad Idumaeos in terram Gabaa; ¹⁵accepitque civitates eorum, et sedit ibi per triginta dies; in quibus diebus adunari praecepit universum exercitum virtutis suae.

Filii Israel occupant loca munita.

4 ¹Tunc audientes haec filii Israel qui habitabant in terra Iuda, timuerunt valde a facie eius. ²Tremor et horror invasit sensus eorum, ne hoc faceret Ierusalem et templo Domini, quod fecerat ceteris civitatibus et templis earum. ³Et miserunt in omnem Samariam per circuitum usque Iericho; et praeoccupaverunt omnes vertices montium, ⁴et muris circumdederunt vicos suos, et congregaverunt frumenta in praeparationem pugnae. ⁵Sacerdos etiam Eliachim scripsit ad universos qui erant contra Esdrelon, quae est contra faciem campi magni iuxta Dothain, et universos per quos viae transitus esse poterat, ⁶ut obtinerent ascensus montium per quos via esse poterat ad Ierusalem, et illic custodirent ubi angustum iter esse poterat inter montes. ⁷Et fecerunt filii Israel secundum quod constituerat eis sacerdos Domini Eliachim.

⁸Et clamavit omnis populus ad Dominum instantia magna, et humiliaverunt animas suas in ieiuniis et orationibus, ipsi et mulieres eorum. ⁹Et induerunt se sacerdotes ciliciis, et infantes prostraverunt contra faciem templi Domini, et altare Domini operuerunt cilicio; ¹⁰et clamaverunt ad Dominum Deum Israel unanimiter, ne darentur in praedam infantes eorum, et uxores eorum in divisionem, et civitates eorum in exterminium, et sancta eorum in pollutionem, et fierent opprobrium gentibus.

Exhortatio Eliachim ad filios Israel.

¹¹Tunc Eliachim, sacerdos Domini magnus, circuivit omnem Israel allocutusque est eos, ¹²dicens:

Scitote quoniam exaudiet Dominus preces vestras, si manentes permanseritis in ieiuniis et orationibus in conspectu Domini. ¹³Memores estote Moysi servi Domini, qui Amalec

confidentem in virtute sua et in potentia sua, et in exercitu
suo et in clypeis suis, et in curribus suis et in equitibus suis,
non ferro pugnando, sed precibus sanctis orando deiecit.
¹⁴Sic erunt universi hostes Israel si perseveraveritis in hoc
opere quod coepistis.

¹⁵Ad hanc igitur exhortationem eius deprecantes Dominum
permanebant in conspectu Domini, ¹⁶ita ut etiam hi qui of-
ferebant Domino holocausta, praecincti ciliciis offerrent sa-
crificia Domino, et erat cinis super capita eorum; ¹⁷et ex toto
corde suo omnes orabant Deum, ut visitaret populum suum
Israel.

Irascitur Holofernes quod resistunt filii Israel.

5   ¹Nuntiatumque est Holoferni principi militiae Assyriorum
quod filii Israel praepararent se ad resistendum, ac montium
itinera conclusissent. ²Et furore nimio exarsit in iracundia
magna, vocavitque omnes principes Moab et duces Ammon,
³et dixit eis: Dicite mihi quis sit populus iste qui montana
obsidet, aut quae et quales et quantae sint civitates eorum;
quae etiam sit virtus eorum, aut quae sit multitudo eorum,
vel quis rex militiae illorum; ⁴et quare, prae omnibus qui
habitant in oriente, isti contempserunt nos et non exierunt
obviam nobis ut susciperent nos cum pace?

Verba Achior de eis.

⁵Tunc Achior, dux omnium filiorum Ammon, respondens
ait: Si digneris audire, domine mi, dicam veritatem in conspectu tuo de populo isto qui in montanis habitat, et non
egredietur verbum falsum ex ore meo. ⁶Populus iste ex
progenie Chaldaeorum est. ⁷Hic primum in Mesopotamia
habitavit, quoniam noluerunt sequi deos patrum suorum qui
erant in terra Chaldaeorum. ⁸Deserentes itaque ceremonias
patrum suorum, quae in multitudine deorum erant, ⁹unum
Deum caeli coluerunt; qui et praecepit eis ut exirent inde, et
habitarent in Charan. Cumque operuisset omnem terram
fames, descenderunt in Aegyptum, illicque per quadringentos

annos sic multiplicati sunt ut dinumerari eorum non posset exercitus.

¹⁰Cumque gravaret eos rex Aegypti, atque in aedificationibus urbium suarum in luto et latere subiugasset eos, clamaverunt ad Dominum suum, et percussit totam terram Aegypti plagis variis. ¹¹Cumque eiecissent eos Aegyptii a se, et cessasset plaga ab eis, et iterum eos vellent capere et ad suum servitium revocare, ¹²fugientibus his Deus caeli mare aperuit, ita ut hinc inde aquae quasi murus solidarentur, et isti pede sicco fundum maris perambulando transirent. ¹³In quo loco dum innumerabilis exercitus Aegyptiorum eos persequeretur, ita aquis coopertus est ut non remaneret vel unus qui factum posteris nuntiaret. ¹⁴Egressi vero mare Rubrum, deserta Sina montis occupaverunt, in quibus numquam homo habitare potuit, vel filius hominis requievit. ¹⁵Illic fontes amari obdulcati sunt eis ad bibendum, et per annos quadraginta annonam de caelo consecuti sunt. ¹⁶Ubicumque ingressi sunt sine arcu et sagitta, et absque scuto et gladio; Deus eorum pugnavit pro eis et vicit.

¹⁷Et non fuit qui insultaret populo isti, nisi quando recessit a cultu Domini Dei sui. ¹⁸Quotiescumque autem praeter ipsum Deum suum alterum coluerunt, dati sunt in praedam et in gladium et in opprobrium; ¹⁹quotiescumque autem paenituerunt se recessisse a cultura Dei sui, dedit eis Deus caeli virtutem resistendi.

²⁰Denique Chananaeum regem et Iebusaeum et Pherezaeum, et Hethaeum et Hevaeum et Amorrhaeum, et omnes potentes in Hesebon prostraverunt; et terras eorum et civitates eorum ipsi possederunt. ²¹Et usque dum non peccarent in conspectu Dei sui, erant cum illis bona, Deus enim illorum odit iniquitatem. ²²Nam et ante hos annos, cum recessissent a via quam dederat illis Deus ut ambularent in ea, exterminati sunt proeliis a multis nationibus; et plurimi eorum captivi abducti sunt in terram non suam.

²³Nuper autem reversi ad Dominum Deum suum, ex dispersione qua dispersi fuerant adunati sunt, et ascenderunt montana haec omnia, et iterum possident Ierusalem ubi sunt sancta eorum.

[24]Nunc ergo, mi domine, perquire: si est aliqua iniquitas eorum in conspectu Dei eorum, ascendamus ad illos, quoniam tradens tradet illos Deus eorum tibi, et subiugati erunt sub iugo potentiae tuae. [25]Si vero non est offensio populi huius coram Deo suo, non poterimus resistere illis, quoniam Deus eorum defendet illos; et erimus in opprobrium universae terrae.

Indignatio magnatum Holofernis contra Achior.

[26]Et factum est, cum cessasset loqui Achior verba haec, irati sunt omnes magnates Holofernis et cogitabant interficere eum, dicentes ad alterutrum: [27]Quis est iste, qui filios Israel posse dicat resistere regi Nabuchodonosor et exercitibus eius, homines inermes et sine virtute, et sine peritia artis pugnae? [28]Ut ergo agnoscat Achior quoniam fallit nos, ascendamus in montana; et cum capti fuerint potentes eorum, tunc cum eisdem gladio transverberabitur, [29]ut sciat omnis gens quoniam Nabuchodonosor deus terrae est, et praeter ipsum alius non est.

Verba Holofernis ad Achior.

6   [1]Factum est autem cum cessassent loqui, indignatus Holofernes vehementer dixit ad Achior: [2]Quoniam prophetasti nobis dicens quod gens Israel defendatur a Deo suo; ut ostendam tibi quoniam non est deus nisi Nabuchodonosor, [3]cum percusserimus eos omnes sicut hominem unum, tunc et ipse cum illis Assyriorum gladio interibis, et omnis Israel tecum perditione disperiet. [4]Et probabis quoniam Nabuchodonosor dominus sit universae terrae; tuncque gladius militiae meae transiet per latera tua, et confixus cades inter vulneratos Israel, et non respirabis ultra donec extermineris cum illis. [5]Porro autem si prophetiam tuam veram existimas, non concidat vultus tuus; et pallor qui faciem tuam obtinet abscedat a te, si verba mea haec putas impleri non posse. [6]Ut autem noveris quia simul cum illis haec experieris, ecce ex hac hora illorum populo sociaberis ut dum dignas mei gladii poenas exceperint, ipse simul ultioni subiaceas.

Traditus filiis Israel Achior.

⁷Tunc Holofernes praecepit servis suis ut comprehenderent Achior et perducerent eum in Bethuliam, et traderent eum in manus filiorum Israel. ⁸Et accipientes eum servi Holofernis profecti sunt per campestria; sed cum appropinquassent ad montana, exierunt contra eos fundibularii. ⁹Illi autem divertentes a latere montis ligaverunt Achior ad arborem manibus et pedibus; et sic vinctum restibus demiserunt eum, et reversi sunt ad dominum suum.

¹⁰Porro filii Israel descendentes de Bethulia venerunt ad eum; quem solventes duxerunt ad Bethuliam, atque in medium populi illum statuentes, percunctati sunt quid rerum esset quod illum vinctum Assyrii reliquissent. ¹¹In diebus illis erant illic principes Ozias filius Micha de tribu Simeon, et Charmi qui et Gothoniel. ¹²In medio itaque seniorum et in conspectu omnium Achior dixit omnia quae¹ locutus ipse fuerat ab Holoferne interrogatus, et qualiter populus Holofernis voluisset propter hoc verbum interficere eum; ¹³et quemadmodum ipse Holofernes iratus iusserit eum Israelitis hac de causa tradi, ut dum vicerit filios Israel, tunc et ipsum Achior diversis iubeat interire suppliciis, propter hoc quod dixisset: Deus caeli defensor eorum est.

Planctus et oratio populi.

¹⁴Cumque Achior universa haec exposuisset, omnis populus cecidit in faciem adorantes Dominum; et communi lamentatione et fletu unanimes preces suas Domino effuderunt ¹⁵dicentes:

Domine, Deus caeli et terrae, intuere superbiam eorum et respice ad nostram humilitatem; et faciem sanctorum tuorum attende, et ostende quoniam non derelinquis praesumentes de te, et praesumentes de se et de sua virtute gloriantes humilias.

¹⁶Finito itaque fletu et per totam diem oratione populorum completa, consolati sunt Achior ¹⁷dicentes:

Deus patrum nostrorum, cuius tu virtutem praedicasti, ipse tibi hanc dabit vicissitudinem ut eorum magis tu inter-

itum videas. ¹⁸Cum vero Dominus Deus noster dederit hanc libertatem servis suis, sit et tecum Deus in medio nostri, ut sicut placuerit tibi ita cum tuis omnibus converseris nobiscum.

¹⁹Tunc Ozias, finito consilio, suscepit eum in domum suam, et fecit ei cenam magnam; ²⁰et, vocatis omnibus presbyteris, simul expleto ieiunio refecerunt. ²¹Postea vero convocatus est omnis populus, et per totam noctem intra ecclesiam oraverunt, petentes auxilium a Deo Israel.

Holofernes exercitum ad Bethuliam admovit.

7 ¹Holofernes autem altera die praecepit exercitibus suis ut ascenderent contra Bethuliam. ²Erant autem pedites bellatorum centum viginti millia, et equites viginti duo millia, praeter praeparationes virorum illorum quos occupaverat captivitas, et abducti fuerant de provinciis et urbibus universae iuventutis. ³Omnes paraverunt se pariter ad pugnam contra filios Israel; et venerunt per crepidinem montis usque ad apicem qui respicit super Dothain, a loco qui dicitur Belma usque ad Chelmon qui est contra Esdrelon.

⁴Filii autem Israel, ut viderunt multitudinem illorum, prostraverunt se super terram, mittentes cinerem super capita sua, unanimes orantes ut Deus Israel misericordiam suam ostenderet super populum suum. ⁵Et assumentes arma sua bellica, sederunt per loca quae ad angusti itineris tramitem dirigunt inter montosa, et erant custodientes ea tota die et nocte.

Incidit aquaeductum.

⁶Porro Holofernes, dum circuit per gyrum, reperit quod fons qui influebat aquaeductum illorum a parte australi extra civitatem dirigeret; et incidi praecepit aquaeductum illorum. ⁷Erant tamen non longe a muris fontes ex quibus furtim videbantur haurire aquam, ad refocillandum potius quam ad potandum. ⁸Sed filii Ammon et Moab accesserunt ad Holofernem, dicentes:

Filii Israel non in lancea nec in sagitta confidunt, sed

montes defendunt illos et muniunt illos colles in praecipitio constituti. ⁹Ut ergo sine congressione pugnae possis superare eos, pone custodes fontium ut non hauriant aquam ex eis; et sine gladio interficies eos, vel certe fatigati tradent civitatem suam, quam putant in montibus positam superari non posse.

¹⁰Et placuerunt verba haec coram Holoferne et coram satellitibus eius, et constituit per gyrum centenarios per singulos fontes. ¹¹Cumque ista custodia per dies viginti fuisset expleta, defecerunt cisternae et collectiones aquarum omnibus habitantibus Bethuliam, ita ut non esset intra civitatem unde satiarentur vel una die, quoniam ad mensuram dabatur populis aqua quotidie.

Querelae populi contra Oziam.

¹²Tunc ad Oziam congregati omnes viri feminaeque, iuvenes et parvuli, omnes simul una voce ¹³dixerunt:

Iudicet Deus inter nos et te, quoniam fecisti in nos mala, nolens loqui pacifice cum Assyriis; et propter hoc vendidit nos Deus in manibus eorum: ¹⁴et ideo non est qui adiuvet, cum prosternamur ante oculos eorum in siti et perditione magna. ¹⁵Et nunc congregate universos qui in civitate sunt, ut sponte tradamus nos omnes populo Holofernis; ¹⁶melius est enim ut captivi benedicamus Dominum viventes, quam moriamur et simus opprobrium omni carni, cum viderimus uxores nostras et infantes nostros mori ante oculos nostros. ¹⁷Contestamur hodie caelum et terram et Deum patrum nostrorum qui ulciscitur nos secundum peccata nostra, ut iam tradatis civitatem in manu militiae Holofernis, et sit finis noster brevis in ore gladii qui longior efficitur in ariditate sitis.

¹⁸Et cum haec dixissent, factus est fletus et ululatus magnus in ecclesia ab omnibus; et per multas horas una voce clamaverunt ad Deum, dicentes:

¹⁹Peccavimus cum patribus nostris, iniuste egimus, iniquitatem fecimus. ²⁰Tu, quia pius es, miserere nostri, aut in tuo flagello vindica iniquitates nostras; et noli tradere confitentes te populo qui ignorat te, ²¹ut non dicant inter gentes: Ubi est deus eorum?

²²Et cum fatigati his clamoribus et his fletibus lassati siluissent, ²³exurgens Ozias infusus lacrimis dixit:

Aequo animo estote, fratres, et hos quinque dies expectemus a Domino misericordiam; ²⁴forsitan enim indignationem suam abscindet, et dabit gloriam nomini suo: ²⁵si autem transactis quinque diebus non venerit adiutorium, faciemus haec verba quae locuti estis.

8   ¹Et factum est, cum audisset haec verba Iudith vidua, quae erat filia Merari, filii Idox, filii Ioseph, filii Oziae, filii Elai, filii Iamnor, filii Gedeon, filii Raphaim, filii Achitob, filii Melchiae, filii Enan, filii Nathaniae, filii Salathiel, filii Simeon, filii Ruben; ²et vir eius fuit Manasses, qui mortuus est in diebus messis hordeacceae: ³instabat enim super alligantes manipulos in campo, et venit aestus super caput eius, et mortuus est in Bethulia civitate sua, et sepultus est illic cum patribus suis.

⁴Erat autem Iudith relicta eius vidua iam annis tribus et mensibus sex. ⁵Et in superioribus domus suae fecit sibi secretum cubiculum, in quo cum puellis suis clausa morabatur. Et, habens super lumbos suos cilicium, ieiunabat omnibus diebus vitae suae, praeter sabbata et neomenias et festa domus Israel. ⁷Erat autem eleganti aspectu nimis; cui vir suus reliquerat divitias multas et familiam copiosam, ac possessiones armentis boum et gregibus ovium plenas. ⁸Et erat haec in omnibus famosissima, quoniam timebat Dominum valde, nec erat qui loqueretur de illa verbum malum.

Audiens Iudith irascitur contra Oziam.

⁹Haec itaque, cum audisset quoniam Ozias promisisset quod transacto quinto die traderet civitatem, misit ad presbyteros Chabri et Charmi. ¹⁰Et venerunt ad illam, et dixit illis:

Quod est hoc verbum in quo consensit Ozias, ut tradat civitatem Assyriis si intra quinque dies non venerit vobis adiutorium? ¹¹Et qui estis vos qui tentatis Dominum? ¹²Non est iste sermo qui misericordiam provocet, sed potius qui iram

excitet et furorem accendat. ¹³Posuistis vos tempus miserationis Domini, et in arbitrium vestrum diem constituistis ei. ¹⁴Sed quia patiens Dominus est, in hoc ipso paeniteamus, et indulgentiam eius fusis lacrimis postulemus.

¹⁵Non enim quasi homo sic Deus comminabitur, neque sicut filius hominis ad iracundiam inflammabitur. ¹⁶Et, ideo humiliemus illi animas nostras, et in spiritu constituti humiliato, servientes illi, ¹⁷dicamus flentes Domino, ut secundum voluntatem suam sic faciat nobiscum misericordiam suam, ut sicut conturbatum est cor nostrum in superbia eorum, ita etiam de nostra humilitate gloriemur.

¹⁸Quoniam non sumus secuti peccata patrum nostrorum, qui dereliquerunt Deum suum et adoraverunt deos alienos; ¹⁹pro quo scelere dati sunt in gladium et in rapinam et in confusionem inimicis suis: nos autem alterum deum nescimus praeter ipsum. ²⁰Expectemus humiles consolationem eius, et exquiret sanguinem nostrum de afflictionibus inimicorum nostrorum; et humiliabit omnes gentes, quaecumque insurgunt contra nos, et faciet illas sine honore Dominus Deus noster.

²¹Et nunc, fratres, quoniam vos estis presbyteri in populo Dei, et ex vobis pendet anima illorum; ad eloquium vestrum corda eorum erigite, ut memores sint quia tentati sunt patres nostri, ut probarentur si vere colerent Deum suum. ²²Memores esse debent quomodo pater noster Abraham tentatus est; et, per multas tribulationes probatus, Dei amicus effectus est. ²³Sic Isaac, sic Iacob, sic Moyses et omnes qui placuerunt Deo, per multas tribulationes transierunt fideles.

²⁴Illi autem qui tentationes non susceperunt cum timore Domini, et impatientiam suam et improperium murmurationis suae contra Dominum protulerunt, ²⁵exterminati sunt ab exterminatore, et a serpentibus perierunt. ²⁶Et nos ergo, non ulciscamur nos pro his quae patimur; ²⁷sed reputantes peccatis nostris haec ipsa supplicia minora esse, flagella Domini quibus quasi servi corripimur, ad emendationem et non ad perditionem nostram evenisse credamus.

[28]Et dixerunt illi Ozias et presbyteri: Omnia quae locuta es vera sunt, et non est in sermonibus tuis ulla reprehensio; [29]nunc ergo ora pro nobis, quoniam mulier sancta es et timens Deum. [30]Et dixit illis Iudith:

Sicut quod potui loqui, Dei esse cognoscitis, [31]ita quod facere disposui probate si ex Deo est, et orate ut firmum faciat Deus consilium meum. [32]Stabitis vos ad portam nocte ista, et ego exeam cum abra mea; et orate, ut sicut dixistis, in diebus quinque respiciat Dominus populum suum Israel. [33]Vos autem nolo ut scrutemini actum meum, et usque dum renuntiem vobis, nihil aliud fiat nisi oratio pro me ad Dominum deum nostrum.

[34]Et dixit ad eam Ozias princeps Iuda: Vade in pace, et Dominus sit tecum in ultionem inimicorum nostrorum. Et revertentes abierunt.

Induit se Iudith cilicio.

9 [1]Quibus abscedentibus, Iudith ingressa est oratorium suum, et induens se cilicio posuit cinerem super caput suum, et prosternens se Domino, clamabat ad Dominum, dicens:

[2]Domine, Deus patris mei Simeon,
 qui dedisti illi gladium in defensionem alienigenarum
 qui violatores extiterunt in coinquinatione sua,
 et denudaverunt femur virginis in confusionem,
[3]et dedisti mulieres illorum in praedam
 et filias illorum in captivitatem,
 et omnem praedam in divisionem servis tuis
 qui zelaverunt zelum tuum;
 subveni quaeso te, Domine Deus meus, mihi viduae.
[4]Tu enim fecisti priora,
 et illa post illa cogitasti, et hoc factum est quod ipse voluisti.
[5]Omnes enim viae tuae paratae sunt,
 et tua iudicia in tua providentia posuisti.
[6]Respice castra Assyriorum nunc,
 sicut tunc castra Aegyptiorum videre dignatus es,

quando post servos tuos armati currebant,
confidentes in quadrigis et in equitatu suo
et in multitudine bellatorum.
⁷Sed aspexisti super castra eorum,
et tenebrae fatigaverunt eos;
⁸tenuit pedes eorum abyssus, et aquae operuerunt eos.

⁹Sic fiant et isti, Domine,
qui confidunt in multitudine sua et in curribus suis,
et in contis et in scutis,
et in sagittis suis et in lanceis gloriantur;
¹⁰et nesciunt quia tu ipse es Deus noster,
qui conteris bella ab initio,
et Dominus nomen est tibi.
¹¹Erige brachium tuum sicut ab initio,
et allide virtutem illorum in virtute tua;
cadat virtus eorum in iracundia tua,
qui promittunt se violare sancta tua,
et polluere tabernaculum nominis tui,
et deiicere gladio suo cornu altaris tui.

¹²Fac, Domine, ut gladio proprio eius superbia amputetur.
¹³Capiatur laqueo oculorum suorum in me,
et percuties eum ex labiis caritatis meae.
¹⁴Da mihi in animo constantiam ut contemnam illum,
et virtutem ut evertam illum.
¹⁵Erit enim hoc memoriale nominis tui,
cum manus feminae deiecerit eum.
¹⁶Non enim in multitudine est virtus tua, Domine,
neque in equorum viribus voluntas tua est;
nec superbi ab initio placuerunt tibi,
sed humilium et mansuetorum semper tibi placuit deprecatio.

¹⁷Deus caelorum, creator aquarum et dominus totius creaturae,
exaudi me miseram deprecantem,
et de tua misericordia praesumentem.

¹⁸Memento, Domine, testamenti tui,
et da verbum in ore meo;
et in corde meo consilium corrobora,
ut domus tua in sanctificatione tua permaneat,
¹⁹et omnes gentes agnoscant quia tu es Deus,
et non est alius praeter te.

Post orationem ornata egreditur cum abra sua.

10 ¹Factum est autem, cum cessasset clamare ad Dominum, surrexit de loco in quo iacuerat prostrata ad Dominum; ²vocavitque abram suam, et descendens in domum suam abstulit a se cilicium, et exuit se vestimentis viduitatis suae. ³Et lavit corpus suum et unxit se myro optimo, et discriminavit crinem capitis sui et imposuit mitram super caput suum; et induit se vestimentis iucunditatis suae, induitque sandalia pedibus suis, assumpsitque dextraliola et lilia et inaures et annulos, et omnibus ornamentis suis ornavit se. ⁴Cui etiam Dominus contulit splendorem, quoniam omnis ista compositio non ex libidine sed ex virtute pendebat, et ideo Dominus hanc in illam pulchritudinem ampliavit, ut incomparabili decore omnium oculis appareret. ⁵Imposuit itaque abrae suae ascoperam vini et vas olei, et polentam et palathas et panes et caseum; et profecta est.

⁶Cumque venissent ad portam civitatis, invenerunt exspectantem Oziam et presbyteros civitatis. ⁷Qui cum vidissent eam, stupentes mirati sunt nimis pulchritudinem eius; ⁸nihil tamen interrogantes eam, dimiserunt transire dicentes: Deus patrum nostrorum det tibi gratiam, et omne consilium tui cordis sua virtute corroboret, ut glorietur super te Ierusalem et sit nomen tuum in numero sanctorum et iustorum. ⁹Et dixerunt hi qui illic erant omnes una voce: Fiat, fiat. ¹⁰Iudith vero, orans Dominum, transivit per portas, ipsa et abra eius.

Mane ducitur ad tabernaculum Holofernis.

¹¹Factum est autem, cum descenderet montem circa ortum diei, occurrerunt ei exploratores Assyriorum; et tenuerunt eam

dicentes: Unde venis, aut quo vadis? ¹²Quae respondit: Filia sum Hebraeorum; ideo ego fugi a facie eorum, quoniam futurum agnovi quod dentur vobis in depraedationem, pro eo quod contemnentes vos noluerunt ultro tradere seipsos, ut invenirent misericordiam in conspectu vestro. ¹³Hac de causa cogitavi mecum dicens: Vadam ad faciem principis Holofernis ut indicem illi secreta illorum, et ostendam illi quo aditu possit obtinere eos, ita ut non cadat vir unus de exercitu eius.

¹⁴Et cum audissent viri illi verba eius, considerabant faciem eius; et erat in oculis eorum stupor, quoniam pulchritudinem eius mirabantur nimis. ¹⁵Et dixerunt ad eam: Conservasti animam tuam, eo quod tale reperisti consilium, ut descenderes ad dominum nostrum. ¹⁶Hoc autem scias quoniam, cum steteris in conspectu eius, bene tibi faciet; et eris gratissima in corde eius. Duxeruntque illam ad tabernaculum Holofernis, annuntiantes eam.

¹⁷Cumque intrasset ante faciem eius, statim captus est in suis oculis Holofernes. ¹⁸Dixeruntque ad eum satellites eius: Quis contemnat populum Hebraeorum, qui tam decoras mulieres eos debeamus? ¹⁹Videns itaque Iudith Holofernem sedentem in conopoeo, quod erat ex purpura et auro et smaragdo et lapidibus pretiosis intextum, ²⁰et cum in faciem eius intendisset adoravit eum, prosternens se super terram; et elevaverunt eam servi Holofernis, iubente domino suo.

Blanditur ei Holofernes et verba Iudith ad eum.

11 ¹Tunc Holofernes dixit ei: Aequo animo esto, et noli pavere in corde tuo, quoniam ego numquam nocui viro qui voluit servire Nabuchodonosor regi. ²Populus autem tuus si non contempsisset me, non levassem lanceam meam super eum. ³Nunc autem, dic mihi qua ex causa recessisti ab illis, et placuit tibi ut venires ad nos.

⁴Et dixit illi Iudith: Sume verba ancillae tuae, quoniam si secutus fueris verba ancillae tuae, perfectam rem faciet Dominus tecum. ⁵Vivit enim Nabuchodonosor rex terrae, et vivit virtus eius quae est in te ad correptionem omnium animarum errantium; quoniam non solum homines serviunt illi

per te, sed et bestiae agri obtemperant illi. ⁶Nuntiatur enim
animi tui industria universis gentibus; et indicatum est omni
saeculo, quoniam tu solus bonus et potens es in omni regno
eius, et disciplina tua omnibus provinciis praedicatur.

⁷Nec hoc latet quod locutus est Achior, nec illud ignoratur
quod ei iusseris evenire. ⁸Constat enim Deum nostrum sic
peccatis offensum, ut mandaverit per prophetas suos ad
populum quod tradat eum pro peccatis suis. ⁹Et quoniam
sciunt se offendisse Deum suum filii Israel, tremor tuus super
ipsos est. ¹⁰Insuper etiam fames invasit eos, et ab ariditate
aquae iam inter mortuos computantur. ¹¹Denique hoc ordi-
nant ut interficiant pecora sua, et bibant sanguinem eorum.
¹²Et sancta Domini Dei sui quae praecepit Deus non contingi,
in frumento vino et oleo haec cogitaverunt impendere; et
volunt consumere quae nec manibus deberent contingere. Ergo,
quoniam haec faciunt, certum est quod in perditionem dabuntur.

¹³Quod ego ancilla tua cognoscens fugi ab illis, et misit me
Dominus haec ipsa nuntiare tibi. ¹⁴Ego enim ancilla tua Deum
colo etiam nunc apud te, et exiet ancilla tua et orabo Deum.
¹⁵Et dicet mihi quando eis reddat peccatum suum; et veniens
nuntiabo tibi, ita ut ego adducam te per mediam Ierusalem, et
habebis omnem populum Israel sicut oves quibus non est
pastor: et non latrabit vel unus canis contra te, ¹⁶quoniam
haec mihi dicta sunt per providentiam Dei. ¹⁷Et quoniam
iratus est illis Deus, haec ipsa missa sum nuntiare tibi.

¹⁸Placuerunt autem omnia verba haec coram Holoferne et
coram pueris eius; et mirabantur sapientiam eius, et dicebant
alter ad alterum: ¹⁹Non est talis mulier super terram in
aspectu, in pulchritudine et in sensu verborum. ²⁰Et dixit ad
illam Holofernes: Benefecit Deus qui misit te ante populum,
ut des illum tu in manibus nostris. ²¹Et quoniam bona est pro-
missio tua; si fecerit mihi hoc, Deus tuus erit et Deus meus, et
tu in domo Nabuchodonosor magna eris, et nomen tuum
nominabitur in universa terra.

Iubet Holofernes ei dari de cibis suis.

12 ¹Tunc iussit eam introire ubi repositi erant thesauri eius, et

iussit illic manere eam; et constituit quid daretur illi de convivio suo. ²Cui respondit Iudith et dixit: Nunc non potero manducare ex his quae mihi praecipis tribui, ne veniat super me offensio; ex his autem quae mihi detuli manducabo. ³Cui Holofernes ait: Si defecerint tibi ista quae tecum detulisti, quid faciemus tibi? ⁴Et dixit Iudith: Vivit anima tua, domine meus, quoniam non expendet omnia haec ancilla tua, donec faciat Deus in manu mea haec quae cogitavi. Et induxerunt illam servi eius in tabernaculum quod praeceperat.

⁵Et petiit dum introiret, ut daretur ei copia nocte et ante lucem egrediendi foras ad orationem, et deprecandi Dominum. ⁶Et praecepit cubiculariis suis, ut sicut placeret illi exiret et introiret ad adorandum Deum suum per triduum. ⁷Et exibat noctibus in vallem Bethuliae, et baptizabat se in fonte aquae. ⁸Et ut ascendebat orabat Dominum Deum Israel, ut dirigeret viam eius ad liberationem populi sui. ⁹Et introiens munda manebat in tabernaculo, usque dum acciperet escam suam in vespere.

Ubi Holofernes rogat Iudith sibi in coniugium.

¹⁰Et factum est in quarto die, Holofernes fecit cenam servis suis, et dixit ad Vagao eunuchum suum: Vade, et suade Hebraeam illam, ut sponte consentiat habitare mecum. ¹¹Foedum est enim apud Assyrios si femina irrideat virum, agendo ut immunis ab eo transeat. ¹²Tunc introivit Vagao ad Iudith et dixit: Non vereatur bona puella introire ad dominum meum, ut honorificetur ante faciem eius, ut manducet cum eo et bibat vinum in iucunditate.

¹³Cui Iudith respondit: Quae ego sum ut contradicam domino meo? ¹⁴Omne quod erit ante oculos eius bonum et optimum faciam; quidquid autem illi placuerit, hoc mihi erit optimum omnibus diebus vitae meae. ¹⁵Et surrexit et ornavit se vestimento suo, et ingressa stetit ante faciem eius. ¹⁶Cor autem Holofernis concussum est; erat enim ardens in concupiscentia eius. ¹⁷Et dixit ad eam Holofernes: Bibe nunc et accumbe in iucunditate, quoniam invenisti gratiam coram me. ¹⁸Et dixit Iudith: Bibam, domine, quoniam magnificata est

anima mea hodie prae omnibus diebus meis. [19]Et accepit et
manducavit et bibit coram ipso, ea quae paraverat illi ancilla
eius; [20]et iucundus factus est Holofernes ad eam, bibitque
vinum multum nimis, quantum numquam biberat in vita sua.

Iudith oratione facta caput eius abscidit.

13 [1]Ut autem sero factum est, festinaverunt servi illius ad
hospitia sua; et conclusit Vagao ostia cubiculi, et abiit.
[2]Erant autem omnes fatigati a vino. [3]Eratque Iudith sola in
cubiculo; [4]porro Holofernes iacebat in lecto, nimia ebrietate
sopitus.

[5]Dixitque Iudith puellae suae, ut staret foris ante cubiculum et observaret. [6]Stetique Iudith ante lectum, orans cum
lacrimis et labiorum motu in silentio [7]dicens: Confirma me,
Domine Deus Israel, et respice in hac hora ad opera manuum
mearum, ut sicut promisisti, Ierusalem civitatem tuam erigas,
et hoc, quod credens per te posse fieri cogitavi, perficiam.

[8]Et cum haec dixisset, accessit ad columnam quae erat ad
caput lectuli eius, et pugionem eius qui in ea ligatus pendebat
exsolvit. [9]Cumque evaginasset illum, apprehendit comam capitis eius, et ait: confirma me, Domine Deus, in hac hora.
[10]Et percussit bis in cervicem eius, et abscidit caput eius; et
abstulit conopoeum eius a columnis, et evolvit corpus eius
truncum. [11]Et post pusillum exivit, et tradidit caput Holofernis ancillae suae; et iussit ut mitteret illud in peram suam.

[12]Et exierunt duae secundum consuetudinem suam, quasi
ad orationem; et transierunt castra, et gyrantes vallem venerunt ad portam civitatis. [13]Et dixit Iudith a longe custodibus
murorum: Aperite portas, quoniam nobiscum est Deus, qui
fecit virtutem in Israel.

[14]Et factum est, cum audissent viri vocem eius, vocaverunt
presbyteros civitatis; [15]et concurrerunt ad eam omnes, a
minimo usque ad maximum, quoniam sperabant eam iam non
esse venturam. [16]Et accendentes luminaria, congyraverunt
circa eam universi; illa autem ascendens in eminentiorem
locum, iussit fieri silentium. Cumque omnes tacuissent,
[17]dixit Iudith:

Laudate Dominum Deum nostrum,
    qui non deseruit sperantes in se,
[18]et in me ancilla sua adimplevit misericordiam suam,
    quam promisit domui Israel;
    et interfecit in manu mea hostem populi sui hac nocte.

[19]Et proferens de pera caput Holofernis, ostendit illis,
dicens: Ecce caput Holofernis, principis militiae Assyriorum;
et ecce conopoeum illius, in quo recumbebat in ebrietate sua,
ubi per manum feminae percussit illum Dominus Deus noster.

[20]Vivit autem ipse Dominus,
    quoniam custodivit me angelus eius,
    et hinc euntem et ibi commorantem,
    et inde huc revertentem;
    et non permisit me Dominus ancillam suam coinquinari,
    sed sine pollutione peccati revocavit me
    vobis gaudentem in victoria sua,
    in evasione mea, et in liberatione vestra.
[21]Confitemini illi omnes, quoniam bonus,
    quoniam in saeculum misericordia eius.
[22]Universi autem adorantes Dominum dixerunt ad eam:
Benedixit te Dominus in virtute sua, quia per te ad nihilum
redegit inimicos nostros.

Laudes Domino concrepantes benedixerunt Iudith.

[23]Porro Ozias, princeps populi Israel, dixit ad eam:

Benedicta es tu, filia, a Domino Deo excelso,
prae omnibus mulieribus super terram.
    [24]Benedictus Dominus qui creavit caelum et terram,
    qui te direxit in vulnera capitis principis inimicorum
        nostrorum;
    [25]quia hodie nomen tuum ita magnificavit,
    ut non recedat laus tua de ore hominum
    qui memores fuerint virtutis Domini in aeternum:
    pro quibus non pepercisti animae tuae
    propter angustias et tribulationem generis tui,

sed subvenisti ruinae ante conspectum Dei nostri.

[26]Et dixit omnis populus: Fiat, fiat. [27]Porro Achior vocatus venit; et dixit ei Iudith:

Deus Israel, cui tu testimonium dedisti quod ulciscatur se de inimicis suis, ipse caput omnium incredulorum incidit hac nocte in manu mea. [28]Et, ut probes quia ita est, ecce caput Holofernis qui in contemptu superbiae suae Deum Israel contempsit, et tibi interitum minabatur dicens: Cum captus fuerit populus Israel, gladio perforari praecipiam latera tua.

[29]Videns autem Achior caput Holofernis, angustiatus prae pavore cecidit in faciem suam super terram; et aestuavit anima eius. [30]Postea vero quam resumpto spiritu recreatus est, procidit ad pedes eius et adoravit eam, et dixit: [31]Benedicta tu a Deo tuo in omni tabernaculo Iacob, quoniam in omni gente quae audierit nomen tuum magnificabitur super te Deus Israel.

Ubi suspendit caput Holofernis in porta.

14   [1]Dixit autem Iudith ad omnem populum: Audite me fratres. Suspendite caput hoc super muros nostros; [2]et erit, cum exierit sol, accipiat unusquisque arma sua, et exite cum impetu; non ut descendatis deorsum, sed quasi impetum facientes. [3]Tunc exploratores necesse erit ut fugiant ad principem suum excitandum ad pugnam. [4]Cumque duces eorum cucurrerint ad tabernaculum Holofernis et invenerint eum truncum in suo sanguine volutatum, decidet super eos timor. [5]Cumque cognoveritis fugere eos, ite post illos securi; quoniam Dominus conteret eos sub pedibus vestris.

[6]Tunc Achior videns virtutem quam fecit Deus Israel, relicto gentilitatis ritu, credidit Deo et circumcidit carnem praeputii sui, et appositus est ad populum Israel, et omnis successio generis eius usque in hodiernum diem.

[7]Mox autem ut ortus est dies, suspenderunt super muros caput Holofernis, accepitque unusquisque vir arma sua; et egressi sunt cum grandi strepitu et ululatu. [8]Quod videntes exploratores, ad tabernaculum Holofernis cucurrerunt. [9]Porro

hi qui in tabernaculo erant, venientes et ante ingressum cubiculi perstrepentes, excitandi gratia inquietudinem arte moliebantur, ut non ab excitantibus sed a sonantibus Holofernes evigilaret. [10]Nullus enim audebat cubiculum virtutis Assyriorum pulsando aut intrando aperire. [11]Sed cum venissent eius duces ac tribuni et universi maiores exercitus regis Assyriorum, dixerunt cubiculariis: [12]Intrate et excitate illum, quoniam egressi mures de cavernis suis ausi sunt provocare nos ad proelium.

[13]Tunc ingressus Vagao cubiculum eius, stetit ante cortinam et plausum fecit manibus suis; suspicabatur enim illum cum Iudith dormire. [14]Sed cum nullum motum iacentis sensu aurium caperet, accessit proximans ad cortinam, et elevans eam, vidensque cadaver absque capite Holofernis in suo sanguine tabefactum iacere super terram, exclamavit voce magna cum fletu, et scidit vestimenta sua. [15]Et ingressus tabernaculum Iudith non invenit eam; et exiliit foras ad populum, [16]et dixit: Una mulier hebraea fecit confusionem in domo regis Nabuchodonosor: ecce enim Holofernes iacet in terra, et caput eius non est in illo. [17]Quod cum audissent principes virtutis Assyriorum, sciderunt omnes vestimenta sua; et intolerabilis timor et tremor cecidit super eos, et turbati sunt animi eorum valde, [18]et factus est clamor incomparabilis in medio castrorum eorum.

Assyrii videntes turbati fugerunt.

15 [1]Cumque omnis exercitus decollatum Holofernem audisset, fugit mens et consilium ab eis; et solo tremore et metu agitati, fugae praesidium sumunt, [2]ita ut nullus loqueretur cum proximo suo, sed inclinato capite relictis omnibus, evadere festinabant Hebraeos quos armatos super se venire audiebant fugientes per vias camporum et semitas collium. [3]Videntes itaque filii Israel fugientes, secuti sunt illos, descenderuntque clangentes tubis et ululantes post ipsos. [4]Et quoniam Assyrii non adunati in fugam ibant praecipites, filii autem Israel uno agmine persequentes debilitabant omnes quos invenire potuissent.

⁵Misit itaque Ozias nuntios per omnes civitates et regiones Israel, ⁶omnis itaque regio omnisque urbs electam iuventutem armatam misit post eos; et persecuti sunt eos in ore gladii, quousque pervenirent ad extremitatem finium suorum.

Persequentes Assyrios praedam eorum acceperunt.

⁷Reliqui autem qui erant in Bethulia ingressi sunt castra Assyriorum; et praedam quam fugientes Assyrii reliquerant abstulerunt, et onustati sunt valde. ⁸Hi vero qui victores reversi sunt ad Bethuliam omnia quae erant illorum attulerunt secum, ita ut non esset numerus in pecoribus et iumentis et universis mobilibus eorum, ut a minimo usque ad maximum omnes divites fierent de praedationibus eorum.

⁹Ioachim autem summus pontifex de Ierusalem venit in Bethuliam cum universis presbyteris suis, ut videret Iudith. ¹⁰Quae cum exisset ad illum, benedixerunt eam omnes una voce dicentes:

Tu gloria Ierusalem,
tu laetitia Israel
tu honorificentia populi nostri.
¹¹Quia fecisti viriliter
et confortatum est cor tuum,
eo quod castitatem amaveris
et post virum tuum alterum nescieris;
ideo et manus Domini confortavit te,
et ideo eris benedicta in aeternum.

¹²Et dixit omnis populus: Fiat, fiat. ¹³Per dies autem triginta vix collecta sunt spolia Assyriorum a populo Israel. ¹⁴Porro autem universa quae Holofernis peculiaria fuisse probata sunt dederunt Iudith, in auro et argento et vestibus et gemmis et omni supellectili, et tradita sunt omnia illi a populo. ¹⁵Et omnes populi gaudebant, cum mulieribus et virginibus et iuvenibus, in organis et citharis.

Canticum Iudith.

16 ¹Tunc cantavit canticum hoc Domino Iudith dicens:

²Incipite Domino in tympanis,
cantate Domino in cymbalis;
modulamini illi psalmum novum,
exaltate et invocate nomen eius.
³Dominus conterens bella,
Dominus nomen est illi.
⁴Qui posuit castra sua in medio populi sui,
ut eriperet nos de manu omnium inimicorum nostrorum.
⁵Venit Assur ex montibus ab aquilone
in multitudine fortitudinis suae;
cuius multitudo obturavit torrentes,
et equi eorum cooperuerunt valles.
⁶Dixit se incensurum fines meos,
et iuvenes meos occisurum gladio,
infantes meos dare in praedam,
et virgines in captivitatem.
⁷Dominus autem omnipotens nocuit eum;
et tradidit eum in manus feminae, et confodit eum.
⁸Non enim cecidit potens eorum a iuvenibus,
nec filii Titan percusserunt eum,
nec excelsi gigantes opposuerunt se illi;
sed Iudith filia Merari in specie faciei suae dissolvit eum.
⁹Exuit enim se vestimento viduitatis,
et induit se vestimento laetitiae
in exultatione filiorum Israel.
¹⁰Unxit faciem suam unguento,
et colligavit cincinnos suos mitra;
accepit stolam novam ad decipiendum illum.
¹¹Sandalia eius rapuerunt oculos eius,
pulchritudo eius captivam fecit animam eius;
amputavit pugione cervicem eius.

¹²Horruerunt Persae constantiam eius,
et Medi audaciam eius.
¹³Tunc ululaverunt castra Assyriorum,
quando apparuerunt humiles mei arescentes in siti.
¹⁴Filii puellarum compunxerunt eos,

et sicut pueros fugientes occiderunt eos.
Perierunt in proelio a facie Domini Dei mei.

[15]Hymnum cantemus Domino,
hymnum novum cantemus Deo nostro.
[16]Adonai Domine, magnus es tu,
et praeclarus in virtute tua,
et quem superare nemo potest.
[17]Tibi serviat omnis creatura tua,
quia dixisti et facta sunt,
misisti spiritum tuum et creata sunt,
et non est qui resistat voci tuae.

[18]Montes a fundamentis movebuntur cum aquis,
petrae sicut cera liquescent ante faciem tuam.
[19]Qui autem timent te
magni erunt apud te per omnia.

[20]Vae genti insurgenti super genus meum!
Dominus enim omnipotens vindicabit in eis, in die iudicii
visitabit illos.
[21]Dabit enim ignem et vermes in carnes eorum, ut urantur et
sentiant usque in sempiternum.

[22]Et factum est post haec, omnis populus post victoriam
venit in Ierusalem adorare Dominum; et mox ut purificati
sunt, obtulerunt omnes holocausta et vota et repromissiones
suas. [23]Porro Iudith universa vasa bellica Holofernis quae
dedit illi populus, et conopoeum quod ipsa sustulerat de
cubili ipsius obtulit in anathema oblivionis. [24]Erat autem
populus iucundus secundum faciem sanctorum; et per tres
menses gaudium huius victoriae celebratum est cum Iudith.

Dies festus instituitur in posteros.

[25]Post dies autem illos unusquisque rediit in domum suam;
et Iudith magna facta est in Bethulia, et praeclarior erat
universae terrae Israel. [26]Erat etiam virtuti castitas adiuncta,
ita ut non cognosceret virum omnibus diebus vitae suae, ex
quo defunctus est Manasses vir eius. [27]Erat autem diebus

festis procedens cum magna gloria. [28]Mansit autem in domo
viri sui annos centum quinque, et dimisit abram suam liberam,
et defuncta est ac sepulta cum viro suo in Bethulia; [29]luxitque
illam omnis populus diebus septem.

[30]In omni autem spatio vitae eius non fuit qui perturbaret
Israel, et post mortem eius annis multis. [31]Dies autem victoriae huius festivitatis ab Hebraeis in numero sanctorum
dierum accipitur, et colitur a Iudaeis ex illo tempore usque in
praesentem diem.

✒ BIBLIOGRAPHY ✒

L. E. T. André, *Les Apocryphes de l'Ancien Testament* (Florence, 1903).
R. Arnald, *Commentary on Apocrypha*² (London, 1760).
C. J. Ball, *Judith* in Henry Wace, *The Holy Bible, Apocrypha* ("Speaker's Commentary," London, 1888).
André Barucq, *Judith-Esther* (Paris, 1959).
Gottfried Brunner, *Der Nabuchodonosor des Buches Judith* (Berlin, 1940).
L. Cappellus, *Commentarii et Notae Criticae in Lib. Judith* (Amsterdam, 1689).
H. Cazelles, "Le personage d'Achior dans le livre de Judith," in *Mel. Levreton* (Paris, 1951), pp. 125-137.
A. E. Cowley, *Judith*, in R. H. Charles, *Apocrypha and Pseudepigrapha of the Old Testament* (Oxford, 1913), I, pp. 242-267.
A. M. Dubarle, *Judith, formes et sens des diverses traditions* (2 vols., Rome, 1966).
J. A. Duncan, "A Hebrew Political Romance," in *Biblical World* (1894), pp. 429ff.
J. G. Eichhorn, *Einleitung in die Apokryphischenschriften des A.T.* (Leipzig, 1795).
J. A. Fabricius, *Bibliotheca Graeca*, ed. Harles (Leipzig, 1838), iii, pp. 736-738.
O. F. Fritzsche, *Die Bücher Tobi und Judith erklärt* (Leipzig, 1853).
M. Gaster, "An Unknown Hebrew Version of the History of Judith," in *Proceedings of the Society of Biblical Archaeology* (March 6, 1894), pp. 156-163.
"Judith," in *Encyclopaedia Biblica*, cols. 2642-2646.
C. D. Ginsburg, *Judith*, in Kitto's *Cyclop. Bibl. Lit.*
Y. M. Grintz, *Sepher Jehudith* (Jerusalem, 1957).
R. E. Glaymen, *Recent Judith Drama and its Analogues* (Philadelphia, 1930).
E. L. Hicks, "Judith and Holofernes," in *J. Hell. St.*, 6 (1885), pp. 261-274.
J. Jahn, *Einleitung in die göttl. Bücher des Altes Bundes* (Vienna, 1802-03).
A. Jellinek, Beth Ha-Midrasch (1853-78).
R. A. Lipsius, "Über das Buch Judith und seinen neuesten Dolmetscher," in *Zeitschr. für wissenschaftl. Theol.* (1858), pp. 39-121.
Max Löhr, "Judith," in E. F. Kautzsch, *Die Apokryphen und Pseudepigraphen des A.T.* (Tübingen, 1900).
B. M. Metzger, *An Introduction to the Apocrypha*² (New York, 1963).
C. Meyer, "Zur Entstehungsgeschichte des Buches Judith" in *Bibl.*, 3 (1922), pp. 193-203.
A. Miller, *Das Buch Judith übersetzt und erklärt* (Bonn, 1940).
C. F. Movers, "Über die Ursprache der deuterokanonischen Bücher des A.T.," in *Zeitschr. für philos. u. kathol. Theol.*, 13 (Cologne, 1935).

J. Nickes, *De Libro Judithae* (Wratislaviae, 1854).

Henry Pentin, *Judith* (London, 1908).

R. H. Pfeiffer, "The Book of Judith," in *History of N.T. Times* (New York, 1949), pp. 285-303.

F. C. Porter, "Judith," in *HBD*, ii, pp. 822-824.

G. Priero, *Giuditta* (Torino, 1958).

Edna Purdie, *The Story of Judith in German and English Literature* (Paris, 1927).

A. Scholz, *Das Buch Judith eine Prophetie* (Cologne, 1885).

Emil Schürer, *HJP* (Edinburgh, 1897), II, iii, pp. 32ff.

P. W. Skehan, "The Hand of Judith," in *CBQ*, 25 (1963), pp. 94-110.

L. Soubigou, *Judith* (Paris, 1949).

J. Steinmann, *Lecture de Judith* (Paris, 1953).

F. Steinmetzer, *Neue Untersuchung über die Geschichtlichkeit der Judith-erzählung* (Leipzig, 1907).

F. Stummer, *Geographie des Buches Judith* (Stuttgart, 1947).

C. C. Torrey, *The Apocryphal Literature* (New Haven, 1945).

"The Site of Bethulia," in *JAOS*, 20 (1899), pp. 160ff.

"The Surroundings of Bethulia," in *Florilegium Melchior de Vogüe* (Paris, 1909), pp. 599-605.

E. E. Voigt, *The Latin Versions of Judith* (Leipzig, 1925).

G. Volkmar, "Die Composition des Buches Judith," in *Theol. Jahrb.* (1857), pp. 441-498.

Judith, in *Handb. der Einleitung in die Apokryphen* I, i (Tübingen, 1860).

S. Weissmann, *Das Buch Judith, historisch-kritisch beleuchtet* (Vienna, 1890).

O. Wolff, *Das Buch Judith als geschichtliche Urkunde verteidigt und erklärt* (Leipzig, 1861).

S. Zeitlin, *An Historical Study of the Canonization of the Hebrew Ssriptures* (New York, 1933), pp. 31-34.

—, "Jewish Apocryphal Literature," in *JQR*, (1950), pp. 237-239.

F. Zimmermann, "Aids for the Recovery of the Hebrew Original of Judith," in *JBL*, 57 (1938), pp. 67-74.

O. Zöckler, *Judith*, in *Die Apokryphen des A.T.* (Munich, 1891).